T0366584

TRANSFORMATIVE MEDIA

TRANSFORMATIVE MEDIA
Intersectional Technopolitics from Indymedia to #BlackLivesMatter

Sandra Jeppesen

1971–2021

30 29 28 27 26 25 24 23 22 21   5 4 3 2 1

Printed in Canada on FSC-certified ancient-forest-free paper (100% post-consumer recycled) that is processed chlorine- and acid-free.

Library and Archives Canada Cataloguing in Publication

Title: Transformative media : intersectional technopolitics from indymedia to #BlackLivesMatter / Sandra Jeppesen.
Names: Jeppesen, Sandra, author.
Description: Includes bibliographical references and index.
Identifiers: Canadiana (print) 20210230487 | Canadiana (ebook) 20210230592 |
    ISBN 9780774865913 (hardcover) | ISBN 9780774865937 (PDF) |
    ISBN 9780774865944 (EPUB)
Subjects: LCSH: Alternative mass media – Political aspects. | LCSH: Technology – Political aspects. | LCSH: Social movements – Political aspects.
Classification: LCC P96.A44 J47 2021 | DDC 302.23—dc23

Canadä

UBC Press gratefully acknowledges the financial support for our publishing program of the Government of Canada (through the Canada Book Fund), the Canada Council for the Arts, and the British Columbia Arts Council.

This book has been published with the help of a grant from the Canadian Federation for the Humanities and Social Sciences, through the Awards to Scholarly Publications Program, using funds provided by the Social Sciences and Humanities Research Council of Canada.

Printed and bound in Canada by Friesens
Set in Futura Condensed and Warnock by Apex CoVantage, LLC
Copy editor: Lesley Erickson
Proofreader: Judith Earnshaw
Indexer: Margaret de Boer
Cover designer: Gerilee McBride
Cover image: Coco Riot

UBC Press
The University of British Columbia
2029 West Mall
Vancouver, BC V6T 1Z2
www.ubcpress.ca

This book is dedicated to Christopher Petersen

Contents

Preface

Where I Stand

When engaging in qualitative research, it is important that the researcher be transparent about standpoint, perspective, identity, and experience and how these might impact the research. I would therefore like to take a moment to briefly explain, as bell hooks says, "where I stand."

I have been an anarchist organizer for more than twenty years (for details, please refer to the Appendix). Anarchists critique all forms of oppression, exploitation, domination, and hierarchies. We also work to construct alternative liberatory systems and practices in everyday life. This political approach has several impacts on this book. First, it shapes the range and types of groups, networks, texts, theories, and organizations included in my research, which focuses on grassroots autonomous social movements and media projects that tend to reject political parties, capitalism, NGOs, the state, and other top-down institutions. These movements and projects are contesting neoliberal capitalism, corporate globalization, poverty, racism, colonialism, ableism, heteronormativity, eco-destruction, and more. Not just my research but also my activism has focused on these contestations. Second, my activism shapes the theoretical frameworks I find salient. In particular, anticapitalist and anti-state analyses are strong in anarchist organizing and thought, but intersectionality, political economy, and several other disciplines such as feminism, queer studies, critical race theory, and decolonization, in their most radical forms, also inform the analysis in this book, my activism, and my life more generally.

My education lends me a certain amount of privilege; however, my relationship to this privilege is complex. I grew up in a rough-and-tumble lower-middle-class family with working-class relatives. As an adult I have lived in poverty with a street-involved life including periods of precarious housing, homelessness, and squatting. In graduate school and as a professor, my background and politics have shaped experiences of non-belonging in academia. I have been considered too loud, too political, biased in my research, not respectable, and so on. At the same time, for the past ten years I have been working as a professor at a small rural university and have held several research grants (see Acknowledgments below). I have progressed through the ranks – a hierarchy that sits uneasily with me – and have recently been promoted to Full Professor. As someone who has never been at home in academia, I have felt the need to work harder to prove my worth in an institution I find smothering. At the same time, living in a rural area means I am cut off from radical movements and must leave home to be with comrades in struggle. This isolation creates an emotional tax and a feeling of non-belonging where I live and work, a feeling further exacerbated by the pandemic.

My education did not start in the social sciences and humanities. My undergraduate degree is in systems design engineering from the University of Waterloo, which shapes my understanding of technologies, algorithms, and so on. I subsequently completed a master's degree in English and creative writing at Concordia University (and published a novel, *Kiss Painting*, about anarchist punk activists), attempting to carve out liberatory spaces and practices in creative production within academia. This was followed by a PhD in English literature at York University where I wrote a thesis on "guerrilla texts," or media and culture produced within an anti-authoritarian cultural logic. My thesis was influenced by the emergent field of alternative media, as well as my involvement in the punk and anarchist scenes in Toronto, Montreal, Germany, and beyond. Upon completing my PhD, I was fortunate to land a precarious gig as a limited-term appointment in the Communication Studies department at Concordia University in Montreal, during which time I was involved in organizing the Montreal Anarchist Bookfair, among other things. I now work in the Media, Film, and Communications program in the Interdisciplinary Studies department at Lakehead University Orillia. In this book, I attempt to draw together and draw from these formative educational trajectories.

In terms of intersecting axes of identity, I am a white ciswoman with experiences of poverty. As an adult my poverty has been mitigated by communities practising mutual aid, anti-consumerism, and gift, barter, and sharing economies (the old-fashioned kind that involved no monetary exchange). They have included polyamorous, queer, trans, disabled, and multiracial communities. My partner lives with a life-long disability, and I have made the conscious choice not to write about disability here because it is too personal. For that, I will need more time.

As researchers, our identities mean we write about some movements as participants and others as allies or accomplices, considering all movements crucial for the liberation of all people. This is grounded in a value-based practice that those most affected should be at the forefront of movements. However, to ensure the liberation of all, it is important that we are in solidarity as accomplices with movements that our identities and lived experience do not inform.

I participate in and write about multi-issue, multi-identity, and meta-issue movements that challenge all structures of oppression. At the same time, I do not claim to speak on anyone's behalf. Therefore, my research relies most heavily on the following inspirations: texts and research produced by writers and theorists internal to social movements whose work has sustained me; experience in grassroots organizing with amazing activists who give me hope; and ideas gleaned through participatory action research, also with incredibly inspiring people. As Dwyer and Buckle (2009) state: "Whether the researcher is an insider, sharing the characteristic, role, or experience under study with the participants, or an outsider to the commonality shared by participants, the personhood of the researcher, including [their] membership status in relation to those participating in the research, is an essential and ever-present aspect of the investigation."

It is my responsibility, then, as an accomplice, to do the work of interrogating whiteness, racism, colonialism, heteronormativity, and binary genderism, participating in the work of bringing these issues forward in organizational and theoretical ways, alongside those who have direct experience and are at the forefront of these movements. Like many of these movements and scholars, I engage with intersectionality because it helps us to better understand and challenge systems of oppression, working in solidarity with others. The objective of this book is not just to understand how intersectional technopolitics are taken up by social movement and media activists, but to use research to support ongoing global social transformation projects.

I am situated within the global meta-issue movements that are the subject of my research, but I am not active within all of the media projects, so, in this sense, I share the roles, experiences, and identities of some but not all movement and media activists covered here. I sometimes use "their"/"our" or "they"/"we" to signal this belonging/non-belonging.

The challenge in writing a book about intersectionality is to organize the research into chapters. When issues are intersectional, rather than silos, how do we separate them into chapters in the linear progression of a book that belies their interconnectedness? In making these decisions, I have decided, using an activist strategy, to focus on the foregrounded issue of the movement around which the other intersectional axes are organized.

Though I have stated my own standpoint, we are not all born knowing or sharing identical identities or experiences, so we must find a path through this material somehow, from beyond our own angle of vision. But our angle of vision is also really where we must start. This can be a challenge for writers and readers alike. We may have conceptions about how the world works, and these may be challenged. While I have done my best to critically analyze and make sense of the material, there will be gaps and spaces into which I have as yet found no viewpoint.

But here is what I hope for, as we work through this material together. For readers such as myself – white ciswomen who may be academics and who may have complicated class privilege, organizing as anticapitalist or anarchist feminists who are also accomplices in antiracist, anticolonial, and 2LGBTQ+[1] movements – this book maps an opportunity for learning more about movements in ways that I hope will contribute to them. It should also support thinking about working as accomplices in meta-issue movements.

For readers (for example, cismen) who come from racialized, Indigenous, and BIPOC (Black, Indigenous, and people of colour) groups, or from 2LGBTQ+ groups (people who are not feminist or who have not thought about misogyny, rape culture, gender binaries, or women's issues), the objective is to provide a better understanding of how the structures of race, colonialism, and sex are connected to capitalism, sexuality, and gender, offering insight into what media and social movement activists are doing about it.

---

1 I use "2LGBTQ+" to indicate "two-spirit," "lesbian," "gay," "bisexual," "trans," "queer," and so on. The "+" is an inadequate placeholder for many identities, and this is discussed in Chapter 5.

For readers who come from intersecting privilege (for example, white, middle-class cismen or ciswomen who have mostly stable immigration status, mostly hetero relationships, mostly stable economic situations in terms of income, housing, and jobs), and who may have never thought about intersectional experiences and structures, reading some chapters might be challenging. This is an invitation to read with an open mind and to consider reaching out in different ways to better understand and support intersectional movements.

For readers who come from experiences of multiple intersecting oppressions, this book may provide new moments of identification and insight, or it may not present anything new. The objective is for it to be a synthesis of some global contemporary meta-issue and media movements, bringing together many different examples of grassroots projects. I hope it might be useful, whether it is to reinforce, foreground, and recentre intersectional movements that you are involved in already, or whether it is to reveal gaps in my knowledge and perspective that can be addressed and expanded elsewhere in discussions that spill out beyond these pages.

Because there will be gaps. And I hope there will be critiques. My angle of vision is what it is and cannot be different. My knowledge of feminism comes from experience together with research, whereas my knowledge of 2LGBTQ+ and BIPOC issues and movements comes from research, allied social movement experiences, and everyday life. While my whiteness, my education, my cis gender and sex, my anarchist experiences, and other elements of my angle of vision provide insights by proximity, they also prevent me from knowing things through distance. If these moments prove hurtful (and I hope this does not happen but acknowledge that it may), I hope and trust that they are also openings into greater dialogue and learning beyond the book, whether it is in the classroom, in workshops, in movements, in informal discussions, in the next person's book, in activist media, and so on.

It is a difficult series of choices that inform this book. Although I experience white and other intersecting layers of privilege, I aim to decentre whiteness. At the same time, in writing about intersectional BIPOC and 2LGBTQ+ movements and media, there is a risk of appropriation of voice, getting it wrong, white saviourism, being a white-hating white person or a race traitor, and more.

This is research-activism. It is messy and complex. It sits in tension with the traditional view of research, which requires an impossible objectivity. It sits in tension with social movements, whose members' knowledge has in the past been extracted from them for the benefit of researchers' careers. It sits in tension with the conflicting desire to celebrate activists while also engaging in critical reflection so that activist work might be more effective in realizing its goals. It sits in tension with my desire to be more active in the movements I write about as I take time away from them to do this writing. In producing this book, writing about movements is my indirect way of contributing to activism.

As a result of these and other tensions, this book is not perfect. It is not the beginning or the end of anything but a snapshot of something in motion; thus, like a moving target, it feels hard to hit with any accuracy. Nonetheless, I hope the dialogues it generates extend its usefulness beyond these pages to researchers and activists alike, in making some modest contribution to the complex intersectional technopolitical struggles of our time.

Acknowledgments

I would like to thank members of the MARG collective over the years for their contributions to the project. They include (in order of appearance in the collective) Holly Nazar, Adrienne Hurley, Kate Milberry, Joanna Adamiak, Sharmeen Khan, Chloe Verner, Samantha Pritchard, Christina Petsinis, Kameela Amer, Cassidy Croft, Toni Hounslow, Kamilla Petrick, Emilie Michalik, Ellen Craig, Jaina Kelly, and Cassandra Witteman, as well as our two MITACS GlobaLink students from Brazil, Luiza Aikawa and Barbara Monfrinato. In addition, I would like to thank the community media activists who supported our work and worked with us within their communities: Annie Clair, Geordie Dent, Rebecca Granovsky-Larsen, Carolin Huang, Darya Marchenkova, and Shelagh Pizey-Allen. I would like to thank the international activists who co-facilitated workshops with me: Seamus Farrell, in Dublin, and Laura Na-Blankholm, in Copenhagen. Also, special thanks to Aruna Boodram, who facilitated MARG visioning meetings and got us through some complex conversations. While MARG members have not contributed to writing this book, they have produced many publications in scholarly journals, books, and popular media and have presented findings at various types of conferences, from scholarly to activist. However, we collectively decided not to write a book collectively.

Thanks also to the publisher, UBC Press; James McNevin, the acquiring editor, and Ann Macklem, the production manager, whom I worked with at UBC Press; the anonymous peer reviewers; and the Lakehead University

Senate Research Committee Grant in Aid of Publication. Special thanks to the ZeMKI Centre for Media, Communication, and Information Research at the University of Bremen, Germany, for supporting my work through a research fellowship in the summer of 2018, and particularly to my mentor there, Dr. Christian Pentzold, who provided feedback on an earlier version of the Introduction. Thanks to ZeMKI as well for publishing that earlier draft as part of their Working Papers series. A version of some parts of the Introduction has been published in the *International Journal of Communication* (Jeppesen 2021).

This research was supported by the Social Sciences and Humanities Research Council of Canada (SSHRC) with an Insight Grant (435–2013–1385), Indymedia 2.0: New media activism in the global digital economy; an Insight Development Grant (430–2014–00181), Protest Media Ecologies: Communicative affordances for social change in the digital era, with Dr. Alice Mattoni; and a Standard Research Grant (410–2010–2257), Communicating Social Change: Changing communication forms in Quebec anti-authoritarian feminist groups and coalition, 1999–2009. Thanks to the many colleagues with whom I have worked on these projects, including Émilie Breton, Anna Kruzynski, Aaron Lakoff, Alice Mattoni, Coco Riot, Rachel Sarrasin, and Emiliano Treré.

Thanks also to various community members who have taken the time to read and provide feedback on drafts of the book, including Monica Mitra Chaudhuri, Sydney Neuman, and Dave Struthers. Your input and insights have been invaluable. Any mistakes that remain in the book are my own.

I would also like to express profound gratitude to the global social movement and media activists I have organized with over the many years, and to those whom I have had the pleasure to meet, work with, interview, facilitate workshops with, or get to know in other ways. You are an inspiration.

And, finally, a profound thanks to my life partner, Christopher Petersen. There are no words.

Abbreviations

2LGBTQ+	two-spirit, lesbian, gay, bisexual, trans, queer, and many other sexual identities
ACAR	anticolonial and antiracist
ADB	Asian Development Bank
BIPOC	Black, Indigenous, and people of colour
BLM	Black Lives Matter
BRICS	Brazil, Russia, India, China, and South Africa
CEDAW	Committee on the Elimination of Discrimination against Women
CLAC	*La Convergence des luttes anticapitalistes* [Montreal]
CRAC	*Collectif de recherche sur l'autonomie collective*
DDOS	direct-denial-of-service
DRY!	Democracia Real Ya!
DSM	*Diagnostic and Statistical Manual of Mental Disorders*
ELN	National Liberation Army [Colombia]
FARC	Revolutionary Armed Forces of Colombia
FCM	free-culture movement
FTAA	Free Trade Area of the Americas
F2F	face-to-face
GA	general assembly
GIFCT	Global Internet Forum to Counter Terrorism
GJM	global justice movement

HHH	Hijabs, Hoodies and Hotpants
ICT	information and communications technology
IGO	intergovernmental organization
IMC	Independent Media Centre
IMF	International Monetary Fund
IWD	International Women's Day
MARG	Media Action Research Group
MMIWG	Missing and murdered Indigenous women and girls
MMIWG2S	Missing and Murdered Indigenous women, girls, and two-spirit people
MST	*Movimento dos Trabalhadores Rurais Sem Terra* [Brazil]
NAFTA	North American Free Trade Agreement
NGO	non-governmental organization
NPIC	non-profit industrial complex
NWSA	National Women's Studies Association
P2P	peer-to-peer
PGA	People's Global Action
POC	people of colour
QSS	Quebec Student Strike
QTPOC	queer and trans people of colour
QUIP	Queer Undocumented Immigrant Project
SAP	structural adjustment program
SMO	social movement organization
SPVM	Service de Police de la Ville de Montréal
SPWM	Samut Prakarn Wastewater Management
STAR	Street Transvestites Action Revolutionaries
TERF	trans exclusionary radical feminism
WB	World Bank
WDO	Women of Diverse Origins
WSF	World Social Forum
WTO	World Trade Organization
WWOS	Walking With Our Sisters

TRANSFORMATIVE MEDIA

1

Intersectional Technopolitics

Intersectional technopolitics is emblematic of our time. Intersectional activists increasingly use digital technologies to support their political objectives. From fledgling livestream and digital activism by Indymedia and the global justice movement two decades ago, to the full-fledged digitally facilitated anti-austerity and Arab Spring protests of a decade ago, to the current wave of hashtag activism, including #MeToo, #IdleNoMore, and #BlackLivesMatter, intersectional technopolitics has become a mainstay in global activism.

A growing body of scholarship considers social movements and digital media together; however, this book aims to address three gaps in the literature. First, while scholars of the movements of the squares have investigated digitally facilitated activism (G. Brown et al. 2017; Gerbaudo 2012; Treré, Jeppesen, and Mattoni 2017), only a few studies note that meta-issue or intersectional groups have contributed critical discourses and organizing structures to these movements (Fuster Morell 2012; Gámez Fuentes 2015; Talcott and Collins 2012). The growing meta-issue character of global social movements and media activism remains understudied.

Second, the scholarship suggests that traditional forms of collective action have been superseded by a fragmented, individualistic connective action framework based on a widespread reliance on social media (Bennett and Segerberg 2012). However, as some scholars have noted, this claim elides the histories and current organizing of collective actors who have adopted digital strategies (Dessewffy and Nagy 2016; M. Lim 2013; Sartoretto 2016). While acknowledging the connective power of social media, we neglect collective organizing at our peril. This book interrogates the continued existence of media collectives and their connective and collective actions at the confluence of digital technologies and grassroots mobilizations.

Third, intersectionality theory has long been used to study systems and structures of oppression and exclusion (Collins and Bilge 2016; Crenshaw 1989, 1991; Kaijser and Kronsell 2013; Williamson 2015), with recent studies showing that intersectionality is a growing activist politics of liberation (Breton et al. 2012a; Chun, Lipsitz, and Shin 2013; Cruells and Ruiz García 2014; Laperrière and Lépinard 2016) also used in community organizing and media projects (Costanza-Chock, Schweidler, and TMOP 2017). There is a gap in the literature, however, regarding intersectional, digital media activist practices (Mundt, Ross, and Burnett 2018), which this book also aims to address.

These three gaps in the research were identified by a research collective called Media Action Research Group (MARG) when we began a multi-year global study of intersectional movement and media activist projects. We combined participatory action research methods with integrated media activist activities, which included the following: facilitating media activist workshops; participating in activist gatherings and conferences; hiring media activists to join the collective to conduct research, produce media, design the website, and write articles; and reciprocating with the contribution of research labour to media and movement groups.

Research questions and processes alike were grounded in intersectionality theory and practice, with five pillars: feminism, antiracism, anticolonialism, anticapitalism, and 2LGBTQ+ liberation. Intersectionality provided the theoretical, practical, and methodological framework, structuring engagements with participants. Inclusion criteria were also intersectional: participants self-identified as working within intersectional movement and media projects.

Research questions covered three specific themes: intersectional antioppression practices, material and immaterial resources, and collective memory.

The research included three phases, each producing a data set: (1) six focus-group workshops (2014–15); (2) semi-structured interviews with eighty-nine research participants in eleven countries (2016–17); and (3) knowledge-mobilization workshops in five countries (2018). These three data sets were transcribed and coded in NVivo. We have produced findings on methods; autonomous journalism; political economies in intersectional media activism; and gender, sexuality, and power in anarchist movements (Aikawa, Jeppesen, and MARG 2020; Jeppesen 2019; Jeppesen and MARG 2018; Jeppesen and Nazar 2012, 2018; Jeppesen et al. 2017).

In addition, I have been a member of the *Collectif de recherche sur l'autonomie collective* (CRAC) in Montreal, in which 123 activists, including media activists in the anti-authoritarian movement in Quebec, Canada, were involved in a horizontal participatory co-research project. Further, I have participated in a research team with Emiliano Treré and Alice Mattoni on protest-media ecologies in Spain, Italy, and Greece consisting of sixty interviews with media and movement activists. These two interview data sets also inform my working knowledge of social movement and media activism, the former having produced findings on intersectionality (Breton et al. 2012a, 2012b; Jeppesen et al. 2013, 2014; Jeppesen, Kruzynski, and Riot 2016) and the latter on technopolitics (Treré, Jeppesen, and Mattoni 2017).

The alignment of the researcher and research participants has provided a unique opportunity for critical research from within social movement and media activist milieus, allowing for insights through proximity. Despite this solidarity model of research, to be of service to activists, a critical analysis of not just successes but also challenges and contradictions is provided. In this book, it is presumed that the reader will be familiar with mainstream discourses, and therefore, rather than rehearse them, the focus will be on the social movement and media activists' discourses. Consequently, I take the strategy of intentional subjectivity, following media activist practices that have emerged from my research (Jeppesen 2016a). Media activists argue that all news media is subjective and cannot reach its ideal of objectivity because of the subject position of the journalist, news framing, editorial decisions, the bias in journalism schools in the post-secondary education system, the lack of diversity in the newsroom, and so on. This premise is further supported by scholars and journalists alike (Herman and Chomsky 2010; Perez 2019; Schudson and Anderson 2009; Thorburn 2014). Therefore, to expose the subjectivity of all journalism, some media activists will intentionally write from a clearly articulated subject position. Similarly, to expose the subjectivity of all research, feminist, Black, Indigenous and People of Colour (BIPOC), and 2LGBTQ+ researchers will sometimes also state their subject position (Cahill 2007; S. Harding 1992; TallBear 2019; Ye 2016). This is the strategy I take here in providing the standpoint above and restating my subject position through reflexive statements in relation to the material as necessary throughout this book. Brazilian communications and social movement scholar Paola Sartoretto and I have argued elsewhere that a standpoint of proximity allows for closer insights in some ways but may also prevent the critical insights an outsider may be able to offer (Jeppesen and Sartoretto 2020). For these reasons, I acknowledge the limits of this approach while hoping the analysis developed here is still of use to scholars, journalists, and activists alike.

The ideas articulated in this book are based on my own analysis of aggregate data, unless media practices or statements are attributed to a specific media or movement project. While I do not repeat the findings of MARG's previous publications, this book in part aims to synthesize and extend them.

Based on this synthesis, I propose an empirically grounded theoretical framework that starts to map together key dimensions of media practices that combine intersectionality and technopolitics. This book is informed by key shifts in two areas. We have seen a profound shift in social movements from single-issue, coalition-building movements toward integrated meta-issue, intersectional movements. At the same time, we have seen a profound shift from fragmented, ad-hoc media practices toward coordinated, networked, digital, transmedia, technopolitical media practices.

Thus, my proposal is that intersectional technopolitics has emerged as the predominant set of integrated practices used in social movement media activism today. It offers many nuanced strengths and opportunities to movement and media activists while also being fraught with contradictions and challenges. Reflecting on both strengths and challenges, the book aims to map the range of intersectional technopolitical practices of many global groups, some of whom were interviewed and some of whom were encountered in the scholarly research.

Intersectionality in Meta-issue Movements

"Intersectionality" is a term increasingly used in both public discourse and social movements. Intersectionality theory describes the complex dynamics of multiple intersecting micro and macro systems of oppression. The term "intersectionality" was first coined by Kimberlé Crenshaw (1989), who articulated a legal framework for considering anti-Black racism in the context of gender oppression, arguing that race and gender had intersectional constructions, making Black women's oppression different from the oppression of Black men, on the one hand, and white women, on the other.

However, the observation that oppressions of gender and race must be considered together can be dated much further back. For example, in 1851, Sojourner Truth's famous speech "Ain't I a Woman?" articulated the differences in social position between white and Black women at the time and called for feminist liberation, inclusive of Black women, an early example of intersectional advocacy (Brah and Phoenix 2013). Further, Indigenous women noted the intersecting gendered, economic, and age-based effects of colonialism and capitalism in the early 1900s, demanding that land be returned to them as Indigenous women (Clark 2016). Black feminist scholars analyzed intersectionality beyond race and gender to include capitalism in what bell hooks labels "white supremacist patriarchal capitalism" (hooks 1982). This triangulation has been extended to include intersections with queer embodiment (Rice et al. 2020), nation (Collins 1998), decolonization (Clark 2016), decolonizing antiracism (Dhamoon 2015), transfeminism (Araneta and Fernández Garrido 2016), and intersectional affinities (Ahmed 2016), among many more trends and tendencies explored in this book.

Intersectionality theory has thus grown from a legal framework for intersectional identities (Crenshaw 1991) to a broader theoretical perspective on interlocking systems of oppression (Razack, Thobani, and Smith 2010). Critical race theorists Collins and Bilge (2016, 2) offer the following extended definition:

> Intersectionality is a way of understanding and analyzing the complexity in the world, in people, and in human experiences. The events and conditions of social and political life and the self can seldom be understood as shaped by one factor. They are generally shaped by many factors in diverse and mutually influencing ways. When it comes to social inequality, people's lives and the organization of power in a given society are better understood as being shaped not by a single axis of social division, be it race or gender or class, but by many axes that work together and influence each other.

Collins and Bilge's global approach to intersectionality is now taken seriously in many societies as a framework for challenging complex layers of social division in situations as divergent as social democratic policies in the European Union (La Barbera 2017), speeches at the Hollywood Academy Awards ceremonies (Kornhaber 2018), and media activist groups in Latin America (Aikawa, Jeppesen, and MARG 2020).

Particularly in social movements and media, intersectionality has its own genealogies. Black feminist movements in the 1970s advocated for the rights of Black women as distinct from the demands of white women. For example, white women were vying to enter the workforce, whereas Black women had long been working to feed their families. Similarly, the white-dominated feminist movement was advocating for birth control and abortion rights, whereas racialized and Indigenous women were fighting for reproductive justice, to keep their children, and to end coercive sterilization programs (Stote 2017). The Combahee River Collective famously produced a statement outlining "the historical reality of Afro-American women's life-and-death struggles for survival and liberation" (1977, para. 3), providing a history of Black feminist activism.

Another genealogy traces intersectional movements to anticapitalist and anarchist movements. The anticapitalist concerns of meta-issue movements are evident. Related anarchist movements are increasingly intersectional, with feminist, 2LGBTQ+, and BIPOC activists mobilizing in autonomous collectives. However, while Black feminists started with intersectional identities, anarchists have tended to prioritize capital and the state, therefore feminists, 2LGBTQ+, and BIPOC participants in anarchist and socialist movements have long struggled to render them more than superficially feminist, antiracist, queer, and nonbinary (Ackelsberg 2005; Breton et al. 2012a, 2012b; Crass 2013; Farrow and Bear 1977; Shannon et al. 2013). In both genealogies, intersectionality can be understood as a series of liberatory practices engaged by social movement and media activist projects dating back at least to the 1970s.

Despite the negotiation of complex intersectional identities and critiques of interlocking structures of oppression in social movements, scholarly accounts of media activism and protest movements tend to encode a universal subject in considerations of collective identity. The Indignados in Spain, YoSoy132 in Mexico, and the 99% in Occupy have been identified as collective identities (Fuster Morell 2012; Treré 2015), with few studies breaking this down to a greater level of granularity to examine how complex identities and subject positions might influence mobilization and media practices (Cruells and Ruiz García 2014; Talcott and Collins 2012).

This research reveals that intersectionality has been used as a collective identity and as a set of liberatory practices in movement and media activist collectives. Projects foreground a particular issue while working from an intersectional perspective. Costanza-Chock and colleagues (2017) have found that 2LGBTQ+ organizations receive funding for a single focus, whereas the groups studied used an intersectional approach, including antiracist, anti-poverty, youth, housing, and other initiatives. Moreover, groups in North America such as UndocuQueer, Queer Undocumented Immigrant Project (QUIP), and Ste-Emilie Skillshare have organized around intersectional representations of queer and trans people of colour (Gentile and

Salerno 2019; Jeppesen, Kruzynski, and Riot 2016; Salgado n.d.). Thus, we can understand that the subjectivities and collectivities are intrinsically intersectional rather than aspirationally coalitional.

Intersectional digital transfeminism movements such as #MeToo and #MosqueMeToo (Gash and Harding 2018; Mendes, Ringrose, and Keller 2018; Point 2019), as well as digital antiracism movements such as #Black-LivesMatter and #SayHerName, the latter co-founded by Crenshaw (M. Brown et al. 2017; Crenshaw and Ritchie 2015; Mundt, Ross, and Burnett 2018; S. Williams 2016), substantiate the claim that collective action is increasingly intersectional. Sirma Bilge (2016, 2020) cautions that intersectionality should not serve ornamental or appropriative purposes, an issue the #MeToo movement has been accused of, given the predominance of white women and celebrities using the hashtag. However, the fact that #MeToo was in fact started by African American Tarana Burke, who leads a sexual assault initiative called MeToo (without the #), indicates the layers of complexity in intersectional movements. In other words, the movement was foundationally intersectional and later became appropriated by white women and celebrities. This illustrates the complexities of understanding ornamental intersectionality in movements that are fluid and change over time.

Intersectional Waves of Contention

Within social movement scholarship, waves of contention are understood to produce their own protest repertoires, with the repertoire of contention being a set of modes of engagement available to the general population for making political demands. Intensified moments of civil unrest produce new modes of contestation or social movement practices, extending the repertoire of contention. Meta-issue movements in the newest global waves of contention, I argue, have begun to contribute intersectional practices to these repertoires.

One such practice is the format of teach-ins, which increasingly foreground intersectional issues. Participating in a World Economic Forum protest convergence as part of the global justice movement (GJM) in Cologne, Germany, in 1998, was one of my earliest experiences of activist convergence teach-ins. I attended workshops facilitated by people from across the globe – India, Russia, Argentina, South Africa. They revealed how many social movement concerns were connected to neoliberal capitalism in the growing GJM characterized as a "movement of movements" (Mertes and Bello 2004). This naming of the GJM as a movement that integrated many interrelated movements signified the fledgling global grassroots meta-issue networks foregrounding the meta-issue of neoliberal capitalism and its intersectional issues such as race, colonialism, gender, labour, poverty, farming, sex work, and more.

Ten years later, in the anti-austerity wave of contention, we see information spread not just through in-person teach-ins on the squares but also on social media. Spanish digital-movements scholar Mayo Fuster Morell (2012) notes the emergence of "meta-politics" in the 2011 Indignados or 15M movement of the squares in Spain. The meta-issue of austerity was indicated by the slogan "We are not commodities in the hands of politicians and bankers." Related movements brought together by 15M included housing, unemployment, student debt, net neutrality, and anticapitalism (Fuster Morell 2012, 391). Also intersecting with austerity, issues such as feminism, antiracism, anti-Islamophobia, decolonization, and 2LGBTQ+ rights were taken up by some participants in 15M, according to the research participants we interviewed.

Another ten years later, in the era of social media platform dominance, the hashtag activism wave of contention has gained prominence. Scholarship identifies Indigenous intersectionality (Clark 2016), intersectional 2LGBTQ+ movement and media activism (Costanza-Chock, Schweidler, and TMOP 2017), intersectional transfeminism (Ahmed 2016; J. Lim and Fanghanel 2013), and intersectional anti-Black racism (Garza 2014; Mundt, Ross, and Burnett 2018) as key social movement concerns in the wave of contention that foregrounds austerity.

Forefront Strategies

In grassroots meta-issue movements, horizontal organizing tends to be the accepted structure, but the question remains: Who should be at the forefront of a movement? Related questions arise regarding everyday practices. Whose word is given weight in meetings? Who is empowered as a media spokesperson? And who speaks at events including workshops and protests? Practices related to speaking, both within movements and in public events, embody power regarding who speaks and is therefore understood to be at the forefront or an informal leader.

Many movement groups articulate "forefront" strategies based on the principle that those most affected by an issue should be at the forefront serving as horizontal leaders. Some groups such as Black Lives Matter call themselves leaderful rather than leaderless (Khan-Cullors and Bandele 2018), providing strategic and tactical direction for the movement, exercising "power with" rather than "power over" through spheres of influence (Gordon 2008; Jeppesen 2019).

The question of who should be a media spokesperson is a key forefront media practice, with activist groups using a variety of practices. Some groups come to a consensus on media strategy in a general assembly, and choose a media committee to develop talking points, create media releases, and give interviews aligned with the larger group's consensus. Some groups agree that anyone within the group should be empowered to speak on behalf of the group, with mutual trust ensuring the group is accurately represented. Other groups will have a rotating spokesperson and offer skillshares so new members may also serve as spokespeople. This last was the predominant practice mentioned by interviewees.

Contradictions and tensions can arise in these forefront strategies. Racialized spokespeople have been violently attacked by racist police. For example, one person's multiracial antiracism group had decided to empower a spokesperson of colour; however, this was reconsidered after their experience of violence. Racialized spokespeople were also condescended to by mainstream journalists, who said they were "very articulate" or "spoke English well," racially inflected codes that erase the expertise of BIPOC activists. Further challenges arise in relation to mainstream media. Journalists are accustomed to a group having a leader and are often confused by leaderless groups. Journalists may therefore contact a random group member they know, ignoring the group's designated spokesperson, or a non-spokesperson activist might speak to the media on their own initiative. In both cases, this creates a cycle in which they are the one upon whom journalists will continue to call. Journalists circumventing the designated spokesperson can create power dynamics within the group that are counter to horizontal principles.

Internal power dynamics might also lead to a person being tokenized by their group as a racialized or gendered forefront spokesperson. When such individuals are encouraged to take a forefront role, they may already be overtaxed in terms of time, resources, or capacities precisely because of their marginalization, and may therefore experience the intended support as a form of unwanted pressure. While collectives might need to navigate tensions in forefront organizing, it is the predominant mode of dealing with leadership in horizontal multi-issue activist groups in relation to the media because it empowers people most affected by an issue to speak out, take on horizontal leadership, and shape their own futures.

Foreground Strategies

Most multi-issue organizations foreground a single issue while also working with intersectional approaches to that issue.

Regarding 2LGBTQ+ rights and intersectionality, Sasha Costanza-Chock, Chris Schweidler, and the Transformation Media Organizing Project (2017, 167) have found that "many LGBTQ and Two-Spirit organizations have an intersectional analysis and do intersectional media work." Organizations that foreground 2LGBTQ+ issues, in other words, deal with intersectional issues 2LGBTQ+ people experience, related not just to heteronormativity and transnormativity, but also to housing, racism, violence, policing, refugee rights, mental health, employment, and more.

Further, regarding Indigenous intersectionality, Natalie Clark (2016, 47) argues that "Indigenous feminists remind us again and again in their writing that violence has always been gendered, aged, and linked to access to land." Thus, activist media focusing on Indigenous issues must acknowledge that for Indigenous people who are "writing and speaking out today, this knowledge of the interlocking arteries of colonialism has always been part of our truth-telling" (Clark 2016, 47). Decolonizing movements thus foreground Indigenous rights while integrating intersectional concerns about gender, age, sexualities, health outcomes, and so on (Hargreaves 2017).

Moreover, regarding anti-Black racism and intersectionality, Alicia Garza, one of the co-founders of Black Lives Matter, notes how the movement foregrounds anti-Black racism while also centring the contributions of Black queer women, maintaining an intersectional emphasis that links anti-Black systemic racism to profiling, police violence (Weissinger, Mack, and Watson 2017), the school-to-prison pipeline (Crenshaw 2011), mental health, poverty, education, trans rights, disability, and more (Garza 2014).

Finally, regarding intersectional transfeminism, movements such as SlutWalk and #MeToo foreground gender issues including sexual assault and rape culture, with some activists making space for articulations of Islamophobia, youth, antiracism, education, transmisogyny, misogynoir, cisnormativity, and so on.

Foregrounding can thus be defined as a liberatory intersectional practice that allows a group to focus on one primary issue while also working on the many issues that intersect with it. It intrinsically includes intersectional identities and provides a mechanism for considering the intersectional character of systems of oppression.

Translocal Strategies
Forefronting and foregrounding are used in tandem with translocal strategies that connect local and global movements. Activists share strategies, tactics, and practices globally through digital media, and they organize autonomously to reflect local issues. There is often no direct coordination or interaction among global organizations or groups except through media consumption – they learn about one another's movements and tactics online.

Translocal Networks
Whereas the global justice movement is seen to include summit hopping and coalition building, in anti-austerity and hashtag contestations, this is supplanted by virtual summit hopping using livestreaming and live tweeting of protests for global participation through translocal strategies (H.-T. Chen, Ping, and Chen 2015). On international days of solidarity, for example, such as the March 8th International Women's Day March, mass mobilizations are supported translocally through linked convergences in many cities, each framed according to local issues.

Protest Camps
Tahrir Square, Occupy, Gezi Park, the Indignados, and Aganaktismenoi have created ongoing camps in the squares, supported by micro-infrastructures such as community kitchens, media tents, general assemblies, and so on (G. Brown et al. 2017; Feigenbaum, Frenzel, and McCurdy 2013; Fuster Morell 2012). While earlier protest camps organized by activist groups or NGOs tended to focus on a single issue, camps are now meta-issue and multigenerational, with citizens participating who had not considered themselves activists before (G. Brown et al. 2017; Feigenbaum, Frenzel, and McCurdy 2013; Treré, Jeppesen, and Mattoni 2017). Movements such as the Indignados and Occupy mobilize camps in many cities, and on critical days, they call for solidarity translocal actions by international supporters.

The Logic of Connective Action
Social media similarly allows participants to organize translocally through affective friend and family networks using the logic of connective action (Bennett and Segerberg 2012). Digital networks generate a generalized collective identity that sustains meta-movements and provides space for the expression of intersectional issues. Individual participants use connective

action to foreground salient issues, working with like-minded individuals to develop forefront strategies. These participants use translocal organizing strategies to connect digitally with global movements interested in similar issues without co-organizing, without asking for permission to use a similar group name, such as Occupy, and without even communicating directly with one another.

Distributive Organizing

The structure used by translocal networks is to organize through distributive networks, with many groups participating in local movements to organize local and global actions, develop analysis, create content, and call events. In the Quebec Student Strike of 2012, for example, Facebook was used by strike participants (rather than elected student leadership) to call a "Naked March," which was festive and highly attended, drawing attention to queer, trans, and feminist issues in relation to student debt. To take other examples, the distributive leadership of the Indignados across Spain in 15M and globally in Occupy focused on shared overall objectives such as the affect or emotion of indignation in the Indignados or the class-based identity of the 99% in Occupy, while also organizing around specific local issues such as housing, gentrification, education, free culture, austerity, and so on.

Intersectional Leadership

The newest waves of contention combine the above strategies with a commitment to intersectionality. They are often founded by people experiencing multiple intersectional oppressions, such as the intersectional leadership of Black Lives Matter described above. Similarly, Idle No More was started by four women, of whom three are Indigenous and one non-Indigenous, signifying intersectional leadership across Indigeneity and gender. This can be complex, as we saw in the case of #MeToo which is seen to have two initiators, Tarana Burke and Alyssa Milano, who may be understood as engaging distributive leadership by instantiating and approaching intersectionality in different ways. Intersectional translocal leadership in grassroots horizontal organizations can also create tensions as people work to create new organizing relationships.

Intersectional Dimensions

In light of these interwoven strands of intersectionality, six key dimensions characterizing intersectional media practices have been identified (see Table 1).

Table 1 Key dimensions of intersectionality

Dimension	Intersectional media practices
Anticapitalist collective subjects	Against state-capital-communications complex; disavowal of the economic; contest digital divide; intersectional digital feminisms
Intersectional counterpublics	Online-offline counterpublics; antiracist; queer; trans and non-binary genders; feminist; anticolonial; disability politics
Translocal cartographies	Refugee and (im)migrant justice; no-border networks; queer immigrations; media transgress borders
Participatory creation and ownership	Collective self-ownership of cultural production; creation of self-owned technologies and infrastructures; creative experimentation
Intersectional solidarity	Intersectional solidarity economies; data justice; solidarity values in technological design; post-scarcity; mutual aid
Distributed horizontalist rhizomes	Distributive infrastructures of horizontality; rhizomatic distributive leadership; multipolitical architectures of practice

First, in the political economy of intersectional anticapitalism, media activists disavow the economic imperative of production, creating media as a labour of love and valuing cooperative creative expression over competitive capitalist accumulation. However, a disavowal of the economic is only possible with class privilege, as noted by many media activists interviewed. Some undertook unpaid media labour with family financial support, while others required paid media labour for subsistence, an issue that played out along intersectional lines. Media activist projects facilitated participation opportunities for intersectional marginalized groups through practices including a queer and trans people of colour (QTPOC) mentorship program, an Indigenous journalism fund, and media technology skillshare workshops for female and/or 2LGBTQ+ participants. Media activist projects challenged systemic oppressions by both representing intersectional political content and supporting intersectional practitioners.

Second, interviewees noted the importance of intersectional counterpublics, confirming how "statistics and surveys indicate that many more women, people of colour, seniors and individuals from marginalized groups are becoming increasingly active" (Kahn and Kellner 2007) in media activism. For example, in Athens, the intersectional feminist collective called Burnt Bras developed both a blog and a Facebook page to disseminate theoretical analysis of intersectional meta-issue movements, focusing on how antiausterity and feminist issues articulate with antiracism, no-border politics, disability, and mental health to foster intersectional counterpublics. Similarly, Groundwire in Canada, Smaschieramenti in Italy, Dotterbolaget in Sweden, Strike in the United Kingdom, and Mídia NINJA and Capitolina in Brazil, among others, organized as horizontal media collectives producing intersectional feminist media and counterpublics. This is not to erase key differences in the local, historical, and national spaces they inhabit but rather to suggest that they produce intersectional counterpublics in similar ways.

Third, translocal, borderless digital-activist cartographies support (im)migrant self-representations against capitalist and state austerity through digital technologies such as mesh networks, portable WiFi routers, and no-border networks that support international migration, challenging global antimigration racialization structures. For example, a nonprofit media initiative in Athens called Solomon supports refugees and migrants by offering free four-month media production labs, with opportunities to report in the magazine and join the production team. Similarly, Calais Migrant Solidarity and No Borders Iceland activists created solidarity networks supporting migrant cross-border travel and refugee claims, integrating migrants into activist networks, sharing media skills and technologies, and supporting their self-articulated objectives. And in Greece, feminist groups provided print media about women's rights to female refugees, addressing gender in the context of migration. Thus, no-border politics intersects with racialization, social class, and gender through translocal cartographies that map global migration across international borders to intersectional meta-issue media and movements.

Fourth, participatory autonomous digital alternatives are key, as Vlachokyriakos and colleagues (2016, 1097) argue: "Clearly, there is a role that digital technology can play in reconfiguring citizen participation" that is attentive to "the various power relations at play." This connects to the work of an interviewee with Open Lab Athens in the solidarity economy network, who designed and coded technologies based on horizontal, participatory values that amplified the distributive leadership of intersectional groups through technologies of horizontality. Recognizing that digital technologies are neither neutral nor instrumental, but encode political meanings, the solidarity network recoded digital technologies to increase participation, collaboration, and collective self-determination, consistent with the values of intersectional anticapitalist solidarity economies.

Fifth, building solidarity economies based on post-scarcity and mutual aid is linked to intersectional media content, structures, and digital technologies. An interviewee from Open Lab Athens noted that collectives organized using solidarity, barter, and gift economies through networks of solidarity health clinics, schools, theatres, farm-to-table groups, and more. This created a transition "from transactional to relational service models" (Vlachokyriakos et al. 2016, 1096), grounding actions in reciprocity, mutuality, self-organization, and deep diversity. Within these networks, Open Lab Athens coded software to "embed the logic and values of solidarity both socially and economically in the systems" (Vlachokyriakos et al. 2017, 3135). These digital solidarity networks – fostering both connective and collective action – encoded intersectional solidarity logics into software, platforms, and apps, challenging the capitalist logic of digital platforms. Their media practices were not only technological but also material, affective, epistemological, and intersectional, including data justice practices such as encryption and data privacy (Dencik, Hintz, and Cable 2016).

Finally, the sixth dimension encompasses prefigurative distributed infrastructures fostering intersectional horizontality through metapolitical architectures of technology. In Greece, for example, interviewees used the Facebook group "Indignados of Syntagma Square" for peer-to-peer (P2P) debates of issues on which decisions were later made face-to-face (F2F) in the Syntagma Square protest camp general assemblies. This provided space for in-depth deliberation online, with general assemblies focused on decision making. We also interviewed members of Omnia TV in Athens, an autonomous, horizontal, antifascist digital TV station set up in the shared living room of two tech activists. Their leadership countered the risk of informal hierarchies of elites (Costanza-Chock 2012; Wolfson 2013); collective members perceived these two participants not as taking more power but rather as shouldering more responsibility. From antifascism to anticolonialism, media projects such as Xnet in Spain; Mídia NINJA and Capitolina in Brazil; Groundwire, the Media Co-op, and Ricochet in Canada; and Marronage in Denmark have generated specific internal technical, economic, labour, and discursive collective processes to foster intersectional decolonizing distributive leadership structures for production of both media content and social movement actions. These six dimensions of intersectional media practices are increasingly embedded in technopolitics.

Technopolitics Theory
Media activists engage in technopolitics by rendering the political elements of technologies visible. In doing so, "the technopolitics of social movements strives to guarantee the democratization of social media in order to create a

space where subjects can exercise their rights and obligations" (Caballero and Gravante 2017, 6). Technopolitics fosters opportunities for the equitable communication and self-expression of collective counterpublics.

Technopolitics was a key media and movement practice in the anti-austerity wave of contention, particularly within both Latin America and the Spanish Indignados (Caballero and Gravante 2017; Gerbaudo 2012; Toret et al. 2013; Treré, Jeppesen, and Mattoni 2017). However, this was not the only provenance of technopolitcs. Rather, technopolitics had emerged in the global justice movement of the early 2000s, most notably in Indymedia (Hanke 2005; Kidd 2003; Milioni 2009; Pickard 2006; Pickerill 2007), the free culture movement (Fuster Morell 2012; Milberry and Anderson 2009), and early video activism (T. Harding 1998).

Two decades ago, Kellner (2003, 182) suggested that "technopolitics can be and is being used for anti-capitalist contestation." He defined technopolitics as "the use of new technologies such as computers and the Internet to advance political goals" (Kellner 2003, 182), a basic definition that remains salient for media activists. More recently, Toret and Calleja (2014, 15) have also traced the genealogy of technopolitics to the livestreamed anti-World Trade Organization (WTO) protests of Seattle Indymedia in 1999, in "Web 1.0, at the very edge of the Web 2.0, at the very height of the anti-corporate globalization movement." These practices, including Independent Media Centres (IMCs), "open[ed] new terrains of political struggle for voices and groups excluded from the mainstream media and thus increase[d] potential for intervention by oppositional groups" (Kellner 2003, 182).

At the same time, Kellner (2003, 184) cautions "that the computerization of society will intensify the current inequalities in relations of class, race and gender power." In noting these intersectional inequalities, he counterposes dangers to participatory affordances in the capitalist domination of the internet (Curran, Fenton, and Freedman 2016; Fuchs 2009), opening an as-yet-unresolved debate about the contradictions inherent in the political economy of participatory media.

Kurban, Peña-Lopez, and Haberer (2017, 6) emphasize that this contradiction necessitates a consideration of power: "Technopolitics allows us to translate the complexity surrounding the integration of new technologies into power dynamics among political actors." As with Kellner (2003), this formulation considers power in the political economy of media activism; however, it takes political power and technologies as separate spheres, with technologies having instrumental affordances for political action.

But technopolitics is not a practice of accessing neutral digital affordances to create communicative action. Rather, technopolitical activists mobilize digital technologies as both the tool and terrain of struggle. Edwards and Hecht (2010, 619) argue that technopolitics signals already-integrated "hybrids of technical systems and political practices that produce new forms of power and agency." Unlike Kellner (2003) or Kurban and colleagues (2017), Edwards and Hecht (2010) see technological designs as having generative embedded politics. Analyzing technologies in apartheid South Africa, they found that the state integrated oppressive political objectives into technological design, with, for example, "computerised population registers serving to displace the (political) denaturalisation of millions of black South Africans into a (technical) matter of recordkeeping" (Edwards and Hecht 2010, 638). These systems included biometric fingerprinting and mandatory passes – both violently enforced through racialized policing – illustrating the embedded politics of racialized social control in imperialist technologies.

We see the emergence of similar technopolitical passes in the new COVID-19 passports, for example, in Israel-Palestine, where it has been predominantly Israelis who have been vaccinated and thus have access to the freedom of movement granted by the passport, a freedom not available to the predominantly unvaccinated Palestinians, particularly those living in the West Bank and Gaza (Reality Check 2021). The controversy of vaccination passports is that they may divide populations into two distinct socioeconomic futures of the haves and have-nots, and, further, that this will likely play out along intersectional racialized lines.

Although technologies can often be reconfigured for oppositional uses, and media activists may "find ways of reshaping them (within limits) for purposes for which they were never intended" (Fominaya and Gillan 2017, 385), this is not always the case. Edwards and Hecht (2010) argue that anti-apartheid activists could not produce countertechnologies to challenge racialized technopolitical state power. As Vlachokyriakos and colleagues (2017, 3135) have found, state and capitalist technologies "promote and sustain a logic that is adverse to principles of solidarity – fostering individualism, the simplification of human relations and a market logic with significant negative effects on social and welfare justice." This technopolitical state and capitalist logic paradoxically both disguises and underlines the ideological function of digital technologies from above.

In opposition to these structures, grassroots technopolitical collective swarms (Toret et al. 2013) have challenged the hypercapitalist enclosure of

the internet, providing avenues for democratic, cultural, political, and epistemological multidirectional interactive dialogue and exchange, and rejecting
profit-oriented monetization systems based in advertising, data mining, and
unpaid media activist labour (Dowling, Nunes, and Trott 2007; McRobbie
2011). Thus, despite Kellner's (2003) early observation of the importance of
technopolitics to intersectional groups, within social movements of the early
2000s the politics within technopolitics was predominantly anticapitalist.

As neoliberal globalization produced intensifying enclosures of the
internet through communicative cybercapitalism (Dean 2009; Dyer-Witheford 1999), anticapitalist technopolitical activists developed "a set of preeminent practices of what may potentially be a multitudinous re-appropriation
of the political, economic, and communicative spheres" (Toret and Calleja
2014, 4). Collective action, in the subsequent era of social media platform
dominance, merged into connective action (Bennett and Segerberg 2012). In
the context of austerity in Latin America and the Indignados in Spain, Toret
and Calleja (2014, 25) define technopolitics as exclusively liberatory, "the tactical and strategic, multitudinous deployment of ICTs for the organization,
communication and unfolding of collective action." They suggest, contra
Edwards and Hecht (2010), that technopolitics is a tactic always used by
activists (not available to state or capital) to reappropriate power.

Building from and within anticapitalist movements, the politics of technopolitics increasingly includes intersectional meta-issues (Breton et al.
2012a; Costanza-Chock, Schweidler, and TMOP 2017; Cruells and Ruiz
García 2014; Ezquerra 2012; Mendes, Ringrose, and Keller 2018; Williamson
2015). The seemingly paradoxical incorporation of hypercapitalist social
media platforms into grassroots activist media practices does not belie the
fact that intersectional technopolitics also comes with a commitment to
autonomous media. Capitalist platforms were not used uncritically by the
media activists we interviewed; social media networks were initially
"opposed by many activists because of their corporate character" (Fuster
Morell 2012, 389). Research participants shared critiques of targeted
advertising, a lack of security and data privacy, openness to state surveillance, restricted social affordances, black box algorithms, and so on. They
continued to develop prefigurative, self-managed media in their repertoire
of technopolitical action, consistent with their social values:

> Technopolitics may encompass forms of cyberactivism, but the key differ-
> ence is that technopolitics is not limited to the digital sphere. It feeds from
> and into collective abilities for inventing forms of action that may take place

or start on the internet but that are not confined to it. It enables and inter-
connects the taking of the public urban, digital and mass media spaces.

(Toret and Calleja 2014, 25)

For technopolitical activists, the question of who owns and operates urban,
digital, and media spaces is crucial. The question of ownership draws our attention to the political economy of digital media activism, in particular with respect to media labour and transmedia mobilizations (Costanza-Chock 2013).

Networked Media Labour under Neoliberalism

New patterns of networked digital media labour under neoliberal capitalism
shape the technopolitical media practices of social movements. The contradiction of intersectional anticapitalist activists engaging in platform labour
informs the organizational structures, funding models, and material and
immaterial resources of media activist projects (Jeppesen and Petrick 2018).
Media labourers have joined the flexploited precariat – they're forced into
so-called flexible temporary contracts or part-time work that is beneficial to
the employer but thrusts them into precarious employment (Fuchs 2013).
An admixture of these shifting employment structures and technological
media practices combine to produce an emergent sociotechnical practice of
networked journalism (van der Haak, Parks, and Castells 2012).

Media activists enter this labour force with conflicting objectives. They
predominantly reject mainstream media logics, preferring to take on unpaid
or underpaid media activist labour in independent media while hustling to
get the odd well-paid freelance gig writing about topics consistent with their
values. The types of labour open to media activists are charted briefly below.
Some are clearly useful whereas others are imbued with contradictions for
intersectional technopolitics activists.

The Unpaid Media Internship

Media producers take unpaid media internships hoping for gainful employment; however, "a slim 37 percent of unpaid interns received job offers"
(Evans and Janish 2015). Unpaid media labour is characterized as capitalist
"hyper-exploitation," with 100 percent of the labour converted to surplus
value (Fuchs 2013). Unpaid internships replace entry-level jobs, restructuring media work. Interns with class privilege can leverage parental financial
support into workforce experience, intensifying racialized and gendered
media divides (de Peuter, Cohen, and Brophy 2012) and deepening the
unequal opportunities in media work.

The Invisible Immaterial Labourer

Digital platform labour is immaterial through its "communicative capacities and sociality" (N. Cohen 2013, 181; see also Brophy and de Peuter 2007). Information, cultural content, and affective relations create value for employers and platforms alike as invisible networks, data, and metadata. Media activists are thus engaged in the invisibilized affective labour of social networking. Most often women, 2LGBTQ+, and BIPOC, these media labourers are not guaranteed that any credit or remuneration for their work will accrue to them, noting how their media productions have been used without their consent for profit by people in dominant groups. In techno-politics, the intersectional, immaterial platform activist balances hyper-exploitation with the need for virality.

The Gig Economy Cognitariat

A highly educated segment of the flexploited precariat, often with graduate degrees in communications and culture, the gig economy cognitariat are employed in the highly competitive, insecure conditions of the knowledge and cultural sectors (Dean 2014). Generating innovative epistemological, pedagogical, and cultural forms, their work may advance policy change yet remain underfunded as they survive contract to contract. This is intensified for intersectional producers who challenge the status quo, circulating creative knowledge work in technopolitics activism at the risk of losing gigs and income.

The Entrepreneurial Journalist

With no fixed employment, new journalists are now self-employed, forced to leverage freelance gigs by mobilizing reportage with photography, video, websites, podcasts, and blog posts to create a branded niche while excluded from job security and unions (N. Cohen 2016). Covering political issues creates the risk of losing work despite a long record of journalistic excellence. The intersectional technopolitics activist thus contradictorily engages in competitive, capitalist media markets, whereby if they successfully create an activist-oriented niche brand, it might relegate freelance opportunities to unpaid labour.

The Journalism Start-Up

Entrepreneurial journalists who choose not to work alone but to form a media organization that rejects most advertising have chosen to develop funding streams through grants, crowdfunding, and sustainers

(Jeppesen and Petrick 2018). Community news outlet Bristol Cable in the United Kingdom combines paid and unpaid labour, with the objective of full employment. Athens Live in Greece started with a crowdfunder, reporting on Greek politics in English. Both use a sustainer model, avoid paywalls, mentor racialized youth, and have won journalism awards. Intersectional technopolitics entrepreneurial journalists deploy media and business skills to support social change.

The Citizen Journalist
Passing by an unfolding event, the occasional citizen journalist pulls out a cellphone to livestream it, the 1991 Rodney King bystander video by George Holliday being an early example of this (Deggans 2011). Citizen journalists in China reported on the 2008 earthquake that the government had denied (M. Moore 2008). Citizens also livestream racist police violence, such as Diamond Reynolds' Facebook livestream of the police shooting of her boyfriend, Philando Castile, at a traffic stop in 2016 (Uberti 2016). Intersectional activists can thus mobilize immediate support, but Facebook also benefits through monetizations.

The Freedom-of-Information Journalist
Freedom-of-information legislation facilitates information activism (Halupka 2016), whereby previously privatized, secretive government agency data can be accessed. Email correspondence among government officials can ground in-depth investigative journalism. Intersectional activists use this information as evidence of systemic oppressions in publicly funded organizations. This mode of journalism is time-consuming; requests take months to process; and documents with the best information, from a journalist's perspective, might unfortunately be the most redacted.

The Data Journalist
Data activism is the new media activism (Milan 2017). Reactive data activists mobilize against big-data abuses such as surveillance, invasion of privacy, and algorithms of oppression; proactive data activists exploit open access data to develop civic participation opportunities. Data journalists use open data for investigative journalism and data visualizations. Infographics such as x-y graphs, charts, bar graphs, and scatter-dot maps allow the data journalist to visualize abuses and support social transformation. Intersectional data journalists can turn big data from exploitative to liberatory, but this also requires technical skill.

Whistleblower Journalism

Whistleblowers serve as the moral compass of our times. They work with reporters such as Glenn Greenwald, who reported on Edward Snowden's revelations that the National Security Agency was illegally spying on domestic American citizens (Geist 2015; Hintz, Dencik, and Wahl-Jorgensen 2018; Rosner 2013). Grassroots whistleblower projects include Xnet in Spain, which set up an encrypted dropbox for citizens to anonymously deposit incriminating documents. Whistleblower journalism projects provide the buffer needed to protect whistleblowers from the state while ensuring they reach an audience.

The Documentary Journalist

Documentary filmmaker activists produce in-depth investigative journalism (Canella 2017; Christensen 2009), aesthetic narratives of world events from a critical perspective, including the film about Edward Snowden, *Citizenfour* (Poitras 2014). *State of Exception* (O'Hara 2017) features protests in Rio de Janeiro against the World Cup and Olympics. Director O'Hara foregrounded intersectional decolonization through the production of a participatory documentary in which he worked closely with local Indigenous and activist groups, provided cameras and skillshare workshops, and organized film screenings at community centres, countering the typical extractive model of documentaries. At the same time, intersectional documentary filmmakers such as O'Hara often struggle for recognition and funding to support the creation of content that is highly controversial in a field with high production costs and intact gatekeeping.

The Comics Journalist

Comics are technologies of change. *The Beast* is a research-based graphic novel about Canadian climate activists by anarchist collective Ad Astra, with researcher Patrick McCurdy. Comic artists are also intersectional activists. In Sweden, members of the feminist comics collective Dotterbolaget share work opportunities as they produce comics about the intersections of sex, gender, sex work, poverty, gender violence, and immigration. In Spain, non-binary artist Coco Riot's life-size art project *Gender Poo* deconstructs binary bathroom symbols, inviting viewers to contribute new subjectivities (Riot 2008).

The Hacktivist

Hacker activists, such as the Electronic Frontier Foundation, mobilize through technologies as a site of contestation. Arising in the global free culture movements of the 1980s and '90s, early hacktivists coordinated direct-denial-of-service (DDOS) attacks in solidarity with the Zapatistas uprising, taking down the Mexican government's website. Some members of hacker groups such as Anonymous use hacking to hold corporations accountable; others do it just for the lulz or laughs (G. Coleman 2014). Hacktivists are at the centre of technopolitics media activism, sharing advanced digital skills and contesting who owns the internet.

In the era of COVID-19, media labour is increasingly troubled by fake news, misinformation, and disinformation. Discredited films such as *Plandemic*, conspiracy theories promoted by the group QAnon, and social media proliferation of anti-mask and anti-vaccination hype have wreaked havoc with attempts to curb the spread of the virus. This explosion of disinformation also runs the risk that critics of the current global effort to combat COVID-19 will be dismissed as conspiracy theorists.

In this complex technosocial mediascape, intersectional media activist projects must find a balance between capitalist hyperexploitation and intersectional liberation as they engage in digital transmedia mobilizations.

Digital Transmedia Mobilizations

Social movements have shifted toward transmedia mobilizations using social-media-platform affordances and mobile technologies. Researcher-activist Sasha Costanza-Chock (2014, 50) provides a working definition of transmedia organizing: "The creation of a narrative of social transformation across multiple media platforms, involving the movement's base in participatory media making, and linking attention directly to concrete opportunities for action." They use digital media to support political objectives, relying on five key practices: cross-platform linkability, transformation narratives, accessible participation, creation of movement actions, and accountability to the movement. Transmedia mobilizations are thus technopolitical.

However, the political economy of capitalist platform ownership reveals a contradiction inherent in the use of social media by grassroots activists (Curran, Fenton, and Freedman 2016; Fuchs 2009, 2012). As activists mobilize political content to create virality, platforms are datafying and monetizing activists' human relationships and social behaviours (Milan 2017). Technology researcher and critic Jaron Lanier suggests that because digital platforms are structured to provide instantaneous feedback loops, they are no longer social networks but rather "behavior modification empires," amplifying negative emotions to keep users' eyes on platforms longer, as well as using psychological techniques to create addictive responses (Lanier

2018). Advertising on social media sites is increasingly lucrative – Facebook's 2020 revenue was US$85.97 billion (Tankovska 2021a); Twitter's was US$3.71 billion (Tankovska 2021b); and YouTube's was $US19.77 billion (Tankovska 2021c). Techno-sociologist Zeynep Tupfekci (2017) argues that the advertising model of social media is creating an algorithmic social dystopia that is negatively impacting our everyday lives from social behaviour to political participation and beyond.

At the same time, social media is crucial for social and political participation for intersectional groups. US journalist Imani Gandy argues that Twitter is the epicentre of communication for marginalized communities who don't tend to participate in mainstream politics, such as young and/or BIPOC people (Amnesty International 2018, 9). Popularized during the Arab Spring, sometimes dubbed the "Twitter revolution" (Wolfsfeld, Segev, and Sheafer 2013), hashtag activism has been adopted by global digital movements, including #BlackLivesMatter and #MeToo. Twitter allows for both the immediacy of short bursts of timely information, such as live tweeting from the scene of protests, and the long-term aggregation of links to more in-depth media reports and critical analysis. At the same time, Twitter is inhabited by misogynist, racist, and transphobic trolls (Amnesty International 2018). The Greek Indignados, or Aganaktismenoi, abandoned Twitter in 2011 when it became overrun by trolls (Treré, Jeppesen, and Mattoni 2017, 417). The consequences for those targeted can be damaging, especially when trolling moves offline through doxing, described below. Trolling thus functions as a technology of control against people in intersectional groups. Facebook, YouTube, and many other platforms are also rife with trolls.

The technological affordances, political economies, participatory opportunities, and risks inherent to transmedia mobilization give rise to important questions. Media activists are faced with a "'real digital divide' [that] is the result of a social shaping of new media toward the interests of already powerful social groups, marked by class-specific characteristics, including profound individualization" (Burgess and Green 2013, 78). Activists negotiate this divide carefully, deciding when and how to use Twitter, Facebook, or YouTube to promote their campaigns. Platform users are found to be strong influencers of the development of social media algorithms and functionality (van Dijck and Poell 2013). Digital movements shape social media practices, as "a rise in the number of extensive protests is more likely to precede changes in the use of social media than to follow [them]" (Wolfsfeld, Segev, and Sheafer 2013, 116).

José van Dijck and Thomas Poell (2013, 2) argue that the "constellation of power relationships in which social media practices unfold" needs to be accounted for. Social media logic is based on programmability, popularity, connectivity, and datafication, dimensions that impact who can benefit from social media's opportunities. These dimensions of social media logic extend into society, establishing themselves in public and institutional spheres as "natural" processes, which are not natural but have been ideologically shaped by the priorities of capital and state power. As van Dijck and Poell (2013, 11) state, "The double-edged sword of empowerment – of users and platforms – is a recurring trope in the evolving socio-technical logic of social media." Questions of power are pivotal in the patterns of networked media labour that enable and delimit the technopolitical dimensions of media activist practices.

Technopolitical Dimensions

Seven key dimensions characterizing technopolitical media practices have been identified (see Table 2).

First, P2P digital infrastructures are key to collective media activist practices by the connected multitude, facilitating engagement with technologies and audiences of scale (Mundt, Ross, and Burnett 2018), and coordinating technological appropriations to achieve planned viralities. For example, technopolitical activists interviewed by MARG at Xnet in Spain used P2P infrastructures for hacking, hijacking, or riding the Facebook and Twitter trending algorithms to maximize social movement mobilizations and achieve widespread mainstream media coverage (see also Treré, Jeppesen, and Mattoni 2017). In Black Lives Matter and earlier protests against anti-Black racism, media activists paired up to simultaneously livestream and

Table 2 Key dimensions of technopolitics

Dimension	Technopolitical media practices
P2P	Peer-to-peer infrastructure; technologies of scale; global reach
Multitech	Multigenre, multiplatform, multidevice technologies
Motile	Online-offline motility; websites linked to spaces
Translocal	Technologies, identities, affect, and knowledge production without borders
Open	Open source; free culture; net neutrality; hacktivism
Secure	Antisurveillance; data privacy; data justice; antidatafication
Distributive	Distributive technological architectures; distributive leadership potentiation

live-tweet protest events on social media as modes of protest witnessing and police countersurveillance (Hermida and Hernández-Santaolalla 2018; Wilson and Serisier 2010). These technopolitical practices often achieved global reach, with social media providing architectures of scale to small autonomous media collectives.

Second, technopolitics relies on multiple technologies along three axes of practice: genres, platforms/apps, and devices. Research participants predominantly produced one media genre, such as a blog, magazine, or TV station, but engaged multiple genres to mobilize their media content. Practices included being interviewed on podcasts; writing; and creating videos, music, photos, artwork, theatre performances, and memes, as well as residual media for offline publics, such as posters and flyers (also digitized and shared online). Their media project's success was sublimated to an overall virality of meta-issue movement messaging through multiplatform transmedia mobilizations (Costanza-Chock 2014). Technologies were multidevice, using corporate laptops, tablets, and smartphones but also solidarity technologies such as independent media centres, open WiFi hubs, mesh networks, portable WiFi routers, and activist internet service providers (Monterde and Postill 2014).

Third, media activist interviewees noted the importance of online-offline motility (Toret et al. 2013), or the ability to move easily between positions in online and offline public spheres.

Online P2P technologies, apps, and devices thus facilitated offline F2F engagements, including collectively produced F2F technologies such as the people's mike, where a group repeats and collectively amplifies a speaker's words (Costanza-Chock 2012). Contours and textures of groups and social movements in online apps, devices, genres, and networks are recognizable in their offline contours, and vice versa. Translation, mobilization, construction, disruption, and deterritorialization all transmogrify through online-offline motility portals, moving through material space and cyberspace, self-propelled as recognizable collective intersectional subjectivities. Websites link to autonomous social centres; Facebook groups link to media collectives; #GreekRiot links to actual riots in the streets of Greece. From hybrid media activism (Treré 2019), a complex multiplicity emerges of motile unalike subjectivities collectively self-propelling through camps, streets, riots, protests, solidarity networks, social media platforms, devices, discourses, affective media labour, and multimodal actions. For example, Bristol Cable is a journalist collective in the United Kingdom that produces a monthly print broadsheet in a space donated by a community member. It hosts community launches that also offer audiences opportunities to join the media project, produced in a space both digital and physical. Print articles are available online, and the collective offers in-person media production workshops. No longer differentiating media practices as online or offline, their designs, politics, activists, events, and actions self-propel liminally between the two.

Fourth, multiplicitous P2P and F2F technologies create translocal synergies across protests, cultures, movements, and uprisings, mobilizing affective unities (Apoifis 2017), collective intelligences (Toret and Calleja 2014), subaltern epistemologies (Santos 2015), and transborder knowledge production (Bennett 2004). Translocal mobilizations transgress borders digitally in solidarity technologies of no-border networks, increasingly pivotal in meta-issue movements. For example, an interviewee with Calais Migrant Solidarity organized digital technologies for migrants to communicate about possible transportation, which borders had permeable membranes, and how to get there, providing legal information on cross-border migration on its website in multiple languages. Calais Migrant Solidarity also offered video-editing skillshares for migrants to produce self-representations and mobilized protests through digital action call-outs, where global movements organized simultaneous solidarity actions linked to local issues. This replaced summit hopping and subverted the gatekeeping role of calling protests, previously the purview of large civil society organizations. Translocal digital technology and media synergies thus propel both actions and subjects across borders in cross-border collectively organized connective actions.

Fifth, self-owned autonomous platforms are free and open. Free culture movements have contributed to the technopolitical "development of the concept of the digital commons" (Fuster Morell 2012, 390), in which digital communicative spaces are shared for the common good (Kidd 2003). Code is open source; websites are open editorial, and technologies are oriented toward public inhabitation. Hacktivists mobilize digital technologies (Milan 2013) to secure protester data and communications from state and corporate surveillance as data activists struggle to enact digital citizenship (Hintz, Dencik, and Wahl-Jorgensen 2018; Siapera 2016). Media activists at Xnet in Spain whom we interviewed, for example, created an encrypted drop box for citizens to become whistleblowers and crowdfunded legal fees to prosecute corrupt politicians, providing an open access spreadsheet of funds spent, producing multiplicitous open technologies of accountability.

Sixth, a balance is negotiated among open access, editorial, and membership collectives and technologies, and secure, encrypted, and antisurveillant

formations in surveillance capitalism (Zuboff 2019) intersecting with surveillant democracy. Proactive and reactive data activism push surveillant
technologies toward social justice, using big data to contest power (Milan
2017). Interview participants with Athens Live used big data journalism to
produce an exposé of AirBnB's destruction of long-term rental housing in
Athens (Sideris 2018). Moreover, participants in a grassroots research
collective used public data to monitor white supremacist groups in order to
confront their racist street attacks. Data activism is key to technopolitical
contestations of exploitative mechanisms, data proxies, bad data training,
and proprietary algorithms that both use and generate big data, amplifying
inequalities of race, class, gender, and more (S.U. Noble 2018; O'Neil 2016;
Sandvig et al. 2016; Wachter-Boettcher 2017).

Seventh, technological architectures of distributive leadership potentiate
networked horizontal organizing structures (Toret and Calleja 2014). Anticapitalist solidarity software, for example, was designed by an interviewee
from Open Lab Athens to transgress authoritarian capitalist and state communicative logics (Vlachokyriakos et al. 2017). They instead encoded solidarity into apps to facilitate sharing, collaboration, horizontality, and
multinodal distributive leadership networks. Transgressive digital infrastructures and architectures thus create open-ended experimentality in
anti-oppression systems. Moreover, for many of the media projects we
researched, technologies of distributive leadership were evident in the pivotal role they played in digitally mobilizing critical discourses, popular info-
actions, and multidimensional synergies (Fuster Morell 2012).

These seven dimensions of technopolitics form the second half of the
theoretical framework proposed here.

Intersectional Technopolitics

As illustrated above, technological and intersectional strategies used by
meta-issue movements and media activists are integrated to the extent that
they can no longer be separated. Therefore, mapping an integrated intersectional technopolitics is necessitated (see Table 3).

First, technopolitics is integrally intersectional and anticapitalist, with
meta-issue movements using digital technologies to fight intersecting systems of oppression. Strategies foreground the media power of intersectional
projects undertaken by marginalized groups, playing leadership roles in the
global autonomous mediascape mobilizing simultaneously against intersectional neoliberal capitalism, gender oppression, racism, heteronormativity,
and austerity through a multiplicity of digital technologies.

Table 3 Key dimensions of intersectional technopolitics

Dimension	*Intersectional technopolitics practices*
Intersectional and anticapitalist	Digital accessibility; foreground media projects by marginalized groups; disengage from capital; media are decolonizing, antiracist, feminist, queer-transfeminist, etc.
Distributed online-offline architectures and motility	Online-offline motility; distributive architectures of technology; distributive leadership; connection to social centres, refugee squats, feminist makerspaces, hackerspaces
Multiplicities of technologies and spaces	Multiple genres, platforms, devices, actor-types, groups, spaces, actions, labs, independent media centres; balance openness with security; data, social, and political justice activism
Translocal solidarity economies and technologies	Solidarities without borders; technology-enabled networks across difference; translocal mobilizations; solidarity economies; solidarity software design
Collective autonomy through direct action	Technologies and politics are collectively autonomous; ends achieved through actions; collectively self-owned and self-managed sustainable technological and social infrastructures

Second, leadership within autonomous media projects is through distributive P2P networks with F2F motility. Architectures of distributed technologies are integrated with distributed architectures of autonomous collective self-leadership; these distributive leadership models extend rhizomatically from local to national and global spaces. P2P architectures are connected through hybridity to F2F spaces. These include autonomous social centres, refugee squats, feminist makerspaces, hackerspaces, occupied anarchist theatres, grassroots medical clinics, food security solidarity networks, COVID-19 mutual aid collectives (Pleyers 2020), and more.

Third, technopolitics is multi-issue, multiactor, and multitech. Multiplicities of technological genres, platforms, and devices intersect with multiple actor-types, collectives, and organizations engaged in integrated intersectional collective and connective action. Spaces include material F2F spaces, digital P2P spaces, action camps, independent media centres, hacker labs, protest assemblies, squats, and more. Ease of mobility and motility among multiplicitous politics, platforms, spaces, genres, and groups is key. Technologies and spaces are open, free, and accessible across intersectional identities, nondatafied, secure, encrypted, and protected from intersectional capitalist and state surveillance.

Fourth, translocal horizontal solidarities across borders engage multipolitics, multitechnologies, multispaces, and the multitude, enabling networked media production and distributed communication across intersectional cultural and geopolitical space. Media and movement activists work in conjunction with translocal social movement mobilizations, including no-border networks, migrant rights, Black Lives Matter, #MeToo, 2LGBTQ+ organizations, Indigenous groups, and so on. Technopolitical multiplicities of communicative affect, knowledges, labour, and collective intelligences operate through solidarity logics in intersectional anticapitalist decolonial economies, technologies, cultures, and experimental designs.

Fifth, collective autonomy applies to technologies and politics alike through integration. Autonomous media activists mobilize direct actions, achieving ends through actions, creating collectively self-owned technological and social infrastructures liberatory by design. Through direct actions oppositional to or disengaged from communicative capitalism, activists work toward liberatory technologically and politically integrated P2P and F2F infrastructures using intersectional technopolitics.

Contradictions and Tensions

Thus far, we have articulated an ideal type for intersectional technopolitics, supported in the first instance by empirical evidence. In practice, many contradictions and tensions arise. Here we instantiate three such contradictions related to horizontality.

First, media projects attempt to develop liberatory intersectional anti-oppression practices within horizontal collective spaces fostering equality by rejecting hierarchical leadership models. However, the media projects themselves tend to play a leadership role in broader movements, producing key analytical discourses, mobilizing participants, and framing the movement in ways sometimes picked up by mainstream media. Xnet interviewees, for example, note that in the Indignados movement, established activists act as facilitators for general assemblies and model horizontal practices on social media for newer activists, playing a mentorship role. Similarly, participants in Smaschieramenti in Italy organize gender conscientization workshops on unmasking masculinities in which participants from the broader milieu reflect collectively on deconstructing intersectional masculinities and the gender binary in relation to power within personal and political spheres; as such, the horizontal collective plays a leadership role in mobilizing gender discourses and practices. Activists with Burnt Bras in Greece, to take a third example, write analytical tracts on intersectional feminism for their blog, disseminating them on social media for the broader movement and serving as an "anchor point" for theoretical development

(Jeppesen, Kruzynski, Lakoff, and Sarrasin 2014). The contradiction of rejecting hierarchical leadership models within autonomous collectives that in turn play a leadership role within larger movements indicates that horizontality is not without power relations, but rather shares power outward through spheres of influence (Gordon 2008; Jeppesen 2019).

Second, there is a contradiction between the capitalist political economy of social media and intersectional anticapitalist horizontal media practices. The reach of social media has made its use mandatory for media activists, despite critiques of capitalist platforms. Participants note that algorithms can be oppressive in racist, gendered, classist, heteronormative, and other ways, an argument supported by research (S.U. Noble 2018; O'Neil 2016; Sandvig et al. 2016). Moreover, platform production and labour structures enact intersectional capitalist oppressions through the hierarchies of Silicon Valley. Media activists who use platforms to disseminate intersectional discourses may be exposed to advertising that is racist, sexist, heteronormative, and/or colonial; trolls who mobilize misogynist and racist backlashes; misogynist affordances for partner stalking, threats of sexual violence, and doxing (dumping a person's personal information online with an invocation to do harm); and so on – with offline consequences.

Aware of these contradictions, media activists mobilize against intersectional digital oppressions. One collective, for example, organizes men in their group to confront sexist trolls and take the burden of emotional labour from the shoulders of female activists. In the United Kingdom, Bristol Cable organizes journalists into support pairs so that if someone experiences oppression, they have a mentor for conversations, backed up by collective processes. Burnt Bras limits the time each member spends dealing with online trolls. They post their blog link on social media to direct readers off trolled capitalist platforms and onto their website, which is populated with intersectional analysis and closed to commenting.

In marginalized groups, mental health effects are a key concern. Many groups mention socializing in person as important to recovering from negative affective platform labour, mutually supporting each other's mental health in convivial, relaxing moments. However, this is not universal. Some feel that socializing negatively reinforces social hierarchies within groups. Some mention that they are there to produce media and do not have the emotional capacity or professional training to do mental health support work. Some activists in mental health crisis temporarily or permanently step back from collective commitments. The contradictions between internal liberatory practices of intersectionality in horizontal autonomous media projects and external oppressive practices and hierarchies of social media platforms with which they engage – and the negative affective impacts – thus remain unresolved.

Third, intersectional technopolitics remains in stark contrast to the intersectionally oppressive structures in which these collectives operate in society at large. While many projects have made inroads, and intersectionality is increasingly accepted as important within some societies, much remains to be done. Certainly, social movement and media activists function within systems of oppression, including global and domestic digital divides along intersectional lines of race, class, gender, colonialism, and sexuality. The political economy of these circumstances impinges on activists who may experience reduced access to devices, skills, technologies, employment, infrastructure, and so on. Nonetheless, they continue to do the difficult everyday work of intersectional technopolitical activism, sharing tangible and intangible resources based on an ethos of solidarity and mutual aid (Jeppesen and Petrick 2018; Mundt, Ross, and Burnett 2018).

Despite, or perhaps because of, these and other challenges in intersectional technopolitics, it seems pivotal to understand the integration of meta-issue intersectional politics with multiplicitous digital technologies. Intersectional technopolitical practices have become even more critical as we move through a global pandemic (Pleyers 2020) in which intersectional oppressions have shaped inequitable health outcomes, with movement and media activists organizing collectively and connectively in response.

These are the many concerns that this book addresses.

The Structure of This Book

A complex question emerges in the organization of this book: How can intersectional movements and practices be covered in linear sections and sequences? In other words, how should I organize the representation of intersectional meta-issue movements and media practices that are inherently about connections and overlapping concerns into distinct chapters? Chapters cannot overlap and intersect with one another the way intersectional movements and media do. Following the material itself, I have organized the book in the same way that intersectional movements and media organize, using the organizational practice of foregrounding one issue while linking to others. In some instances, this means a movement may be covered in more than one chapter, focusing on its different elements, and I address this explicitly when it comes up.

In this first chapter, I have argued that the practices of social movements and their repertoires of contention and communication have shifted over the past two decades toward meta-issue intersectional technopolitical mobilizations.

Chapter 2 begins this mapping with the emergence of intersectional technopolitics in the global justice movement. Community radio in Latin America played a pivotal role in the movement, while the global Indymedia network brought together coders with free culture activists. Social movements came together to build an alternative consensus opposing the so-called Washington Consensus, to contest neoliberal globalization through mass protest convergences, and to build alternatives to neoliberal capitalism in everyday life. Movements increasingly integrated anticapitalist concerns with climate, labour, Indigenous, student, sexuality, housing, racism, gender, and other social justice initiatives, fostering an emergent intersectionality. In the same time period, media activists were early adopters of digital media affordances (Castells 2010; Rodriguez 2001), fostering an emergent technopolitics.

With an ever-intensifying neoliberalism rolling out austerity measures, anti-austerity movements, covered in Chapter 3, followed the global justice wave of contention. They are well known for engaging in technopolitics, building on the previous movement's free culture elements, while confronting the contradictions of anticapitalist organizing in a capitalist society. Creating alternatives in everyday life to assert anticapitalist forms of collective living, they took to the streets to contest austerity measures imposed following the 2008 EuroAmerican financial crisis. In Quebec, Canada, in the Maple Spring of 2012, a student uprising against a 75 percent tuition hike saw nightly marches being met with political repression. Activists organized general assemblies, not just in student groups but also in neighbourhoods, moving toward a general social strike. In Spain, the Indignados set up protest camps to fight back against austerity measures, linking intersectional issues and collectively and connectively organizing micro-infrastructures to support the camps on the squares. Both movements engaged horizontal forms of organizing gleaned from the global justice movement, but their media activism was transformed by the dominance of platform activism, including transmedia mobilizations, distributive leadership, livestreaming, and coordinated intersectional technopolitics.

Chapter 4 considers intersectional antiracist and anticolonial movements and media practices. With Black Lives Matter, we see the practice of foregrounding anti-Black racism from an intersectional perspective. Idle No More and Standing Rock, Indigenous resurgence movements happening at the same time as Black Lives Matter, foreground Indigenous issues including territories, framing themselves as environmental protectors rather than protesters. Movements against the crisis of missing and murdered Indigenous women and girls (Saramo 2016) have produced the *Stolen Sisters* report (Amnesty International 2004), which spurred the movement of Sisters in Spirit (Tolley, Martin, and Gilchrist 2012) and the travelling crowdsourced art show *Walking With Our Sisters* (Walking With Our Sisters n.d.). They integrated crowdfunding into an artistic strategy, creating networked art in the material world. Theorists consider relationships between anti-Black racism and anti-Indigenous racism, cautioning against the race to innocence, in which individuals may choose to foreground one axis of oppression and discount others (Fellows and Razack 1998). Moreover, the "Oppression Olympics," which creates hierarchies of oppression in which subjects jockey for position as the most oppressed, serves only to keep people feeling increasingly more oppressed (Dhamoon 2015). Finally, both Indigenous movements and movements against anti-Black racism focus on healing justice, integrating culturally specific teachings, education, epistemologies, and knowledge production.

Linking race to heteronormativity, Chapter 5 analyzes intersectional 2LGBTQ+ movements and media practices, from the Queer Nation, ACT UP, and marriage-equality movements of the 1990s and early 2000s to the radical queer, trans, and non-binary movements of today. 2LGBTQ+ movements contest the capitalist shift toward so-called pink dollars, in which businesses cater to the stereotype of the professional, wealthy, childless gay male in commercial "gay villages." While queer geographies are liberatory for those who can participate, for others, the stereotype of a homonormative body, lifestyle, and subject-position is problematic as it serves to invisibilize 2LGBTQ+ identities who don't conform to dominant categories related to race, class, gender, beauty norms, parental status, immigration status, and so on. Queer and trans people of colour movements such as #Free_CeCe have achieved some forms of virality but tend to experience a slower burn than the rapid rise experienced by other movements, perhaps indicative of a latent or overt transphobia. Non-binary and trans movements advocate against trans pathologization and for the decolonization of trans bodies, with movements foregrounding non-Western sexualities, including North American two-spirit gender sexualities, the Brazilian *travesti*, or the Pakistani gender-ambiguous *khwaja sira*.

2LGBTQ+ intersectional mobilizations include trans and non-binary art projects, incorporating the body-as-media-text, using the body as both the site and the subject of contestation.

In relation to antiracist, anticolonial, and 2LGBTQ+ movements, Chapter 6 considers the emergence of digital transfeminist movements, from the cyberfeminism of the 1980s and '90s, to the social media mobilizations of contemporary hashtag feminism. The contradictions of #MeToo are explored, as the digital affective labour of discussing sexual assault online takes an emotional toll, sometimes leading to burnout. This can be worse for BIPOC and 2LGBTQ+ groups; moreover, some participants feel #MeToo does not speak to racialized groups. With hashtags such as #MosqueMeToo, participants suggest that Islamic feminism must challenge patriarchal structures in ways that confront both Western feminism and Islamic religious and gender oppression (Point 2019). Similarly, SlutWalk contests rape culture, but unlike #MeToo, it has a street presence, mobilizing translocal protests, each with its own unique flavour and mobilization strategy (Carr 2013; Ringrose and Renold 2012). As with other online intersectional movements, these approaches to digital feminism and transfeminism are subject to the violence of misogynist, transmisogynist, racist-misogynist, and misogynoir backlash and trolls. Some activists have developed controversial hackback strategies, from blocker bots to digilante justice. While the effectiveness of online activism is sometimes called into question, I examine three qualitative metrics to evaluate the successes of intersectional technopolitical transfeminist movements.

In conclusion, Chapter 7 synthesizes several questions regarding contemporary intersectional technopolitics. Are digital movements simply recreating the society of the spectacle in an intensified online format, where everyday social activities, including intersectional activist and affective activities, are monetized by capitalist platform corporations, supporting structures that tend to be intersectionally capitalist, that is, racialized, gendered, heteronormative, and colonial? Does this, in some ways, defeat or recuperate intersectional technopolitics movements? Or are there ways in which technologies of control can be extracted from control by movements and the technopolitics of embodied movements can be transformed into the embodiment of intersectional technopolitics? From the perspective of technopolitics, activists struggle to find a balance between self-owned, self-determined media outlets for collective action and capitalist social-media platforms for connective action and the loss of autonomy they entail. And from the perspective of intersectionality, activists may consider Sara

Ahmed's proposition of an "affinity of hammers," where people pick up hammers and chip away at the walls that separate us from one another and our fullest capacities and empowerment (Ahmed 2016). Current initiatives to create international tech ambassador positions and big tech anti-terrorism initiatives are interrogated as attempts to exercise technologies of control or to exert control over technologies from a position of increasingly undemocratic capitalist power.

2

Global Justice

_____

The global justice movement (GJM) in the late 1990s and early 2000s is an important place and time to start a genealogy of intersectional technopolitics. This movement built on earlier siloed feminist, anti-nuclear, environmental, civil rights, antiracist, 2LGBTQ+, and labour movements, spearheading a shift toward new interconnected meta-issue movements. It also increasingly relied on emergent digital technologies to mobilize and report on mass mobilizations. It was a flashpoint that would eventually bring about the intersectional technopolitics media practices of today.

The GJM had two simultaneous starting points in what at the time was called the "Global North" and the "Global South." Some people still use these terms, acknowledging that their implied geographical orientation is better understood as an economic relationship. This includes some activists and scholars from the "Global South" who may shorten it to "North" and "South" (see for example, Santos [2015], *Epistemologies of the South*). Earlier, terms such as "developing," "underdeveloped," and "developed" were used to signify economic differences, as were "First," "Second," and "Third" world. These have largely fallen out of use as they are value-laden, dividing the world into hierarchies. Today people may use "Majority World" to refer to countries in Africa, Latin America, Asia, and the Middle East where there are higher populations. This term acknowledges that, while the G20 countries may be more politically powerful, they are not the largest populations, but rather a small group of elite countries not representative of the majority of the world's population (Silver 2015). The terms "high-income" and "low-income" countries are also used to indicate economic disparities. On one hand, this pair of terms allows for gradation, such as middle-income or lower-middle-income countries, but on the other hand, it erases the imperialistic relationship between the two that has caused the income disparities. We also see the emergence of new economic power blocks beyond the G20 states, such as BRICS: Brazil, Russia, India, China, and South Africa. When geographies of power arise in this book, I will either use the terms of the authors cited or name the specific countries and regions where possible. I use the term "EuroAmerica" to refer to the European Union, the UK, the United States and Canada, and it can also be understood to include Australia, New Zealand, Japan, and other high-income countries.

On January 1, 1994, heralding the start of the anti-globalization or global justice movement, the Zapatista Liberation Army launched a coordinated uprising in which they took over five cities in Mexico, the day the North American Free Trade Agreement went into effect. With the cry "Ya Basta!" (Enough!), they declared war on the Mexican government (Goodman 2004) and reclaimed these cities for Indigenous self-governance. This led to the establishment of the autonomy of the Zapatistas in Chiapas, Mexico. The subsequent 1996 Encounter for Humanity and against Neoliberalism launched the GJM with the slogan "For humanity and against neoliberalism," taken up by global activists for its critique of neoliberalism.

Shortly thereafter, led by movements in the United Kingdom, in 1997 the Multilateral Agreement on Investment was proposed but soon defeated by global civil society groups. On the heels of this activist victory, American-led social movements organized what would later be called the Battle of Seattle, a mass protest mobilization against the World Trade Organization (WTO) meetings in November-December 1999. In Seattle, Indymedia activists set up a livestream network and independent media centre, launching the Indymedia network. Media activists in Seattle used nascent cell-phone communications, network-facilitated livestreaming, video activism, and hacktivism, elements of the free culture movement and predecessors of the digital communications media that would be central to subsequent waves of contention.

This joining together of global movements, with leadership from Latin America, shapes my analysis of social movements and media activism. I therefore foreground voices of scholars from Latin America, particularly those in communication for social change, dependency theory, and so on, to contest the EuroAmerican domination of the field of communications. Moreover, I foreground voices of global social movements and media activists, recognizing Latin American leadership in intersectional technopolitics, which can go unacknowledged in the dominant communications literature (Treré and Barranquero 2018).

In this context, it is important to develop a definition of "neoliberal globalization." In political theories of development that labelled some countries "developed" and others "developing" or "underdeveloped," it was presumed that industrial development took place evenly across all countries and that some countries were simply ahead of others in this process. This was the development paradigm dominant in communication studies and international development research in the mid-twentieth century.

In the 1970s, however, Latin American dependency-theory scholars made a key intervention against this paradigm. Scholars argued that instead of following similar trajectories on different timelines, countries were differentially developed as a result of "static and inequitable international capitalist relations" (Clayton 2004, 278). These inequitable relations were not natural but derived from territorial colonialism and resource exploitation of colonized countries in the Global South by imperial powers from the Global North. The initial phase of territorial colonization was followed by neocolonial economic relations, which reinforced unequal development economically rather than territorially.

Neocolonialism today has been reinforced through neoliberal supranational institutions such as the WTO, the World Bank (WB), and the International Monetary Fund (IMF). Neoliberalism continues to benefit so-called developed nations (the G20 states, for example), to the detriment of the Majority World (parts of Latin America, Africa, and Asia, for example): "The evolution of this global system of underdevelopment-development has, over a period of time, given rise to two great polarizations which have found their main expression in geographical terms" (Sunkel and Girvan 1973, 136) – "the core" (Global North or high-income countries) and "the periphery" (Global South, Majority World, or low-income countries).

This set of global relationships was not accidental but orchestrated through the historical and ongoing processes of colonization:

> It is postulated that underdevelopment is part and parcel of the historical process of global development of the international system, and therefore, that underdevelopment and development are simply the two faces of one single universal process. Furthermore, underdevelopment and development have been, historically, simultaneous processes which have been

linked in a functional way, that is, which have interacted and conditioned themselves mutually.

(Sunkel and Girvan 1973, 135–36)

Historically, it was the violence of colonialism, resource extraction, and slavery that led to development and wealth in EuroAmerica by producing underdevelopment and poverty in much of Asia, Africa, and Latin America.

The core and the periphery therefore also represent two polarized social classes in two different configurations. The first configuration is "a polarization of the world between countries: with the developed, industrialized, advanced, 'central northern' ones on one side, and the underdeveloped, poor, dependent, and 'peripheral southern' ones on the other" (Sunkel and Girvan 1973, 136) – thus core and periphery.

The second configuration is the establishment of discrepancies of wealth and social class within countries, by which marginalized groups in core nations can be understood as belonging to the periphery (for example, some Indigenous groups, refugees, homeless people, etc.). The intersectional axes of race, class, immigration status, colonialism, and capitalism play out in uneven economic access within high-income countries. Some activists we interviewed – for example, in Spain and Greece – referred to themselves as living in the Global South within the Global North – the periphery in the core. At the same time, within periphery countries, elite classes benefit from development and therefore belong to the core, also known as the metropole, an apt name as the elite classes are often situated in urban metropolises – the core in the periphery. In other words, there is also "a polarization within countries, between advanced and modern groups, regions and activities and . . . marginal and dependent groups, regions and activities" (Sunkel and Girvan 1973, 136).

While this system of uneven development is not new, it has intensified with the growth of neoliberal institutions that have developed and continue to develop multilateral free-trade agreements and impose structural adjustment programs (SAPs) on countries in the periphery, or in the case of Greece, the periphery in the core.

The actual functioning of globalization, thus, directly contradicts the objectives stated by nation-states and organizations in the core such as the G20 and the World Economic Forum. SAPs imposed by the IMF and WB in exchange for debt relief, ostensibly to help countries develop economically, instead force periphery countries to change their economic and social structures to benefit capitalists in the core (both domestically and globally), maintaining the structures of dependency, worsening underdevelopment, and more deeply impoverishing people in the periphery. This has happened in many countries, the most recent being Greece, the first country within the EU to be forced to accept a bailout and SAPs imposed by the IMF, precipitating the so-called Grexit crisis. The crisis led to a referendum on the IMF imposition of austerity measures, which precipitated social unrest due to the widespread intensification of poverty, as the minimum wage was sent on a downward spiral and health care and social services were gutted. The Greek anti-austerity protests arose in response to the imposition of SAPs.

Specific examples of the adjustments imposed by SAPs include mandatory defunding of social programs such as health care, welfare, and education; imposition of monocrops for export to global markets, which debilitates local subsistence farming and destroys ecosystems; reduced labour standards so that semi-industrialized factories owned by multinational corporations can benefit from low production costs, such as the *maquiladora* sweatshops on the border between the United States and Mexico; and the reduction of environmental protections so that multinational corporations in extraction industries such as mining, oil, and gas need not be responsible for so-called environmental externalities. This environmental devastation has been well documented by international activist organizations such as the Mining Injustice Solidarity Network. In these ways, and many others, top-down "globalization promotes a destructive competition in which . . . countries are forced to cut labor, social and environmental costs to attract mobile capital. When many countries do so, the result is a disastrous 'race to the bottom'" (Brecher, Costello, and Smith 2000, 5).

Countering this race to the bottom, activists across the globe set out to challenge the ways in which neoliberal globalization has been intensifying domestic and global inequalities. This was a surprisingly prescient movement: "Just under 10 years later we would be in the grips of a financial crisis brought about by some of the very forces they were objecting to" (Fenton 2020, 1052).

Toward Intersectionality

In addition to environmentalists, labour organizers, and grassroots anarchist and anticapitalist groups, "the anti-globalisation movement was made up of non-governmental organisations (NGOs), debt campaigners, students and Indigenous peoples" who formed coalitions, shared movement demands and strategies at convergence workshops, and found "common cause in the harms committed by forms of trade liberalisation that undermine local economies, decimate communities and serve global corporate expansion" (Fenton 2020, 1052), destroying the environment and driving an intensifying wedge between the poor and the wealthy. The GJM is thus often referred to as "a movement of movements" (Mertes and Bello 2004) that developed a shared diagnostic frame (Ayres 2004) identifying key issues in neoliberal trade policies to target.

However, the prognostic frame (Ayres 2004) was more complex, as civil society actors engaged in debates oversimplified in the media as "fix it or nix it." Some activists felt trade policies should be fixed by holding them to higher standards, whereas others believed neoliberal institutions should be nixed altogether because they are structurally incommensurate with global relations of equality. Both groups argued that world issues might better be addressed through attention to key factors such as climate, migrant, gender, and economic justice – that is, the global justice that named the movement. Although the label "anti-globalization movement" was used in the mainstream media, most activists were not against globalization per se, but rather against the capitalist co-optation of globalization. Consequently, their preferred movement labels included "global justice" (the one I use here) as well as "alterglobalization," "anti-corporate-globalization" or "globalization from below."

In their book *Globalization from Below*, Brecher, Costello, and Smith (2000, 6–9) argue that neoliberal globalization was neither inexorable nor desirable but rather intensified global inequalities, created economic volatilities leading to financial crises, degraded democracy, and accelerated the climate crisis. In India, the Save Narmada Movement provided a framework for critiquing globalization from above, challenging the hidden ideological relations in neoliberal globalization that perpetuated uneven development (Roy 2004). These relations included centralized, undemocratic processes in which unaccountable, exploitative decisions were taken behind closed doors without the knowledge or consultation of constituencies (Bose 2004, 156). Many social movement organizations (SMOs) from Latin America and Asia – including the Save Narmada Movement, farmers in India contesting Monsanto's patenting of seeds and the creation of terminator genes for seedless crops, and more – were joined by those from EuroAmerica in demanding that neoliberal institutions be nixed. "Nix it" organizations were typically more radical, revolutionary, or anticapitalist, with critiques of systems of oppression that they thought were not fixable. But many groups did not fit easily into the nix-it or fix-it binary. Consisting of reformist and revolutionary contingents – and many along the complex spectrum in between – mass protest mobilizations began to take place globally against meetings of neoliberal organizations. These movements gradually formed into broad-based global networked organizations such as the World Social Forum and People's Global Action.

The GJM expanded the use of horizontal decision making at mass protest mobilizations, including spokescouncils and *consultas* (open forums) that facilitated the organization of mass protest convergences in the weeks and months leading up to the days of demonstrations. The use of camping in public spaces, used in the anti-nuclear and feminist movements of the 1970s and '80s (Downing 1988; Feigenbaum 2010; Roseneil 1995), became an established form of contestation in GJM-related squatter movements, homeless tent cities, no-border networks, and other protest camps (Kadir 2016; Kraus 2010; Rigby 2010). This practice was also used to house partici-pants of mass protest mobilizations who converged on the city to contest the legitimacy of the organization meeting there. The spokescouncils and public camps were SMO practices that gradually evolved into the general assemblies of the camps and protests of the squares during the anti-auster-ity, Occupy, Arab Spring, and other movements.

In this context, three key dimensions of the GJM emerged that framed the movement's demands, tactics, and strategies: consensus, contestation, and construction.

Consensus: For Humanity and against Neoliberalism

The GJM shaped its demands based on a shared basis of unity grounded in alternative values, emerging out of the 1996 Zapatista Encounter for Human-ity and against Neoliberalism. Movements agreed that "Another world is possible" (McNally 2002; Mertes and Bello 2004) and developed a consen-sus on alternative economic, environmental, and social justice values. Coali-tion building was premised on collaboration, recognizing that "cooperation need not presuppose uniformity" (Brecher, Costello, and Smith 2000, 16).

Coalitions were "generally multi-issue, and even when participants focus[ed] on particular issues, they reflect[ed] a broader perspective" (Brecher, Costello, and Smith 2000, 16). The tentative consensus was developed through long debates at convergences by global groups and included five important hallmarks, or what I have elsewhere called "value practices" (Jeppesen 2010a).

Direct Democracy

Decision making put leadership of the movement in the hands of those most affected by decisions, based on the forefront principle, explained above. Move-ment practices such as talking circles or go-arounds provided mechanisms for everyone to speak, raise dissenting ideas, and contribute to the direction of the movement through horizontal structures and consensus decision making. Distinct from electoral democracy, in which citizens vote infrequently (e.g., once every three or four years), direct democracy allows people to be involved in ongoing community decision making, contributing to discussions, developing suitable solutions to local problems, and working together to shape the fabric of society in a way that benefits the community. These directly democratic mechanisms would grow to shape today's social movement practices.

Solidarity

Coalitions of solidarity strengthened new global networks, rejecting not just top-down globalization but also the hierarchical charity model, recognizing that handouts do not transform but rather reinforce inequalities. Instead of charity, activists worked to build capacity and empowerment within and across global communities: "Solidarity based on mutuality and common interest increasingly form[ed] the basis for the relationships among different parts of the movement" (Brecher, Costello, and Smith 2000, 16).

For example, at an alterglobalization workshop, as union organizers with CUPE 3903, my colleagues and I talked to garment and sweatshop workers from Bangladesh who were fighting for safer working conditions and higher wages. Our union was starting to organize a boycott of Walmart because of their poor treatment of workers in their supply chain. However, the workers themselves asked us to mobilize support from unions in Canada by calling for safer working conditions and supporting their other specific demands. They also asked us to drop the boycott of Walmart, who was one of their factory's biggest customers, as it might put their jobs at risk. This illustrates why forefront organizing is so important – the Bangladeshi garment workers needed to be at the forefront of developing strategies for improving their labour conditions. Solidarity in Canada required that we develop not just an understanding of the interconnectedness of global issues, which is fairly abstract, but also a working relationship with those most affected whose lead we could follow to support concrete demands. Our "solidarity" boycott, it turned out, might have done more harm than good.

Respect for Life

Extending respect for all life to include protection of the environment and non-human animals, climate justice, animal rights, vegan diets, deep ecology, and more came to be integrated into political demands. Labour organizers began to see the contradictory logics of the treatment of the environment and the labour needs of their members in industries that put them at risk, such as the mining, oil, and gas industries. The famous "teamsters and turtles" coalition was formed at the Battle of Seattle, allowing groups once at odds to work together to find common ground. Increasingly, activists started to follow Indigenous leadership in taking the long view of decision making for seven generations. Life, dignity, respect, and the Latin American principle of *buen vivir*, or living in harmony with all beings, including respect for the rights of nature, are foundational values, increasingly salient in global intersectional movements today.

Rejection of All Systems of Domination

Activists gradually recognized the overarching problem of interconnected systems of domination, in relation to neoliberal capitalism, beginning a shift to meta-issue politics in which intersectional issues would be increasingly understood as key to liberation movements (Collins and Bilge 2016). Activists moved toward critically analyzing systemic oppression rather than trying to root out the one "bad apple" in the system. These systemic critiques moved toward a consensus, with connections among systems becoming increasingly salient in movement demands, organizational processes, and structures, all moving toward intersectionality.

Affinity Models of Organizing

Grassroots groups formed loose-knit organizations based on a consensus of shared values and objectives, in other words, a sense of affinity. Activists began to appear at mass mobilizations already self-organized into autonomous affinity groups, formations in which activists make collective decisions regarding participation and contribute to conversations about the strategies, tactics, and political objectives of the movement or mobilization. Affinity groups do not build membership lists; rather, people join by participating. Affinity is also a model for community organizing on everyday issues such as housing, climate justice, poverty, racism, and refugee rights. Building affinities is a way to put these shared concerns into practice in small horizontal groups working in solidarity toward common objectives. Their basis in close overlapping friendship groups and networks would go on to shape the social logic of connective action that emerged in the anti-austerity wave of contention through social-media affordances.

Consisting of many different global affinity groups, NGOs, SMOs, grassroots organizations, and so on, this civil society consensus was a somewhat

uneasy one. People's Global Action and the World Social Forum were networks that fit loosely into the more revolutionary anticapitalist category and
the more reformist tendency, respectively. This sometimes led to conflicts
over protest tactics of direct action, civil disobedience, sit-ins, flying squads,
anarchist black blocs, vigils, and more. With their own histories, trajectories, and politics, the two groups nonetheless served as hubs to develop
alternative social, environmental, and economic models. The values of this
tentative consensus were put into practice in two ways: the immediate contestation of mass protests, and the longer-term organizing of alternative
structures in everyday life in latency periods between protests.

Contestation: Mass Protest Mobilizations

While consensus developed values, contestation put them into action. Mass
protest mobilizations and the convergences leading up to them tended to
contest three types of neoliberal summits: (1) multilateral meetings of
elected government officials from elite countries, such as the G20, the European Union, or the Association of Petroleum Exporting Countries; (2)
meetings of global neoliberal financial institutions such as the WTO, WB,
IMF, World Economic Forum, or the Asian Development Bank; and (3)
meetings to adopt free-trade agreements such as the Multilaterial Agreement on Investment, the Free Trade Area of the Americas, or the Trans
Pacific Partnership.

Contestations consisted of a multi-day convergence, often a week long,
before the mass protests began in earnest (Starr, Fernandez, and Scholl
2011). A convergence space would be organized, usually in conjunction with
an Alternative Media Centre, for local and out-of-town activists to hook
into the mobilization. There would be workshops on topics of neoliberalism
with opportunities to network with like-minded global activists and learn
about their struggles, and others on how to participate in the days of action
that provided legal information, lawyer phone numbers, and civil disobedience training. There would also tend to be a daily spokescouncil or consulta
for affinity groups to participate in making collective decisions about how
the days of action would be organized, including how they themselves would
engage.

As a short autobiographical note, during many global protest convergences (see Appendix A), I have taken on participatory and organizational roles.
This included presenting and attending workshops, participating in consultas and spokescouncils, being on the "day of demo" committee, organizing a coalition, and participating in affinity groups, some of which used

black bloc tactics (Dupuis-Déri 2019). While this experience is too complex to encapsulate here, I mention it because it informs my understanding of these events. The experience of participating in mass protest convergences can have a profound effect not just on a person's understanding of global issues but also on the way they engage with the world, live with other people, and challenge the underlying assumptions of everyday life. It can also connect people in irrevocable ways, change personal and professional relationships, and shift the direction of people's lives, particularly if they are arrested, but also in terms of the type of activist and advocacy work that is subsequently taken on, and how it is approached.

Below, I explore two key mass protest mobilizations, the first in Asia and the second in North America (which I participated in), analyzing their objectives, strategies, tactics, and outcomes.

ADB, Thailand, 2000

This mass protest mobilization and convergence included a People's Social Forum, which was organized in Chiang Mai in the weeks leading up to the Asian Development Bank's (ADB's) Annual Governors' Meeting in 2000. It took place in the double context of the "democratization process taking place in Thailand which began with the middle class uprising against the Thai dictatorship in May 1992" (Tadem 2012, 460) and the Asian financial crisis of 1997.

. Theresa S. Encarnacion Tadem (2012) argues that the Asian economic crisis revealed deep contradictions in neoliberal capitalism in the broader Asian context, while the fall of several Asian dictators in the 1980s and 1990s, a complex political situation in and of itself, allowed for the return of democratic civil society contestations. In Thailand, this paved the way for the rise of several Thai grassroots mobilizations, including the campaign of Klong Dan villagers against the ADB-funded Samut Prakarn Wastewater Management project (SPWM) in their village. This significant local movement was widely supported by NGOs such as Greenpeace, Focus on the Global South (a regional NGO in Bangkok), and other national and international NGOs, as well as grassroots movements such as the Assembly of the Poor and the People's Network (Tadem 2012).

This ADB development project was accused of a lack of local consultation, corruption in management, environmental impacts negatively affecting local food and fishing sources, and intensifying poverty in the area (Tadem 2012, 458): "No environmental impact assessment had been undertaken before the implementation of the project, which is required by Thai law" (Tadem 2012, 458). A mass mobilization was therefore organized against the 2000 ADB Annual Governors' Meeting in Chiang Mai, widely attended by global participants and covered by independent and foreign media. From high-level international meetings to grassroots mobilizations, a "boomerang" pattern developed by which local repression was mobilized in a "spiral" model to develop international audiences and alliances (Tadem 2012, 479). This led to mass protests at the Governors' Meeting, bringing the campaign into the international spotlight.

The mass protest convergence provided space for debates at the People's Forum leading up to the main days of protest and for converging activists to share global political information about different movements and the ADB more generally. It also allowed them to develop a shared understanding of how the local SPWM project was "exacerbating poverty, destroying the environment and undermining the rights, livelihoods and food security of local communities through the region" (Tadem 2012, 467–68).

Tadem (2012, 459) argues that alterglobalization mobilizations at summits held by neoliberal organizations such as the ADB provide opportunities and sites for interaction between global movements and local campaigns, "where ideas could be exchanged, debated, and reformulated," providing space for shared critical analysis and building international solidarity. "The effectiveness of the campaigns against the Asian Development Bank policies in Thailand in particular and in the region in general depended on the capability of anti-globalization movements to develop sites of interaction where ideas could be exchanged, debated, and reformulated" (Tadem 2012, 459). Moreover, the dialogues were mutual, creating solidarity with activists and movements in Asia and beyond.

The Chiang Mai protests against the ADB were the perfect opportunity for the Klong Dan villagers to contest the SPWM in conjunction with the support of global environmental actors in the GJM. The villagers wanted to stop the project, whereas global civil society actors wanted variously to reform the ADB or to abolish it. Participants thus had differing objectives, which, while seeming to fall on different sides of the oversimplified fix-it or nix-it debate, worked in conjunction to contest the local SPWM project. Despite these debates within the movement, participants came together in "a common site of interaction" and contestation of the neoliberal development paradigm (Tadem 2012, 474). The outcome was mixed: "Affected communities filed an inspection request, which was approved in July 2001, when it became evident that the ADB had violated its own policies during project preparation and implementation" (Bank Information Centre n.d.). The project was reduced from two sites to one and remains highly contested. The mixed result demonstrates one of the challenges in contesting neoliberal intensifications that do not go away when the protesters do.

FTAA, Canada, 2001

Mass protests in Quebec City, Canada, against the Free Trade Area of the Americas (FTAA) in April 2001 saw over twenty thousand global activists participating, including unstructured grassroots groups, NGOs, SMOs, labour unions, student groups, other civil society organizations, and unorganized local Quebec City citizens. Three days of protest focused largely on a three-metre fence around the meeting site, which was pulled down by direct-action affinity groups (mine included) on the first day of the protest, as well as a record-setting deployment of tear gas against activists, in three days of marches, sit-ins, celebratory protests, and street fighting that went late into the night, with hundreds of arrests.

The FTAA, liberalizing trade in North, Central, and South America, was widely referred to as "NAFTA on steroids," NAFTA being the existent North American Free Trade Agreement at the time. Activists organized and participated in a series of consultas, or open forums, in Quebec City and Montreal leading up to the protests. These, along with the protest mobilization itself, were co-organized by the Quebec City group, Summit of the Areas Welcoming Committee (CASA in French), in conjunction with the Montreal-based *La Convergence des luttes anticapitalistes* (CLAC). Similar to the Chiang Mai protest convergence, civil society groups came together at the Second Peoples' Summit of the Americas in the days leading up to the protests to discuss global campaigns and build networks and coalitions based on shared affinities.

The mass mobilization was the first globally to organize under the principle of respect for a diversity of tactics. Whereas the 1999 Seattle anti-WTO protests had debated the principle of non-violent civil disobedience, not everyone at the protest agreed to it, causing conflict between non-violent and black bloc activists. To avoid this conflict, and to accommodate different tactics, the CASA and CLAC consultas together made the decision to organize the city into colour-coded protest zones: red for direct action, yellow for civil disobedience, and green as a safe zone for parties and protest. This did not prevent the police from attacking the green zone with tear gas and more.

Ultimately, the FTAA was defeated that week, due in part to mass protests and in part to the rejection of the proposal by meeting participants from Latin America, Africa, and Asia. However, some have argued that long after the activists declared victory and went home, many of the FTAA's original proposals were implemented piecemeal in other contexts, calling into question the possibility of defeating neoliberalism writ large, as with the case in Chiang Mai.

Nonetheless, there are key things to consider regarding contestation through mass protest mobilizations. Working together on campaigns with like-minded organizers, both the anti-SPWM and the anti-FTAA mobilizations linked local struggles with global solidarity movements based on a consensus regarding alternative values. They held discussion forums using direct democracy, called for the autonomy of local communities to self-determine, and organized through affinity and international solidarity groups with shared objectives based on respect for life, equality, dignity, and the environment.

The various modes of contestation in the GJM were not without controversy. Some activists were critical of the privileged practice of summit hopping, whereby activists travelled to urban centres to join protests where summits were taking place. Others argued that a better way to organize would be to stay home and strengthen movements in our local communities, fighting neoliberalism in everyday life. Still others suggested that the politics of everyday life – such as living in housing collectives, organizing workers' collectives, and other community organizing – is a kind of lifestyle activism that cannot effect change. While yet others believe that the means must be consistent with the ends; therefore, to organize against neoliberal capitalism in structures that are hierarchical, exploitative, and oppressive is hypocritical and defeatist. And finally, there were ongoing and unresolved debates about tactics, which tended to polarize groups, particularly those who engaged in black bloc tactics such as property destruction and those who preferred non-violent or party-and-protest modes of contestation.

Despite being only partially successful in their stated objectives, GJM mass protest contestations demonstrated the importance of global horizontal networks, discussed below.

Construction: Horizontal Networks

The GJM constructed a massive number of informal and formal SMOs, organizations, networks, and counter-institutions as alternatives to neoliberal capitalism. Information about these initiatives was shared through alternative media and personal connections made at counter-summits organized during the types of mass protest convergences of contestation discussed above. The Zapatista Encounters, the People's Global Action gatherings, and the World Social Forum (WSF) all worked to create a horizontal movement of movements without top-down leadership. Here, we see the emergence of the multi-issue politics mentioned in the Introduction, where intersectional connections between differently focused movements start to be forged.

The WSF is an interesting case of an SMO that attempted to construct a horizontal network to support the GJM. The first WSF was organized in Porto Alegre, Brazil, in 2001 by a loose network of Brazilian and French GJM organizations that shared the objective of countering the power of the World Economic Forum. Its development "can be seen in the context of the emerging protests against the World Trade Organization, the IMF and the World Bank in 1998 and 1999" (Kerswell 2012, 74). Emphasizing the creation of alternatives, the WSF opened up a space in global civil society to emerge as a "new political actor" (Kerswell 2012, 76) on the global stage. It includes not only traditional participants in civil society, such as labour unions and NGOs, but also grassroots, loose-knit, autonomous, and horizontal SMOs and networks.

The 2002 WSF, also held in Porto Alegre, featured 800 workshops and 150 large seminars, as well as protest marches in the streets. Keynote speakers at the WSF have included well-known writers, researchers, and critics of neoliberal capitalist globalization such as Noam Chomsky, Rigoberta Menchu, and Arundathi Roy. Local, regional, and national Social Forums were subsequently organized, as well as themed social forums on pressing topics. For example, the Argentina uprising was the focus of the Buenos Aires Social Forum in 2002, which attracted more than ten thousand participants (Correa Leite 2003, 39).

The WSF works according to principles of direct democracy, with a horizontally organized international board. It "is an alternative to liberal democracy, but also the state system in general" (Kerswell 2012, 76). It was created as a non-hierarchical "'open space' for discussion and networking for organizations opposed to neoliberal globalization, capitalism and imperialism" (Kerswell 2012, 76). Conceived as a space and process rather than an organization (Correa Leite 2003, 41; WSF charter), it did not invite participants but issued an open call for participation, with a few explicit exclusions (e.g., military organizations, political parties). For those from the north who had previously organized in isolation, an objective of the WSF was to cultivate "an informed sense of our mutual dependence with the people in the south" (Eldred and Tuckett 2003, 102), by learning about issues in the south, a dialogue facilitated by the creation of a global democratic body that might challenge neoliberalism through the objective of creating a system of global equality.

The WSF "accepts that there will be no single grand discourse in imagining another world and making it possible. Discourses will be plural, overlapping, challenging; and that common strengths derive from the diversity of solutions people grounded in different cultural contexts will make for themselves" (Eldred and Tuckett 2003, 104). This is a strength of the WSF's charter and objectives.

The question remains whether the WSF is as open and inclusive as it aims to be. The registration fees can exclude the participation of people from lower income countries. For example, during the 2007 WSF in Kenya, the fee of five Euros was the equivalent of a week's wages for local Kenyans, making participation for people in the local region inaccessible (Kerswell 2012, 89). In addition, the costs of registration and travel to attend the WSF can be prohibitively expensive for members of underfunded or unfunded grassroots organizations. A third issue emerged in Montreal in 2016, when approximately two hundred potential participants were denied visas to enter Canada (Marchand 2016). Fourth, people question the viability of flying globally to attend a forum that has climate justice on its agenda. Thus, while the objective is to be inclusive and open, its implementation has run up against its limits.

Despite critiques, the existence of the WSF indicates that coordinated action across meta-issue movements previously thought to be disconnected can be facilitated through the development of a civil society network. Further, it illustrates the beginning of international social movements connecting the intersectional dots. Moreover, it demonstrates the possibility of coordinating mass global actions on intersectional issues aimed at and interactive with many levels of governance, from the municipality and local neighbourhood to city-wide, regional, national, international, and supranational bodies.

The People's Global Action (PGA) network, rooted in Latin America, is a second case of interest, as it approaches organizing from a more grassroots perspective than the WSF. The PGA has remained much more open and fluid with respect to participation, strategies, and tactics while generating a loose consensus in terms of values, principles, and affinities. The network's development of global solidarity movements and coalitions was based on the adoption of shared values, articulated in the PGA Hallmarks, which could be signed onto by any organization that agreed to them.

The five PGA Hallmarks, adopted in 2001 (see website) in Cochabamba, Bolivia, are:

1 A rejection of capitalism and destructive globalization
2 A rejection of all systems of domination
3 A confrontational attitude
4 Direct action and civil disobedience tactics
5 Autonomous organization.

The GJM, including both the WSF and the PGA, was initiated in large part by organizations and activist groups in Latin America, in particular Mexico and Brazil, including many Indigenous groups, yet, as it progressed, it seemed to move away from those roots, growing increasingly inaccessible to marginalized participants, including the very people who started it.

Nonetheless, the GJM saw the rise of intersectional counterpublics organized by the WSF, People's Global Action, the People's Social Forum, and related regional forums and organizations. The six intersectional movement practices outlined in Chapter 1 had their formative beginnings during the early years of the GJM in the emergence of intersectional, anticapitalist subjectivities opposing neoliberalism within these groups and the grassroots and SMOs that contributed to them. An awareness of refugee and immigration movements and the enclosure of increasingly militarized borders rendered translocal cartographies an important space of contestation. Solidarity movements and economies, participatory creation and ownership of the means of epistemological production through independent digital media, and distributed horizontal rhizomatic networks were on the rise, with the roots of horizontality developed in Argentina quickly spreading throughout the GJM. As community media scholar Arne Hintz (2011, 149) notes, "The creation of networks and collaborations across movements, both domestically and transnationally, has been identified as one of the key factors for gaining political influence." These early manifestations of intersectional horizontal networks would lead to the rise of anticapitalist alternatives in the anti-austerity wave of contention. In the GJM, they relied on an emergent form of technopolitical media activism.

Toward Technopolitics

Two key media practices emerged from the GJM that laid a foundation for technopolitics. The first practice was participatory communication for social change from the grassroots, such as community radio projects in

Latin America. The second practice was digitally facilitated communication where media activists could connect, organize, analyze, and mobilize through autonomous platform networks such as Indymedia.

Communication for Social Change

Proponents of development communication argued that communication technologies were both an index and a mode of modernization in the global periphery. The scholarly field of development communication was largely situated in Europe and North America, with the dominant language being English. Considering communication as an index, proponents measured how many media outlets (radio stations, TV stations, newspapers, etc.) there were in order to label countries or cities more or less developed. Considering communication as a mode of development and identifying under-developed sites, they brought new media and communications technologies to communities aiming to improve development. They labelled people in the communities as either "early adopters," seen as leaders of change, or "laggards," seen as being more traditional and unwilling to change.

Scholars in Latin America recognized this "modernization of communication" process as one of colonization, as a process that created ongoing dependencies, and introduced several critiques of the political economy of development communication. First, they noted that media systems in Latin America are configured differently and that communication technologies are used in culturally specific ways that may not be accounted for in measurements taken by those from EuroAmerica. Second, they observed that development communication specialists did not consult with local communities in Latin America to identify local needs. Little space was allocated for participation by community members, particularly in decision making and technological implementation and maintenance.

Third, scholars noted that the labels "early adopters" and "laggards" were themselves colonizing, failing to account for a politics of resistance to colonization that might be exercised by people making an informed decision not to adopt new technologies imposed from the outside, preferring instead to develop their own local communications processes and cultures. Early adopters were often people who belonged to the metropole, elite leaders who served to benefit economically and socially from the new technologies, and experienced privilege through proximity to whiteness, whereas laggards might be racialized groups who saw this system of unequal development as corrupt and racist, and therefore refused to participate.

Finally, there was a critique of the short-sightedness of these projects in that although funds were typically raised in EuroAmerica by NGOs and covered the cost of communications technologies, there were seldom funds to train people to use, maintain, repair, or update them as systems broke down or needs changed. This work required further visits by "experts" from EuroAmerican NGOs who hoarded information, skills, and capacities, creating a deepening dependency and more often resulting in technologies remaining unused or broken.

While the dominant paradigm of development communication sought to measure the early adoption of communications as a way of evaluating the progress of a developing country toward industrialization, the unspoken expectation was that the forms of communication introduced would also be used to disseminate the dominant ideology of EuroAmerica and to develop a conforming community that would follow its ideological development designs.

However, community radio projects demonstrated that some early adopters of communicative technologies engaged in communicative actions of resistance to development, while others resisted through refusal to adopt imposed modes of communication. Brazilian communications scholar Paola Sartoretto (2016) has found that the Brazilian *Movimento dos Trabalhadores Rurais Sem Terra* (MST) or Landless Rural Workers' Movement, rejected the individualist social media paradigm of Facebook and Twitter in favour of a collective mode of face-to-face organizing that did not separate people on individual computers or personal Facebook pages. They instead brought people together to strategize and organize collectively, expressing a cultural rejection of both social media platforms and the individualized action frames implicit in the logic of connective action (Bennett and Segerberg 2012).

Rejecting the development communication paradigm, key Latin American scholars such as Clemencia Rodriguez (2001) in Colombia have proposed a new field they call communication for social change. This is a key field in alternative media research that has emerged in Latin America and focuses on participatory production and decision making with explicit social-change objectives in both the media production and the research process itself. Addressing the primary critique regarding leadership and decision making, activists and researchers advocate for the participation of the local community at every stage in the implementation of new communications and media technologies. This involves consultation from the start and playing a leadership role in decision making. It also involves reconceiving the process of technology implementation as a cyclical, iterative process that includes ongoing training and capacity building.

Participatory communication involves five stages, with the fifth stage circling back to the first: (1) relationship building, (2) community consultation and community leadership development, (3) communication strategy design, (4) communication strategy implementation, including training and capacity building, (5) and a community feedback process.

As this process implies, a key element of communication for social change is the ongoing development of skills and capacities in the local community. For Rodriguez (2001), a key actor in the process is the citizen-journalist, a local community member who may have little to no training in journalism but knows a great deal about the social and political situation in their community and is therefore able to use the media to mobilize people to take action together on local issues. Community-based leaders (typically not elected leaders or organizational leaders) often play a key role in creating media, opening spaces for others to create media to share their experiences and opinions on issues in the community. They create opportunities for citizens to become citizen journalists who can work in many genres, including radio, TV, print, documentary, and blogs.

A second key element in communication for social change is the emphasis on providing an avenue by which local community members in marginalized groups can come to voice and become empowered to make change in their communities through media and communications. One of the most successful practices for this in Latin America is community radio, where everyone can come down to the station and speak on the radio about what is happening in their community. Community radio is perceived as being easier to produce than print media (which requires advanced literacy skills) or TV production (which requires technological skill and equipment). The theories and practices of communication for social change are therefore attentive to processes of community empowerment.

In this context, we will consider two forms of media practice key to the fledgling technopolitics of the GJM era: community radio in Latin America, and the Indymedia network. Both are early examples of technopolitics, beginning to integrate the politics of content, participation, and community ownership and control of media production into the technologies and processes of communications. Because the GJM and the field of communication for social change are both largely driven by organizations in Latin America, it is important to consider examples of media projects initiated in Latin America. In this way, we can better understand the interplay between global media activist initiatives and how they learn about, support, and interact with one another.

Participatory Community Radio in Latin America

Policy frameworks affecting several countries in Latin America have been highlighted by many supra-regulatory bodies interested in the governance of community media: "The European Parliament (in 2008) and the Council of Europe (in 2009) adopted declarations in which they highlighted the important role of community media in advancing social cohesion, media pluralism, and intercultural dialogue" (Hintz 2011, 150). Moreover, community communication scholar Arne Hintz has found that community radio stations are popular throughout Latin America because of their low costs and local programming, particularly in rural areas. At the same time, many countries in Latin America have outlawed community radio or made the process of applying for a licence and funding prohibitive (Hintz 2011, 151).

Social movements have become engaged with the issue of communication rights, with the World Association of Community Broadcasters playing a pivotal role in demanding community radio licences for global grassroots organizations (AMARC 2007). Several community radio stations in Latin America, discussed below, have achieved legitimacy as outlets of communication for social change: Radio Favela, in Brazil and in Colombia; Radio Andaquí, in southern Colombia; Juventud Stereo, in Guaviare; and the seventeen-station network AREDMAG, in Magdalena Medio.

Radio Favela

In 1998, Brazil was one of the earliest countries in Latin America to legalize community radio. However, licences were difficult to obtain; thus, "thousands of community radio stations are broadcasting in Brazil without licences, making it one of the most vibrant grass-roots radio landscapes worldwide" (Hintz 2011, 155). Bailey, Cammaerts, and Carpentier (2008) examine the representation of Radio Favela, a youth-led radio station in Brazil, as told through a narrative film of the same name. While *Radio Favela* is a filmic representation of the station, it is based on a true story of four young men who started an unlicensed community radio station in the Belo Horizonte *favela* (community[1]) of Brazil in 1980.

---

1 Sometimes *favela* is translated as "slum" in popular media, however, as "slum" is denigrating, people who live in the favelas prefer to use the word "community." I follow their lead here.

This radio station provided coverage of, by, and for the local favela community members. It engaged audience members in various ways: reading letters from friends in jail on drug charges; broadcasting a plea for free dental work, answered by a dentist who called the station; broadcasting a phone call from a local woman who lost her pet parrot; discussing community-housing issues with inhabitants; and warning people when a large police force entered the favela. As these examples illustrate, "The community is seen to structurally participate in the radio station. The co-ownership of the community is made evident when, after the studio has been destroyed in the police raid, the favela gets the money together to rebuild" (O. Bailey, Cammaerts, and Carpentier 2008, 39). The station not only serves the community but also belongs directly to it. It creates space for participation in civil society, creating counterpublics and providing both a physical space and a media space for subaltern voices to meet and talk about their own experiences to an audience with whom these experiences may be shared. It also provides a space to contest the oppression of the state, to participate in translocal organizing with other networked radio stations, and to contribute to broader global struggles.

Radio Andaquí

Colombia community radio in the early 2000s developed in the context of the ongoing conflict among several armed groups including, variously, the state military, paramilitary groups such as the Revolutionary Armed Forces of Colombia (FARC) and the National Liberation Army (ELN), narcotraffickers, and the US military, from roughly 1964 until a tentative truce beginning in 2015, during which "on average, between 2,100 and 3,000 people [we]re killed each year for political reasons" (Murillo 2003, 123). These killings were met with impunity, and people lived in extreme fear of everyday gun violence. Nevertheless, Murillo (2003) confirms the existence of over two hundred community radio stations in Colombia in the early 2000s.

The conflict imposed limitations on speech, and the public sphere had become somewhat demobilized. As Rodriguez, Ferron, and Shamas (2014, 10) observe, "Local public spheres are among the first casualties when unarmed communities are caught in the fighting of warring groups." Communities had abandoned public squares and streets, seeking the safety of private life. The mainstream media at the time were largely controlled by political parties, and some people came to call Colombia a "democra-tatorship" (Murillo 2003, 123). Community radio initiatives intervened in this context to reinstill a sense of community.

Radio Andaquí was founded in June 1994 in Belén de los Andaquíes, Caqueta, in southern Colombia, where the population had largely abandoned all sense of public life out of fear. To counter this, the radio station announced a Christmas decorating contest based on neighbourhoods rather than individuals, with the prize being a block party. Neighbours would have to work together to create decorations on their block and come together to celebrate the winner. To promote the contest, "the station then used its radiocycle, a mobile unit mounted on a tandem bicycle, to transmit from a different block every night. Little by little, neighbors began coming and going from one block to another, comparing decorating strategies" (Kidd, Barker-Plummer, and Rodriguez 2006, 10). They also participated in the radiocycle broadcasts. In this way, the station generated greater social cohesion in the community, providing a safe means for people to participate in the public sphere and together reclaim their streets for celebratory purposes.

This serves as an example of the subaltern counterpublic that, although not explicitly confrontational against the state or globalization, nonetheless challenges the effects of globalization (the globalized militarized drug trade, globalized policing, the US intervention in the region, and so forth) by creating alternatives to a fear-based existence. Radio Andaquí created social communication beyond the simple production of media by bringing people together and using mobile broadcasts to create a series of public events contesting ownership of the public squares and streets by those with greater fire power.

The Juventud Stereo radio station took a similar approach. Founded in 1995 in Guaviare by the Movimiento Juventud por el Guaviare (Movement for Guaviare youth), it was granted an official licence in 1997 and started broadcasting in 1998. At the time Guaviare was considered a "red zone" rife with conflict, and for some the growing coca industry was the only realistic economic future. In this context, Juventud Stereo took up the struggles of the youth movement, working with other individuals and organizations in the community to deal with the negative impacts of the coca industry, including the US-backed spraying of herbicides, environmental issues, human rights, Indigenous rights, and agricultural-worker activism.

The radio station provided capacity-building workshops for youths aged thirteen to twenty-five, including both media literacy and radio-production skills (Murillo 2003, 135). In addition, the station organized cultural events, youth leadership workshops, political candidate forums, and community building events. The youth thus produced social communication in three ways: among those participating in the station; between radio producers and the audience; and laterally among audience members (Murillo 2003, 135). Through social communication, they connected with social movements and those in political power, generating an ever-wider sphere of influence. In the context of globalization, they provide an excellent example of a translocal, subaltern media counterpublic.

Radio stations also organize into networks for collective advocacy and sharing experiences and expertise. AREDMAG is a case in point in Latin America. A network of seventeen community radio stations in Magdalena Medio, they engaged with three academic researchers in a process of participatory self-evaluation. The process revealed that the network serves the community through social communication and relationship building in multiple ways, for example, as a space for connecting social movements and audiences and as peace builders engaged in conflict resolution. They mediated among local individuals or groups in conflict within the community; between citizens and authorities; and between civilians and paramilitary groups.

As an example, one of the station directors was detained by a guerrilla group called ELN. The radio station was used to broadcast various types of messages: (1) a communiqué to the guerrillas to respect the director's life, (2) messages from the community to the guerrillas urging them to free the director, and (3) supportive messages to the director himself. In the end, the guerrillas agreed to release the director if people from the radio would go to the guerrilla camp to pick him up. But some were afraid of what might happen if only one or two people went.

The solution? They organized a caravan of 480 community members to travel fifteen hours into the Andes mountains; the station director returned with them two days later (Kidd, Barker-Plummer, and Rodriguez 2006, 11). In this example, the radio was literally used by the community to save a person's life by mediating between the citizens and the guerrilla group.

The self-evaluation research process revealed that radio stations in the network shared the objective of creating connections to social movements and civil society, although, in reality, very few actually were (Kidd, Barker-Plummer, and Rodriguez 2006, 1). They struggled with the tension between producing grassroots programming for local or regional audiences, and the desire to reach a national popular audience. However, through collaborative discussions fostered by the research, they came to realize "that it was much more important to reach tight levels of connectedness and articulations with other progressive social movements and grassroots organizations in the region than to reach large audiences" (Kidd, Barker-Plummer, and Rodriguez 2006, 11).

The participatory evaluation process culminated in bringing together sixty radio station workers for a three-day workshop, providing space for self-reflection so stations could become more aware of their successes and make changes to bring their media practices in line with their values and objectives. They were also able to present the researchers' evaluation of their achievements to outside funders to maintain the radio network (Kidd, Barker-Plummer, and Rodriguez 2006, 12). The network itself was strengthened through the research process, and their peace-building and social movement support amplified, confirming that "these Colombian community communicators have a profound understanding of the communication and information needs of their community in times of war" (Rodriguez et al. 2014, 10). They used radio to mesh together the social fabric and generate engagement through empowered collective social action.

This case illustrates how radio stations allow people to begin experiencing non-violence: "Instead of sending messages describing non-violence or trying to persuade people to live non-violently in a war-torn community, a radio station triggers a process of non-violent conflict resolution in the community" (Rodriguez, Ferron, and Shamas 2014, 12). There is a mechanism of accountability, as the community supports the process and becomes directly or indirectly engaged. This attempts to shift "the political culture that forced people to remain complacent and silent as a result of years of stagnation and war" (Murillo 2003, 135).

What we see in community radio then is the emergence of technopolitical practices that integrate politics into technologies. These practices include scale-shifting from the local to the regional and national, integrating political concerns into media practices, featuring translocal mobilizations that produce affect, knowledge, and "epistemologies from the South" (Santos 2015). These radio practices also illustrate the principles of ownership and control of media open to community participation and they contest police surveillance and violence while fostering distributive leadership through horizontal networks of radio producers sharing media practices and technological expertise. These practices, important in their own right, have helped pave the way for the technopolitical media practices integral to the Indymedia network.

The Network Society as Globalization

The network society has influenced movements for social change. The network society can be defined as "the social structure resulting from the interaction between the new technological paradigm and social organization at large" (Castells 2005b, 3). This new paradigm has caused a profound restructuring of social arrangements in society. We have thus not just entered a new economic form with neoliberal globalization but also a new form of social structure and practice with the dominance of the internet. Castells (2005a, 693–94) suggests there have been six interrelated dimensions of change from the 1970s to the 1990s: a technological shift; globalization; the demise of nation-state sovereignty; the crisis of patriarchy; and ecological consciousness – all driven by the information and communications technology (ICT) revolution, massive restructuring of states and capitalism, and the legacy of radical 1960s cultural and social movements. Like technopolitics, this network society encompasses a communicative paradigm shift that has been produced in tandem with a profound shift in social structures.

The network society is inherently global, with social, governance, and communicative structures all reorganized on a global scale. Global networks rely not just on the ICT nodes of global platforms, sites, and content, or the technological backbone of communications such as fibre-optic cables, transmission towers, and internet service providers, but also on the nodes and structures of global cities and the physical spaces that organize people and technologies together.

Counter to what one might think, and similar to technopolitics, the network society is neither technologically nor ideologically deterministic: "Technology does not determine society: it is society. Society shapes technology according to the needs, values, and interests of people who use the technology. Furthermore, information and communication technologies are particularly sensitive to the effects of social uses on technology itself" (Castells 2005b, 3).

The transformation of media practices in the network society engendered by the widespread use of mobile technologies, WiFi, 4G and 5G data plans, and smartphones is referred to by Mark Deuze (2012) as the integrated assemblage of "media life," and by Clay Shirky (2008) who proclaims, "Here comes everybody," joining the techno-optimists. On the other hand, techno-pessimists warn of the hegemonic power embedded in this connectivity, as it has failed to deliver on its promise to democratize media (Curran, Fenton, and Freedman 2016).

Within this network society, global social movement media activists have mobilized in the GJM in two predominant ways: through glocalization (Robertson 1995) or translocal (Appadurai 1990) frameworks. Social movement media have a growing consciousness of the global implications of their local efforts.

As mass social movement mobilizations at global summits have brought together hundreds of thousands of activists, strategies are not transferred from one location to another; rather, they are developed together in translocal solidarities. News produced by media activists can also be translocal, combining local mediatization of global events and global mediatization of local events. In translocal media, "although the homogenizing effects of global culture exist, they are absorbed by local political and cultural economies and reappear as heterogeneous dialogues with the original versions. The homogenous and heterogeneous, and the global and the local, find themselves in permanent fields of tensions" (O. Bailey, Cammaerts, and Carpentier 2008, 123). Translocal mobilizations, as we saw in Chapter 1, take place when multiple mobilizations occur with similar strategies, tactics, and objectives in different locations organized by specific, local protest cultures. Occupy is an example of this: following the first Occupy Wall Street protest in New York City, which led to the Zucotti Park occupation, multiple Occupy movements sprang up across the United States, Canada, the United Kingdom, and beyond, each with their own flavour but all contesting the oppression of the 99% by the 1%. Despite this broadly inclusive collective identity calling attention to social class, the Occupy movement was also critiqued for its domination by white, male organizers by feminists, antiracist organizers and Indigenous people who experienced tensions. In particular, Indigenous groups called attention to the term "Occupy" as encoding yet another settler re-occupation of Indigenous lands (Tuck and Yang 2012).

Many movements now call for global days of action as well, such as the October 2011 global day of action against austerity called by the Spanish Indignados, or the global Women's March that took place two days after Donald Trump's inauguration as president of the United States in January 2016 (Wallace and Parlapiano 2017). While protests are linked through organizing strategies, objectives combine the exigencies of local organizing initiatives with shared intersectional objectives and technopolitical strategies. Translocal networks are particularly salient in the Indymedia network.

Indymedia and the Rise of Global Technopolitics

The Indymedia network, explored briefly in the Introduction, emerged during the Seattle anti-WTO protests in 1999. Seattle Indymedia was started "with only $30,000 in donations and borrowed equipment" (Kidd 2003, 50), including cutting-edge livestreaming equipment donated by an ex-Microsoft techie. According to media and communications scholar Dorothy Kidd, the independent media centre (IMC) in Seattle brought together four groups: alterglobalization social movements, local Seattle social movements, alternative media activists, and tech activists in the open source, free culture movement (Kidd 2003, 59–60). They were critical of enclosures of the commons under neoliberalism through the privatization of the digital commons and the corporatization of the internet. Tech activists in the open source movement, who believe that information wants to be free and who share a "common code" (Kidd 2003, 57) or value system, also shared political values with many GJM activists.

The Seattle IMC was "created by media democracy activists who gathered in a downtown Seattle storefront during the weeks leading up to the WTO protests; the IMC was fashioned as a grassroots news organization to provide non-corporate accounts of street-level events" (Pickard 2006, 20). The website received over one million hits during the week of the Seattle protests. Their open editorial format proved effective, and Indymedia collectives soon sprang up across the globe: "Within the first year, 24 new IMCs emerged around the world in places like Quebec City, Prague, and Washington, DC, often in conjunction with large global justice protests against neoliberal institutions such as the IMF and World Bank or the G8" (Pickard 2006, 20).

Indymedia quickly became a network of tech and media activists engaged in two types of organizing: (1) those who run online technology for websites that report on and support radical activism, producing content for these websites as well as providing tech support; and (2) those who set up and run temporary IMCs for mass protest convergences or communications tents at protest camps such as the Occupy and Indignados square occupations. Already by 2005, the Indymedia network included a translocal network of "over 150 sites in 50 countries across six continents" (Pickard 2006, 20).

The IMC movement is global in both its network and its political commitments, rooted as it is in the GJM: "The IMC [in Seattle] enabled independent journalists and media producers of print, radio, video, and photos from around the world to produce and distribute stories from the perspectives of the growing anti-corporate globalization movement" (Kidd 2003, 50). Similarly, Canadian communications scholar Bob Hanke (2005, 44), in a case study of Canada's Ontario Indymedia collective, notes that "the same 'real time' hypermedia environment that is a precondition for the transpolitical empire of speed has also given rise to transnational campaigns, alliances of activists across borders." And Greek media activist and researcher Dimitra Milioni (2009, 425) notes in her case study of Indymedia Athens that it serves as a counterpublic sphere intertwining the local and global, representing broader collective action frames: "The emphasis is upon global activity regarding not only the locale in which action is taking place, but also the issues of concern. Indymedia Athens does not encourage a retreat to localization either as a shelter from globalization or resistance to globalization." For Milioni (2009, 426), it is therefore important to recognize that Indymedia "resembles a transnational coalition that connects local identities to global considerations and builds a global solidarity." This translocal model of Indymedia is based on the autonomy of local collectives regarding production and dissemination of their own journalism, within a horizontal, global, decentralized network organized through distributive leadership.

An Emergent Intersectional Technopolitics

The GJM brings together nascent interconnected meta-issue movements organizing against global neoliberal capital and cutting-edge participatory digital technologies and practices used by increasingly globally connected activists, creating an emergent intersectional technopolitics (see Table 4).

In terms of the movement and media practices mapped in Chapter 1, we can see the GJM beginning to formulate intersectional technopolitical strategies that will lead to their widespread use in contemporary moments. The open editorial system of Indymedia was an innovative peer-to-peer (P2P) architecture by which people could both post and read news without the filters of

Table 4 Key dimensions of intersectional technopolitics in the GJM

Dimension	Intersectional technopolitics in the GJM
Intersectional and anticapitalist	Contesting neoliberal capitalism; voices of marginalized global groups; meta-issue global movement starts to become intersectional
Distributed online-offline architectures and motility	Online-offline community connections; distributive architectures of Indymedia platform; distributive leadership in global movement; offline connection to squatted social centres, IMCs
Multiplicities of technologies and spaces	Multiple genres (radio, website, zines, etc.); many actor types in GJM, including NGOs, SMOs, grassroots groups; global actions; open media technologies; emergence of tech activism
Translocal solidarity economies and technologies	Solidarities without borders in GJM; technology-enabled networks of Indymedia; translocal mobilizations and summit hopping; solidarity platform design
Collective autonomy through direct action	Technologies and politics are collectively autonomous; collectively self-organized technological and social infrastructures in community radio and Indymedia

mainstream media gatekeepers. This P2P architecture achieved technologies of scale with a global reach. It promoted multitech usages, included multigenre posting, and facilitated work on multiple platforms; however, it was not yet multi-device, as smartphone technologies were not yet widespread.

Community radio facilitated offline participation in community decision making, empowering activism through sociotechnical assemblages. Indymedia also created offline and online motility, with websites linked to the real-world spaces of global grassroots collectives. Virtual spaces, such as IRC chat rooms, were coupled with the material space of IMCs at protest convergences, with some Indymedia collectives creating longer-term hubs in local communities. Indymedia facilitated translocal technologies without borders, hosting servers for one country physically located in another. And the GJM facilitated translocal mobilizations during summits, including summit hopping and solidarity marches. It balanced the openness of the free culture open source movement's hacktivism with anti-surveillance security culture, attempting to protect against activist surveillance by the state, while rejecting the nascent capitalist social media platforms, with Facebook starting in 2004 and Twitter in 2006. Finally, distributive technologies were combined with distributive leadership potential, although not always fully actualizing horizontality due to social and technological exclusions alike.

These technopolitical media practices, combined with the increasingly intersectional meta-issue focus of the global social movement and media activism, were signs of an emergent intersectional technopolitics that would come to fruition in subsequent global waves of contention. With the twenty-year anniversary in 2019 of the founding of Indymedia, an outpouring of reflections on its legacies have shown that it had important global impacts on media activist practices, and some Indymedia collectives continue to function to this day (Aikawa, Jeppesen, and MARG 2020; Baú 2020; Fenton 2020; Robé and Wolfson 2020; Van Leeckwyck et al. 2020).

Challenges and Successes

The translocal network characteristics of Indymedia have led to both successes and challenges. First the successes. As many alternative media scholars and activists observe, independent media produces and amplifies the voices of the otherwise voiceless, including GJM activists who were often marginalized in mainstream reporting on globalization. Through Indymedia's open editorial policy, where anyone can post stories to the site, "activists who are not regarded as primary sources of political news because they operate outside of official channels for political action are given a voice" (Hanke 2005, 57). Indymedia's widespread anticapitalist economic model, promoting community-owned and self-organized digital technologies for marginalized groups, illustrates how it is one of the key harbingers of technopolitics.

Another success, as Pickard argues, is that Indymedia has proven to be an effective example of direct democracy through three discursive, technical, and institutional media constructions: an interactive, web-based interface and open editorial policy; its horizontalism and attention to power dynamics through consensus decision making; and its commitment to open source software (Pickard 2006, 20). To this I would add a fourth key media practice – maintaining rootedness within social movements grounded in the alternative consensus discussed above: "Such radical democratic practices as Indymedia's consensus decision making and open internet technology are invested with values of inclusiveness, diversity, openness, co-operation, transparency, and collective decision-making" (Pickard 2006, 23).

Dorothy Kidd (2003, 60) similarly links their democratic structure to values, arguing that "the IMC network is based on a nonhierarchical structure that relies on highly complex processes of networked consensus," resulting in "a high level of democratic processing" that is "drawn from the direct-action wing of the anti-globalization movement" and thus "represents a new level of development of a communications commons." Moreover, she suggests that the success of Indymedia was partially due to the open storefront, which brought in many different groups of people: "The storefront provided the personal and technological interface to bridge the rivalries between different media, different organizations, and different generations" (Kidd 2003, 61). Thus Indymedia signalled an early tendency toward recognizing the importance of intersectional anti-oppression practices across age and diversity.

The successes of Indymedia also involved the sharing of emerging digital technologies, including both hardware such as the livestream video technology and lightweight digital cameras and software such as the open editorial platform interface. Seattle Indymedia overcame previous experiences of competitive space limitations for media production, as "the site could accept an unlimited amount of content, including text, photos, graphics, video, and audio" (Kidd 2003, 62). This may have contributed to a further success, which was the reach they achieved: "During the anti-WTO protests in Seattle, the site had a million and a half hits, and the entire network is now [in

2002] estimated to receive about four-hundred-thousand page views a day"
(Kidd 2003, 62), just three years after its inception.

On the other hand, the IMC network was not without its challenges and
contradictions. First, the site's open editorial policy proved challenging. As
Hanke (2005, 45) argues, online "development and uses are fraught with
tensions between open and closed systems." The lack of moderation, while
providing open participation for activists, also allows for hateful, off-topic,
or otherwise inappropriate posts by anyone and everyone. To address this
issue, some IMCs filter out hate posts or hide off-topic articles or comments
in a near-unreachable part of the site. Others engage in mild moderation to
weed out the most egregious material. However, the problem has never
been completely resolved because of the paradox at its root – an anti-
authoritarian newsgroup does not want to engage in authoritarian solutions
that contravene its own editorial policy and political commitments, even if
it is to remove authoritarian (fascist, racist, sexist, homophobic, etc.)
content.

The second challenge is the digital divide. Although many people might
have access to computers, leading to the claim that anyone can post on the
site, in reality, not everyone in the world has such access. Challenges in
using Indymedia and its discussion board wikis have been identified as
leading to a "lack of access, expertise, and confidence" among those
attempting to participate, perhaps due to the fact that "Indymedia's tech-
nocentric means of communication seems to privilege white North
American males, a recurring grievance" (Pickard 2006, 28). Furthermore,
IMCs are dependent on volunteer or unpaid labour, meaning that only people who hold paid employment elsewhere, don't have primary child-care
responsibilities, or are supported by partners or parents, as mentioned in
Chapter 1, can do Indymedia work. Therefore, it requires a certain level of
class and gender privilege. If a person works on the site while also holding
down a full-time job or other gendered and/or racialized responsibilities,
this can easily lead to the burnout of some participants more than others.
This also causes a lack of financial sustainability for both the collective,
which depends on volunteer labour, and the media activists, who contribute
unpaid labour to the site.

To address the global digital divide, early on in the IMC network, at the
request of and in dialogue with activists from Latin America, an effort was
made by those in EuroAmerica to share technologies and skills. Specifically,
networks of solidarity were created between Seattle and media activists in
Latin America engaged in community radio. Within IMC collectives,

recognizing the skills divide as well, skillshare workshops were organized for the most skilled members to train the less skilled members. These workshops also happened within EuroAmerican collectives.

Arising from differences in skills and tech savviness, a challenge to the avowed practices of horizontality, a third challenge becomes evident – the risk of informal hierarchies. The structurelessness of horizontality sometimes leads to the development of elite, informal in-groups or cliques, also creating exclusions, which are tricky to identify and even harder to address (Pickard 2006, 32). This applies not just at the local level but also in the global Indymedia network. Sometimes, open editorial structures promote openness more effectively for those in the dominant group (Costanza-Chock 2012; Wolfson 2013), reproducing the very structures of inequality they claim to be challenging, a finding that many Media Action Research Group (MARG) research participants have reiterated.

A fourth challenge that we see in both community radio in Latin America and the Indymedia network is that struggles for freedom of communication are yoked to a prevalence of police brutality and state repression. Indymedia has often had its website under police surveillance (Hanke 2005, 57). Kidd (2003, 63) has also found that IMC activists themselves were not just under surveillance but also under a growing risk of physical attacks by police. For example, the FBI raided Indymedia Seattle after the 2001 Quebec City anti-Free Trade Area of the Americas protests. And there were violent police raids on the Genoa IMC at the Armando Diaz School during the G8 protests in Italy 2001, hospitalizing many activists, some with broken bones, and jailing many others. Similarly, Radio Favela was under constant threat of being shut down by police. One of the four founders was arrested for pirate-radio broadcasting and subjected to police violence in jail. In Brazil, "unlicensed community radio stations are heavily repressed. According to some accounts, up to 10 radio stations are shut down every day, and up to several thousand per year" (Hintz 2011, 155).

With the September 11, 2001, attack on the New York World Trade Centre, now known as 9/11, the GJM was supplanted by a wave of protests against the War on Terror, followed a decade or so later by the Occupy and anti-austerity mobilizations after the 2008 economic crisis. Some Indymedia activists slowly shifted to other pursuits while resisting the use of capitalist social media platforms, and intersectional technopolitics would go underground in a latency phase to emerge rhizomatically in unexpected ways in the years to come.

3 Anti-austerity

Anticapitalists in a Capitalist World

The Riot Hipster meme, featuring a bearded male protester taking a selfie at the 2017 G20 protests in Hamburg, went viral with the tagline "That feeling when you're overthrowing capitalism but just can't resist taking a selfie on your iPhone 7." The meme, as Christina Neumayer and David Struthers (2018) argue, exemplifies a nascent politics of technologies introduced by increasing media activist reliance on capitalist social media platforms and expensive digital devices that calls into question the class privilege that may be required to participate fully in anticapitalist movements. It also indirectly questions the lens of communications scholarship, which tends to engage predominantly with middle-class EuroAmerican media movements and, even within that, does not always engage with antiracist or anticolonial movements, a critique amplified by the hashtag #CommunicationSoWhite.

The Riot Hipster meme symbolizes the contradiction of anticapitalist and anti-austerity activists who are in open contestation of a capitalist system in which they are undeniably locked. Tools of the media activist today – including multigenre digital devices and genre-specific technologies – are produced and distributed by global capitalism and tend to be more available to those with class privilege. Alternative media activists tend to use the same tools as the mainstream media, appropriating them for anticapitalist purposes (e.g., culture jamming, data justice, hacktivism) and social movement reporting. Media activists, however, unlike mainstream journalists, have to supply their own devices or find ways to access expensive technologies from software and servers to printing presses and radio stations. Some media activists, particularly those in the free culture movement, use open source platforms and apps, but this seems a limited – if quite critical – option, as these, too, have been coded on expensive computers by skilled workers, and require expensive devices to use, with access divided across intersectional class, gender, colonial, and race lines.

The Riot Hipster meme begs the question whether a person can have both anticapitalist politics and class privilege, contesting a system from which they benefit, and which forces them to compromise their ideals in everyday life. Certainly, there are examples of this throughout history, from anarchist aristocrat Peter Kropotkin to Situationist Guy Debord, to US Democratic senator and self-proclaimed socialist Bernie Sanders who reportedly has a net worth of USD$2.5 million (Peterson-Withorn 2019).

However, the complications of the anticapitalist and anti-austerity movements cut deeper than the social-class issue parodied by the Riot Hipster meme. The meme calls into question the controversial labour practices of Apple and its subsidiary Foxconn in China, known for extreme working conditions and high suicide rates, with employees who likely could not afford the newest iPhone. The meme might thus also be interpreted as a sub-viral marketing strategy by Apple iPhone, appealing to those most critical of its marketing and manufacturing practices.

Who has the right, and who has the opportunity, in a globalized world, to be an anticapitalist – and to be represented as such? Moreover, if the European male hipster, with his new iPhone – the most privileged global activist, one might say – has forfeited the right to be considered an anticapitalist, then must all media activists reject the newest tools of communication to be seen as correctly anticapitalist – and thereby lose their voices? Where does this leave intersectionally marginalized activists who scramble for resources, skills, capacities, and paid labour to support their activism? Does this mean that activists who, for example, live in poverty, must remain impoverished to become empowered? There is a problematic politics in judging activists for not properly embodying oppression, a position-taking called the Oppression Olympics (Dhamoon 2015), discussed further in Chapter 5. Instead of calling out privileged activists, perhaps we should figure out how to combat barriers to participation for the most marginalized, including pathways out of poverty.

Considering these questions and more, this chapter examines the integration of intersectional technopolitics into anticapitalist movements. What are the material conditions in which intersectional anti-austerity and anti-capitalist movements are engaged in the production and dissemination of meanings? Anticapitalists are not always good at reconciling certain contradictions, nor do they always foreground transfeminist, 2LGBTQ+, antiracist, and Indigenous concerns. Here I focus on the entanglements intersectional participants introduce to anticapitalist movements and media projects when they are active on issues such as labour, poverty, youth and student rights, gender, race, immigration, housing, health care, or anti-Black racism that are intersectional to the meta-issue of austerity.

The media and economic, social, and political contexts of contention shifted considerably between the global justice movement (GJM) era that ended around 2001 and the rise of anti-austerity protests after 2008. The digital media context shifted to Web 2.0, characterized by the dominance of interactivity and social media (Fuchs 2010; Jarrett 2008). Mainstream media experienced an intensification of technological and ownership convergence in increasingly global media systems (Jenkins 2006). Widespread distrust of mainstream media escalated (N.S. Cohen 2016; Ferris 2001) as people turned increasingly to alternative media for news and entertainment, with a rise in peer-to-peer (P2P) downloading for entertainment and using social media as a news source (Andersson 2009; Atton and Wickenden 2006; Carrier 2010; Poell and Borra 2012). *Prosumers,* who produce as much media as they consume, became the dominant media user, with activists being no exception (Atkinson 2008; Downing 2003; Min 2004; Rauch 2007). People had also started to consume news in echo chambers that serve to reinforce their already-existing political positions, with algorithms using filter bubbles to maintain or even exacerbate growing political divisions.

The debate between techno-optimists and techno-pessimists had further escalated. Rather than reinforcing this false dichotomy, it is important to consider who has power with respect to media and technologies, and how dominant media power is being contested as meanings are circulated. The mediascape in the mid- to late 2000s also saw a shift toward the dominance of mobile media and devices to the point that having a smartphone is seen as a necessity of life, and a media activist would require one to engage in street activism, for example, livestreaming, live tweeting, communicating with their affinity group, and learning where protest hot spots are.

The Riot Hipster meme belies the fact that many people living in relative poverty, precarious labour situations, and so on will nonetheless have expensive mobile phones. Brazilian locative media scholars Tharsila

Dallabona-Fariniuk and Rodrigo Firmino (2018, 2) have found that individuals are increasingly immersed in a "personal data ecosystem, when the awareness of 'being connected' *full time* becomes very important," with populations in EuroAmerica and Latin America projected to own 2.8 and 1.5 devices per capita in 2020, respectively. Although the digital divide is telling, the crucial point is that, on a global scale, individuals can now be expected to own at least one device to manage their personal-data ecosystem. This ownership is also a dependency that creates a sense of identity, belonging, and sociality, and it can even generate addictions. The meme captures a common sentiment among younger generations such as iGens or GenZs and millennials that a selfie is necessary to authenticate any event, leading to a social compulsion to constantly document everyday events through the personal-data ecosystem, which is now also an image ecosystem. These are the new material conditions of existence that serve as a backdrop to the anti-austerity wave of contention, a very different sociotechnological context to that of the GJM. We must therefore consider who has access to the means of production of representation and how, in this wave of contention, their visibility might be, on the one hand, differently limited via the new platform algorithms, smartphone and data surveillance, and other social-control mechanisms and, on the other hand, differently extended via the new discoverability and viral affordances of their personal data and image ecosystems.

After the slow demise of the GJM, the economic field intensified neoliberal capitalism, precipitating the 2008 EuroAmerican financial crisis and subsequent imposition of austerity measures by the neoliberal institutions the GJM wave of contention had been contesting. After the crash, G20 nation-states decided at their highly contested 2010 Toronto meeting to impose intense austerity measures. This involved retrenching the power of the banks and capital while cutting social welfare; increasing personal and government debt loads, particularly in Latin America, Africa, and parts of Asia, but also in Greece; and implementing further systemic policies and structures to protect capitalism, most often at the expense of the ordinary citizen. Bailouts were provided from governments to large corporations, such as banks, while governments simultaneously rolled out drastic cuts to social-welfare nets, including education, health care, social supports, employment insurance, pensions, minimum wage, and so on. Latent community organizing, which had continued after the decline of the GJM, quickly shifted its focus post-2008 to addressing austerity as a meta-issue.

Linked to shifts in media and economics, the political context saw complex transformations for intersectional marginalized groups across race, Indigeneity, sexuality, and gender. The election of Barack Obama as president of the United States introduced the problematic discourse of a postracial world, juxtaposed with growing contestations of racism. Beyond the United States, global uprisings took place in the Arab and African Spring in Tunisia, Egypt, Turkey, and so on. The landmark United Nations Declaration on the Rights of Indigenous Peoples (UNDRIP 2007) was adopted, supporting an already ongoing rise in Indigenous cultural resurgence and resistance to colonialism that had been growing in response to specific threats such as pipelines, fracking, mining, and so on. Around the same time, intersecting with issues of antiracism and anticolonialism, 2LGBTQ+ rights rose to the forefront of global social movements. Same-sex marriage was legalized in a variety of countries, starting in 2001 in the Netherlands, and continuing in 2003 in Belgium, 2005 in Canada, 2009 in Sweden, 2012 in Denmark, and 2015 in the United States, with intersectional 2LGBTQ+ movements taking shape. Non-binary and transgender identities were catapulted onto the main stage of politics with the participation of intersex South African Olympic athlete Caster Semenya at the 2009 World Championships, transgender woman Laverne Cox's popularity in the 2013 TV series *Orange Is the New Black*, and the 2015 gender transition of American Olympic athlete Caitlyn Jenner. These widely popularized celebrity media representations played out in tandem with the rise in trans, non-binary, and two-spirit activism globally.

At the same time, a rise in populism was starting to be reflected in the election of right-wing governments and the rise of alt-right movements, including pro-lifers, climate deniers, Incels (involuntary celibates, who are highly misogynistic), white supremacists, and transphobic, heteronormative, and antifeminist movements, leading to an escalation of systemic and interpersonal violence informed by "intersectional hate" (Browne 2016). EuroAmerica was increasingly characterized as a polarized world where people located at two ends of the right-left political spectrum were no longer on speaking terms, nor were they reading each other's media, leading to a decline in the shared sense of a national imaginary.

In the context of these three major shifts toward the dominance of mobile media, the intensification of neoliberalism via austerity measures, and the increase in rights for marginalized groups amid the violent backlash of alt-right populism, critiques of GJM summit hopping led to social action in local communities of a more sustained nature. Taken together, this meant that in the anti-austerity wave of contention, longer-term campaigns of constant contention would supplant shorter-term mass protest convergence mobilizations, facilitated through the everyday use of social media networks. Social movement and media practices alike became intensely integrated into everyday life as the dual strategy of contestation and construction melded into an integrated protest form that took place in the online and offline public sphere.

Anti-austerity in Constant Contention

Austerity hit every sector of life, causing many community groups and activist organizations to contest the specific impositions of austerity measures affecting them. Movements for housing, students, minimum-wage and basic-income, Indigenous rights, and so on were all engaged in contesting the harsh impacts of austerity. The anti-austerity rubric was thus an almost ready-made umbrella providing the structure for a meta-issue movement that created a coherent amalgamation of many disparate movements. Unlike Occupy, which was accused of being an incoherent movement with no particular demands, the Indignados were seen as a coherent movement contesting a clear target – austerity – through an emotional action frame that society could understand and get behind – indignation.

The politics of the anti-austerity wave of contention thus included a shift toward local organizing around local issues in solidarity networks framed by a critical analysis of intersectional systemic oppressions linked to capitalism and austerity. Thus, while anticapitalists were certainly engaged in the GJM, the capitalist imposition of austerity measures combined with the increasingly widespread critiques of capitalism previously mobilized by the GJM catapulted explicitly anticapitalist organizers to the forefront of anti-austerity movements.

The austerity wave of contention contested the fact that neoliberal capitalism was now openly benefitting from state regulatory frameworks under the auspices of the double-speak process of deregulation, which enacted not deregulation but new regulations that favoured capital. Free-trade regulatory frameworks provided mechanisms by which corporations could bypass national regulations such as environmental protections or labour law, with corporations able to sue states, overturning the capacity of democratically elected governments to domestically regulate industry, labour, taxes, trade, and the environment. Consequently, supra-national, non-elected organizations such as the World Trade Organization, International Monetary Fund, Asian Development Bank, and World Bank began to supersede the autonomy of states, resulting in a lack of democratic accountability. Thus, anticapitalist movements connected critiques of austerity measures to critiques of corrupt states and the neoliberal institutions that dominate them, with anticorruption becoming a key axis of analysis and action.

Anticapitalist critiques also began to shift beyond considering that employees were not paid enough under austerity measures, or that working conditions were unsafe or insecure, toward identifying the fundamental unequal relationship of employer-employee as the root problem. Rather than organizing unions, anticapitalists argued that unions were negotiating the terms of their own exploitation; consequently, their working conditions would never be fully under their own control. They therefore organized into worker's co-operatives and worker-controlled labour formations in a growing form of direct-action, forefront labour organizing. At the same time, they demanded a basic income or a living wage through community protest movements. Moreover, in the organization of everyday life, they created solidarity structures and economies in the movements of the squares and beyond.

Developing this analysis of movement structures (and the context of the detailed media labour practices of Chapter 1) profoundly shifted social movement strategies. Movements continued to work toward both creating the commons and taking to the streets. As Marisol Sandoval argues, this "double strategy combines immediate and immanent change with working towards systemic transformations" (Sandoval 2016, 58). What we see in the anti-austerity wave of contention, however, is a joining of these two strategies in a very public way through the politics of constant contention. Protest camps of the anti-austerity wave of contention – and other similar ongoing or sustained strategies, such as the nightly protest marches of the Quebec Student Stike or the weekly Fridays for Future climate strikes – served as longer-term strategies for creating the commons.

I therefore contend that constant contention became the new mode of organizing initiated by the anti-austerity wave of contention, whereby protests took place for a longer, sustained period of time, or on a frequent, regular basis, the timing of which was defined by the protest organizers themselves based on an activist rather than a capitalist event or logic. Constant contention bears similarities to a temporary autonomous zone, establishing a given space and time for people to come together under their own local community logics such as a protest camp. It is thus a mode not just of contestation but also of creating alternative values, logics, infrastructures, relationships, and media mobilizations.

The Anticapitalist Commons

Under neoliberal capitalism, the commons has slowly been enclosed, sold off to private interests to be used in for-profit ventures. Public squares have been branded, and communities must apply and pay for permits to use them. Public parks have been sold to corporations and closed at night, limiting public access and outlawing open-air sleeping, often the only recourse for homeless people. Air, water, roadways, education, the media, and other public goods have become increasingly privatized, branded, closed off, and monetized (Dean 2009; Giroux 2002).

Following the GJM wave of contention, we saw a growing trend toward rebuilding and reclaiming the commons. Activists built community gardens to extract themselves from commercial food systems and capitalist property relations to land, which is instead reclaimed as a commons to create community food security (Caffentzis and Federici 2014; Federici 2011; Harvey 2011; Jeppesen et al. 2013). Similarly, cafés, schools, daycares, book fairs, publishers, houses, and other infrastructures were organized as horizontal collectives or co-operatives. These are connected increasingly to a commitment to minimalist degrowth lifestyles, mutual aid and solidarity economies, and other horizontal, direct engagements that collectively organize everyday life. The politics of reclaiming the public commons gave its name to a popular global protest movement – Reclaim the Streets.

In the anti-austerity wave of contention, the protest camp became a new commons, a space in which social life could be reproduced to create, reclaim, and rebuild society in a new way. Collective autonomy practices focused on the collective ownership of the means of production, representation, and social reproduction within the camps on the squares. The latent stage of mobilization between mass protests was brought to the forefront on the squares to such a degree that entire micro-villages were created that attempted to establish themselves as autonomous from state and capital, organized according to horizontal, anticapitalist frameworks. The means of production were reclaimed to creatively fulfill basic needs for food, clothing, shelter, and so on. The means of representation, the image and discursive or text-based systems that document movement histories and collective memories, were reclaimed through media and communications committees grounded in technopolitical strategies. And social reproduction – the means of interaction, dialogue, and relationship building – was redesigned so everyone had a way to participate in public discourse and decision making, for example through general assemblies. As many Media Action Research Group (MARG) interview subjects mentioned, all you needed to do to be a member of the camp was to participate, whether it was by cooking food, speaking at the general assembly, producing media, or looking after children. Autonomy did not, in this sense, refer to individualized independence or separate rights but rather collective independence from state governance and capitalist control, while organizing to create positive social relationships of lived equality, respect, and dignity.

Similar projects that the protest camps drew inspiration from included land takeovers by the Movimento dos Trabalhadores Sem Terra (MST), or landless rural workers in Brazil (Sartoretto 2016); the squatters' movements that occupied abandoned buildings, particularly in the Netherlands and the United Kingdom (Kadir 2016); the takeover of unused land for community gardens (Caffentzis and Federici 2014); and no-border protest camps. In addition, antiracist and 2LGBTQ+ contributions were noted by our interviewees. For example, there are currently many Indigenous land reclamation projects, such as the Tiny House Warriors, who set up Tiny Houses to reclaim Indigenous lands and "stop the Trans Mountain pipeline from crossing unceded Secwepemc Territory" (Tiny House Warriors 2019). There were also a range of temporary autonomous zones that reclaimed spaces for 2LGBTQ+ people such as Queeruption (G. Brown 2007), including intersectional identities such as queer and trans people of colour (Jeppesen, Kruzynski, and Riot 2016).

Protest camps in the squares engaged in prefigurative horizontal organizing of the commons, contributing to the creation of counter-institutions with a shared anticapitalist political culture (G. Brown et al. 2017; Feigenbaum, Frenzel, and McCurdy 2013). The anticapitalist commons in the anti-austerity wave of contention, rather than being relegated to latent phases of movement organizing between protests, actually became the mode of protest mobilization itself. The camps integrated everyday-life models of organizing and creating alternatives as a crucial mode of constant contention. Creating alternatives and mobilizing protests were inexorably integrated, and both took place in the public sphere, online and offline, in an ongoing, sustained, and continuous mode of everyday anticapitalist protest.

Protest Camps

Along with creating and taking back the commons, anticapitalists used the direct-action strategy of taking back the streets, building protest camps and employing other strategies to reclaim public spaces. Marisol Sandoval (2016,

55) argues that global anticapitalist protests gained popularity and strength after the 2008 economic collapse:

> In the context of the economic crisis of 2008 and the rise of debt, poverty and unemployment we are witnessing indications of a revival of the social critique. The Occupy movement's famous slogan "We are the 99 per cent" poignantly criticises the inequality of a capitalist system that disproportionally benefits a small number of people at the expense of the majority. Similarly, the *Indignados* movement in Spain and the protests in Greece clearly highlighted the profound discontent of a generation whose life is shaped by job insecurity, debt and lack of democracy.

As anticapitalist contention and the creation of alternatives were joined together in anti-austerity movements, activists created comprehensive mini-infrastructures in many cities based on horizontality, self-organization, and autonomous actions in the camps, which served as base camps for launching frequent protest marches. Many protest strategies emerged, such as encampments, nightly marches, diversity of tactics, square occupations, cooperatives, technopolitics, artistic resistance, and more.

The mobility and tactical ephemerality of earlier protest tactics, such as mass protest convergences and mobilizations, Reclaim the Streets, snake marches, and flash mobs, morphed into other forms of street protest. Two key anticapitalist protest movements that engaged in constant contention are analyzed below in terms of mobilization strategies that extended a single protest march into a period of constant contention over a series of several months.

15M, Spain, 2011

On May 15, 2011, protests were called across Spain, with tens of thousands of people showing up to form a protest movement named after this day, 15M for 15 May. While crowds dispersed in most cities, in Madrid an overnight camp opened up in the Puerta del Sol:

> Nothing was planned to take place after the demonstration, but a very small group decided to camp that night in the Puerta del Sol, a large plaza in Madrid's historical centre, filming their actions and streaming them on the web. On the second night, with no warning or possibility for negotiation, the police kicked them out of the plaza. That same night, in an instance of the "Streisand effect," thousands of people came out to the Puerta del

Sol, many of whom decided to stay the night and sleep. Thus was born #spanishrevolution.

(Sanchez Cedillo 2012, 574)

The 15M movement, as it was known to activists, or the Indignados, as it was known in the media, was famous for and popularized the use of technopolitics. This included hijacking corporate social media sites and also organizing through a key movement website, Democracia Real Ya! (www.democraciarealya.es).

The livestreaming of the initial camp in Puerta del Sol played a key role in spreading news of the camp and mobilizing thousands of participants to join it. However, the 15M movement was not simply a camp: "It was as much encampment as demonstration; as much network swarm as neighbourhood assembly; as much Facebook group as *marcha indignada*" (Sanchez Cedillo 2012, 576). Raul Sanchez Cedillo (2012, 574–75) suggests that this wave of contention in Spain was constituent of a new multitude, what he calls, after Hardt and Negri, "a prototype for constituent power," consisting of "a multitude that has behaved and organized itself toward the foundation of a new political order that would invalidate and remove the current one."

As we learned in interviews with 15M activists, the movement was nonhierarchical and prefigurative, bringing together people from all walks of life – regular people who had not been activists before but who could no longer abide government corruption, the impact of austerity on their lives, or the control by capitalists of the processes of democratic decision making. 15M spread like wildfire across Spain and was not limited to the already mobilized urban centres such as Madrid and Barcelona.

The initial slogan, "We Are Not Commodities in the Hands of Politicians and Bankers" (Sanchez Cedillo 2012, 577), defined the movement as explicitly anticapitalist, rejecting not just their own subjugation and commodification but also the country's democratic and economic leadership, largely seen as corrupt, and in their place, constructing horizontal mechanisms of lived equality, reclaiming collective dignity, and taking back the power to make collective democratic decisions themselves.

The protest camps provided space for activists to set up a tent and live for several months. The mobilization also allowed for online participation through technopolitical strategies: "The new technologies enhanced the capacity of self-organisation, disintermediation, and viral knowledge, and triggered the emergence of a new collective actor, dubbed as connected multitudes" (Treré 2019, 144). The connected multitudes were linked through social media as well as other digital technologies such as blogs, digital radio, email lists, shared digital documents, and so on. They rejected the participation of traditional top-down social movement organizations, based on critiques of the World Social Forum. 15M discouraged existing political parties from participating in the camps in any official capacity but at the same time, the movement eventually gave rise to the emergence of Podemos, a political party that subsequently rose to power.

The 15M movement created multi-dimensional synergies through its engagement with multiple generations of activists (Fuster Morell 2012). This included new participants who had not considered themselves activists but got involved by visiting the encampments; GJM activists who had mobilized around the issues of free culture, net neutrality, copyright law, housing, capitalism, and more in the latent phase; and grandparents who had lived through the oppression and fascism of the Franco years, and were enthusiastic to see public dissent legitimated.

Multi-dimensional synergies yoked together multiple generations of experienced and inexperienced activists who were all affected in different ways by austerity but who had different capacities, skills, and interests in social movement and media activism. Also yoked together were activists across a range of intersectional issues, including those from the free culture movement who would inform the technopolitical media strategies, as well as a range of intersectional activists, including transfeminists, people of colour, and 2LGBTQ+ participants who introduced intersectional demands (Asara 2020; Cruells and Ruiz García 2014). Thus, the digital, multi-dimensional synergies of 15M contributed to an intersectional politics of liberation enacted as an everyday organizational strategy of constant contention.

The Quebec Student Strike, Canada, 2012

As 15M continued to build its movement, in 2012, in the province of Quebec, Canada, the government announced a 75 percent tuition hike, sending tens of thousands of college and university students into the streets in protest. Demanding not just a tuition freeze but free tuition, and mobilizing critiques that extended beyond education, they linked tuition hikes to policies of austerity under neoliberal capitalism.

The Quebec Student Strike, known in French as the "Printemps Érable," a francophone homonym of "Printemps Arabe" or "Arab Spring," began on March 22, 2012, with a massive walkout and protest march of two hundred thousand students in the bilingual English-French city of Montreal. Almost four hundred thousand students – and some of their professors, myself included – across the province eventually engaged in the strike by walking out of classes and participating in political and social actions such as nightly protest marches, general assemblies at colleges and universities, neigh-bourhood assemblies, and *casseroles* marches, which involved marching in the streets banging on pots and pans.

The nightly protest marches are what characterized the Quebec Student Strike as a mode of constant contention. From the day the tuition hike was announced, nightly protest marches departed from the same square in downtown Montreal. Each night, a different group would call a march, giv-ing it a particular flavour, but even if no group sent out a call, everyone knew the march details. If you arrived late, you could always find the protest, as it was being livestreamed on CUTV, the Concordia University digital TV sta-tion (Thorburn 2014).

Recognizing the limitations of traditional top-down student unions, student organizers quickly formed a new grassroots coalition called CLASSÉ (La Coalition large de l'Association pour une solidarité syndicale étudiante, or Broad Coalition for the Solidarity of Student Unions), which worked through a diversity of tactics, horizontal organizing, and respect for the autonomy of grassroots student groups to call actions using social media.

Students and their supporters pinned on small red felt squares to show their solidarity, based on the francophone expression "carré dans la rouge" or "squarely in the red," pointing to escalating levels of student debt. When the National Assembly of Quebec, overwhelmed by the nightly marches and feeling the pressure of the mass arrests, passed Bill 78, "La Loi Spéciale," restricting the right to protest or express support for the protest by wearing a red square, the student strike transformed into a social uprising across the province. Generally thought by students, lawyers, and the general public to be a contravention of the Canadian Charter of Rights and Freedoms, the Special Law spurred community groups to join the constant contestation.

When the Special Law was passed, the distributive, horizontal organiz-ing model of the students spread to local neighbourhoods, which organized general assemblies to discuss issues related to the student strike, including housing, gentrification, racism, and policing, depending on the ideas con-tributed by neighbours. Neighbourhood assemblies also discussed how to participate in demonstrations such as the May 1 international Labour Day march, the anti-Indianapolis-500 protest, the nightly student marches, and the student strike in general. The community marches joined the nightly marches, which were soon taking place throughout Quebec as well as throughout the city of Montreal. No longer departing from one location, night marches started throughout the city and used a snake-march mode of wending their way through the streets, meeting up with other marches in adjacent neighbourhoods or making their way to the city centre to join the main march.

The success of the Printemps Érable was partially due to the fact that it was the first time that English students – including two large anglophone universities in Montreal, Concordia and McGill – joined their francophone counterparts in large numbers to contest tuition hikes, with organizing, meetings, and media spokespeople operating in both national languages. The CLASSÉ coalition, moreover, made several key decisions to continue working together at specific junctures of discord when strategic divergences arose, fighting back against the provincial government and the media, which seemed to be working hard to divide the groups.

The student strike also enabled the organization of actions through Facebook and other social media so that student leadership did not control the marches, resulting in different flavours of protest, from a naked march to a family-friendly march to an extraordinary silent march of judges and lawyers against the Special Law.

The anticapitalist group *La Convergence des luttes anticapitalistes* (CLAC), the Montreal group that had co-organized the anti-Free Trade Area of the Americas (FTAA) protests, was rejuvenated, adding to the students' repertoire of contention through training and holding monthly meetings to support the student strike and inject an anticapitalist analysis. A women's caucus within CLAC also started, signalling the growing commitment to intersectionality in anticapitalist movements.

By the end of the student strike, a new slogan had emerged: "La grève est étudiante, la lutte est populaire" (Student strike, social struggle), signalling the importance of the broader anticapitalist social struggle against neoliberal austerity measures. Activists made important connections between the intensification of neoliberalism, job precarity, neighbourhood gentrification, affordable housing, immigration and borders, police brutality, the racialized, colonial, and gendered hierarchies in universities and their relationship to tuition and student debt, and other complex issues that connected intersectional capitalism to the student strike. This constant contention was also an intersectional intervention.

The strike culminated in the defeat of the Liberal government on August 1, 2012, when leader Jean Charest called an election, and on September 4 the Parti Québécois was elected, quickly repealing the Special Law and cancelling the proposed tuition hike. The new government has, nonetheless, continued to increase tuition fees over the years since 2012 and has also passed racist laws such as the prohibition against wearing religious garb (such as the hijab) at work for those in public service. Nonetheless at the time, the Quebec Student Strike was celebrated as a huge success by students and supporters across the province.

The Spanish 15M and the Quebec Student Strike expanded the methods and modes of protest mobilization that had emerged in the GJM, but they also deviated from that repertoire of contention, which predominantly consisted of mass protest convergences and mobilizations at summits, introducing strategies of constant contention through protest camps and nightly marches. These social movement strategies also shaped anticapitalist, anti-austerity practices with respect to an increasingly complex set of technopolitical practices.

Anticapitalist Technopolitics

Working with and within anticapitalist social movements, anticapitalist media practices are based on many of the same organizational, structural, and value-based practices, including collective autonomy, horizontalism, prefiguration, and the media and communications commons. What is important to consider is how these shared movement practices reject, challenge, shift, or reconfigure media power by claiming and articulating media power in ways that are non-hierarchical, distributed, decentralized, and anti-oppressive.

Power reconfigurations through media construct not only new media relations but also new social relations articulated to media power, including cultural, political, and economic relations. These power shifts take place on four levels: internal to media networks, between media producers and the subjects they interview and depict, between media networks and audiences, and between autonomous media and mainstream media. The reconfigurations more often than not reflect the alternative value practices mapped out in our consideration of the GJM.

Internal to media networks, we see media practices emerge that challenge the hierarchical top-down power structures of traditional journalism. Autonomous journalism practices allow for greater participation, particularly in terms of decision making and setting the direction of media content and reportage. They include reportage teams working together on projects, skillsharing among members, and authoring media collaboratively.

Power is shared among individuals within a horizontal working relationship that is generative of a media labour commons. The media labour commons is professional and committed to producing high-quality, ethical journalism; media activists we interviewed were often highly educated with master's degrees in communications and so on. The basic conception of media activist journalism is that it is a public service and a public good, in other words, something society holds in common and benefits from. It is oriented toward critiquing inequalities, corruption, and the like and thereby toward improving society through critical content, and it contests top-down media power through horizontal, prefigurative media projects. This relationship anchors the others.

Between media producers, the topics they cover, and their subjects or the people they interview, there is a sense of accountability achieved through horizontal relationship building. Those interviewed by media activists tend to be in long-term relationships of trust with media activists, active in the same communities, with shared values and collective identities. Co-interviews may be conducted, questions may be shared with participants ahead of time, and decisions about content of the final media piece will be taken together. Non–media activists can be invited to produce their own media, as we saw in the example of community radio, above. Power is shared among producers and subjects of news within a transparent, horizontal, community-based relationship. There are nonetheless challenges in creating horizontalism, as discussed earlier.

Between media producers and audiences, we see shifts in the expectation of audiences for horizontal many-to-many relations rooted in the notion of the *produser*, in contrast to the top-down point-to-many model of mainstream media. Audiences now demand immediacy, insider perspectives, and news that is both honest and subjective, and media activists offer improved analysis through approachable media frames that include audience members in the framing. The audience is no longer the elite Habermasian public; instead, it is an agglomeration of multiplicitous counterpublics generating, sharing, and commenting on new discursive regimes that challenge dominant social norms, discourses, and media practices.

It is now the audience, using digital technologies, that is ubiquitously making mass contributions of concrete news items, breaking news, investigative reporting, and other forms of intersectional anticapitalist autonomous journalism. Power is shared between journalists and audiences, where the audience is now both a critical journalist and a critical news subject, co-creating the knowledge commons through the horizontal media labour commons.

In these new relationships, autonomous media activists are attempting to challenge the hegemonic power of mainstream media. Non-dominant perspectives are breaking the regimes of truth and semiotic subjugation of mainstream media frames. Media activists break through the gatekeepers of mainstream media and even become interview sources for mainstream journalists. Thus, power is shared through the cracks in mainstream media, and the floodgates of anti-austerity, anticapitalist journalism open in a surprising direction – via social media and the logic of connective action (Bennett and Segerberg 2012). How this logic, including seemingly contradictory social media logics and technopolitical logics, played out in 15M and the Quebec Student Strike is analyzed below.

Technopolitics in 15M

15M is a movement well known for engaging technopolitics (Treré and Barranquero 2018) through a commitment to deepening and expanding these practices. The use of social media is combined with collectively self-owned media in interesting and sometimes contradictory ways related to the challenges of being an anticapitalist in a capitalist world, as discussed above in relation to the Riot Hipster meme.

Collective Self-Ownership of Media

It is significant that the 15M movement was started by a protest call-out shared on the activist-run platform Democracia Real Ya! (DRY!). The slogan for this call-out was two-fold, the first being the platform name, "Real Democracy Now!," signalling non-confidence in government, and the second being a phrase that would become the movement's slogan, "We Are Not Commodities in the Hands of the Bankers and Politicians!" – an anticapitalist message identifiable as such through the use of the term "commodity."

DRY! was at that time a new activist platform created by an umbrella group formed by pro-democracy, hacktivist, and free culture groups. First, the online pro-democracy activist group #NoLesVotes (Do not vote for them) had been formed to mobilize around the lack of democracy in the government's passing of a regressive anti-copyright law, *La Sinde*, which the majority of the population opposed. Second, hacktivists from the global group Anonymous and the local group Isaac Hacksimov were also active in the DRY! Collective. And third, activists from grassroots groups in the free culture movement (FCM) were also part of DRY! These three activist micro-cohorts joined together and mobilized using the DRY! platform with other free culture, squatter, nerd, geek, anarchist, autonomous, and loose-knit or grassroots groups and non-aligned individuals.

On May 15, 2011, the DRY! call-out generated a protest of fifty thousand people in Madrid and multiple thousands in many cities across Spain, and a campaign of constant contention. This call-out is quite different from that of other countries in the anti-austerity wave of contention, such as Greece, where the call-out that kicked off the Aganaktismenoi or Greek Indignados movement was sent on Facebook by a small, anonymous group of Facebook friends, an action that in many ways shaped their media practices according to a pragmatic (not anticapitalist or technopolitical) social media logic (Treré, Jeppesen, and Mattoni 2017).

The Free Culture Movement

Protest media practices in Spain have long been rooted in the FCM, activists against corporate control of culture, and in favour of net neutrality, open source politics, and a free open access digital commons (Fuster Morell 2012). The free culture centre, Conservas, in Barcelona, and the anti-authoritarian hackerspace, Patio Maravillas, in Madrid, were spaces in which DRY! collective members were engaged. In other words, the 15M media practices, from the very beginning, were grounded in activist-owned and -run web platforms and anti-authoritarian and anticapitalist media practices. Social media was also used extensively; to take an early example, Twitter was used to send the call-out for backup in the fledgling encampment in the first few days of 15M. However, the fact that hacktivists and free culture activists had created DRY! ahead of 15M and were able to use this anticapitalist platform to inspire hundreds of thousands of people across Spain to march in the streets is a testament to the strength of autonomous media and communications technologies in the technopolitical strategies of 15M.

Geeks and Anarchists

The free culture movement in 15M was supported by geek or nerd culture, on the one hand, and anarchist culture, on the other. Some have argued that 15M's technopolitical practices were structured in anticapitalist ways because of the long-term influence of autonomous Marxists and anarchists, although the movement overall was not ideologically aligned. At the same time, the influence of anarchists in Spain has important historical roots, with anarchists active in the 1920s against Franco, engaged in developing anarchist collectives including anarchist-feminist collectives (Ackelsberg 2005), and therefore multiple generations of anarchists can be understood to have influenced, whether directly or indirectly, the media practices of 15M.

Squatted Social Centres

Related to the anarchist influence, there is a well-known history in Spain of squatted or occupied social centres, with over thirty in Madrid alone. These social centres are typically anarchist or anti-authoritarian – they are horizontally organized and use consensus decision making and prefigurative anti-oppression politics. They are often used as independent media centres during mass mobilization convergences, where autonomous media activists set up digital networks for reporting on protests. The links between squatted social centres, the free culture movement, and hacktivist ethics and cultures demonstrate how mobilized political actions such as squatting work in concert with technologies for communicative action. This further illustrates how online-offline motility works, as squatted social centres have corresponding online spaces occupied by the same people who go to events or otherwise inhabit them in the material world.

Technopolitics

The combination of anti-authoritarian, anticapitalist politics, cultures, and social spaces with horizontally organized technological practices is fundamental to the 15M's protest media practices of "technopolitics," a term that the activists themselves used (Treré, Jeppesen, and Mattoni 2017). In 15M, "technopolitics" played out through the explicit politicization of technologies, including (a) horizontal, grassroots ownership of media and the development of platforms such as DRY!; (b) open source politics that influenced modes of use, including open access, net neutrality, and free culture; (c) horizontal social relations influencing digital technology and media practices; and (d) intersectional anticapitalist politics that produce horizontality in both media content and digital media practices.

Technopolitics in 15M, for Emiliano Treré (2019), required a convergence of several key factors. The movement appropriated digital technologies in a political opportunity structure in which "state actors were late in catching up with technological innovation" (Treré 2019, 193), which meant they avoided, in part, the surveillance and social control subsequent movements have experienced. The movement also disrupted the strategy of personalization, whereby mainstream journalists look for a charismatic leader to interview, as in the GJM, where different spokesperson strategies were developed (see Chapter 2). While activists in 15M did not refuse to speak to mainstream media as some activist groups do, they instead interacted humorously by, for example, sending them on a wild goose chase through the camps to find an elusive (fictional) leader (Treré 2019, 194). Moreover, taking up the anti-austerity meta-issues allowed 15M to create interventions in mainstream media through the dispersion of many related issues. Treré notes that these tactics led to a nightmare for journalists looking for a single coherent story. At the same time, I suggest that it forced mainstream journalists to work harder to understand the complex intersectional layers of the movement. Finally, 15M used displacement as a strategy to redirect mainstream journalists to its own media websites and the sophisticated movement-led analysis and mapping of complex issues they contained. In these strategies, media activists used their own self-determined media practices, and if journalists took an interest, so be it.

Intersectional Technopolitics

Although much has been made of the 15M use of social media in anti-austerity protests, media activists also created viral messages that effectively mobilized an incredibly large public through their own autonomous media platforms, including DRY! and others. This can be understood through an examination of the protest media imaginary of 15M (Treré 2019; Treré, Jeppesen, and Mattoni 2017).

As John Postill (2014, 354) argues, "In the 15M imaginary, today's viral sophistication portends tomorrow's political emancipation. The indignados' exaltation of virality is a form of discourse in which technology and grassroots politics are seen as being inextricably tied."[1] Thus the grassroots technology of their own platform, which could not be co-opted by capitalist advertising, data mining, state dataveillance, or other exploitations. The adoption of collectively self-owned platforms and autonomous media projects is a key media practice of 15M and pivotal to their technopolitical practices.

Moreover, the linking of a variety of intersectional issues under the meta-issue of austerity led the 15M to be one of the earliest broad-based intersectional movements. Although not everyone in the movement was conversant with intersectionality, many media practices developed by intersectional antiracist feminist activists were taken up by 15M, such as general assemblies

---

1 Postill's premise that 15M was a non-violent movement is not supported; in fact, he himself demonstrates that there was a constant tension between non-violent civil disobedience and more confrontational tactics, and he cites activists saying that there was never a decision taken at a general assembly in favour of non-violence.

with prioritized speakers' lists, an emphasis on power sharing, an attention to building relationships across seemingly disparate movements such as 2LGBTQ+ and anti-Islamophobia movements. Viviana Asara (2020) found that 15M had a high level of environmental consciousness, linking ecologies and degrowth movements to consumerism and social class through the anti-capitalist practice of rebuilding the ecological commons.

Within 15M, "equality assemblies were organized around class, gender, sexual orientation and identity, disability, and national origin" eventually amalgamating to focus on "four inequality dimensions: class, gender, sexual orientation, and gender identity" (Cruells and Ruiz García 2014, 9). With respect to intersectionality, a group of self-defined migrant women brought the issues of race and immigration to the feminist assembly and included them in the antiracist feminist anti-austerity manifesto, and intersectional 2LGBTQ+ groups and assemblies were also formed. Intersectionality was thus fundamental to the 15M movement focusing on intersectional identities in discussions related to austerity such as labour, economics, everyday life, and sexed-gendered-racialized embodiments (Cruells and Ruiz García 2014, 12). The equality assemblies produced political tracts and disseminated them online, participating as digital media activists in the 15M technopolitical mobilization of political discourses. The general assemblies of the 15M camps attempted to be inclusive of the equality assemblies, integrating people with intersectional identities and politics into the overall collective identity of the movement.

The technopolitical strategy our interviewees spoke about most was hijacking (sometimes called hacking or riding) the Facebook and Twitter trending algorithms. Activists had figured out how the trending algorithms worked and subsequently devised a way to collectively generate trending topics on Facebook and Twitter through coordinated actions. Slogans and hashtags were devised collectively through online brainstorming sessions, and coordinated timing was planned for each campaign by media activists with many years of experience. The capacity to achieve virality was widely responsible for the movement messaging reaching a mainstream audience and for 15M becoming a widespread movement throughout Spain with a global reputation that spawned global solidarity networks and actions. Moreover, technopolitical tactics transformed the need for activists to garner mainstream media coverage into a need on the part of mainstream media journalists to cover the 15M movement. Finally, technopolitics illustrates the integration of digital media strategies into political activism to such a degree that activists could no longer say whether they were movement or media activists, as the entire 15M movement was deeply engaged in media action.

Contradictions and Tensions

While the 15M's intersectional political strategies seem seminal, we must be careful not to suggest that the 15M connection to both free culture and intersectional participants led them to reject capitalist media uses altogether or to achieve an unmitigated intersectional practice. While anticapitalists were originally quite skeptical about the use of platforms such as Twitter and Facebook, this opposition predominantly came from GJM activists familiar with the Indymedia model of activist-owned platforms.

However, while some 15M participants were developing and mobilizing via anticapitalist, anti-state technopolitical platforms such as DRY! and NoLesVotes.com, these sites in turn linked their content on Facebook. Media activists also used Twitter for live-tweeting and protest mobilization, suggesting that other movement participants share the content widely and also that they create and share their own content (Postill 2013, 342).

At the same time, 15M struggled to fully realize intersectionality. This is because "incorporating an intersectional perspective involves the challenge of dealing with a complex reality and recognizing the various forms of oppression experienced by participants, in order to avoid reproducing or reinforcing certain inequalities" (Treré 2019, 197). 15M also needed to combat the development of a generalized collective identity, in this case, the Indignados or indignant ones, who had a presumed uniformity, whereas, in fact, the movement consisted of a broad range of groups of social actors and identities who were named and articulated in the tentative development of intersectional social relationships. The equality assemblies were a space to foreground these specific identities. However, they also created issues for those living with multiple intersectional identities – for example, should a transgender woman organize with the feminist or the 2LGBTQ+ assembly? The production of tracts by the equality assemblies and their integration into the movement was important in terms of identifying and naming the specifics of the fabric of Spanish society participating in 15M, albeit in these often-imperfect ways. At the same time, many dominant activists in the larger general assemblies pushed back against the gender manifestos, transfeminist banner hangs, and 2LGBTQ+ actions, as they did not see them as salient to the overall identity of 15M.

That said, 15M's intersectional technopolitical practices were very sophisticated, allowing for the production of media by nerds, hackers, anarchists, autonomists, free-culturists, feminists, and other radical media makers, as well as anybody who wanted to produce media. This could be done on activist-owned platforms, then posted on social media to exploit the reach of platforms for distribution; further, technopolitical activists encouraged others to create and share their own content via smartphone technologies. At the same time, as Treré (2019, 155) has noted, "there were frequent clashes between on one side the technopolitical sublime with its ideals of leaderlessness, openness, and spontaneity, and on the other side the sometimes hierarchical dynamics of the media teams that manage social movement communications." This conflict is based on the disjunction, discussed in Chapter 1, between the horizontal organization of media teams, which themselves are leaderless, and their relationship to the broader social movement in which they play a leadership role. Groups such as Xnet, pivotal in developing the algorithm hijacking practices, also provided the 15M movement with media and movement activist mentorship and training, meeting facilitation for the general assemblies, and a growing intersectional transfeminist perspective.

A further dimension generating tensions in 15M media teams was the fact that austerity measures imposed by the European Bank produced a large number of unemployed people, from youth (at nearly 50 percent unemployment at the time) to university graduates and experienced journalists, many of whom created media content during the anti-austerity movement and helped develop the complex, online-offline hybrid of technopolitics. These individuals contributed sophisticated journalistic expertise to the movement's media strategies, however their expertise also generated disparities between their professionalism and the grassroots nature of the broader movement.

This happened in Greece as well, with groups such as the Omikron project getting their direction and creative expertise from graphic design, communications, and film-making experts in dialogue with those in the project more interested in debating politics. This sometimes led to moments of refocus by professionals who became adept at facilitating decision making in a horizontal mode, aided by the professional skill of getting tasks accomplished to deadline – admittedly an issue, at times, within leaderless organizations notorious for their endless meetings and lack of attention to timelines.

15M will long be remembered for its technopolitical strategies, although it remains to be seen whether the confluence of conditions shaping the constant contention and digital media practices that flourished in 2011 will ever be repeated.

Technopolitics in the Quebec Student Strike

For the Quebec Student Strike (QSS), in addition to the connective action coordinated by ad hoc collective general assemblies, a unique technopolitical practice was the livestreaming of nightly protests by the Concordia University Television station, CUTV, in Montreal. Livestreaming uses a wireless connection, available either from a smartphone data plan or an HD or DLSR video camera uplink system such as Livestream, to transmit video live to the internet. W. Lance Bennett and Alexandra Segerberg (2013, 25) argue that the news media are unable to capture authentic, immediate coverage of protest actions whereas media activists participating in the protests themselves produce excellent reportage. As journalist Gordon Mangum argues,

> Livestreaming is a unique medium because it is highly authentic, raw, uncut, and unprocessed. It allows the viewer to see events happen in real time through the eyes of a participant. In some ways it occupies the highest sense of technological immediacy which has resulted from faster internet speeds, pervasive data connection, and the increasingly sophisticated technology crammed into smart phones. It is as close as you can get to being there without actually being there.
>
> (Mangum 2015)

Livestreaming was used by anticapitalists in the QSS to reach a wide audience. Journalist and communications researcher Chenjerai Kumanyika (2016a, 2016c) argues that the livestreamer, through a specific video documentation practice, plays multiple roles as a media activist, citizen journalist, protester, documentary archivist, legal observer, and social justice researcher.

Livestreaming

Sasha Costanza-Chock (2012) provides a critical analysis of livestreaming during Occupy, which can help us understand the context of livestreaming in the QSS. Costanza-Chock focuses on the globalrevolution.tv site, which was key during multiple Occupy actions across the United States, Canada, the United Kingdom, and beyond. Their research traces the roots of Occupy livestreams back to Deep Dish TV in the 1990s, which "organized satellite uplinks for live feeds from anti-nuclear and anti-war demonstrations" (Costanza-Chock 2012, 382).

At the end of the 1990s, Indymedia developed the first open editorial media platform for uploading video at the anti-World Trade Organization (WTO) 1999 Seattle protests, discussed in the previous chapter. Subsequently, in 2008, with changing technologies, activists from Indymedia in the Twin Cities worked together with the Glassbead Collective at the Republican National Convention, where citizen-journalists livestreamed protests at theuptake.org using smart-phones (Costanza-Chock 2012).

Media producers from these groups then came together to form Global Revolution to livestream the Occupy protests in 2011. In 2012, livestreaming became a mainstay, capturing the full duration of the nightly marches for several months during the QSS. For Costanza-Chock (2012, 382), the gene-alogy of protest livestreaming demonstrates that "innovative media prac-tices, for the most part, did not spring fully formed from the fertile minds of massed 'digital youth'" but rather there has been a steady development of livestreaming in anticapitalist and other protests over several decades.

Elise Thorburn (2014, 54) suggests that the QSS "was a battle against auster-ity and the logic of capital," during which the most widely diffused form of media did not come from mainstream outlets but instead "the live streaming video footage uploaded instantly to the Internet" was "captured by teams of student reporters and activists" working (paid and unpaid) for CUTV.

Jennifer Spiegel (2015, 54) finds that the QSS generated both symbolic and direct actions, including campus picket lines, nightly marches, and the-atrical interventions, all of which embodied a "performative rejection of the dominant neoliberal culture." On the other hand, many activists felt that stack symbolic actions of the QSS were inadequate, and that winning the strike necessitated economic disruption across the province. Student strikers thus organized protests against different capitalist targets such as Plan North and the Grand Prix, campaigns that were also livestreamed where possible.

Livestreamed video footage thus emerged as the most valued communi-cative action in QSS protests. Activist livestreamers attained close-up foot-age because they were trusted by other protesters. As an emergent media practice of anticapitalist movements, livestreaming shifted the repertoire of constant contention along three dimensions: agency against the spectacle, counter-surveillance of police, and generating the media commons.

Agency against the Spectacle

What is key for Spiegel is the interruption of the alienation of the Spectacle, a concept from Guy Debord that critiques the way image systems under capitalism are indistinguishable from our lives and, at the same time, and paradoxically, draw us away from actually living. Spiegel (2015, 57) argues that livestreaming interrupts the Spectacle:

The image stream generated from the nightly protests ... was not packaged. When things got tense, the camera crew and reporters were frequently the first to bear the brunt of police brutality. Here, those disseminating images were not positioned as outside observers representing the situation; the live streaming created an ethical immediacy whereby the spectator could, in theory and at any point, join the action.

The audience could also be a participant, watching the livestream on a phone, live tweeting, and sharing links, while also participating in the night march, monitoring what was happening in which part of the city to inform their decision making.

Livestreaming further disrupts the Spectacle by producing images of the intersectional self. Whereas for Debord the Spectacle was focused on the capitalist image system generated by fictional narrative film and TV shows, the CUTV livestream was a form of direct-action journalism (Jeppesen 2016a). Rather than representing the unattainable, capitalist images of social positions we are presumed to already inhabit, protest livestream produces anticapitalist images of social positions that students, activists, and community members do inhabit – representing ourselves to ourselves and beyond.

The shift is therefore from external to internal representations, overcoming the alienation of the external-Spectacle image system to instead construct events, images, and social positions as they actually exist. This does not generate agency but reveals an always-already existing agency to its own agentive social movement actors, as well as to a broader public, amplifying the affect of empowered subjectivities. These subjectivities are intersectional, whereby the media activists participating in the livestream are POC, women, and so on, who draw attention to intersectional oppressions, analyzing the links between education, race, class, gender, sexuality, immigration status, disability, police violence, and so on.

Livestreaming as Counterveillance

Technopolitics attempts to challenge the state, capital, and other dominant systems. The images and subjects depicted in livestreaming protests can disrupt the power of the state and the mainstream media system. The provincial government's imposition of tuition hikes was disrupted through representations of grassroots struggles contesting the hikes. The mainstream media, which was predominantly representing the government's position, was disrupted by the CUTV livestream, sometimes interviewing CUTV reporters in an attempt to legitimize their own reporting. Thus, the subjectivity of students and supporters overtook visual and textual discursive formations emanating from the state – the declaration of tuition hikes and the enactment of the Special Law – and supplanted them with a dominant visual discourse of the community in collective struggle against these injustices.

In response, the state, through the armed apparatus of the police, including the SPVM, or local Montreal police, and the provincial Sureté du Québec (SQ), attempted to curtail and delimit – sometimes violently – the protesters' routes, actions, and forms of contestation.

However, like Indymedia in Seattle in 1999, the livestream revealed quite clearly the prevalence of police violence, with CUTV camera operators often targeted, thus clearly inhabiting the subject position of student strikers while also using footage as counterveillance against the police. Sociologist Elise Thorburn (2014, 55) argues that the CUTV livestream was generative of "a new assemblage – the counter-hegemonic surveillance assemblage, that began to challenge and hold accountable the power of the state." Thus, as a technology of technopolitics, livestreaming revealed the corruption of power in its specific uses in the QSS.

Livestreaming protest thus provides counterveillant media. Social media can be used to distribute counterveillant videos to broader audiences, but the platforms themselves are not counterveillant. Indeed, quite the opposite – they were widely known by the activists we interviewed to be vehicles for state surveillance of activists, who are vulnerable when posting videos documenting protest activities, and are open not just to surveillance of posted content but also to metadata tracking by the state.

Here, it is crucial to distinguish between a platform's infrastructural affordances and the content being produced by activists. On the one hand, platform infrastructures are designed and constructed for surveillance of users by capital in what Shoshana Zuboff (2019) calls surveillance capitalism. They do not have affordances for media activists to put the state and capital under surveillance. On the other hand, activists livestreaming police actions, such as CUTV in the QSS and Black Lives Matter in Ferguson, do create videos that can hold the police accountable, a form of state counterveillance also used by 15M (Hermida and Hernández-Santaolalla 2018).

The Political Economy of Livestreaming

In theory, anyone in the QSS could create a livestream video, but in practice it is a specialized skill such that typically only a handful of people do livestreaming. For example, in a study of #G20report at the G20 protests in Toronto, "when the 46 most relevant videos are considered, there is one account that stands out, which contributed 13 (28 percent) of these videos" (Poell and Borra 2012, 701). While hundreds of thousands of people participated in the G20 protests, they were not all producing and uploading peer-to-peer videos; this was also the case in the QSS. The political economy of activist livestreaming is such that participation is in principle quite open but in practice quite limited.

One of the stumbling blocks for livestreaming is cost. Certainly, the cost of video cameras has come down since the early days of livestream video. CUTV had to nonetheless come up with creative income streams to fund the bandwidth and equipment. The CUTV platform therefore offered a donation page that was widely used. However, this was complicated by the fact that CUTV is neither an open access platform with participatory affordances nor a capitalist social media platform with widespread interactivity and discoverability. There is a difference between participatory social media – where everyone shares media during protests due to speed and ease of use – and livestreaming the whole protest, which requires commitment, planning, forethought, skills, and capacities and is best done with a team. Livestreaming is a form of activist content production that often relies on a model of one or a group of livestreamers sending to a mass audience. Thus, who owns media is not the only factor in the political economy of protest media, but in addition activists must consider how they can reach an audience, develop livestreaming labour skills, and so on. To produce livestream video requires skill, video equipment, and expensive livestream technologies. In Occupy, for example, there seemed to be a hierarchy of skills that shaped the type of media interventions activists made, from posting items on social media (done by 77 percent of activists) to signing petitions (62 percent) to writing blog posts (19 percent) to creating video (8 percent) (Costanza-Chock 2012a, 379). With only 8 percent of activists tending to create videos, producing livestream video is not accessible to every activist.

Moreover, livestream is best created by a team of people required to carry the camera, dialogue with protesters, carry the livestream backpack, communicate with activists at other locations, live tweet the links and updates, and rotate tasks so that people can eat or use the toilet without dropping the livestream once it is up online and has an audience. CUTV, similar to the Ferguson livestreamers described by Kumanyika (2016b), often went out in teams of four or five people to maintain a continuous livestream through several hours of protest. Having a team also contributes to better representing an intersectional and complex collective identity and foregrounding a range of issues, with various team members contributing analysis throughout the livestream, posing different questions to students being interviewed, and choosing students or protesters who might bring a different perspective.

These key differences between social media and livestreaming point toward livestreaming being generative of the anticapitalist communications commons in ways that social media platforms are not.

The Anticapitalist Communications Labour Commons

The QSS "had the university, [and] its rapid neoliberalisation as its target, connecting it to the notion of the commons" (Thorburn 2014, 54). Livestream media practices joined and generated the communications labour commons. Self-owned, -managed, and -organized, it allowed protesters to reclaim shared collective self-representations, closing the distance between media subject and object. The communications labour commons can be defined as a shared, collectively owned and operated set of media production practices, including the horizontal social relations in which they are used. At the same time, differences of capacity may be shaped by systemic inequalities that in turn shape who produces livestream video (Costanza-Chock 2012) and thus who can contribute to this commons.

Alternative media activists, through participation in social movements such as 15M and the QSS, have shifted their conception of communications labour within the protest imaginary. Instead of labour being conceived of as individualized, meritocratic, and paid accordingly, work in alternative media is understood as having a social function and, further, as being inextricably linked to sociality. Labour is social because it requires connection to others in terms of those who came before and those with whom one labours (shares resources, conducts interviews, produces media, distributes media, and so on).

Media labour can thus be understood as part of both a communications commons and a labour commons: "Contrary to capital, which is sustained on inequality and competition, the commons connects individuals in networks founded on cooperation, mutualism and equality" (Azzellini 2016, 4). Autonomous media uses these processes to generate an anticapitalist communications labour commons:

> The commons is neither state nor market: it is not a public good administered or regulated by the state, and it is not private property or a source of surplus value extracted by outsiders offering "participation." Commoning is

the alternative to the supposed dualism of state vs. private, which are not opposed to each other but share the same logic.

(Azzellini 2016, 3)

The shared logic of state and capital is the logic of hierarchically organized control of labouring subjects. The communications labour commons has its own distinct logic that contests the logic of domination and instead supports an anticapitalist logic. As such, labour may be paid, unpaid, or partially paid, but never exploitative, as no surplus value is extracted; the fruits of the communications labour commons are held in common by the activists in the social movement.

Anti-austerity Intersectional Technopolitics

What has emerged in the anti-austerity wave of contention (see Table 5) is the pervasive reappropriation by intersectional anticapitalists of capitalist social media platforms. The entanglements of transfeminist, 2LGBTQ+, antiracist, and anticolonial intersectional politics are starting to be visible, integrated into the media activist practices of protest mobilizations and the anticapitalist communications labour commons.

In relation to the five key dimensions of intersectional technopolitics mapped in Chapter 1, the anti-austerity movements studied here built on

Table 5 Key dimensions of anti-austerity intersectional technopolitics

Dimension	Anti-austerity intersectional technopolitics practices
Intersectional anticapitalist meta-issues	Contesting economic crisis caused by intensification of neoliberal capitalism; consolidation of meta-issue movement; focus on intersectional issues in relation to austerity
Distributed online-offline architectures and motility	Online-offline hybrid movement; distributive leadership across many cities; online debates; general assemblies; connection to squatted social centres and camps in the squares
Multiplicities of technologies and spaces	Multiple platforms and devices; many actor types across generations; open media technologies; emergence of social media algorithm hijacking; free culture technopolitics
Translocal solidarity economies and technologies	Solidarities across borders; digitally facilitated networks of connective action; translocal mobilizations and solidarity protests; solidarity technologies and design justice
Collective autonomy through direct action	Politics of collective autonomy in the squares; collectively self-owned websites joined by self-representation and debates on capitalist platforms; direct action camping in squares

the fledgling practices of the global justice movement. Continuing to focus on global intensifications of neoliberal capitalism following the 2008 economic crisis, anti-austerity organizers consolidated a meta-issue movement under the umbrella of austerity, bringing together housing, living wage, food security, homelessness, and employment to contest specific capitalist policies while also addressing the intersectionality of these issues across axes of race, gender, immigration status, age, and more.

We also see the rise of online-offline hybrid media movements where protesters meet online in Facebook groups to discuss the organization in the squares, while shifting those conversations into decision making in the general assemblies constitutive of the governance in the squares (Treré 2019). This hybrid online-offline movement organization facilitates distributive leadership across many cities in both online and offline spaces, with experienced facilitators from the GJM coordinating conversations. Activists engage in relationships of care by providing not just structures for decision-making processes but also collective care tents for massages and chill-outs, supplies of sunscreen and water to stave off the effects of protesting in the heat, and inequality assemblies and manifestos for mutual support.

Online, relations of care and collectivity are developed across multiple platforms, including social media and self-owned activist platforms. The anti-austerity protests take place in the context of the ubiquity of smartphones, devices that are pivotal in fostering massive peer-to-peer communications to and from the squares. We also see participation by many actor types across multiple generations. Technologies are increasingly open editorial despite being corporate-owned, giving rise to the emergence of social-media technopolitics through the tendency of regular activists (rather than student unions, NGOs, social movement organizations (SMOs), or other top-down groups) to call different types of marches, livestreaming the protests in the QSS and hijacking the social media algorithms to gain trending topics in 15M, with both models gaining widespread social support.

As austerity spreads across many countries, solidarities are developed across borders through digitally facilitated networks of connective action. Activists are not in direct communication, but they are engaged intensely with one another's media outputs, following tactics and strategies and integrating them immediately into their own repertoires of contention. This leads to translocal mobilizations and solidarity protests globally, specifically in 15M. Solidarity design and technologies emerge in Athens, where solidarity economies are particularly strong, filling the social support role of failed institutions such as the media, health care, education, employment, housing, and more. Technologies are designed with architectures and functionalities that facilitate sharing and, as such, are explicitly anticapitalist.

Finally, the politics of collective autonomy is put into action in mediatization of the protest camps that occupy the squares or spill out into nightly marches. Collectively self-owned websites such as DRY! are joined by self-representation, debates, and strategizing on capitalist platforms that foster participation, in order to facilitate the many different direct actions of the movements, from camping in squares, organizing protests, and developing community-based media to working on technologies, food, and housing initiatives. The collectivity of the social movement actor expands its collective identity through equality assemblies and integrated media teams who contest capitalism in relation to intersecting identities and oppressions related to austerity in 15M and student struggles in the QSS, with the two movements being connected and reflected in each other's movements.

Challenges and Debates
Several key challenges and debates arise in doing media activist work in the anticapitalist communications labour commons which is fundamentally opposed to communicative surveillance cybercapitalism, while also living within this system. Challenges in particular arise regarding the economics of funding and resourcing media projects, and the precarity of media labour that works to disrupt media power.

Anticapitalist Funding Models
Funding models are varied within autonomous media. Rejecting funding through corporate advertisers, anticapitalist media activists take up different approaches to generating funds: self-funding, ethical grants, sustainer subscriptions, funding drives, and crowd funding (Jeppesen and Petrick 2018).

Grassroots media tend to be self-funded, in other words, they pay for resources themselves and do not receive any pay for the media work undertaken. Some groups will seek out grants consistent with their ethics and mandate, though this can create conflicts over funds and has limited short-term sustainability. A video activist spoke of their project – working on media production with community youth – being offered funding from the police, however, this was rejected because it would have jeopardized the project's relationships with youth and constrained their self-expression. Not wanting to succumb to these ethical dilemmas, media activist groups, from documentary filmmakers to magazine producers to protest media livestreamers, increasingly turn to crowd funding. Economic sustainability is an ongoing issue for anticapitalist media, sometimes leading to a diversion of efforts away from media work toward fundraising temporarily in order to return eventually to the media labour itself.

Anticapitalist Resources

Understanding the political economy of the communications labour commons and acknowledging that media work should not be exploitative, media activists organize in horizontal organizations, as we have seen. Not only the media projects lack funds, but so do the individual media activists themselves. Despite often being well trained and professionalized, many media activists are unpaid or underpaid for their work, falling into the various media-labour categories mapped out in the Introduction. The freelance autonomous media worker "might be free from hierarchical control, but she is also free to starve. In this sense autonomy remains an illusion" (Sandoval 2016, 54). This sums up the tension between the two worlds the media activist labours within: the communications labour commons and the capitalist economy.

Solutions such as the formation of cultural co-operatives seem promising, as Sandoval (2016, 55) argues, organizing communicative and cultural labour to overcome the isolation, hierarchies, and competitiveness in the culture and media industries: "Precarious workers can thus be part of a workers movement to create an alternative that rejects both hierarchical control and alienated labour as well as self-exploitation and precarity." Many of the media projects and activists with whom we researched were caught in some form of this struggle.

Precarious Labour

From a political-economy perspective, which considers ownership structures in relation to media power, there are two very different ways to create alternative media content – through engagement with the existing capitalist platforms, whose ownership models and organizational structures are inherently hierarchical and exploitative, or by creating alternative platforms, whose structures and ownership are in the hands of media activists themselves and are thus self-determined and autonomous to a great extent (Jeppesen 2016b). This is the dual strategy engaged by the 15M movement in both creating their own media platforms and subverting capitalist social media platforms. The desired autonomy, however, can never be fully realized within a capitalist framework – even 15M and the QSS livestreamers used social media to share their messages – but media activists can prioritize a range of specific dimensions of practice on the "sliding scale of autonomy," in which the more autonomous practices they can actualize, the more autonomy they may achieve (Jeppesen 2010a). Autonomy is thus seen not as an absolute but as a matter of degree.

When anticapitalists use capitalist platforms, they risk being reduced to social media prosumers inadvertently generating income for Facebook, Twitter, YouTube, Instagram, and other capitalist corporations (N.S. Cohen 2013, 178; see also Dean 2014, Fuchs 2009), in which "audiences' communicative activity and sociality are captured and commodified, feeding the circuits of flexibilized media production" (N.S. Cohen 2013, 179). They risk a double commodification in (1) the free labour people do in creating content online that serves as data for the platform, and (2) the metadata that users create, which is aggregated by corporations and sold to advertisers (N.S. Cohen 2013, 179).

When media activists organize more formally into creative cultural or media co-operatives, generating their own media technologies or platforms, the humanized and socially just economy "comes into conflict with capitalism as a system that is by definition based on limitless accumulation, a drive for constant growth, exploitation and competition" (Sandoval 60). Conflicts arise while working as a horizontal collective embedded within the hierarchical profit-driven competitive capitalist system. "While at the internal level the members of a co-op can decide how ownership and decision power are organised, they cannot overcome the dependencies that result from operating within a capitalist economic system" (Sandoval 2016, 63). Moreover, intersectional organizing is not always a shared priority for everyone in the group, as we saw in the contestation of the feminist and 2LGBTQ+ interventions in 15M.

Sandoval notes that capitalism is very good at co-opting the movements of its critics. We also see this in the social media co-optation of alternative media, through both ideological and commodification modes (Hebdige 1979). First, social media empties alternative media of its politics while embracing the cultural form of participatory DIY self-representation. Ideologically oppositional or counter-hegemonic production of alternative media is then lost in the deluge of self-absorbed and narcissistic representations reinforcing the already powerful. It's no longer a threat to capitalism because now everybody is doing it – producing the content without the prefigurative, horizontal anticapitalist processes and protests. In terms of commodification, alternative media resists capitalist modes of advertising and media control. However, social media is an intensified advertising machine that uses content production as a means to gather metadata and sell users to advertisers as aggregates of consumer groups. Participatory production is automatically commodified through social-media monetization processes. For social media users who left TV behind to escape advertising, this is a triple defeat.

Anticapitalist Media Power

Anticapitalist media power is a contentious issue full of challenges, contradictions, ambivalences, and ambitions. While there is clearly a deep "power imbalance between those who produce content and provide metadata, and those who profit from it" (N.S. Cohen 2013, 186), many media activists such as those in 15M and the QSS have appropriated corporate and collectively self-owned media to support movements that intend to undermine the capitalist models of platform owners.

At the same time, for Nicole Cohen (2013, 186), on social media "the products of people's productive activity appear to them in an alien form," especially if what they're doing is organizing a protest against austerity while simultaneously contributing capital to the purveyors of austerity. This is not just alienating but disjunctive and contradictory. The result is the naturalization of commodification and surveillance, where we resign ourselves to the fact that every corner of our life, including our social lives and interpersonal relationships, will be commodified and surveilled, and moreover, that it is only from within these commodified and surveilled conditions that we can undertake activism at all.

While a return to exclusively activist-owned, collective, open editorial platforms that function horizontally and do not use advertising or make money for corporate conglomerates is unlikely, there are elements of the anticapitalist communications labour commons – and, importantly, the collective action that organizes it – that remain relevant to movements today. This includes intersectional anticolonial and antiracist movements, which are considered in the next chapter.

4

Anticolonialism and Antiracism

Indigenous decolonization and the Black Lives Matter movements have generated a great deal of coverage in mainstream media. Recent coverage has started to draw attention to the fact that colonialism and anti-Black racism are systemic issues articulated in the intersectional power structures of state, capital, 2LGBTQ+, and gender systems. These two intersectional movements work to centre Black, Indigenous, and people of colour (BIPOC) experiences and perspectives, based on key frameworks from critical race and decolonization theory. Anticolonial and antiracist (henceforth ACAR) concerns are often considered together by academics and activists alike as interrelated disciplines and discourses (Breton et al. 2012b; Dhamoon 2015). In this context, this chapter focuses specifically on anti-Black racism and decolonization movements and their media uses in North America.

Colonization has been imposed through state and structural violence. In North America, this takes place in the context of colonial nation-to-nation relations with Indigenous nations. Colonialism has taken the form of land theft, along with the systematic destruction of Indigenous governance systems, laws, cultural traditions, languages, health expertise, spiritual practices, and even well-documented violent child removal (Wesley-Esquimaux 2009). Moreover, colonial dominance was enacted through several mechanisms, including forced removal of Indigenous peoples from unceded lands, broken treaties, police and military violence, and the structural violence of the legislative management of Indigenous peoples. Part and parcel of colonization is the intersectional enactment of colonial state violence toward women, which has consisted of non-consensual sterilization, ignoring sexual assault and trafficking of Indigenous women and girls, erasure of matrilineal lineages, mistreatment in the health system, and so on. The ongoing epidemic of missing and murdered Indigenous women, girls, and two-spirit people is considered a "deliberate race, identity and gender-based genocide" (National Inquiry into Missing and Murdered Indigenous Women and Girls 2019a, 5). Indigenous intersectional oppressions are furthered through the racialization-sexualization of Indigenous women in particular ways based in "settler-colonial forms of kin, kind, and relating that are hierarchical, anthropocentric, capitalocentric, and hetero- and homonormative" (TallBear and Willey 2019, 5), paired with a failure within North American society to value the lives of Indigenous women, as stereotypes and disrespectful, sometimes violent, behaviours are perpetuated by settlers. This is further exacerbated by media representations.

The Canadian settler nation-state (among others) has a nation-to-nation relationship with Indigenous nations in the land now called Canada. The mechanism of colonization is based in land theft or appropriation and cultural genocide. This differs from other structures of racism, such as forced migration imposed by systems of slavery and migration of subsequent waves of immigrants and refugees.

Black people have a fraught but different relationship to land ownership in Canada. Many Black people's ancestors were brought to the Americas through enslavement, and thus did not have the opportunity to own land or bequeath land to heirs, resulting in intergenerational disinheritance from property ownership that continued long after they freed themselves from slavery (Maynard 2017). Others arrived as Loyalists who fought on the side of the British in the US civil war and were offered land that was subsequently devalued through environmental racism and segregation (Cole 2020).

Anti-Black racism, moreover, has been enacted through specific forms of state and structural violence, some of which also affect Indigenous peoples. These overlapping forms of structural violence include police brutality, the judicial system, the carceral system, the school-to-prison pipeline or school pushout (also experienced intersectionally by 2LGBTQ+ youth), surveillance, everyday policing of racialized communities, racial profiling, and more (Maynard 2017). In addition, Black communities experience state violence through everyday white police patrols in their neighbourhoods, border policing, deportations, or being undocumented. Intersectional to structural violence, experiences of Black people are systemically unequal with respect to poverty, mental health, heteronormativity, gender oppression, sexuality, housing, employment, religion, and more (Khan-Cullors and Bandele 2018).

State oppression further impacts BIPOC people through the racialization of the prison-industrial complex (Davis and Dent 2001), racialized police profiling and violence against Black and Indigenous people and their disproportionate incarceration, including the rising percentages of Black and Indigenous women in prison in Canada (Government of Canada 2020; Policy4Women 2018). Colonial and racist oppressions operate through these macro state and capitalist structures as well as through micro social norms and behaviours, including media and social stereotypes, microaggressions, and so-called casual everyday racism (Chanicka 2018). This is a brief overview of some of the issues, systems, and structures contested by BIPOC people through ACAR social movements and media activism.

Approaches to ACAR movements and media are articulated to frameworks of intersectional technopolitics, as movements reimagine and mobilize sociotechnical systems in specific ways grounded in BIPOC community values, experiences, and liberatory imaginaries, as we have seen with the global justice movement (GJM) and anti-austerity movements. BIPOC groups have also been directly involved in those movements, making key critical ACAR interventions (Martinez 2000; Talcott and Collins 2012). Contemporary Black liberation movements tend to work with an intersectional perspective while foregrounding anti-Black racism. This is logical, given that intersectionality has a genealogy in Black feminism, as discussed in Chapter 1.

In a similar vein, decolonization movements often participate in intersectional coalitions such as the GJM and anti-austerity movements. For example, the 2010 G20 protests in Toronto featured a massive Indigenous Solidarity march. At the same time, some Indigenous groups increasingly take a "land back" sovereignty perspective (Tiny House Warriors 2019), asserting the right to self-governance of land through Indigenous economic systems articulated by the "right to a moderate livelihood" (D.C. Harris and Millerd 2010). Some also link territory to issues such as gender, age, sexuality, and so on (TallBear 2019) through a growing "Red intersectionality" approach (Clark 2016).

Indigenous groups in the Americas are many and varied, therefore, any analysis presented here may hold true for some groups but not others. Rather than a comprehensive analysis, the provisional focus presented here is on intersectional elements of some current Indigenous waves of contention.

Personal Reflexive Statement
As a white settler antiracist and anticolonial accomplice, I attempt to foreground the voices, texts, and movements of BIPOC artists, activists, and academics in this chapter. My politics, perspectives, and identity will

nonetheless influence the texts and concepts I work with, including my angle of vision in relation to ACAR movements and media. I emphasize systemic critiques in alignment with and following the lead of ACAR activism and scholarship. I feel responsible to do the work of researching, understanding, and supporting ACAR movements and media and have been engaged in ACAR intersectional activism and research for many years. This means, like alternative media journalists, I sometimes omit the mainstream perspective, which is widely available elsewhere. At the same time, my white settler identity and mainstream university education mean that, despite supporting a decolonizing perspective, my work is framed by Western epistemologies.

I acknowledge my work is limited and provisional because of my identity. There is knowledge based in experience regarding racism and colonialism that is not available to me, a concept explained below as the "voice-of-colour thesis." When I cite the literature of BIPOC scholars and activists, I do not claim their knowledge as my own. I make no claim to have complete knowledge on ACAR topics, because knowledge production is never the purview of just one person and, moreover, it is never finished but is an ongoing collective task of communities and societies. My objective instead is to introduce some concepts and movements I have learned about, providing what will be by necessity partial and incomplete reflections.

Although I am white and do not have lived experience as a Black or Indigenous person, I feel it is important to integrate antiracism and anticolonialism into my activism and research because racism and colonialism are deep causes for ongoing oppression and inequity. As such, I acknowledge my place within the "insulated environment of racial privilege" (DiAngelo 2018, 100), but I would like to move forward and I am willing to take risks and make mistakes. This chapter is therefore an imperfect attempt to be an ACAR accomplice instead of maintaining a complicit silence.

If there are gaps, things I have not had the space or knowledge to cover, we can look to texts, theorists, and activists beyond these pages; I look forward with respect to hearing those voices. Following Kim TallBear (enrolled Sisseton-Wahpeton Oyate, descended from the Cheyenne and Arapaho Tribes of Oklahoma),[1] a scholar in decolonial sexualities, Indigenous peoples, technoscience, and the environment, I acknowledge the partiality of

---

1 Indigenous tradition suggests a person be named by their ancestry, which often includes land of origin.

my view "and argue for the robust intellectual project of diverse partial standpoints" (TallBear 2019, 494).

ACAR Theory

In this section, key theoretical frameworks in critical race and decolonization theory are introduced to provide context for the interpretation of the movement and media strategies to follow.

The Social Construction of Race

Race is not biological. According to critical race legal scholar Ian Haney-Lopez (1994, 11), "There are no genetic characteristics possessed by all Blacks but not by non-Blacks; similarly, there is no gene or cluster of genes common to all Whites but not to non-Whites." In fact, as Haney-Lopez (1994, 12) finds, "greater genetic variation exists within the populations typically labelled Black and White than between these populations." Race is therefore broadly understood to be socially constructed through an ongoing "process subject to the macro forces of social and political struggle and the micro effects of daily decisions" (Haney-Lopez 1994, 7).

The discredited biological determinist position has been and continues to be constructed by white-dominated institutions to maintain racialized hierarchies by referencing pseudo-scientific legitimation of the so-called natural. However, "the so-called natural is always paramount in settler ideas of appropriate ways to relate, control, and allocate rights and resources that reproduce structural inequities" (TallBear and Willey 2019, 5). In other words, although race is socially constructed, this social construction produces material effects. Thus, anticolonial and antiracist movements contesting colonialism and anti-Black racism have two seemingly contradictory tasks. First, we need to dismantle problematic assumptions about the biological formation of race to illustrate the scientific equality of all racialized groups, and, second, we must denounce and contest the negative material effects of socially constructed race and racism that have shaped the lives of Indigenous and Black people in unequal ways.

Antiracism

Given systemic racism exists, how is our society combating racism? Black activist and scholar Ibram X. Kendi (2019, 13) defines an antiracist as "one who is supporting an antiracist policy through their actions or expressing an antiracist idea." This is an important definition because it puts the emphasis on not just policies and ideas but also everyday actions and practices. For

Kendi, racist policy is responsible for encoding and institutionalizing systemic racism and racial inequity (Kendi 2019, 18). Racial inequity, in turn, is defined as situations where "two or more racial groups are not standing on approximately equal footing" (Kendi 2019,18), such as having equal access to education, home ownership, employment, life opportunities, and the like. Racial inequity is not abstract and cannot be undone by changing racist laws; it must be achieved in practice. Antiracist policy, a requisite of antiracist practice, is "any measure that produces or sustains racial equity between racial groups" (Kendi 2019, 18). For Kendi, all policies are either racist or antiracist. The majority of policies claiming to be "race neutral" have proven to be racist. Antiracism more broadly can thus be understood as "a powerful collection of antiracism policies that lead to racial equity and are substantiated by antiracist ideas" (Kendi 2019, 20). Antiracist organizing often functions at the level of policy and process. The social movement groups we interviewed developed intersectional antiracist practices that accounted for and attempted to mitigate racism through policy, process, and action.

Colourblindness and the Denial of Racism

Denial of racism means ignoring its social, cultural, economic, and political effects. This takes place particularly when white people say things such as, "I don't see race," or "We are all the same race, the human race," or "I am not racist, but . . ." The denial of race and racism by white people erases the experiences of racism endured by racialized groups. This denial is based on a paradox: racism is widely condemned in law, policy, and public discourse, but at the same time racism persists in both systemic and interpersonal forms, facilitating both racist behaviours and their simultaneous denial (A.P. Harris 2012; Jiwani 2006). Calling a white person racist is now seen as more egregious than making racist remarks. This played out recently in Canada when NDP leader Jagmeet Singh was ejected from the House of Commons for calling Bloc MP Alain Therrien racist because he refused to acknowledge systemic racism in the RCMP, Canada's federal policing agency (Zimonjic 2020). Therrien's denial of racism, itself a racist action, was not censured. Antiracist activist movements take place in this complex and fraught context, where the very existence of racism is both patently evident and vehemently denied.

White Fragility

The denial of racism can be attributed to what white antiracist scholar Robin DiAngelo calls "white fragility," the difficulty white people have in engaging in conversations about race and racism (DiAngelo 2018). She argues that North American society is largely racially segregated, to the benefit of white people who do not face racial stress: "The mere suggestion that being white has meaning often [elicits] a range of defensive responses" (DiAngelo 2018, 2), accompanied by behaviours attempting to recentre white entitlement and comfort. She calls this emotional response by white people to conversations about race and racism "white fragility." White fragility, despite how it sounds, is not a position of weakness: "Though white fragility is [elicited] by discomfort and anxiety, it is born of superiority and entitlement ... a powerful means of white racial control and the protection of white advantage" (DiAngelo 2018, 2). Antiracist social movements often come up against white fragility when attempting to initiate conversations about race, be it online or offline, with respondents engaging in moves to white innocence such as tone policing, calls for civility and respectability, claims of colourblindness, or reversion to virtue signalling. For Sara Ahmed (2016), these are mechanisms through which the understandable anger expressed by BIPOC individuals at being targeted by racism is policed by white people in a subtle but persistent form of racist discourse. For example, white activists have turned the use of the term "safe space," which indicates an antiracist space safe for BIPOC people, upside-down to mean a space where a white person should feel "safe" to say racist things, including hateful speech, without reprisal. This leads to everyday microaggressions where white people say subtle but clearly racist things in groups or one-on-one in a casual way without considering the hurt they are causing. Dealing with white fragility and microaggressions is one of the challenges in antiracist social movements and media practices. White fragility and settler fragility (Gilio-Whitaker 2018; Watson and Jeppesen 2020) result in high volumes of discursively violent trolling of Indigenous and racialized groups and ACAR movements in mainstream media comments, alternative media sites, and social media.

Algorithmic Racism

With the rise of algorithms in institutional decision making, systemic racist policies and epistemologies that deny and disguise racism are now increasingly amplified in technological systems. Algorithms used in sentencing and parole decisions have been found to encode an anti-Black racial bias (Chander 2017; S.U. Noble 2018). Banks encode algorithms with "neighbourhood" as a proxy for "race" to redline African Americans from mortgage approvals in a racist-disguised-as-antiracist banking policy that allows for the collection of applicants' addresses but not their race (S.U. Noble 2018, 1). White mortgage applicants with similar incomes and credit ratings are approved for mortgages more often than non-white counterparts, as racist policy pays forward "the wages of whiteness" (Roediger and Roediger 1999). This policy divides secure and insecure futures along racialized lines, revealing intersections of racist-capitalist oppression encoded in digital technologies through proxy algorithms.

The Voice-of-Colour Thesis

ACAR social movements are shaped by specific epistemologies, know-ledges, and discourses generated by racialized and Indigenous peoples. This is because "subordinated groups in any social system have knowledge that the privileged lack" (Delgado and Stefancic 2017, 9). However, the import-ant knowledges of Indigenous groups have been epistemologically invisibil-ized and devalued through colonial processes of subjugation and erasure (Santos 2015). Similarly, Black people's knowledges of whiteness have been both the key to their survival and unacknowledged by white people (hooks 1997). Subjugated knowledges and epistemologies are foregrounded in ACAR social movements through recourse to the "voice-of-color thesis [which] holds that because of their different histories and experiences with oppression, Black, American Indian, Asian, and Latino writers and thinkers may be able to communicate to their white counterparts matters that the whites are unlikely to know" (Delgado and Stefancic 2017, 11). Moreover, scholars have long argued for the legitimacy of subjugated knowledges pro-duced from standpoints outside EuroAmerican whiteness (S. Harding 1998; Santos 2015; Semali and Kincheloe 2002), specifically supporting decolonizing Indigenous pedagogies and research (Denzin, Lincoln, and Smith 2008; Pirbhai-Illich, Pete, and Martin 2017; L.T. Smith 1999; Wesley-Esquimaux 2009). For Maōri scholar Linda Tuhiwai Smith (1999, 45), "colonized peoples share a language of colonization, share knowledge about their colonizers, and, in terms of a political project, share the same struggle for decolonization." Foregrounding BIPOC knowledges and voices that produce liberatory epistemologies is thus a key strategy in ACAR movements for challenging dominant knowledge systems.

Reclaiming Epistemologies

The voice-of-colour thesis carries over to research, including grassroots knowledge production by antiracist and anticolonial movements through experiential theorizing as well as scholarly research led by Indigenous and

Black scholars. Latin American scholar Boaventura de Sousa Santos argues that Western thinking is limited in its ability to provide answers to specific research questions because it cannot see outside its own colonial frameworks (2015, 20). Therefore, knowledge ecologies must attempt to correct and account for absent knowledge, "a form of knowledge that aspires to an expanded conception of realism that includes suppressed, silenced, or marginalized realities" (Santos 2015, 157). ACAR activists problematize knowledge produced by the oppressor as a mechanism of subjugation and in its place resurrect knowledge frameworks that have been sublimated through colonial and racist epistemic violence. Thus, a key intersectional technopolitical practice of ACAR media activists is to foreground voices of colour and amplify BIPOC knowledges.

Restoring Indigenous Families

Epistemic destruction for Indigenous peoples in Canada has been and continues to be enacted through non-consensual child removal of approximately 30 percent of all Indigenous children into residential schools (1876–1996) and subsequently into predominantly white foster families through the Sixties Scoop (Truth and Reconciliation Commission of Canada 2015). While many Canadians believe this is a historical practice, child removal by state agencies continues through to today.

Contesting this and other long-term practices of colonialism, anticolonial movements are fighting to restore families and communities, attentive to issues related to embodied oppressions rooted in the colonial, gendered violence of the state. Feminist geographer Sarah de Leeuw (2016, 14–15) explores the ways in which decolonization movements for community self-determination pay attention to "the intimate, embodied, domestic, microscale geographies of Indigenous women and children." Building on an intersectional analysis of Indigeneity, gender, class, ability, and sexuality as they were encoded in the Canadian Indian Act of 1876, de Leeuw demonstrates how systemic legal and state violence have operated in slow, banal, and hidden ways within the domestic sphere, specifically through the forcible removal of Indigenous children from their families, land, households, and cultures. Having extracted the next generation from the community also results in the broader dispossession of Indigenous lands. Today, more children are being removed from Indigenous homes than in the time of residential schools, despite the fact that "Aboriginal children are *less* likely than non-Aboriginal children to face physical or emotional abuse" (de Leeuw 2016, 18–19). When children are removed by the state because of poor living conditions – such as inadequate housing, non-potable water, or reduced education and health outcomes – these conditions have been created by the state (de Leeuw 2016, 19).

Anticolonial and Antiracist Movements

In light of this briefly sketched history of colonialism and racism in the Americas, the ACAR movements analyzed here include Idle No More and 1492 Land Back Lane in Canada, and the global Black Lives Matter movement.

Idle No More

The Idle No More movement started in the fall of 2012 to contest Bill C-45, an omnibus bill that changed Canada's problematic and controversial Indian Act to allow corporations easier access to Indigenous treaty lands, additionally weakening environmental protections for many lakes and rivers. Alarmed at this unilateral legislation undertaken without the free, prior, and informed Indigenous consent required by law (Ward 2011), four women organized a teach-in on Indigenous land rights to contest the bill. The four women were Nina Wilson (Three Pole People – Nakota, Dakota, and Lakota – and Plains Cree from the Crooked Lake Agency, Kahkewistahaw First Nation, in Treaty 4 Territory in southeast Saskatchewan), Sylvia McAdam (nêhiyaw, Cree from Treaty 6 Territory in northern Saskatchewan), Sheelah McLean (third-generation settler from Saskatoon), and Jessica Gordon (Cree/Saulteaux from Pasqua, in Treaty 4 Territory, Saskatchewan) (Coates 2015, 7–9). Publicized by Facebook and other social media, the teach-in was called Idle No More, launching a national Indigenous resurgence:

> It touched the nerve centre of the Canadian political body, challenging settler Canadians to consider the reality of Indigenous Nationhood, which includes Nation to Nation relationships and at the same time extends an invitation to Indigenous and non-Indigenous Canadians to participate together in protecting the water and environment for the benefit of everyone.
>
> (DaCosta 2014)

Muskrat journalist and radio show host Jamaias DaCosta (2014, n.p.) (Kanien'kehá:ka, Cree, Irish, French, and Jamaican) calls Idle No More "the most unifying Indigenous-led movement social media had ever seen." The organizers emphasized grassroots leadership, provided predominantly by women and young people. While not initiated by the traditional Indigenous leadership, the organizers were often in dialogue with them.

Idle No More's four co-founders organized a grassroots distributive network that emphasized loosely linked, multi-issue campaigns through translocal organizing across countries, states, regions, and urban and rural areas. The movement came together under a shared politics of Indigenous resurgence, foregrounding the contestation of Bill C-45 while making space for specific local Indigenous issues, particularly regarding land and water. After the initial teach-in, the movement relied on three key forms of protest: Round Dances, days of resurgence, and long marches, which were organized in part by using the hashtag #IdleNoMore.

Round Dances

Indigenous Round Dances occurred as shopping-mall flash mobs beginning in the December 2012 Christmas season. The Round Dance is a cultural practice that was integrated into a protest form. A Round Dance protest first occurred in Halifax at an event organized by Molly Jean Peters (Paq'tnkek) and Shelley Young (Eskasoni), two Mi'kmaq mothers. The Round Dance protests focused on reclaiming voice and holding space for Indigenous peoples who had, for decades, been prohibited from performing their ceremonies and cultural traditions publicly. Idle No More speakers often mentioned the importance of cultural teachings in healing from intergenerational traumas, building communities, and Indigenous cultural resurgence, and these were foregrounded in the Round Dance protest actions as well. As Peters stated, "One of the things we made sure that we were doing was infusing culture. We wanted to make sure our Elders were here; we wanted to make sure we had our songs here, our dance here, our medicines" (Coates 2015, 56). Many non-Indigenous people of all races and cultures also participated in solidarity in the Round Dances, which were explicitly open and welcomed everyone. In this sense, the events were an opportunity to build relationships between Indigenous and non-Indigenous people, and for the latter to learn about Indigenous cultures.

Days of Resurgence

Another strategy was holding days of Indigenous resurgence. The first National Day of Solidarity and Resurgence took place on December 10, 2012, with hundreds of communities across Canada organizing translocal actions critical of Bill C-45 in order to raise local or regional issues related to the bill. The Happy Valley–Goose Bay Labrador event, for example, foregrounded Bill C-45 issues while also focusing on local government overspending, the campaign to save Muskrat Falls, and the trampling of Indigenous rights in rural northern areas by capitalist resource-extraction projects (Coates 2015, 51).

Building on the success of the national day of resurgence, on December 21, an International Day of Resurgence and Solidarity took place, where groups across Canada organized protests on the land and Round Dances in urban spaces, with global networks engaging in solidarity actions as far away as Egypt, Los Angeles, and London. These coordinated global days of resurgence had the objective of asserting Indigenous power and calling for a renewed Canadian federal commitment to Indigenous land and treaty rights, as well as generating non-Indigenous global support and solidarity.

Long Marches
A third protest form used by Idle No More and grounded in Indigenous cultural practices was the traditional practice of long marches undertaken from remote Indigenous communities to bring messages and demands to the urban seats of provincial and federal governments. Among these marches was the Journey of the Nishiyuu, taken by fifteen Indigenous youth from Winnipeg to Ottawa from January to March 2013 in the bitter cold of winter. This journey was shared through the hashtag #Nishiyuu. Ben Raven (Running Buffalo), one of the marchers, explained the importance of Idle No More and the impact of the movement and the long march for him: "What Idle No More did for a lot of our people, it shook us to the core; it allowed us to really feel and understand who we are. Because when you understand your culture, you understand yourself, and I got to learn that. When I walked this journey, it taught me so many different aspects of life" (as cited in Coates 2015, 147). The three-month journey of the Nishiyuu allowed for the building of relationships among participants in a shared, traditional cultural experience. Ben Raven emphasized the ways in which community healing from intergenerational trauma takes place, with the healing of the community intertwined with individual healing. Cultural teachings, language, traditions, and knowledge played a key role in establishing the sense of pride, self-worth, and connection that had been lost through the trauma of Indigenous children being non-consensually taken from their families (Archibald et al. 2012; Starks et al. 2010).

Indigenous Cultural Resurgence
In the three forms of protest described above, under the auspices of Idle No More, Indigenous cultural elements were central, including prophecies and knowledges focusing on responsibility for the land for the next seven

generations. As Melaw Nakehk'o in Yellowknife said, Idle No More is "an Indigenous resurgence. We have to maintain our land connectedness; we have to be strong in our culture; we have to be on the land and asserting our treaty rights" (as cited in Coates 2015, 67). Land and culture were integrated with self-determination in protest-movement organizing practices and objectives alike. Resurgence, moreover, is a framework that emphasizes Indigenous cultural traditions for healing and rebuilding; rather than focusing on exclusion, oppression, or disempowerment, resurgence reveals and focuses on the unique strengths and specific forms of power and knowledges of Indigenous peoples.

Sovereignty Summer, 2013

The following summer, Idle No More initiated the Sovereignty Summer campaign, a movement based on the "principles of coexistence and mutual respect between Indigenous and non-Indigenous Peoples" (Coates 2015, 141). Several demands were put forward, including (1) the repeal of Bill C-45 provisions regarding the Indian Act and the Navigable Waters Act, (2) respect for the United Nations' principle of free, prior, and informed consent, (3) the reaffirmation of Indigenous land title and treaty rights, and (4) a demand for a national inquiry into murdered and missing Indigenous women and girls, along with strategies for the prevention of this racialized, gendered violence. This inquiry did eventually take place from 2015 to 2019 (National Inquiry into Missing and Murdered Indigenous Women and Girls 2019a, 2019b).

Linked to Indigenous sovereignty in the Idle No More movement is non-Indigenous solidarity. Solidarity for Idle No More happened both domestically and globally. Non-Indigenous solidarity of Canadians with the Indigenous movement was welcomed and cultivated. As Erica Lee, an Indigenous participant in the first teach-in put it, "We are all at risk when treaty rights are violated. We are all at risk when our government chooses to pass legislation without consent, while stifling protest . . . I don't know if you know this but not just Aboriginal Canadians need to drink water" (as cited in Coates 2015, 12, ellipsis in original). The use of sarcasm and humour seen here is a typical occurrence, used both to break the tension and to make gatherings more convivial. Another participant at the same teach-in, Mark Bigland-Pritchard, noted how happy he was to see the "Indigenous and settler people working together to build the resistance" (Coates 2015, 13). Idle No More Round Dances also saw participation by non-Indigenous people of many cultures dancing in solidarity. Indigenous cultural practices that settlers could learn about through participation included drumming, dancing, and smudging as well as Indigenous knowledges shared in speeches and teachings.

Global solidarity was taken up in protests on the international days of action occurring in many countries. Indigenous groups forged global networks of support for Indigenous land and treaty rights. This support often came from international coalitions focusing on climate justice, looking to Indigenous leadership in their respected (and sometimes exoticized or romanticized) role as custodians of the land and as water protectors.

Idle No More was a meta-issue movement, with the foregrounded issue transforming from Bill C-45 to a more general focus on Indigenous self-determination and land rights. Many local and intersectional issues also appeared in the movement: gender violence (the epidemic of murdered and missing Indigenous women and girls); 2LGBTQ+ (renewed celebrating of two-spirit identities); age and youth (journeys of young people reconnecting to intergenerational communities); social class (contestations of living conditions and poverty on reserves); languages (reclamation of Indigenous languages previously forbidden by colonizers); and creative arts (projects such as *Walking With Our Sisters* and REDress, discussed below).

1492 Land Back Lane

Following Idle No more, a new wave of Indigenous resistance in Canada started on July 19, 2020: the 1492 Land Back Lane movement. Its objective and strategy is to reclaim and re-occupy Indigenous lands in Haudenosaunee Six Nations Territory/Caledonia in a process of decolonization by taking the land back (Talaga 2020). Many decolonization movements do not use the term "decolonization" as a metaphor (e.g., to decolonize one's mind), but rather struggle for a return of Indigenous lands and territories, based on the right to Indigenous sovereignty to secure Indigenous futures (Tuck and Yang 2012). Increasingly, Indigenous movements involve blockades of the land to re-establish Indigenous sovereignty over territories that have never been ceded, where treaty rights are not being respected, or where resource extraction is taking place without proper consultation and consent (Rebick 2011; Tiny House Warriors 2019).

1492 Land Back Lane is such a struggle. Developers are attempting to build housing subdivisions on Haudenosaunee land, in particular a swath of land called the Haldimand Tract. According to a recent article in the *Toronto Star*: "The courts, Haldimand County's local government and the developer do not recognize what the Haudenosaunee see as their well-documented claim to the Haldimand Tract, a 384,000-hectare ribbon of land, running the entire length of the Grand River, that was the subject of a 1784 treaty between the Haudenosaunee and the British Crown" (Kennedy 2020). This denial of land rights is under constant contestation through a blockade and re-occupation of the land by Indigenous people.

The protest strategy of Indigenous blockades is a now familiar one. It is part of a larger strategy to re-occupy Indigenous land and territory to be managed through Indigenous self-governance for the benefit of the seven generations. In this sense, the constant contestation is envisioned as a much longer project than the protest camps of the squares in the anti-austerity and Arab Spring movements. The management-and-governance strategy of 1492 Land Back Lane relies on Indigenous economics, which consists of managing land in precisely the opposite way to capitalists, which is to say by *not* extracting resources, with the understanding that only when they remain unextracted and remain living in healthy ecosystems can the resources provide and sustain life far into the future. This is clearly contrary to the colonial-capitalist system and philosophy of property and resource extraction that destroys the land for short-term profits, leaving it barren and unable to sustain life.

The protest strategy used by 1492 Land Back Lane, the Tiny House Warriors, and other Indigenous groups reclaiming their treaty or unceded lands across Canada is what Kanahus Freedom Manuel (Secwepemc and Ktunaxa) calls a "ransom economy" (Manuel, Williams, and Klein 2020). The concept was originally used by settlers in mainstream media when Indigenous people started blockading railways and highways, suggesting that Indigenous blockades "hold our economy for ransom" (G. Smith 2013). In reality, the reverse is true: the Canadian state is holding Indigenous and treaty lands for ransom (Manuel, Williams, and Klein 2020). The protest strategy of re-occupying treaty and unceded lands is therefore a strategy of ironic reversal. Moreover, consistent with the claim of belonging to sovereign nations, Indigenous people charged with blockade-related infractions are increasingly refusing to acknowledge the legitimacy of the settler Canadian colonial court system. The Canadian courts have placed a permanent injunction against Indigenous people being on the land, an injunction that is seen by the Indigenous people facing it to hold no legitimacy over them. This deep-seated conflict lies between the assertion of two very different governance, legal, and land-ownership systems by the colonial nation-state and Indigenous nations.

The protest imaginary and repertoire of contention are framed differently than a protest that makes demands of the government, or even the

Round Dances of Idle No More, which were focused on raising awareness, cultural resurgence, and building relationships of solidarity. In the land re-occupations, Indigenous people do not make claims on the Canadian state as citizens; rather, they engage as members of a nation equal to Canada demanding that Canada uphold the treaties they have signed with Indigenous peoples and abide by international laws. Indigenous groups are reasserting themselves as sovereign nations on the land they see – and that they have legally proven – as rightfully theirs. To demonstrate that they are rightful owners of the land, they are building on the land, using the land in an Indigenous model of living off the land, while at the same time appropriating a capitalist land ownership approach. They are thus making their land rights visible to the Canadian state through putting up structures such as houses, while also making themselves harder to remove from the land. In conjunction with this strategy, they are documenting court-injunction cases that assign specific dollar values to each day of a blockade in terms of lost development or extraction profits. These specific dollar values are understood as a sign of Indigenous blockade successes, as dollars, the Indigenous groups observe, are what capitalists care about, and their loss makes the strongest impact. They use these facts and figures to provide information to insurance companies – which are being approached for insurance by development and resource-extraction projects – to dissuade them from insuring the projects. Further, they provide these facts and figures to shareholders and the corporate interests of the developers to encourage them to divest from the companies whose developments are being blockaded. In these ways they are holding their own land in a reversal and extension of the notion of a "ransom economy."

The twofold economic imaginary of the strategy of land re-occupation thus quite strategically and knowingly relies on two conflicting economic logics. First, it (re)imagines land through an Indigenous economic epistemological framework as a resource that is most productive and supportive of life when it is not "developed," in the Western sense. Second, it reimagines capitalist ventures through a colonial epistemological framework as vulnerable to economic impacts caused by blockades. Based on this colonial logic, the protest imaginary repurposes the set of financial details in capitalist land developers' court injunctions against Indigenous blockades as both an index and an instrument of success in order to make their land unappealing and unapproachable as a potential place for "development." This strategy of invoking two oppositional economic imaginaries simultaneously reasserts Indigenous logics and value systems in relation to the land

and acknowledges and exploits capitalist logics and value systems to undermine them or, more precisely, to reveal the ways in which they are self-undermining. Further, it renders visible the incommensurability of these two systems under which Indigenous people in Canada (and elsewhere) have long been forced to live. Moreover, it is an extended constant contestation strategy, whereby the strategy of building houses on Indigenous territories in and of itself achieves the objective of self-governance and living on the land, through direct action, rather than asking the Canadian state for permission. The logic is clear – one nation need not ask another nation for permission to be self-governing.

As part of this widespread extended constant contestation strategy, another Indigenous protest camp was set up on Burnaby Mountain to stop Kinder Morgan from developing pipelines on unceded Coast Salish Land. DaCosta (2014, n.p.) argues that the Indigenous camp and the Black Lives Matter movement in Ferguson have similar overlapping historical and contemporary links:

> Colonialism is at the core of both scenarios, with historic and ongoing state violence directed against Indigenous people and Black people intersecting on multiple levels. There are some critically significant distinctions in how the oppression is played out for each respective community. However, there are connections to be made, because for both the Indigenous and Black communities, systemic oppression has resulted in racist violent attacks and one-sided media narratives that include valuing corporate interests over people.

The intersectional connections in ACAR movements should therefore be considered in an analysis of the growing Black Lives Matter movement.

Black Lives Matter

Black Lives Matter (BLM) is a broad-based social movement formed in July 2013 by three queer Black women – Alicia Garza, Patrisse Cullors, and Opal Tometi – to contest the acquittal of the white adult George Zimmerman for killing the unarmed Black youth Trayvon Martin (Garza 2014; Khan-Cullors and Bandele 2018). The three BLM founders came together shortly after the news of Zimmerman's acquittal, when Alicia Garza posted a "love letter to black people" on Facebook, including the catchphrase "black lives matter," which her friend Patrisse Cullors saw and then tweeted out #BlackLives-Matter, creating a hashtag that has been used literally billions of times since then, sometimes more than eight million times per day (J. Cohen 2020). Garza and Cullors joined forces with Opal Tometi to create a movement by the same name (Milkman 2017, 24). Their initial list of demands called for federal charges against Zimmerman, no new jails or prisons to be built in Los Angeles, and community control over law enforcement (Khan-Cullors and Bandele 2018, 198), among others. More generally speaking, Black Lives Matter "represents a civic desire for equality and a human desire for respect" (Lebron 2017, xiii). It is both "a challenge to the criminal justice system" and "a declaration of dignity" (Ellison 2016, 4).

The movement was galvanized the following summer in 2014 when Eric Garner and Michael Brown, two Black men, were killed by police within three weeks of each other, sparking national protests in which "extensive coverage by traditional media had catapulted BLM to the centre of the national political conversation" (Milkman 2017, 24), arguably shifting public debate toward support for the movement, with an increase in white accomplices protesting in solidarity.

When Michael Brown was killed by police officer Darren Wilson in Ferguson, Missouri, BLM organized Freedom Rides to Ferguson to join the protest (Bonilla and Rosa 2015; D.L. Moore and Cullors 2014; Solomon 2014). Critical race theorist Fredrick Harris (2015, n.p.) characterizes BLM as a new civil rights movement, "a multiracial, multi-generational movement asserting black humanity in response to racist police killings and vigilante violence." Ruth Milkman (2017) argues that BLM, along with Occupy Wall Street, the Dreamers, and movements against sexual assault, form a wave of contention in which the millennial generation's participation is crucial, particularly because of their high levels of education and reliance on intersectionality as a protest and analytical framework.

Intersectionality: Anti-Black Racism

Early on in Black Lives Matter, the organization developed a list of five guiding principles and objectives in a movement against systemic anti-Black racism: (1) end anti-Black violence, (2) globalize the movement, (3) engage the leadership of trans- and gender-non-conforming people; (4) end misogyny, cis-privilege, and transmisogyny; and (5) build on intersectional critiques of heteronormativity and ageism. Their work was grounded in the embodiment of empathy, connection, justice, and liberation: "Black Lives Matter affirms the lives of Black queer and trans folks, disabled folks, Black-undocumented folks, folks with records, women and all Black lives along the gender spectrum" (Garza 2014, 2). Clearly, these political commitments are imbued with intersectionality theory and practices.

Intersectional anti-Black racism is also being addressed in global locations beyond the United States. For example, Perry (2016) has found that intersectional approaches to anti-Black racism were key in Afro-Brazilian movements in which Black women were central social actors in intersectional community movements against socio-spatial exclusion while also driving theoretical advances.

Leaderful and Decentralized

In organizing a multi-chapter movement, BLM undertakes a specific form of horizontalism it describes as leaderful, defined as "decentralized, with many leaders" in many locations and chapters (Cullors 2016, 82). With three co-founders who may be considered horizontal leaders, BLM adopts a "group-centered model of leadership, rooted in ideas of participatory democracy" (F. Harris 2015, n.p.) and avoids "the charismatic leadership model" of the 1960s civil rights movement, which may have been successful at the time, but was also critiqued for being a "male-centered hierarchical structure" (F. Harris 2015, n.p.). Instead, BLM "recognize[s] that granting decision-making power to an individual . . . poses a risk to the durability of a movement" (F. Harris 2015, n.p.). Powerful leaders can be co-opted by self-interest or externally by powerful interests, targeted by police and state repression, or even assassinated. Within the group, they can shut down political proposals, which happened, for example, when the concerns of Black women were marginalized by the male-centred leadership of the Black Panther Party. Instead, leaderful decentralized movements develop leadership qualities in as many people as possible, empowering them to make decisions and take action, strengthening the movement to its core.

An example of decentralized leadership is the BLM-TO chapter in Toronto, which shut down Toronto Pride (discussed in Chapter 5). This action took place in July 2016, following a March-April protest of the Toronto police killing of Andrew Loku. According to journalist Desmond Cole (2020, 90): "BLM-TO [organized] a demonstration, which started at Toronto City Hall and then moved to police headquarters. The group demonstrated continuously for fifteen nights and sixteen days, enduring attacks from the police while holding open a space for Black power and defiance it called Tent City." This is an example of decentralized leadership and constant contention, as we saw in the 15M camps, also called tent cities. The BLM-TO Tent City was a healing space and a place for people to gather in contention and solidarity. It ended when then-Premier Kathleen Wynne admitted there was an issue with anti-Black racism in the Toronto police force. However, the struggle continues, as participant Christina Gabriella Griffin said, "I want what anybody else wants: the dismantlement of capitalism, end of racism, sexism, transphobia and for people to really acknowledge that there's an actual problem of anti-Blackness that exists" (*NOW* 2016).

Beyond Black Respectability

Black Lives Matter questions the myth of Black respectability (Cullors 2016, 82), which places responsibility on the personal actions of poor and working-class communities to lift themselves up. The myth is that this is supposed to be done by creating a veneer of polite middle-class behaviour and not complaining about the grinding conditions of everyday racism, police violence, harassment, and poverty. Countering the myth of Black respectability, BLM contests the structural violence that keeps Black people in a perpetual state of everyday brutality, fear, and injustice, described in Patrisse Khan-Cullors' memoir in heart-breaking detail (Khan-Cullors and Bandele 2018). BLM further demands the recognition of Black humanity, that Black peoples' lives actually matter. Hanging out in alleyways or parks, involvement in poverty, street life, selling cigarettes, sex work, or petty crime does not mean Black people should be killed (Obasogie and Newman 2016). Moreover, BLM focuses on collective liberation rather than on a limited individualistic notion of personal freedoms to be won on a case-by-case basis (Cullors 2016).

Racialized State Violence

The phrase "racialized state violence" encompasses the variety of ways in which ideological and repressive state apparatuses, such as bureaucracies, welfare offices, tax bureaus, police, the military, jails, schools, hospitals, and the like are systemically racist and, as such, generate physical and emotional pain and suffering among racialized groups. BLM thus focuses on contesting the over-incarceration of Black people; police brutality against Black bodies, including murder with impunity; and the specific ways that women, queer, trans, non-binary, non-status, neurodiverse, and disabled Black folks are brutalized.

Racialized state violence is most visible in physical attacks by the police on Black bodies. Journalist and communications scholar Chenjerai Kumanyika (2016b, 252) argues that the ongoing long-term regularity of police violence and killings of unarmed Black people has resulted in an emergent "analysis of policing as part of a broader 'war on black bodies' [which] has been commonly accepted and frequently articulated among politicized Black folk and social justice advocates." He demonstrates how the language of war has impacted not just public discourse but also escalating levels of military equipment and dehumanizing violence mobilized against Black people. Kumanyika (2016b, 253) describes his arrival at the BLM protests in Ferguson on November 26, 2014, as part of a livestreaming team. The scene was "a war zone," he writes, with military signifiers such as tanks, helicopters, armoured personnel carriers, National Guard soldiers, road blockades, sirens, and automatic weapons: "Protesters faced off against a long line of officers dressed in the combination of military-style clothing and weaponry that we have come to call 'riot gear'" (2016b, 253). He maps out the role played by three wars – the Cold War, the War on Drugs, and the War on Terror – with vaguely defined enemies in intensifying "the blurring of military intervention and local policing" as police departments increasingly deploy "their own paramilitary wings" (2016b, 255). These strategies of war "become constitutive of material violence against Black and brown bodies, while simultaneously creating the logical possibility of denying that a war on black bodies exists" (2016b, 256–57). This denial of racialized state violence works through the same mechanism as the denial of racism but with more palpable consequences.

Racialized state violence occurs beyond the war on Black bodies in less visible but equally violent everyday institutions. ACAR activist, researcher, and author Robyn Maynard (2017, 7) explains how racialized state violence can be inflicted on people through "institutions regarded by most as administrative" and other extra-legal forms of governmentality that "surveil, confine, control, and punish" Black bodies. For example, BLM aims to stop police street checks or carding based on racial profiling. Racial profiling is the well-documented fact that Black people, particularly young males, are often stopped simply for "walking/driving while Black" rather than any connection to criminal activity.

While young Black men are a common target of police violence, not just in society but also in media representations such as police shows, the #SayHerName campaign draws attention to ways in which Black women, queer and trans people, sexual minorities, and people with disabilities are also under attack in specific, often sexualized, ways (Crenshaw and Ritchie 2015; Ritchie 2017).

Black children are also subject to racialized state violence through street harassment and policing in schools. In Canada, there was a successful campaign to remove police from schools in the Toronto District School Board in 2017, ending the School Resource Officers program begun in 2008 (Nasser 2017), with nearby school boards making similar demands. Removing police from schools and rejecting racist carding systems have the objective of disentangling police from the everyday lives of Black people, particularly Black children and youth.

Healing Justice

Demands in which Black anarchists and anti-Black antiracism movements converge include the prison abolition movement (Davis and Dent 2001), which proposes community alternatives to the state-run prison-industrial complex (Cullors 2016; Davis 2003; Jeppesen and Nazar 2018). In place of incarceration, BLM focuses on "healing justice" (Khan-Cullors and Bandele 2018) to reconnect Black people with their communities and to strengthen those communities, so they may heal from the intergenerational traumas of over-policing, incarceration, and other forms of racialized state violence including slavery. Healing justice works through the integration of healing processes and Black community empowerment into the process of social movement mobilization. It also builds mechanisms for dealing with issues within the community without recourse to the police. This is the backdrop to calls to defund the police that have been taken up by mainstream public discourse and implemented in some municipalities in the United States.

BLM in the Pandemic: George Floyd

BLM as a protest movement seemed to lose momentum in March 2020, when the World Health Organization declared the COVID-19 pandemic and many countries went into lockdown. With statistics showing that BIPOC and other marginalized intersectional groups, including women and trans people, have been hardest hit by the pandemic, protesters' attention turned to supporting those in need in the community through mutual aid and solidarity networks (Pleyers 2020). However, when George Floyd, a forty-six-year-old Black man, was murdered on May 25, 2020, by a white police officer, Derek Chauvin, while in his custody, through the application of his knee to Floyd's neck for nine minutes and twenty-nine seconds, a timeframe corroborated by officers' body-worn cameras, although in popular discourse the time is commemorated as eight minutes and forty-six seconds. The situation was livestreamed by multiple bystanders as it unfolded. Despite the dormancy period of the pandemic lockdowns, BLM could not remain silent. The protest movement mobilized protests not just in Minneapolis, where Floyd was killed, but across the United States and globally, night after night, in ad-hoc forms of constant contention. Portland, Oregon, was particularly notable, as regular protests there were greeted with extreme police violence.

Derek Chauvin was charged with second-degree murder, third-degree murder, and second-degree manslaughter, and the three other former officers involved have been charged with aiding and abetting. All four were fired, which is a departure from the typical response of putting officers involved in killing civilians on paid administrative leave. On April 20, 2021, the jury found Chauvin guilty of all charges, and he was sentenced to 22.5 years in prison.

The movements against Indigenous and anti-Black racism and for community liberation have come together using distributive networks similar to those of the anti-austerity movements. However, there are some key differences that bear investigation. The political-opportunity structure of 15M, in which the state had not adequately mobilized its social movement surveillance technologies, was not an opportunity structure available to the more recent waves of Indigenous and Black Lives Matter movements, which are heavily under police surveillance, treated like terrorists, and exposed to intensifying racialized state violence. How did they engage with technopolitics given this context?

ACAR Technopolitics

The mechanisms of ACAR movements call attention to specific historical and contemporary contexts in which BIPOC organizations, groups, and individuals mobilize against racism. This raises important questions regarding the specific uses of technopolitics. Do historical, social, and cultural contexts impact the types of sociotechnical mobilizations used in ACAR movements in comparison to those in the GJM and anti-austerity movements? Conversely, are digital technologies mobilized in racialized ways to attack BLM and Indigenous movements and communities, and if so, how do they respond? Below I reflect on the technopolitical practices of Indigenous and Black Lives Matter movements, including technologies used for liberation movements and those used to oppress.

Anticolonial Technopolitics

Problematic mainstream media representations of Indigenous peoples illustrate what is at stake in Indigenous self-representation strategies. In a comparative study of the mainstream media coverage of three white and three Indigenous women who were missing and/or murdered, Kristen

Gilchrist (2010, 374) found that "press disparities promote the symbolic annihilation, or systematic exclusion, trivialization, and marginalization of Aboriginal women's experiences." White women were represented to be of higher social status and portrayed as innocent, respectable, and pure "girls next door" with their deaths figured as tragedies, through no fault of their own. Indigenous women were identified as disreputable, and they were covered three and a half times less often than white women, with their victimization deemed their own fault, a classic case of media taking recourse to the myth of victim blaming. The myth of victim blaming is common in rape culture where the circumstances of the victim – their poverty, drug addiction, or street involvement, for example – is articulated as the reason they were sexually assaulted or murdered and thus somehow justified. It is a myth because the perpetrator rather than the victim is always responsible for the murder. Missing and murdered Indigenous women and girls (MMIWG) were covered in shorter articles with smaller photos, often using mug shots rather than the family photos used for white girls. Article placement was subsumed within the newspaper rather than the front page reserved for white victims, and the stories and headlines were less personalized: "The invisibility of missing/murdered Aboriginal women from the news landscape depends on the hyper-visibility of missing/murdered White women," Gilchrist (2010, 385) concludes, perpetuating the binary of worthy-unworthy victims.

An intersectional or structural analysis of gendered-racialized oppression in the case of MMIWG is absent from mainstream media. Male perpetrators of sexualized violence are often portrayed as individually aberrant (Jiwani and Young 2006, 901) rather than as exhibiting behaviour consistent with and condoned within systemic gendered-racialized rape culture. When victims are Indigenous or otherwise racialized, "the issue of racism as a factor influencing the crime is often erased" (Jiwani and Young 2006, 901). The media do not demand better policing, education, or preventative programs to protect Indigenous women. Rather, the media use Indigenous identity as a category that renders all missing women unimportant. Indigenous women's specific identities – which First Nation they belonged to, who their families are, histories of the colonial experience, including residential schools, intergenerational sexualized violence, and trauma, or the fact that the Downtown Eastside (in Vancouver, where many women go missing) is on unceded Coast Salish Territory – are typically not explored in detail, if at all (Jiwani and Young 2006, 910–11). Grassroots movements are challenging this symbolic annihilation but change is slow to come.

There are several risks to the symbolic annihilation of Indigenous women in the mainstream media identified by Jiwani and Young and by Gilchrist. First, it problematically signals to the broader society that Indigenous women lack value despite their individual character and accomplishments. Second, this identifies them to offenders as potential victims. Third, this then signals to law enforcement that their cases are not important enough to investigate. This has "dangerous implications for the safety and well-being of Aboriginal women across Canada" (Gilchrist 2010, 385).

It is in – and up against – this media context that Indigenous media activism takes place.

Everyday Violence through Digital Technologies

While they offer communicative affordances, new media and technologies pose specific challenges for Indigenous people for a host of complex reasons. Jane Bailey and Sara Shayan (2016, 321) argue that while digital technologies offer liberatory affordances for marginalized groups, in the case of missing and murdered Indigenous women, girls, and two-spirit people (MMIWG2S) in Canada, technology plays a role in facilitating violence against Indigenous women. This can include stalking, partner violence, sex trafficking, police surveillance, and online hate.

Trafficking recruitment is facilitated through digital technologies and predatory behaviours online, with Indigenous girls and women over-represented in sex work: "60% of sexually exploited youth" are Indigenous, making sex trafficking a serious issue in Indigenous communities (J. Bailey and Shayan 2016, 328–29). Further, misogynist, racist online hate and harassment are targeted at Indigenous women, leading the CBC to take the unprecedented measure of closing its online comments section for all articles related to Indigenous people. Labelling this cyber-bullying erases race: "Online hatred for, and harassment of, Indigenous women and girls is grounded in interlocking oppressions, including colonialism, misogyny, racism, and homophobia" (J. Bailey and Shayan 2016, 334); these are prohibited grounds for hate speech under the Charter of Rights and Freedoms of Canada.

Rather than protecting Indigenous women from harassment, digital technologies such as DNA collection and digital surveillance are used under the pretext of protection by police in paternalistic and criminalizing ways (J. Bailey and Shayan 2016, 337–40). Coupled with the widespread inaction of the police in investigating MMIWG2S cases, this illustrates how the state is implicated in colonial gender oppression and becomes another form of anti-Indigenous racialized state violence.

At the same time, digital technologies are important for grassroots groups, as we saw with #IdleNoMore which helped mobilize that movement. Thus digital technologies are being developed by NGO and IGO groups such as the UN Committee on the Elimination of Discrimination against Women (CEDAW). CEDAW takes an intersectional approach in its aim "to address the devastating impacts of colonialism, racism, and misogyny by fostering Indigenous pride, self-esteem, and cultural identity" (J. Bailey and Shayan 2016, 335). Grassroots activist initiatives to develop digital media skills and capacities in supportive and culturally appropriate ways are increasingly imperative for the survival and cultural resurgence of Indigenous girls, women, and two-spirit people.

Because of the context of this double-edged sword of digital technologies, the intersectional technopolitics of Indigenous communications thus requires two contradictory tasks. First, secure technologies must be developed that protect Indigenous women, girls, and non-binary people from online intersectional racist, misogynist, and transphobic trolling, cyberstalking, police surveillance, and sex trafficking. And second, some Indigenous communities are engaged in digital resource and skills development to mitigate the digital divide that can put them at a disadvantage – for example, in terms of internet access in rural areas on reserve and other circumstances that can limit access to digital technologies and skills.

Building Tech Capacities in Rural Indigenous Communities
Many Indigenous reserves and rural communities are located in sparsely populated areas and/or in the north of Alaska and Canada, both of which are underserved by digital-communications networks, including telephone land lines, cable TV, internet, WiFi, mobile networks, fibre optics, and other high-tech services typically available in urban areas.

Addressing local community technology needs in their research with Indigenous communities, O'Donnell and colleagues (2007) found that in remote and rural Indigenous areas in Canada, video conferencing was a key technology by the early 2000s. To service these communities, organizations such as the company K-Net and the government-funded Atlantic Help Desk developed "broadband video communications for community development by the remote and rural First Nations on their networks" (O'Donnell et al. 2007, 8). The video communication capacities developed included video conferencing, recording video conference talks, and sharing video online. Digital video networks brought Indigenous groups together, fostering communications and better understanding among Indigenous and between

Indigenous and non-Indigenous groups, as well as supporting the growth of digital media skills and capacities in their communities.

The challenges reported in building capacity were similar to the development of communications challenges in Latin America (see Chapter 2), such as the tendency among development staff to support the network themselves rather than building capacity by teaching Indigenous users how; some resistance to digital technologies within rural Indigenous communities; and a long-standing distrust and distance between Indigenous and non-Indigenous groups that seemed difficult to bridge (O'Donnell et al. 2007, 6–8). This was exacerbated by the fact that non-Indigenous Canadians seemed "uninformed and unaware of the situation of their First Nations neighbour communities" (O'Donnell et al. 2007, 8). Specifically, the authors argued that "urban Canadians need to understand that the rural lifestyle is legitimate and that subsistence living is a viable alternative to mass consumption and a materialistic lifestyle" that is perpetuated, for example, by smartphone technologies and more (O'Donnell et al. 2007, 8). Nonetheless, the video-conferencing technologies provided opportunities for "personal, professional or community development" (O'Donnell et al. 2007, 8), connecting rural and urban people interactively over great distances and fostering relationships between communities.

Technologies are thus playing an important role in Indigenous communities; however, the sociotechnical assemblage plays out in specific cultural ways. Indigenous movements in general seem to be more focused on community building through re-establishing cultural traditions, language, relationships, and land rights; therefore, digital technologies are considered more useful by communities and activists if they can support these objectives.

Social Media Uses by Standing Rock Water Protectors

The Standing Rock and No Dakota Access Pipeline (#NoDAPL) movement that coalesced in the summer of 2016 took a different approach to digital technologies. In a social-media network-analysis study, Gyenes and colleagues (2017) found that news on the #NoDAPL movement was covered predominantly by alternative and non-mainstream media, particularly at the beginning. Mainstream media did not take an interest until the conflict between water protectors and the police intensified. This confirms a tendency in mainstream media, when it comes to Indigenous communities, to report not on the issues at hand but the violent conflict that can ensue with blockades and other direct actions. While the hashtag #NoDAPL is used internationally, media coverage was found to be "local and episodic," with the articles most shared on social media coming from National Public Radio (NPR), the Bismark Tribune, Democracy Now!, and Dakota Access Pipeline Facts (Gyenes et al., 2017).

Three key narratives emerged in transmedia cross-platform mobilizations, focusing on legal issues, environmental issues, and military or government facts. The prominence of specific discourses shifted from the corporate energy, gas, and oil discourses, prevalent in early 2016, to discourses produced by Standing Rock activists themselves, including climate change, water rights, and the language of Indigenous "water protectors" (rather than mainstream media's original use of the term "protesters").

The frame of "water protector" produced by the Standing Rock Sioux Nation articulates their role as protectors of the natural world against encroachment by extraction industries. Moreover, the role of water protector is an intrinsic expression of Indigenous culture, treaty rights, sovereignty, and self-determination. Further, it signals the Indigenous sense of humans being part of nature, and accountable to nature, rather than being opposed to it as per the Western frame of the nature-culture divide.

Sam Levin and Nicky Woolf (2016) consider the complexities of social-media activism in their reporting on the process of checking in at Standing Rock on Facebook. Millions of online protesters or "clicktivists" (mouse-clicking activists, most of them not water protectors) checked in at Standing Rock to shield people on site in Standing Rock from digital police surveillance. Some people at Standing Rock were skeptical about whether this would be effective against police surveillance because of the geotagging of locations at check-in, but others felt it was a good tactic of solidarity. Meanwhile, activists present at Standing Rock mentioned that police surveillance in real life, such as audio eavesdropping and helicopter flyovers, was of greater concern to them than digital surveillance. Others said that it would have been great if those million people could have checked in on the ground at the physical site. At the same time, online activism can eventually connect clicktivists to organizers, serving as a contact mechanism for activism on the ground (Levin and Woolf 2016, 1).

People who checked in on Facebook likely did not have the capacity, time, or resources to participate in person at the time. They may have been involved in on-the-ground organizing in one location but in online activism to support another, such that their check-in at Standing Rock served not just as solidarity but as a form of translocal, transmedia mobilization.

Conversely to the Facebook check-in for #NoDAPL, some intersectional feminist Indigenous media projects are material, as with the REDress project and *Walking With Our Sisters*. These contribute to cultural resurgence and are cognizant of the dangers of digital technologies for Indigenous women. Thus, material media projects are also key to understanding Indigenous intersectional technopolitics beyond the digital sphere and in relation to it.

Walking With Our Sisters

Walking With Our Sisters was a mobile Indigenous art project and/or memorial that displayed over 1,600 moccasin tops or vamps created by community members. It travelled to many different cities across Canada from 2013–19, finally landing in Batoche, Saskatchewan, for the closing ceremonies. Organizers, artists, and supporters used the hashtag #WWOS. According to the WWOS website: "Walking With Our Sisters is a commemorative art installation to honour the lives of missing and murdered Indigenous Women of Canada and the United States; to acknowledge the grief and torment families of these women continue to suffer; and to raise awareness of this issue and create opportunity for broad community-based dialogue on the issue" (Walking With Our Sisters n.d.). The vamps displayed in the exhibition were produced by people all over Canada and the US. They were "intentionally not sewn into moccasins to represent the unfinished lives of the women and girls" (Walking With Our Sisters n.d.). While the exhibition may have been originally conceived as an art project, it quickly became a memorial. It was carefully curated with the involvement of Elders, respecting Indigenous protocols and cultural values, and in the process of development, it became a ceremony (Tabobondung 2014).

The call-out to create the project was posted in June 2012 on Facebook, demonstrating the importance of social media, although the art project itself was a material and ceremonial one: "The call was answered by women, men and children of all ages and races. By July 25, 2013, over 1,600 vamps had been received, almost tripling the initial goal of 600" (Walking With Our Sisters n.d.). The curators used their social relationships on Facebook to crowdsource artwork sent in from around the world. WWOS was crowdfunded and organized by volunteers in the community. The project visited twenty-seven communities, with each location featuring the project on a digital website and/or a Facebook page (Walking With Our Sisters n.d.). In addition, several hashtags were used, such as #WWOS, #MMIW, #MMIWG2S, #WalkingWithOurSisters, and #SistersInSpirit. Posters were designed for each event and cross-posted on social media using transmedia mobilization strategies.

Indigenous artist, curator, and lead coordinator for *Walking With Our Sisters*, Christi Belcourt reminds us that the project was not intended as an art exhibit to be objectified but as an Indigenous ceremony. The exhibit space was smudged, pipes and circles took place in the morning at opening and in the evening at closing, and the space was maintained as a ceremonial space and process throughout, respecting the direction of Elders. Belcourt says that the process of remembering the people represented could not take place through "gawking" or "staring from an outside, outsider's perspective." The moccasin vamps should not be treated as artworks with aesthetic appeal, evaluated and engaged with from a rational evaluative distance. Instead, she says, "We must do it by bringing their lives and the acknowledgment of the value of their lives within us, within our hearts" (Tabobondung 2014).

As the art project moved across the country, it became a space for healing around the loss of so many Indigenous women, girls, two-spirit, and non-binary–gendered people, acknowledging the great losses felt by the many communities. It created a visualization of absences while inviting people to consider the spirits of those whose absences were being represented and called in.

The REDress Project

The REDress Project by Jaime Black creates a visualization of absence as well, by hanging red dresses in urban and rural landscapes to represent missing and murdered girls and women. The title of the exhibit is a wordplay, forming the word "redress," and, as such, the empty red dresses serve as both a memorialization and a call for redress. REDress artistically and symbolically represents the absences felt deeply in Indigenous communities and lives.

By using a combination of material and digital representations and mobilization strategies, *Walking With Our Sisters* and REDress served as calls to action and provided a space for action within communities, including acts of healing, reflecting, and rebuilding communities in a new way, invoking the respect for Indigenous women, girls, and two-spirit people inherent in Indigenous cultures. The red dresses are now increasingly used in protest movements, marches, artwork, and blockades as powerful symbols of the importance of Indigenous women, girls, and two-spirit people.

Red Intersectionality

Indigenous scholar and poet Natalie Clark redirects intersectionality theory toward Indigenous experiences of intersectional oppression and liberation. She reclaims writing about interlocking systems of oppression by Indigenous women more than a century ago, who explored the gendered effects of colonialism, including the effects of age and the relationship to the land. Clark cites Sioux activist Zitkala-Sa, who wrote several texts in the early 1900s, for example, about three young girls who resisted violent attacks and attempts to dispossess them of their oil-rich land (Clark 2016, 2). Here, the mechanisms, violence, and technologies of resource extraction contradict Indigenous relations to one another and to the land as protectors. Red intersectionality is thus grounded in asserting Indigenous epistemologies and ontologies, "committed to work that is anticolonial, activist, and focused on the goals of transformation, Indigenous sovereignty, and liberation" (Clark 2016, 2). Technologies of land ownership and theft – including courts, maps, and the violence of land dispossession – played and continue to play out differently for Indigenous peoples, and in particular women, than they do for white settlers. Movements of decolonization can be enacted through many technologies; however, the key issue is the return to the land through treaties and other land rights.

In addition to historical work, Clark studies the process of disclosure of violence in girls' groups as a space for the healing process of storytelling. In these workshop groups, Indigenous girls create narratives of harm or risk – their experiences of violence and trauma – intertwined with poetic narratives and storytelling about resilience, strength, and resourcefulness. Witnessing is also important as the "listeners or receivers of the stories of young women are essential partners in their resistance" (Clark 2016, 4). Moreover, the stories are not individualized or isolated but contribute to a collective narrative in which each narrative claims its own specific space, together forming a narrativized community that produces belonging in the process. The objective is not just to share stories of violence among girls but to work together to end violence and to transform the impact of the experience by sharing healing conversations and strategies of resistance and survival.

Thus, the technologies of narration, storytelling, and witnessing generate community resilience through self-expression combined with witnessing or sharing. Transmedia mobilizations across digital and material media and art forms in the context of women-centred cultural resistance, resilience, and resurgence are thus key elements of contemporary Indigenous intersectional technopolitics.

Technopolitics in Black Lives Matter

The Black Lives Matter movement has been particularly adept at engaging social media, particularly Twitter, to amplify the voices of BLM activists and mobilize a broad-based protest movement for Black liberation. Black

Twitter provides a platform and opportunities for grassroots leadership networks for Black people who might feel alienated from the traditional political process, such as youth, women and girls, 2LGBTQ+, people in poverty, people with mental health struggles, and so on.

Social media has been used effectively for a range of objectives. Marcia Mundt, Karen Ross, and Charla Burnett (2018) used digital ethnography and interviews to understand how BLM was adopting digital media to develop internal relationships of mutual support, particularly through Facebook groups, and to foster external relationships for movement building, most often through hashtags. Guobin Yang (2016) considers how hashtag activism creates affordances for BLM activists to create and control their own narratives, and Denise Wilkins, Andrew Livingstone, and Mark Levine (2019) similarly consider BLM's development of specific rhetoric through social media. Jonathan Cox (2017) argues that in addition to mobilizing protests through social media, BLM uses social media to create an information source for Black activists and interested communities of local and global allies and accomplices. Deen Freelon, Charlton McIlwain, and Meredith Clark (2016) argue that the key contribution of BLM's use of social media is, in fact, the offline struggle and contestations against systemic racism in the streets. Realizing that mainstream media consistently misrepresent Black lives, #BlackLivesMatter media activists have reclaimed "the ability to frame events and direct the actions" by creating and disseminating their own discursive and image-based systems through multiple modes of technopolitical mobilizations (F. Harris 2015, n.p.). Moreover, they have been able to mobilize social media to scale up the movement to achieve a global reach (Mundt, Ross, and Burnett 2018).

Livestreaming

One of the earliest instances of citizen journalism – surrounding the case of the violent beating of African American Rodney King by white police officers – involved confronting technologies of social control through the digital technology of livestreaming (Deggans 2011). For Black people, livestreaming of everyday events such as this can reveal previously invisibilized police violence. While livestreaming the Quebec Student Strike revealed police violence against protesters in a confrontational, exceptional moment, livestreaming of everyday events such as traffic stops, carding, or other racialized police confrontations reveals the violence of everyday policing of Black bodies. The livestreaming of BLM Ferguson brought the two together in an intensified "war zone" (Kumanyika 2016b). BLM protesters captured video of the protests from a massive number of perspectives through livestreaming and live tweeting in Ferguson. But livestreaming of police killing Black people, such as Philando Castile and George Floyd, also helped to galvanize the BLM movement and render visible the invisible, everyday racialized state violence experienced by Black people.

BLM members, spread across the country in a network of horizontal chapters, have captured "intense reporting on police brutality via social media" (F. Harris 2015, n.p.). An example of this was the livestreaming by Diamond Reynolds of Philando Castile's shooting death by police during a vehicle stop (see Chapter 1) in which she, as his passenger, became a citizen-journalist, commenting on actions in a calm manner, despite the intensity of what was happening. The livestream was picked up by people who were nearby, who came down to the site immediately and served as further witnesses to the event and its aftermath. The Facebook livestream was shared widely, garnering exposure of the event and providing an eyewitness account that could be used in court. The unintended consequences of the livestream, however, must also be considered. The circulation of a video showing someone's death is dehumanizing and, many people would say, inappropriate. It desensitizes people to violence against Black people, which also takes place in fiction through TV shows and film. It takes away the dignity of the deceased and their loved ones and runs the risk of retraumatizing Black communities.

The wide circulation of this and other videos of police killings of Black people serves to generate profits for Facebook and other platforms, as they receive advertising revenue when people view these livestreams. The troubling political economy of this form of video activism for BLM is that the circulation of a video of a racist police officer killing a Black person further supports a capitalist economic structure that has been shown to be intersectionally racist. The conundrum of the political economy of social media is not unique to BLM's social media uses. However, in the case of BLM, the specific racism of big-tech algorithms, platforms, and corporations is at issue (S.U. Noble 2018; Sandvig et al. 2016). Clearly, this contradiction functions counter to BLM's political aims. Moreover, it serves as an example of the historical and ongoing economic exploitation of Black lives by white-dominated corporations that is endemic to sectors such as the music industry. In this sense, the technopolitics of social media activism can sometimes indirectly undermine the very movements the activists are supporting using social media. BLM activists are aware of the need to find a balance between seeking virality to mobilize the movement, respecting the lives lost, and reconsidering support for corporate platforms.

Hashtag Activism

Hashtag activism is another instance of a highly effective transmedia mobilization strategy used by BLM across multiple social media platforms. It can be defined as follows: "Hashtag activism takes place when large numbers of comments and retweets appear on social media in response to a hashtagged word, phrase, or sentence" and has its own temporal narrative structure with a beginning, middle (spiking as a trending topic), and end (Yang 2016, 14). Social movements have their own rhetorical and narrative form whose distinguishing character is confrontation. Narrative agency in hashtag activism is defined by Yang (2016, 14) as "the capacity to create stories on social media by using hashtags in a way that is collective and recognized by the public." There are five dimensions of narrative agency in hashtag activism. First, narrative agency is participatory, communal, and co-operative, as we see hashtag activism as an ongoing collaborative project of participatory communication both online and offline. #BlackLivesMatter and #BLM tweets collectively generate a broader narrative of anti-Black racism and its resistance movements, with participants' relationships not necessarily being with one another but with the hashtag itself (Yang 2016, 15).

Second, narrative agency is inventive based on both the limitations and desires of historically situated subjects, and in #BLM, this happens through the creation and amalgamation of personal narratives and political critiques. Third, it is a set of habits of the mind or heuristic skills, which develop as activists become habituated to tweeting and retweeting during protests, even if they themselves are not in the streets. Fourth, it is produced through genre and form and, therefore, is linked to audiences through a variety of media, including video, audio, photos, slogans, memes, news links, comix, and more. #BLM is used for transmedia mobilizations across genres. Finally, it can sometimes be destructive, as we see when trolls emerge against hashtag-activist campaigns, such as racist and/or misogynist and/or homophobic trolling. For some activists, destructive trolling can serve to further reinforce their commitment (Yang 2016, 16).

Racialized media activists we interviewed often had strategies for dealing with trolls and the negative emotional tax they cause. These included rotating particularly egregious tasks, like responding to social media trolls, after a short period of time; taking a step back for a short time to avoid emotional burnout; having a partner, friend group, or white collective share the responsibility for this negative, affective digital labour of dealing with online racism.

Black Lives Matter also led the protest movement in Ferguson. Focusing on #Ferguson, Yarimar Bonilla and Jonathan Rosa (2015) argue that hashtag activism links the non-place of social media to specific geo-spatial experiences and events, forging a dispersed, shared temporality of political events, thereby providing strategic affordances for contesting racialized police violence both in the streets and in the media. Noting that African Americans use smartphones and Twitter more than white Americans, they suggest that the hashtag activism of #Ferguson, #HandsUpDontShoot, and #NoAngel "became a tool for contesting victim-blaming or respectability narratives rooted in the belief that one can control the perception of one's body and the violence inflicted on it" (Bonilla and Rosa 2015, 5–8). They also point to the campaign #IfTheyGunnedMeDown, which draws attention to the narrative-framing impact of the photo used by mainstream media, as "anyone could be represented as either respectable and innocent or violent or criminal – depending on the staging of the photography" (Bonilla and Rosa 2015, 8). The authors draw attention to the intentional release by his mother of the image of Emmett Till's shattered body to demonstrate the importance of media images; the Till image is largely credited with sparking the civil rights movement (Bonilla and Rosa 2015, 12). This links to the livestreaming of Philando Castile's police-shooting death in terms of its affective capacity to motivate both sorrow and outrage.

The virality of #BLM, #BlackLivesMatter, and many of the hashtags mentioned here as part of the Black Lives Matter movement underlines the fact that there is "an acute awareness among young African Americans of how black bodies are particularly vulnerable to misrepresentation by mainstream media" and simultaneously vulnerable to "state-sanctioned violence" and "ongoing experiences of abject inequality in an age of alleged colorblindness" (Bonilla and Rosa 2015, 9). As such they point to personal and collective experiences that contradict the myth of postracial America.

Whereas police shootings often target young Black men, they have also targeted Black children and youth. A case in point is the fatal police shooting of Tamir Rice, a twelve-year-old playing with a plastic toy gun, exemplary of "state agents' distorted views of black Americans," whereby Black male bodies, even young children, are perceived as a threat by the police, and their hoodies, cigarettes, candy bars, and toys perceived as weapons (Bonilla and Rosa 2015, 11). The Tamir Rice media coverage drew attention to drugs and violence in his family situation, but rather than using these details to sympathetically examine the structural effects of intergenerational violence and poverty, and acknowledging that these details were irrelevant to his murder by the police who would not have been apprised of them, the mainstream media used them to justify police use of lethal force (Bonilla and Rosa 2015, 11).

Hashtags prompted many activists to move from online hashtag activism to join the Ferguson protests in the streets. Some got together to create an activist group, Millenial Activists United, that "shifted their role from 'documenting' their actions to 'generating' new forms of social community" (Bonilla and Rosa 2015, 10). This reveals how digital activism online can manifest in offline movements as activists and protesters move between mutually constitutive virtual and material spaces and forms of organizing (Freelon, McIlwain, and Clark 2016).

The wave of protests contesting George Floyd's death in police custody on May 25, 2020, in the midst of a global pandemic, saw a renewal of BLM protests and the #BlackLivesMatter hashtag climbed to record usage levels. While the hashtag was fairly inactive on the day he died, largely as a result of pandemic shutdowns, in the days immediately following his death it averaged 3.7 million tweets per day and peaked three days later at 8.8 million tweets as global protests escalated (J. Cohen 2020). A new protest slogan and movement demand emerged as well: defund the police.

The success of BLM has been at least partially attributable to its ability to mobilize social media to scale the movement, expanding support and involvement not just for #BlackLivesMatter but also for the Movement for Black Lives offline. Mundt and colleagues (2018) have found that BLM uses social media to create community and personal-political relationships by organizing informal coordination among leaders and organizers of translocal events at the local, national, and global level. These networks are able to provide internal, mutual support beyond the weak ties typically attributed to social media networking through mechanisms that allow for mitigation of leadership burnout due to racist trolls and continued police violence; helping one another solve problems, sending solidarity messages, and sharing success stories; and transmitting ideas and knowledge across distances about what various local chapters are doing (Mundt, Ross, and Burnett 2018). In addition, BLM uses social media to generate external material resources, including fundraising through white allies who mobilize grants, venue spaces, or rideshares and online fundraising such as regular "donate" buttons and crowdfunding campaigns. They also post ad-hoc messages saying, "we need this," which often leads to people providing the item also getting involved in the movement, thus deepening online relationships in the offline contexts. BLM thus uses social media to maintain and scale the movement through creating internal networks among chapters, linking to external networks, and connecting with cross-movement, intersectional, multi-issue global movements (Mundt, Ross, and Burnett 2018).

Fast and Slow Organizing

Black Lives Matter has used various technopolitical practices to engage in both fast and slow organizing. Fast organizing takes place via immediate responses to everyday police violence, shootings, and deaths, where BLM shares livestreams or posts hastily organized events on social media and hundreds or even thousands of people show up within very short time-frames, such as hours or days. This speed is possible because of established BLM social media networks, hashtag activism, and livestreaming, key technopolitical practices of the movement.

BLM also uses slow organizing for long-term, strategic coalition building across a host of intersectional issues, including gender, 2LGBTQ+ rights, immigrant, refugee and undocumented people's rights, housing and home-lessness, mental health, climate justice, prison abolition, and so on. Building coalitions is done not across single-issue groups to create intersectional coalitions, but rather as a movement that is itself internally intersectional. Moreover, it does so with everyday lived experiences of multiple intersect-ing oppressions, while also being a very highly educated and highly empow-ered movement (Milkman 2017). As such BLM uses extremely sophisticated media frames and mobilization strategies.

The media activists in this movement thus join the GJM, anti-austerity movements, the Quebec Student Strike, Idle No More, and 1492 Land Back Lane movements in their inclusion of a large number of highly educated knowledge and cultural workers contributing to their uses of intersectional technopolitics.

ACAR Intersectional Technopolitics

Below, the five key dimensions of ACAR intersectional technopolitics are mapped out (see Table 6).

First, the ACAR movements discussed here foreground Black and Indigenous media and cultures, including magazines, blogs, artwork, and more. The anticapitalism we saw in anti-austerity and GJM movements now has an antiracist and anticolonial intersectionality. Elements of this appeared in the GJM through postcolonial critiques of neoliberal capital-ism, which are now foregrounded in digital hashtag movements such as #BLM, #IdleNoMore, and #MMIWG. As Sherene Razack (2002) maps out, there are distinct ways in which intersections between race, colonialism,

Table 6 Key dimensions of ACAR intersectional technopolitics

Dimension	ACAR intersectional technopolitics
Intersectional and anticapitalist	Foreground antiracist Black and Indigenous media and arts projects; critique racism embedded in colonial capitalism; media decolonization and antiracism, feminist, and 2LGBTQ+ intersections; Red intersectionality; counters the race to innocence and the Oppression Olympics
Distributed online-offline architectures and motility	Online-offline spaces for specific purposes; distributive crowdsourced material artwork; distributive leadership of Black and Indigenous women; connection to traditional cultural values; MMIWG, Idle No More grounded in ceremony and protocols; work with Elders
Multiplicities of technologies and spaces	Multiple genres, platforms, devices, actor types, groups, spaces, actions – rooted in Black and Indigenous resilience and strengths; digital divides, with access being both risk and opportunity; technologies create relationships, connect people with communities, and amplify traditions
Translocal solidarity economies and technologies	Indigenous and antiracist global solidarities; technology supports antiracism and Indigenous networks and accomplices; translocal mobilizations; solidarity transgresses white and settler fragility
Collective autonomy through direct action	Autonomous grassroots collectives and projects for self-determination of communities; BLM freedom schools; resilient social and tech infrastructures; affective healing movements for social transformation

capitalism, and gender play out in rural and urban geographies. Anticolonial movements transfer our thinking to land, territory, treaties, and rural spaces, away from the densities of digital technologies to open spaces of belonging. Red intersectionality notes the importance of solidarities among immigrants, racialized groups who have been in North America many generations, and Indigenous peoples who have been here much longer. This intersectional consciousness also informs technopolitics.

Second, in the balance between online-offline spaces, which was so important in anti-austerity protest movements and hackerspaces, ACAR media and movements may choose to use or avoid certain digital technologies for specific purposes. They may engage in distributive, crowdsourced material artwork projects and emphasize the distributive leadership of Black and Indigenous women and 2LGBTQ+ people. These projects are rooted in their deep connections to traditional cultural values, whether Indigenous or

African American. Indigenous movements such as #MMIWG, #WWOS, and #IdleNoMore, in addition to being hashtags, are interpersonal projects of social transformation grounded in ceremony and protocols, and they work in close connection with and under the guidance of community Elders. Thus online-offline motility can lean toward offline spaces, with online spaces being used to mobilize and communicate, but the key representational spaces are in-person and within the communities of concern. This is consistent with the integration of cultural practices in healing justice, used in Black and Indigenous movements alike, to heal from intergenerational traumas.

Third, multiple genres, platforms, devices, actor types, groups, spaces, and actions are all rooted in Black and Indigenous resilience and strength. There is an end to the victim narrative and a shift toward development and demonstration of great strength and resilience within communities. While there are racialized and gendered digital divides, including those affecting on-reserve and inner-city access to technologies, digital access is considered in some communities to bring both the risk of surveillance and the opportunity to connect with distant community, family members, and movements. In this sense, technology is assessed for its capacity to grow relationships, to connect people with communities, and to support spaces in which cultural traditions and values can be shared and advocated for.

Fourth, intersectional movements of Indigenous and antiracist global solidarities develop as people connect globally, with #BLM and #NoDAPL having solidarity protests around the world. Digital technologies support antiracist and anticolonial networks by fostering translocal mobilizations. These forms of global and local solidarity attempt to dismantle white supremacy and colonialism, as participants engage in challenging conversations. However, the emphasis on solidarity does not eclipse the movements themselves; in other words, white people and settlers are not foregrounded, but rather they take a back seat, following the lead of BIPOC groups in ACAR forefront organizing.

Fifth, autonomous grassroots collectives and projects arise for the self-determination of Black and Indigenous communities throughout North America and beyond. The ends of these projects and movements are achieved not through petitions to the state (although anti-state legal action is sometimes required) but through direct, community-led actions, education, and cultural promotion such as BLM freedom schools for young people, Indigenous powwows and so on. Autonomous groups create and engage with resilient social and technological infrastructures in order to share affective healing justice movements for interconnected personal and social transformation. The autonomy of self-determination is echoed in media transformations.

Discussion and Debates

While Indigenous and Black histories have many differences, Black Lives Matter, Idle No More, Standing Rock, *Walking With Our Sisters*, 1492 Land Back Lane, and other Indigenous movements have also stood in solidarity with one another. This solidarity at the intersection of antiracism and anti-colonialism bears further examination.

Beyond the Race to Innocence

Confronting debates over competing marginalizations in feminist work, Mary Louise Fellows and Sherene Razack (1998, 335) argue that to develop solidarity among women, it is necessary for all women to understand how interlocking systems of oppression inevitably lead us to be "implicated in the subordination of other women." More succinctly, "feminists committed to social change must feel compelled to transcend the race to innocence" (Fellows and Razack 1998, 336). The race to innocence ensures that all women remain subordinated. If some women are able to establish their "toehold on respectability" at the expense of others, the feminist project of liberation is doomed to fail. Fellows and Razack (1998, 338) emphasize "the connection between what we know and the interests we protect through our ignorance," an argument taken up by Bobby Noble (2007), to be discussed in the chapter on 2LGBTQ+ movements. Some women, despite being oppressed by gender, also participate in the systemic oppression of other women through axes such as race, class, sexuality, and so on. When challenged about positions of domination (for example, in terms of race or class) the tendency is to restate a position of subordination (for example, as a woman), denying the ways in which these systems of oppression are mutually constitutive (Fellows and Razack 1998, 339). While this self-repositioning as subordinated is understandable, because articulating a marginalized position is the first step in a liberatory framework against erasure and invisibilization, at the same time, competing for the position of most oppressed is counter-productive for all involved.

Fellows and Razack (1998, 342) raise the important notion that some categories are marked (Blackness, lesbian, disabled) while others establish their dominance by remaining unmarked (whiteness, heterosexuality, able-bodiedness), revealing a troubling paradox at the centre of liberal notions of equality: the structures of domination required to produce the equality presumed to inhere in the middle class exclude many categories of people from accessing precisely this equality. Indeed, the formation of liberal nation-states that claim to secure equality of civic participation for all citizens has depended on four imperial projects: enslavement of Africans, genocide and dispossession of Indigenous peoples from their lands, exploitation of the working class, and subjugation of women in reproductive labour – all of which have combined to produce the economic wealth of the imperial centre (Fellows and Razack 1998, 344).

The gender hierarchies established among women through these mutually influencing processes were constitutive of and shaped by the perceived purity of the white, middle-class housewife, whose respectability was established in contradistinction to the degeneracy of Othered women, who took up or were forced into positions as factory workers, domestic workers, sex workers, enslaved workers, undocumented workers, and more. However, "a claim for justice cannot be transformative if it depends for its success on marking the distinction between ourselves and other women who can then be labelled degenerate" (Fellows and Razack 1998, 350). Rather, Fellows and Razack (1998, 352) argue we must transcend our latent desire "to maintain our innocence and to consider that the systems that oppress us are unconnected from the ones in which we are privileged" in order to take seriously "our task as scholars and activists [which] is to trace all the hierarchical connections for the purpose of developing strategies for change."

The foregrounding strategy described above can help with this objective and avoid the race to innocence. Foregrounding in intersectional movements allows for an acknowledgment of the importance of one particular issue while connecting it to other issues through intersectionality. Foregrounding, therefore, is an intersectional practice that can mitigate the race to innocence with respect to anti-Black racism; moreover, as we will see below, it can also mitigate settler moves to innocence in relation to Indigenous peoples that attempt to secure settler futurity (Tuck and Yang 2012).

Beyond the Oppression Olympics

While Fellows and Razack considered the intersections of race and gender, Rita Kaur Dhamoon (2015) adds a layer of complexity as she intervenes at the intersection of antiracist and anticolonial feminisms that may also be seen as competing in a race to innocence. She identifies a debate between, on the one hand, anticolonial activists and scholars who suggest that all inhabitants on colonized land in the Americas – including white people and people of colour – in some ways benefit from structures of settler privilege and, on the other hand, antiracist activists and scholars who draw attention to the ways in which people of colour may have entered colonial nation-states to find themselves targets of systemic racism, and as such cannot be seen to benefit from settler privilege – and, moreover, according to some, must not be seen as settlers at all. She calls this jockeying for position the "Oppression Olympics." Dhamoon suggests that, rather than make claims to be the most oppressed, engaging a transnational, intersectional analysis can help us better tease out and understand the complex set of power relations at play here between Indigenous anticolonial politics and antiracist politics in the ongoing material conditions of settler colonialism.

She suggests, first, that transnationalism must be reconceived to account for Indigenous conceptions of nation, disarticulated from the nation-state, which is "itself a settler-colonial structure and form of governmentality" (Dhamoon 2015, 27) rooted in heteropatriarchy, racism, and capitalist dispossession and control of Indigenous lands, and instead rearticulated as "visions of Indigenous nationhood [that] are based on care and responsibility for land that all can share" (Dhamoon 2015, 27) in mutually accountable relationships. By doing so, she intends to "disrupt the presumed/naturalized legitimacy of heteropatriarchal settler nation-states" as the sole way to understand and legitimate nations and in its place posits the notion of lateral transnationalism, where the nation can serve as a potential site of liberation without claiming an oppressive nation-state configuration or power structure (Dhamoon 2015, 28).

Second, she argues that intersectionality is useful here but that it must move beyond liberal and legal arguments based on identities to better incorporate and interrogate the interlocking power structures, or what Patricia Hill Collins (2000) analyzes as the "matrix of domination," being addressed by anticolonial, antiracist feminist scholars and activists "to counter oppressive and exclusionary forms of white western feminisms" (Dhamoon 2015, 29). From this perspective, considering Jodi Byrd's (2011, 30) notion of cacophony, the matrix of domination reveals "multiple co-constituting horizontal struggles of gendering, sexuality and desire, capitalism, and ableism that interact with the cacophony of colonizer-colonized and other minority oppressions."

Addressing these multiple forms of privilege-oppression (e.g., white colonizers/Indigenous peoples, people of colour/Indigenous peoples, white supremacy/non-Indigenous people of colour, etc.) as binaries is insufficient because they also intersect with gender, sex, sexuality, and social class. For

Dhamoon (2015, 31), who extends the argument of Fellows and Razack, "a feminist praxis of decolonizing anti-racism cannot obscure one struggle at the expense of others because they mutually (albeit differently) structure white-supremacist capitalist heteronormativities." She cautions against what she calls the trade-off model inherent in the Oppression Olympics, which is not just a race to innocence but also a race to the bottom, requiring people to remain oppressed to remain in the movement.

Rather, we must consciously consider "the presumed ontologies and epistemologies that frame practices of liberation" (Dhamoon 2015, 34). This can lead to solidarity and cooperative rather than competitive strategies between Indigenous and Black activists (Sefa Dei 2017), which are emerging increasingly, for example, as Black Lives Matter stood in solidarity with Standing Rock. Patrisse Cullors (2016, 86) notes that Black Lives Matter also advocates for the development of "Black communities in deep solidarity with Indigenous people, given how much Black people have been displaced and given that we end up occupying other people's land." Natalie Clark (2016), as we recall, refers to these complex solidarities as "Red intersectionality," and they must be considered a work-in-progress.

ACAR movements still face many challenges today, despite the rise in mobilizations and solidarities. These include anti-Black and anti-Indigenous racist backlash, everyday challenges of working together across large intersectional groups and networks, the retrenchment of state racism with the rise of right-wing populism, and more. Yet the extensions and revisions of intersectional technopolitics from the anti-austerity and GJM movements by ACAR movements remain noteworthy. These extensions must themselves be extended by understanding how they link to 2LGBTQ+ and transfeminist transformative media and social movements.

5

2LGBTQ+

In this chapter, 2LGBTQ+ movements and media are foregrounded. These movements intersect with and have been mentioned in relation to the activism discussed in previous chapters, and additionally will have intersections with transfeminism, covered in Chapter 6.

Thus far, I have used the generalized term "2LGBTQ+" to indicate a broader collective identity; however, a note on terminology is called for now to understand it at a more granular level. In this chapter, I use the two terms "queer and trans" and "2LGBTQ+" as an admittedly imperfect, inclusive reference to sexualities and genders. I place the "2" for two-spirit in front to prioritize the importance of global Indigenous two-spirit identities and decolonizing queer and trans movements.

Currently, a more comprehensive term might look something like this: LGBTQQIP2SAA – lesbian, gay, bisexual, trans, queer, questioning, intersex, pansexual, two-spirit, asexual, and accomplices.[1] Certainly, there are queer and trans identities omitted from this long list, such as non-binary, gender non-conforming, transsexual, queer and trans people of colour (QTPOC), greysexual, queercrip, femmegimp, Indigiqueer, undocuqueer,

---

1 In using the terms "queer and trans" and "2LGBTQ+" interchangeably, I also intend that these two short forms signify an inclusive reference to new terms and identities that may arise or may already be in use in specific contexts.

and so on, each with different resonances, intersections, and politics (Erickson 2007, 2015; B. Noble 2007; Salgado n.d.; Tallie 2014). In this chapter I will use the language of the scholars and activists that I reference.

By the time this book makes it into print, shifting norms may have already impacted the terminologies being used. If you are reading this long after its original publication, the terminology may seem quaint or even politically charged. If the terms used here have shortcomings, that is perhaps unsurprising, as the terminology is regularly contested and critiqued as the identities and needs of the 2LGBTQ+ community shift and change.

My position in relation to 2LGBTQ+ communities and research should be addressed. I am a cisgender woman and dis-identify with heteronormativity, including the binary gendered, sexualized, racialized and able-bodied norms it encodes. Nonetheless, I am most often read as heterosexual, with a long-term cismale partner. My gender presentation is not static but varies among feminine, masculine, and non-binary. For many years, I have participated in queer culture and relationships, and I acknowledge the importance of queering heterosexuality from an intersectional perspective. I understand myself to have a partial, incomplete, and incoherent queer subjectivity. I take what early queer theorist Eve Sedgwick (1990) calls a "universalizing" view that maintains the importance of queer and trans theories, concepts, and practices for the broader society, including and also beyond 2LGBTQ+ communities.

Global movements for intersectional 2LGBTQ+ liberation have emerged over the past several decades and have gradually become intersectional movements, producing complex media and technologies, including technologies of the body as a site of resistance. Globally there are complex differentiations within the national cultural, political, legal, medical, and social contexts in which queer and trans movements and subjectivities struggle. Therefore, one set of theories or concepts will not necessarily apply to other contexts where specific social movements and media practices may be quite varied. More specifically, Western 2LGBTQ+ frameworks do not necessarily apply to queer and trans movements and media in non-Western or Indigenous global locations.

2LGBTQ+ Movements

Contemporary queer and trans movements were active for decades before they exploded in the United States during the Stonewall Riots of 1969. Famously, one of the leaders within these early 2LGBTQ+ movements was Sylvia Rivera, a trans woman of colour who identified as a drag queen, and co-founded Street Transvestites Action Revolutionaries (STAR) with Marsha P. Johnson in New York City.

Early approaches to LGBT movements tended to be assimilationist, acknowledging that LGBT people were "just like everyone else" and should be accepted
into mainstream culture (Sullivan 2003). In Canada, this was expressed in 1967
by the young justice minister Pierre Trudeau, who would soon go on to become
prime minister, when he said, "There is no place for the state in the bedrooms of
the nation" (CBC 1967). However, the assimilationist approach has been contested by a liberationist perspective (Sullivan 2003) as early as the 1960s with
STAR and other groups such as the Gay Liberation Front founded in 1969.

Fast forward to the 1990s. Queer and trans liberationist movements
asserted that 2LGBTQ+ people are in some ways not like heterosexuals in
terms of both historical experiences and contemporary relationships. Social
movements focused on expressing queer and trans rights through pride,
presence, and visibility in mainstream cultural public spaces (Sullivan 2003).
Movements organized Pride Marches to contest police brutality against
queer and trans people, and public events celebrating 2LGBTQ+ liberation,
staking a claim in spaces such as "the village" or the "gayborhood," commercial areas in metropolitan cities such as New York, Montreal, and San Francisco (Sycamore 2008). Groups such as Queer Nation engaged in mall zaps
and kiss-ins in mainstream public spaces, and the Pink Panthers patrolled
the gay village to "bash back" or protect people who were targeted by homophobic and transphobic violence (Berlant and Freeman 1992; Slagle 1995).
Queer theory emerged in tandem with these movements, sometimes
following them, with Eve K. Sedgwick's (1990) seminal text, *Epistemology of
the Closet*, suggesting that anti-homophobic inquiry needed to develop its
own intellectual trajectories distinct from the concerns of feminist studies,
out of which lesbian and gay studies had emerged.

Sedgwick argued that "hetero-homo" is a constructed binary that first
appeared with the invention of the term "homosexual" in the late nineteenth
century ("heterosexual" came much later). Although this binary has been the
defining dimension of Western sexuality for the past century, she argued, there
are many dimensions along which sexual activity can be differentiated beyond
partner choice. Moreover, the hetero-homo categorical imperative was not neutral, but rather took place within a context of "urgent homophobic pressure to
devalue one of the nominally symmetrical forms of choice" (Sedgwick 1990, 9).
Heterosexuals (without reflexively naming themselves as such) categorized so-
called homosexuals in order to separate, castigate, medicalize, imprison, pathol-
ogize, institutionalize, ostracize, attempt to "cure" (impossible as being
homosexual is not a disease), and otherwise target them through systemic, emotional, and physical forms of abuse and violence (Sedgwick 1990).

Sedgwick (1990, 11) used a post-structuralist approach to argue that the devalued signifiers in binary pairs such as white-racialized, knowledge-ignorance, and private-public, which discursively circulated "an entire cultural network of normative definitions," were placed in a precarious position, open to manipulation by unequal power relations and structures, particularly by those with greater power. This is an argument we are now familiar with, as a similarly structured argument is used by Indigenous and Black scholars to deconstruct the binaries Western-Indigenous and white-Black and, moreover, to reveal these binaries as inflected with power. Deconstruction of these binaries always concludes by reclaiming the power of the previously devalued marker – Indigenous, Black, and, in this case, 2LGBTQ+ – in the binary between cis-heterosexual and 2LGBTQ+ (M. Ross 2005; TallBear 2019). 2LGBTQ+ movements challenge precisely these binary power structures.

Radical queer, trans, and non-binary movements in EuroAmerica have developed through a series of shifts in focus against a range of dominant patterns: from anti-homophobia to anti-heteronormativity (Jeppesen 2010b); to radical queer anticapitalism (G. Brown 2007; Daring et al. 2012; Heckert, Shannon, and Willis 2012; Sycamore 2008; Windpassinger 2010); and then to anti-homonormativity, with growing challenges to the white, middle-class, cis-male domination of 2LGBTQ+ movements (B. Noble 2007; Sullivan 2003). In the 2000s, building on these shifts, we see the emergence of global movements for a range of genders, sexes, and sexualities, including transgender, transsexual, gender-nonconforming, genderqueer, non-binary, intersex, and pansexual (Feinberg 2006; Khoo 2014; Lepischak 2004; B. Noble 2007; Spade 2006; Vade 2005). 2LGBTQ+ movements also work with allied transfeminist movements against gender normativity, transnormativity, and more (Ahmed 2016; Ruin 2016; White 2013).

Anticolonialism and antiracism are concerns within intersectional 2LGBTQ+ movements, with struggles to bring these concerns into more mainstream LGBT movements. In the North American context, Indigenous two-spirited movements have emerged, foregrounding long-established Indigenous identities related to sexualities and genders such as two-spirit or Indigiqueer (Boellstorff et al. 2014; Depelteau and Giroux 2015; Driskill 2011; Innes and Anderson 2015; Ortner and Whitehead 1981; TallBear and Willey 2019; Tallie 2014; Whitehead 1981). Further, anti-colonial queer and trans concerns have been taken up that challenge dominant EuroAmerican and settler-centric theories, terms, and practices (Araneta and Fernández Garrido 2016; Chavez 2016; Garriga-López 2016; Kaas 2016; Ravine 2014; Ruin 2016; Silva and Ornat 2016). Antiracist queer and trans movements have also emerged within the United States and beyond (Alimahomed 2010; Evans and Janish 2015; Jeppesen, Kruzynski, and Riot 2016; Johnson and Henderson 2005; L. Ross 2008). These include 2LGBTQ+ undocumented, immigrant, and refugee movements such as UndocuQueer, the Queer Undocumented Immigrant Program (QUIP), and more (Costanza-Chock 2014; Gentile and Salerno 2019; Salgado n.d.; White 2013).

Intersectional initiatives and complexities in global 2LGBTQ+ transformative movement and media activism are mapped below.

From Marriage Equality to Anti-heteronormativity

In early 2LGBTQ+ movements one goal was to legalize partner relationships through nation-state laws protecting marriage-equality rights. Nation-states on several continents have done so: Netherlands (2001), Canada (2005), South Africa (2006), Iceland and Argentina (2010), New Zealand (2013), United States (2015), Germany (2017), Taiwan (2019), and Costa Rica (2020), to mention but a few. In some countries such as Mexico there may be anti-discrimination laws and it may be possible for 2LGBTQ+ couples to get married in certain states, despite having no national law. In other countries, such as Yemen, Iran, Brunei, Nigeria, Saudi Arabia, Afghanistan, Pakistan, UAE, and Uganda, "homosexuality" is punishable by death. Marriage equality guaranteed under nation-state law goes beyond anti-discrimination legislation and often guarantees rights such as parenting, adoption, inheritance, medical benefits, and so on; however, in practice, these may lag behind the law.

Marriage equality provides the opportunity to consecrate relationships based on a heterosexual two-partner model in which the stereotype, presumption, or expectation is that one partner is masculine and the other feminine. Some 2LGBTQ+ activists have critiqued marriage equality from an intersectional ACAR perspective, arguing that it encodes whiteness, replicates a constrained heteronormative relationship model, and ignores complex intersectional issues in communities of colour such as legal status (Alimahomed 2010), police brutality (J. Khan 2016), health care, and housing (Sycamore 2008). Other activists have argued that marriage-equality rights are important because they allow partners to get together across borders through refugee claims, particularly when one partner lives in a 2LGBTQ+ death-penalty country (Jeppesen, Kruzynski, and Riot 2016; White 2013).

Marriage equality, however, according to Melissa Autumn White (2013), is an ambivalent position for couples moving together across borders. The nation-state promises a liberatory space, but once the partner or couple arrives, homophobia and transphobia continue to play out in everyday life, including systemic heteronormativity. Moreover, for trans, intersex, gender-queer, gender-variant, gender-nonconforming, and non-binary genders and sexes, the notion of "same-sex" marriage is complicated, implying that a partner must have the "same" body. But how is sameness determinable for non-binary or incoherently gendered and sexed subjects (B. Noble 2007)? Thus, the term "same-sex" has been critiqued, whereby the term "marriage equality" seems to better provide equal rights, but also to demand conformity to heteronormative marriage ideals.

Thus, while some 2LGBTQ+ groups advocate for marriage equality, others call it into question. Some argue that, having achieved hard-fought access to marriage equality, it is important to critically analyze the multiple interlocking systems of oppression through which state power, capitalism, racism, colonialism, and heteronormativity continue to circumscribe queer and trans lives, before, during, after, and outside of marriage.

Queer theorist Michael Warner (1993) observes how queer movements have shifted concerns from homophobia to heteronormativity, the organization of society around the presumed norm that intimate relationships will be heterosexual. Heteronormativity requires the stabilization of bodies into two cisgender categories (male, female) and sexual practices into monogamous, heterosexual, and married sex, but its norms also extend beyond sexuality and gender: "Heteronormativity does not exist as a discrete and easily identifiable body of thought" (Sullivan 2003, 132). Rather it "is more than ideology, or prejudice, or phobia against gays and lesbians; it is produced in almost every aspect of the forms and arrangements of social life" (Berlant and Warner 1998, 554). Challenging heteronormativity, oppositional queer counterpublics render queer sexualities visible in public and produce opportunities for the circulation of discourses resistant to heteronormativity (Berlant and Warner 1998; Heckert and Cleminson 2011).

Queer and Trans Visibility and Counterpublics

While early 2LGBTQ+ cultures emerged in particular neighbourhoods in large urban cities, activists have also made interventions in mainstream public spaces. Two American activist groups shaped social movement strategies around public visibility and counterpublics in the 1980s and 1990s. The AIDS Coalition to Unleash Power (ACT UP) was formed in 1987, as feminists and gay men joined under the slogan "silence = death" to confront the failure of global governments to deal with the AIDS crisis (France 2012).

They integrated the body as text into protest, using "die-ins" or death postures of bodies representing a symbolic graveyard.

Queer Nation, founded in 1990, promoted 2LGBTQ+ visibility through mall zaps, kiss-ins, and queer nights out in bars outside the so-called gay village. Queer Nation's members playfully rendered queer sexualities publicly visible by acting like heterosexuals in public, demonstrating intimacies that countered heteronormative domination. Activists then critiqued these actions for their emphasis on consumerist spaces, leading to the queer anticapitalist slogan "We're here, we're queer, and we're not going shopping" and the more provocative "Not gay as in happy, but queer as in fuck you!" Some groups, such as the Lesbian Avengers and the Pink Panthers, used a bash-back strategy of patrolling the gay village at night to confront homophobic and transphobic verbal and physical violence. Both direct-action tactics – mall zaps and bash backs – enacted queerness in public by directly forming queer counterpublics and taking back both public space and collective power rather than demanding rights from the state (Berlant and Freeman 1992; Slagle 1995).

Anticapitalism: Queeruption and Gay Shame

Building on but also deviating from Queer Nation, Queeruption and Gay Shame grew out of anti-heteronormative, anticapitalist, and anti-homonormative critiques, drawing attention to intersections of race, gender, trans, intersex, two-spirit identities, and more (Jeppesen 2010b).

Queeruption is an event that started in London, UK, in 1998 as an anti-capitalist queer and trans safe(r) social weekend in a squatted building. Elements of the event included queercore punk bands, sex cabarets, dance parties, vegan food, DIY workshops, and an anti-consumerist ethos based on bartering and a gift economy (G. Brown 2007). Since then, Queeruption and a similar event called Gay Shame (Sycamore 2008) have taken place in EuroAmerican cities such as New York, Berlin, San Francisco, and Amsterdam. Developing temporary autonomous zones governed by intersectional practices and policies, these events engaged in the project of queer anti-spectacle world making, creating liberatory, anticapitalist queer counterpublic spaces in everyday life (G. Brown 2007). In Montreal, groups with whom I researched in the *Collectif de recherche sur l'autonomie collective* (CRAC), QTeam, and *Les Panthères Roses* organized along intersectional lines while emphasizing queer anticapitalism. Similarly, also in Montreal, grassroots organization *Pervers/Cité* organized an alternative 2LGBTQ+ festival, contesting the capitalist homonormativity of *Divers/Cité*, the mainstream LGBT pride arts festival in Montreal. While *Divers/Cité* has been superseded by *Fierté Montréal, Pervers/Cité* has continued to organize. QTeam, *Les Panthères Roses,* and *Pervers/Cité,* among other groups in Montreal, have mobilized intersectional ACAR and anticapitalist 2LGBTQ+ politics.

QTPOC Intersections: ACAR Movements

In early work on queer and trans people of colour intersections of immigration, race, and 2LGBTQ+ identities, Gloria Anzaldúa (1987) observed that the hybrid identity of *Mestiza* is fluid and contested. The *Mestiza* identity expresses itself in the borderlands between two sides of the many binaries of language, nation-state, gender, and sexuality, in which the subject belongs to both sides of the binary but is at home in neither. Similarly, queer women of colour (Alimahomed 2010), queer Black men (M. Ross 2005), and queer Indigenous people (Driskill 2011) have articulated double exclusions, challenging the dominant 2LGBTQ+ identity. Queer women of colour, for example, are doubly marginalized as "outsiders within" (Collins 1986) both mainstream white-dominated 2LGBTQ+ organizations and their racial or ethnic communities, with the perception in racialized communities being that "queerness" is a white identity (Alimahomed 2010, 151, 162). However, while racialized 2LGBTQ+ individuals may experience alienation from or rejection by their families, there is a misperception that racial and ethnic communities are more transphobic or homophobic than the perceived liberal inclusivity of white-dominated American society. Countering stereotypes in mainstream media TV and film, quantitative research shows that this is statistically unproven (Grant et al. 2011; Thomas 2019).

Sabrina Alimahomed (2010, 153) has found in her research with racialized queer women in California that they resist hegemonic notions of gender, race, ethnicity, and queer representations, rejecting the "assumption that everyone experiences being gay in the same way." Historically "issues of race, gender, and class . . . central to the lives of lesbians of color, were seen as irrelevant" to mainstream LGBT movements, causing a circular argument that Black, Indigenous, and people of colour (BIPOC) were not involved in the 2LGBTQ+ movement and "their absence was further used as a legitimating factor in their marginalization" (Alimahomed 2010, 153, 163).

In response, queer women of colour advanced intersectional "multi-issue social justice politics that combated sexism, racism, homophobia, and class exploitation" (Alimahomed 2010, 153–54). Rather than concluding that experiences of exclusion, invisibility, and silencing within mainstream feminist, queer, and antiracist movements were disempowering, precisely in these moments queer women of colour organized "alternative knowledge formations and representations of resistance" (Alimahomed 2010, 154). For example, Alimahomed (2010, 165) illustrates how a group of queer women of colour at an 80 percent POC-majority campus challenged the fact that although the "LGBT center catered to gendered differences among queers on campus, the queer women's support group was exclusively facilitated by white women, and white women students were consistently the largest groups being served."

This is indicative of what Ibram Kendi (2019, 166) calls "space racism," defined as "a powerful collection of racist policies that lead to resource inequity between racialized spaces or the elimination of certain racialized spaces." Kendi makes a key distinction between segregated spaces and separate spaces, arguing in favour of the latter. Segregation is a racist policy that mandates that people of different races – specifically white and Black in the United States – must circulate in different spheres, including neighbourhoods, schools, restaurants, workplaces, and shops. Segregation is enacted by the dominant race to protect itself from the perceived negative influences of the excluded group: consequently, "just as racist power racializes people, racist power racializes space" (Kendi 2019, 169). This has not just exclusionary but also economic effects. Black spaces in the United States have always been under-resourced in relation to white spaces, particularly schools, real estate, universities, and clubs: "Ideas of space racism justify resource inequity through creating a racial hierarchy of space" (Kendi 2019, 169).

When Black people create separate spaces, these are "spaces of Black solidarity created to separate Black people from racism" (Kendi 2019, 175). White people can feel threatened by separate spaces because they are not used to being excluded, as per the earlier discussion of white fragility (DiAngelo 2018), and they can see them as spaces of anti-white politics. Kendi (2019, 175) argues that white integrationists assume that the mechanism of racial hatred fuelling segregation is the same mechanism of racial separation fuelling solidarity separatism against racism. In practice, these two ways of creating racialized apartness have quite the opposite generative objectives and outcomes.

It might be noted that this chapter is about 2LGBTQ+ organizing, whereas the concept of space racism is about antiracism. It is included here (and not in the previous chapter) because this is one of those times when the intersection of an issue – space racism within 2LGBTQ+ movements – demanded the explanation be placed in an intersectional chapter. This demonstrates the intersectional characteristic of these issues and under-lines the challenge of dividing material on intersectionality into chapters.

The LGBT centre mentioned above, and its queer women's support group, were instituted through space racism. When confronted, "The [white] director refused to institute a queer women of color support group" because it would exclude white people (Alimahomed 2010, 165), demon-strating the white fragility DiAngelo (2018) and Kendi (2019) point to. Rather than engaging further in this oppositional exercise, which only seemed to strengthen the power of the dominant group (Heckert and Clem-inson 2011), QTPOC participants left the centre, "an empowering act . . . to create a space that was able to cater to their own needs" (Alimahomed 2010, 165). This is a similar contestation to the collectively self-empowering devel-opment of *Pervers/Cité* in Montreal, mentioned earlier. Similarly, Black Lives Matter Toronto shut down the pride parade in 2016 to draw attention to anti-Black racism in the organization and police participation in the parade, contesting events-based space racism that can be experienced by Black people in 2LGBTQ+ movements (Craven 2016; J. Khan 2016).

These examples illustrate how intersectionality moves beyond coalition building between 2LGBTQ+ groups and Black groups, to foreground specific intersecting identities of QTPOC individuals and groups contesting the racialized homonormativity and transnormativity of mainstream 2LGBTQ+ movements.

Global Trans Movements

Hegemonies of global capitalism, religion, culture, and so on have created strictly enforced binary gender codes evident in mainstream media and everyday social norms. However, non-binary gender expressions have his-torically been respected in many countries. Leslie Feinberg (2006) has mapped a range of transgender identities, bodies, and expressions related to gender presentation in the context of gender identity. Trans lawyer and activist Dylan Vade (2005, 261) argues that "the ways to be transgender are endless." For Vade, there is no linear relationship between gender, sex, and sexuality. Vade has found that in attempting to establish and stabilize a per-son's gender, the legal system reverts to transnormativity, discussed above, which is "a picture in which all transgender people look the same" (Vade 2005, 255). This finding is corroborated by Korean trans activist Ruin (2016). Both scholars note that the law typically protects only specific legi-ble transnormative bodies, a tendency that has left trans and non-binary people unprotected by the legal system in many countries, and at risk of employment loss, housing and health care discrimination, and transphobic physical violence, including state-sanctioned police violence. In San Francisco, for example, 50 percent of transphobic violence was found to have been perpetrated by the police (Vade 2005, 257). While laws are slowly changing in some countries, transphobia is still very real in many societies, even after legal protections have been enacted.

Gender and sexuality theorist Bobby Noble (2007, 170, 171) also rejects simplistically coherent conceptions of trans or non-binary sex, gender, and sexualities, proposing "post-queer, trans-ed practices of in-coherence," as follows:

> To render something in-coherent . . . means two things simultaneously: first, it means a lack of organization, or a failure of organization so as to make that thing difficult to comprehend; but it also means failing to cohere as a mass or entity . . . rendering bodies and subject positions as in-coherent as possible to refuse to let power work through bodies the way it needs to. It can, in other words, disrupt the coherence mandated by the neatly and dualistically triangulated male/female, gay/straight, sex/gender binary systems.

Bobby Noble rejects the transnormativity enforced by these three interlocking binaries and instead proposes "disturbing the ground of intelligibility" of gender, sex, and sexuality (B. Noble 2007, 173). As a way to visualize an unintelligibilized sex/gender/sexuality system, we can refer to Dylan Vade's (2005, 261) proposition of a gender galaxy, "a three-dimensional non-linear space in which every gender has a location that may or may not be fixed." Moreover, for both Noble and Vade, intersectional experiences of trans people "span all communities, cultures, races, ages, sexual orientations, and genders" (Vade 2005, 264). By corollary, we may propose a sex galaxy, and a sexuality galaxy.

One trans movement imaginary riffing in this direction proposes:

> A proliferation of new femininities and masculinities, of "abnormal" and monstrous bodies inserted into biopolitics, which overflow the fictional but foundational dualism at the heart of capitalist modernity – so-called "sexual difference." [It] traffics in actually existing nonbinary lives, bodies, identities, and genders on a collective social level . . . [which] makes visible the lie of sexual dualism . . . countering the neoliberal privatization of the

sexual sphere by publicly exposing the many ways in which the logic of binary sexual difference routinely fails.

(Espineira and Bourcier 2016, 89)

Further contestations of transnormativity include Indigenous two-spirit movements challenging Western LGBT movements through calls to decolonize trans movements (Boellstorff et al. 2014; Depelteau and Giroux 2015; TallBear 2019; Tallie 2014). Contemporary global trans movements, constricted by neoliberal capitalism, colonialism, racism, transmisogyny, and more, are increasingly taking an intersectional approach to challenge interlocking oppressions.

Below, several specific global trans and non-binary liberation movements are mapped in relation to subjectivities, political demands, and the ways in which they contest gender norms and EuroAmerican aspects of transnormativity.

Gender Ambiguous *Khwaja Sira* (Pakistan)

Challenging transnormativities requires looking beyond EuroAmerican non-binary and trans movements. To illustrate a range of global trans experiences and subjectivities, including specific contexts of oppression, resistance, and empowerment, my first example is from Pakistan, where speaking publicly about sexuality is considered taboo. Ethnographer Faris Khan (2016, 158) has interviewed three *khwaja sira* activists, a "category of gender-ambiguous people" in Pakistan who have gained legal recognition through the right to choose one of three trans genders on their identification: "male (khwaja sira)," "female (khwaja sira)," and *"khunsa-e-mushkil."* These are not identical to EuroAmerican identities, but can be loosely and inadequately translated as transmasculine, transfeminine, and intersex (F.A. Khan 2016, 159).

Within Pakistan, *khwaja sira* have gained the interest of the general public and are often interviewed by the media, despite the taboo of speaking about sex in public. Rather than sexuality, however, the *khwaja sira* interviewers and interviewees together construct discourses related to what can be safely spoken about, such as "feelings" or "love" (F.A. Khan 2016, 161), maintaining ambiguity by explaining relationships through spiritual rather than sexual discourses. In this way they both conform to social norms, as it is taboo to speak of "these things" on TV, but also challenge conformity by pushing back against the demand to speak about sex on TV when cismen and ciswomen do not have to.

Thus, Khan (2016, 162) argues, *khwaja sira* assert their rights differently than the explicit medical, physiological, and hormonal discourses of trans movements in EuroAmerica, where no level of specificity is considered too detailed: "Situated between the poles of normativity and queerness, gender ambiguity offers a form of productive power over mainstream society by preserving the mysterious aura of *khwaja siras*" to maintain the gender and sex of the body ambiguous, unknowable except to oneself, and thus a private concern. This intentional "mysterious" ambiguity provides a method of advocating for the inclusion of non-binary genders in state institutions (e.g., ID cards) but also, with echoes of Bobby Noble's call for incoherencies, "aims to collapse all sense of knowable types . . . in defiance of being rendered socially and legally legible" (F.A. Khan 2016, 163). It is this illegibility, incoherence, and unknowability that lend gender ambiguity its "radical transformative potential" (F.A. Khan 2016, 163). As such it re-centres *khwaja sira* subjectivities as primarily knowable and accountable only to themselves.

Despite these self-determined accounts and accountabilities, *khwaja sira* people remain an extremely marginalized group in Pakistan in relation to mainstream society as well as in relation to mainstream gay and lesbian movements. The politics of culturally specific non-binary self-determination are discussed further below with respect to *travestis* in Brazil and non-binary gender identification in Ecuador.

Trans Pathologization (US, Spain)

Trans pathologization is a term used to problematize the fact that trans or non-binary gender identity has been medically labelled a disorder (i.e., pathologized), exemplified by its inclusion in the *Diagnostic and Statistical Manual of Mental Disorders*, or DSM III (1980), using the term gender identity disorder. However, with the DSM V (2013), this was removed and replaced by two new terms: gender dysphoria, which implies there is stress associated with a person's non-binary or transgender identity, and transsexualism, which implies a person who wants to change their sex is pathological. In some countries, such as the United States, trans people may be forced to be diagnosed with one of these so-called disorders in order to be granted access to medical care, such as hormones or sex-reassignment surgery. However, many people would prefer not to be diagnosed with a disorder, feeling that the disorder is in society, not in the individual.

Trans theorist Jason Cromwell (2006) contests the pathologization of trans people, which stigmatizes trans and non-binary people, and presumes they are asexual because of genital disidentification. Whereas "asexual" is a sexual identity that some binary gendered and non-binary people may identity with, genital disidentification is not necessarily inherent to trans or non-binary identities. Cromwell's interviewees discuss sexual practices connected to the specific trans bodies of their partners, revealing that trans people are indeed sexually active and motivated and that their partners, rather than experiencing trans bodies as lacking, deviant, or pathological, are erotically attracted to their specific bodies and sexualities. Critiques of people predominantly attracted to trans bodies, denouncing them as "tranny-chasers," must therefore be called into question. Avery Brooks Tompkins (2014, 766) argues that "a sex-positive trans politics cannot emerge in trans and transallied communities if the rhetoric of the 'tranny chaser' continues to inform discourses of desire and attraction to trans people." These writers thus demand that trans sexualities be taken seriously rather than discounted, erased, or pathologized.

The triangulated pathologizations of non-binary sexes, genders, and sexualities are further amplified through the health care system. Trans activist and researcher Dean Spade (2006) critically analyzes the complexities of navigating the medical system for trans or non-binary people. Those seeking sex-reassignment surgery have been required by medical practitioners to reference and reify the linearly triangulated sex/gender/sexuality system to demonstrate their need to fully (meaning both surgically and performatively) transition from "one side" of the binary to "the other": "The medical regime permits only the production of gender-normative altered bodies, and seeks to screen out alterations that are resistant to a dichotomized, naturalized view of gender" (Spade 2006, 319). Self-determined gender and sexual identity or expression do not necessarily codify disidentification with the sex/gender assigned at birth. Rather, Spade has found that self-determined gender and sexual identities may be shaped by a range of social influences and formative experiences that may include parenting, religion, poverty, race, body shape, size, and so on, and perhaps, at the same time, they may be shaped by experiences of consciousness building and support in activist groups with a focus on 2LGBTQ+ rights, intersectionality, anticapitalism, anarchism, and/or feminism (Spade 2006, 319).

Contemporary movements against trans pathologization and cisheteropatriarchy are considered by Spanish trans activists Aitzole Araneta and Sandra Fernández Garrido (2016) in their local context to consist of a series of three movements. The first (2006–10) encompassed the "rise and consolidation of the trans-depathologization movement," with the second (2010–13) manifesting in "the consolidation of the transfeminist movement" as trans and feminist movements joined forces. A third "officialist" set of activities included 2LGBTQ+ groups advocating for trans rights in institutional and legal spaces with "some parameters of their struggle determined by their dialogue with established social institutions and/or political parties" (Araneta and Fernández Garrido 2016, 35–36). Thus, global anti-transpathologization movements have worked with allies and developed intersectional coalitions.

Queer and Trans Disability

At the intersection of queer and disability studies, anticapitalist queer-disability theorist Loree Erickson (2007) argues for subject positions of "queercrip," indicating a queer-disabled subjectivity, and "femmegimp," indicating a feminine-disabled subjectivity, both reclaiming once-negative terminology and signalling the intersectionality of these hybrid identities (West 2013). As a filmmaker, Erickson challenges the assumption that disabled people are asexual and confirms specific queer and trans sexualities and desires engaged by disabled people through the DIY self-production of what she calls "queercrip porn" (Erickson 2007, 2015). Thus, she reclaims the term "queercrip" as a critique of ableism, while also reclaiming the terrain of pornography and erotica for disabled subjects, removing it from capitalist circuits through producing DIY porn. Erickson thus underlines and undermines the double assumption of queer ability and heteronormative disability.

Similarly social work researcher Alexandre Baril (2015) argues that trans disability studies have been forced to engage with trans or non-binary studies that assume an able-bodied trans identity, on the one hand, and disability studies that assume a cisgender disabled identity, on the other hand. To complicate and enrich both areas of study it is imperative to problematize the ableist assumptions in trans anti-pathologization movements that stake out a claim for the normative ablebodiedness of trans bodies.

Non-binary Gender ID (Ecuador)

In Ecuador, trans people have demanded changes to the ID card regime for trans and non-binary people. Claudia Sofia Garriga-López (2016) has found that trans movements in Ecuador took advantage of President Rafael Correa's process of nation building to make legal changes regarding gender identification. A key participant in the process was a grassroots organization called Legal Patrol, founded in 2002 by law student Elizabeth Vasquez and trans sex worker Yelina Lafayette. Legal Patrol "supports the social, civil, and economic empowerment of trans sex workers in Quito" by informing trans sex workers in the streets of their legal rights. It challenges police abuses of trans sex workers through "direct interventions during altercations with the police, [and] public denouncements of police abuse" and engages with the police bureaucracy, providing "police sensitivity trainings, and the inclusion of guidelines for proper treatment of trans people in the police human rights handbook" (Garriga-López 2016, 105–6). The group mobilized under the slogan "Gender for All," arguing that sex is private and should not be forcibly disclosed via an ID card, whereas gender is public, affects everyone, and therefore should be on ID cards.

They achieved a new ID system in Ecuador, legislated through the 2015 Organic Law of National Identity and Civil Data Management; however, it is considered a partial win, as it retains a notation of the person's sex. An individual may (1) have the notation of sex removed and have no sex on their ID and/or (2) have it replaced with a gender of either "masculine" or "feminine" (Garriga-López 2016, 113). However, both options will indirectly mark a person as trans through either the absence of the sex notation in the first option, or reference to a binary notion of gender in the second.

We can understand this legislation in the context of the power of trans activism beyond the level of law and policy in influencing public opinion, changing police behaviours, education of trans sex workers, but also education by trans sex workers of those in the legal system regarding trans rights, and shaping a constitutional amendment regarding identity cards. Moreover, as trans people have gained the legal right to change their name on their ID in Ecuador, the number of trans people attending university and obtaining social benefits has greatly increased (Garriga-López 2016, 107).

Decolonizing Trans (North America)

In North America, Indigenous theorists Julie Depelteau and Dalie Giroux (2015) have found that colonization included a process led by the church, capitalism, and the state to suppress Indigenous modes of sex, gender, sexuality, intimacy, and relationship expression. Indigenous peoples have long practised a multiplicity of non-binary genders and sexualities, including fluid kinship, marital, and sexual arrangements. Historically, gender-variant people held positions of high esteem in Indigenous communities that practised "multiple-gender traditions" as well as nonpatriarchal family relations, including polygamy, same-sex marriage, divorce, remarriage, matrilineal lineages, and more (Depelteau and Giroux 2015, 65, 69).

Daniel Brittany Chavez (2016, 60) observes that "advances in multigender inclusion travel very differently between the Global North and the Global

South." Living in Mexico, and self-identifying as transmasculine, the author argues that his masculinity is misinterpreted by feminists as an embrace of patriarchy and stereotypical macho culture. Feminism in Chiapas, Mexico, he argues, relies on the gender binary to determine inclusion criteria, politics, and advocacy within movements, a transphobic practice known as transexclusion and denounced by transfeminists as trans exclusionary radical feminism (TERF). In Chiapas, trans exclusion is complicated through an intersectional emphasis on Indigenous inclusion within feminist movements, acknowledging the key role of Indigenous ciswomen within the Zapatista movement, including demands for access to contraception and security from domestic violence. However, Chavez (2016, 60–61) argues, "this should not come at the expense of diverse gender and sexual" identities, expressions, and politics. Adding to the complex intersectional layers of his activism and communities, Chavez has encountered trans solidarity from the Afro-descendant community, with which he also identifies. He advocates for reclaiming a two-spirit, decolonized trans identity to claim a "sovereign eroticism" (Chavez 2016, 63), a politics that can be strengthened through the formation of deeper solidarities of global intersectional transfeminist coalitions and alliances with ACAR and QTPOC commitments. Calls for decolonizing trans movements and conceptions are increasingly widespread, bringing Indigenous two-spirit sovereign eroticisms and intimacies to the forefront of 2LGBTQ+ movements (Boellstorff et al. 2014; TallBear and Willey 2019; Tallie 2014).

Travesti (Brazil)

Hailey Kaas (2016, 146), one of the first Latina transfeminists in Brazil, introduced the concept of transfeminism into the Brazilian context in 2012 through a Facebook page and blog at a time when there were neither transinclusive nor transexclusive feminist groups in Brazil. She wanted to avoid importing irrelevant US concepts but felt some concepts could be provisionally adopted by adapting them to the specific context and needs of Brazil (Kaas 2016, 148). Using the starting points of intersectionality and agency, Kaas worked to develop a Brazil-specific transfeminism toward the liberation of *travestis*, a non-binary identity specific to Brazil – again, like *khwahja sira*, not easily translated into English. The oppression of *travestis* is constituted by transphobia in the context of racism, poverty, and sex worker status (Kaas 2016, 148).

Joseli Maria Silva and Marcio Jose Ornat (2016, 222) have found that *travestis* and female transsexuals are among the most socially marginalized groups in Brazil, "marked by extreme social and economic exclusion" as well as being "the most vulnerable to violent and untimely death." Through ethnographic interviews with three people who identify as *travestis*, referred to through pseudonyms as Diamante, Perola, and Rubi, Silva and Ornat find that tensions arise in organizing within 2LGBTQ+ groups, as well as within trans advocacy groups, and the three interviewees are not in agreement on the best approach. Some activists oppose the adoption of a trans identity from "Anglo-American" institutions, against which they assert the more authentically Brazilian identity of *travestis*, while others prefer the identity of "trans," noting that there are new possibilities for medical and legal changes to one's gender and sex in Brazil.

According to Silva and Ornat (2016, 223), Perola, on the one hand, articulates a preference to remain *travesti*, preferring to articulate a position of gender subversion, whereas they feel that the identity of being transsexual has been accepted and "forgiven by society." Rubi, on the other hand, notes that adopting a transsexual or transgender identity might distance oneself from the association by the public of *travesti* "with prostitution, violence, poverty, and disease" (Silva and Ornat 2016, 223). Both Perola and Rubi articulate the difference between *travesti* and transsexual identities as a relationship to the body, the former rejecting bodily binaries, and the latter reserving the potential to conform to the gender binary when they so choose in some spaces and times.

Diamante articulates a third position, in which they choose to be *travesti* because they do not want to erase the long history of this subject-position. For Diamante, the relationship to the body is not a determining factor. They argue that although transsexuals may say they feel a disassociation with the penis, they still masturbate and take pleasure from it (Silva and Ornat 2016, 223). This articulates a complex relationship of both *travesti* and transsexual activists to the depathologization movement because many fear depathologization "might jeopardize their inclusion in the National Health System in Brazil" (Silva and Ornat 2016, 224).

Tensions also arise regarding the inclusion of *travesti* in the dictionary. Some transsexuals propose deleting the word altogether, whereas some *travestis* argue that it would erase their identity and history. *Travestis* thus use their identities to "resist gender norms, through epistemic disobedience, using one's own body as a battleground for the achievement of social recognition" (Silva and Ornat 2016, 224).

The movement foregrounding *travestis*, in advocating for a complex transformative gender paradigm appropriate to the multiple gender identities expressed and lived in the Brazilian context, demonstrates how attentiveness to intersectional global grassroots organizing is key to decolonizing trans movements. Indeed in the many complex debates articulated above in relation to trans and non-binary activism in different countries, we see the emergence of the trans body as a resistant communicative text generative of subversive gender epistemologies that contest not just transphobia but also EuroAmerican transnormativity.

2LGBTQ+ Technopolitics

Intersectional 2LGBTQ+ movements are generative of self-representations, working to confront the silos of identity they are presumed to fit into by society. Sasha Costanza-Chock, Chris Schweidler, and TMOP (2017) note the success of 2LGBTQ+ media mobilizations in the United States, emphasizing their "brilliance and resilience" while also noting continued experiences of oppression. For example, the *Undocuqueer* poster series created by undocumented queer and trans youth to represent their specific intersectional identities and shared on Tumblr through transmedia mobilizations served to challenge Trump's attacks on undocumented youth (Salgado n.d.). "Know Your Rights" pamphlets for 2LGBTQ+ youth developed and distributed in the streets, with condoms attached, have provided legal tips for handling themselves in interactions with police (Costanza-Chock, Schweidler, and TMOP 2017). These pamphlets have stirred up controversy and are disliked by the police themselves, who often, in my personal experience, do not respond well to individuals asserting their legal rights in the streets. However, at the same time, it is clearly important that people are aware of their rights and push back against police transgressions. These intersectional 2LGBTQ+ media productions, including analogue posters and pamphlets as well as digital transmedia and social media mobilizations, illustrate the complexities of the new queer and trans technopolitics.

Mangos with Chili (USA and Canada)

QTPOC movement building takes place in some instances through cultural production, which, according to Anabel Khoo (2014, 9–10) can create spaces of healing through public performances and relationship building with an ethos of love, countering intersectional homophobia, racism, transphobia, transmisogyny, capitalism, and colonialism with actions of care. Using this approach, the QTPOC group Mangos with Chili is creatively generating its own power rather than contesting existing power structures:

"Media production does not simply constitute forms of resistance or mere survival, but it also engenders deep transformation" (Khoo 2014, 6) and empowerment for individuals and communities. According to its Facebook page, the performance group, founded in 2006, aims to develop counter-power "through negotiations among non-normative identity, histories of colonialism, and spirituality." On tour, the group's media and art practices have offered "a complex politics and a set of practices that hold difference affirmatively while leaving enough space to imagine and enact new worlds" (Khoo 2014, 9). Prefigurative cultural politics are enacted through performance pieces, imagining new worlds and putting them on stage in embodied form as if they already exist. By doing so, they are bringing these worlds into existence, "offer[ing] a variety of media forms that together create a practice of worldmaking on stage" (Khoo 2014, 24). This queer worldmaking is reminiscent of the objectives and practices of Queeruption and Gay Shame, and explicitly foregrounds the 2LGBTQ+ intersections with race, colonialism, social class, and disability. The travelling performances also create collective autonomy through direct actions in self-organized tours and solidarity economies within the 2LGBTQ+ communities visited.

Love Is Love (USA)

Consistent with the emphasis on participatory 2LGBTQ+ collective self-representation in UndocuQueer and Mangos with Chili, an intersectional 2LGBTQ+ media project described by Lori Kido Lopez (2016) engaged participatory-action research with youth of colour in Madison, Wisconsin. They co-organized to develop the "Love Is Love" campaign with the objective of representing queer and non-binary Black and Hmong youth to raise visibility and naturalize 2LGBTQ+ identities within their communities. Working with Freedom Inc., youth in various groups, including "Black Beauties (Black girls), Nkauj Hmoob (Hmong girls), FreeMen (Hmong boys) and PLUS (queer Black youth) were asked what problems their community faced, and what it would take to make them feel healthy" (Lopez 2016, 232). In the consultations, many participants noted "a desire to see more images of happy, healthy queer people of color in their communities" (Lopez 2016, 232). In response, a media project to define, develop, and circulate these types of images was initiated. The project was started by a media researcher volunteering for Freedom Inc. who noted the organization did not have an overall media strategy but conducted most of its outreach by word of mouth. The development of the media campaign was conducted with consultation and ownership of the youth community. The outcomes derived from the co-development of media images in the process of research were "two-pronged, leading to skill development and capacity-building for the organization as well as learning for the larger targeted community" (Lopez 2016, 232).

The group decided to focus on creating printed posters and postcards featuring "images of queer people hanging out as part of the community, laughing, talking and looking natural" (Lopez 2016, 233). A staff member at Freedom Inc. took photos of youth who felt comfortable being featured in the campaign. The top six photos were selected in consultation with the youth community, and posters were developed with the slogan "Love Is Love" and additional messaging specific to each poster. A round of audience feedback among the broader community narrowed down the posters to those whose preferred reading was in line with the generated interpretations. The posters were then put up in the neighbourhood.

The project outcomes included building capacity and skills for strategic media campaigns for the organization itself and among queer and trans youth of colour; distributing images and messages in the community as a focal point for self-representation, with the objective of slowly shifting visibility and values; building acceptance within the broader community; and creating opportunities for community dialogues through the processes of production and soliciting audience feedback.

The project also "allowed the community to deepen its interactions with the actual stories depicted in the posters" (Lopez 2016, 239). Some participants in the project subsequently worked on the Out for Change: Transformative Media Organizing Project (Costanza-Chock, Schweidler, and TMOP 2017), while others went on to facilitate a webinar on media campaigns. Freedom Inc. moved forward to work on a participatory video production project. The "Love Is Love" project and the subsequent spin-off media projects together demonstrate the importance of digital media literacy campaigns as impactful technopolitical strategies among queer and trans youth of colour, following critiques of Khoo and others regarding the racialized digital divide that can sometimes exclude them from 2LGBTQ+ media production.

Gender Poo (Canada, Spain)

A strong flashpoint for genderqueer, trans, nonbinary, and gender nonconforming individuals is the so-called bathroom question. Which bathroom a person should use is not an easy question to answer, given all the barriers put in place by cisnormative societies. Some school systems in the United States, for example, refuse to allow non-binary or trans students to access the bathroom consistent with their gender expression or to provide gender-neutral bathrooms. Often trans people will be perceived as a threat when using the binary system of bathrooms standard in most countries. As Sheila Cavanagh (2010, 1–2) explains, "Anxiety about gender variance is keenly felt in public washrooms and often projected onto trans folk, . . . and nowhere are the signifiers of gender more painfully acute and subject to surveillance than in sex-segregated washrooms," despite the fact that "there is nothing rational or legitimate about gender panic in modern facilities."

The misperception by cisgender people, however, remains that there is something to be anxious about. As sexuality and gender scholar Cael M. Keegan (2016, 152) argues, "Cisgender women's physical protection from cisgender men continues to be the principal reason cited for sex segregation of bathrooms, although the current structure of most women's rooms does nothing to prevent ill-intended actors from entering."

In fact, the real problem experienced in bathrooms is that trans rather than cis people have something to fear. Antitrans aggression often leads to violent responses by cis people, ranging from verbal to physical assault of trans people, sometimes even resulting in death. In the United States, there have recently been "legislative attempts to prevent or criminalize transgender bathroom access in North Carolina, Utah, Minnesota, Texas, Kentucky, and Florida" (Keegan 2016, 152). Workplaces and schools in these states will only offer one binary set of bathrooms, and trans or non-binary people do not always feel safe accessing them. Sometimes, a workplace may designate a non-binary bathroom, but it might not be conveniently located or accessible to those who need it.

Moreover, people often assume "that all transgender people should ideally use men's rooms" (Keegan 2016, 152). As a case in point, Keegan cites the 2014 National Women's Studies Association (NWSA) conference in which the men's bathrooms were affixed with the supplemental label "gender-neutral bathroom" whereas the women's bathrooms were not presumed to be gender-neutral. This led to a great deal of confusion among conference attendees who wondered if trans women were then being directed toward the "men's + gender-neutral" bathroom, or if cis women should also use the men's room, and so on. When attendees attempted to move the "gender-neutral" sign so that it applied to both the men's and the women's rooms, the signs were repeatedly moved back to the men's side, without covering the original "men's" sign. The system of directing all non-binary people to the men's room "purports to keep cis women 'safe' while obviating transphobic harm" (Keegan 2016, 153). In other words, "trans women are faced with an impossible choice between two potentially treacherous situations: if a trans woman seeks to avoid [gender] policing, accusations, and possible violence in the women's room," presumably at the hands of transexclusionary radical feminists, "she can only do so by entering a 'neutral' space that immediately outs her and may expose her to violence by men" (Keegan 2016, 154).

Drawing attention to these issues, the *Gender Poo* multi-media arts project by non-binary artist Coco Riot (whose artwork is reproduced on this book's cover) produces a multitude of gender signs for bathrooms based on non-binary variations of the typical binary bathroom signs (Riot 2008). These have been exhibited at art shows in professional public art galleries, squatted social centres, and actual bathrooms. Additionally, the artist facilitates participatory creative events where people can design their own self-image as a toilet sign. There is an online gallery of the images, including representations of the various art show locations and other ephemera associated with the shows. The *Gender Poo* images and the various ways and spaces in which they have been made accessible highlight the intersectionality of trans experiences and oppressions while also rendering visible the wide range of trans bodies, on a variation of the body-as-media-text theme. The iconographic, self-embodied depictions of bathroom door signs serve to visualize Dylan Vade's gender galaxy and highlight the importance of self-representation, self-determination, and collective autonomy in creating public discourses and cultural counterpublics that contest gender binaries as social control. The use of the term "poo" in the title creates a playful child-like overtone to what is, in fact, a very serious piece of artwork calling attention to transphobic violence. The term evokes a similar juxtaposition of serious and playful qualities as the song by non-binary Canadian musician Rae Spoon, "Do Whatever the Heck You Want." These strategies push for the reclaiming of offline spaces, with online motility, for image systems that are intersectional, trans, non-binary, and gender non-conforming.

Blogueiras Feministas and Blogueiras Negras (Brazil)

Building a transfeminist movement, the Blogueiras Feministas (Feminist Bloggers) in Brazil have been writing about trans movements on their blog for some time. Some have received transphobic backlash on Google Groups, against which Google did not intervene (Kaas 2016, 148). As such, the 2LGBTQ+ movement in Brazil was found to be only partially supportive of the inclusion of *travestis* and transsexuals in their political advocacy agendas while also being resistant to the adoption of transfeminist principles more generally. Hailey Kaas (2016) concludes that the reluctance of feminist and 2LGBTQ+ movements to adopt an intersectional transfeminist perspective and to engage in solidarity struggles was evidence that a new type of organizing and expression was required.

For Kaas, intersectional approaches, as in the Mangos with Chili project described above, seemed to offer greater opportunities for coalitional trans mobilizations. She worked to develop an intersectional, transfeminist alliance with the "preeminent Black feminist group Blogueiras Negras [Black Bloggers in the feminine] – not only because they, as did we, denounced racist exclusions within feminisms that resemble our own but also because we identified ourselves with the same fight they were fighting: the same plight approached from distinct fronts" (Kaas 2016, 148–49). At the same time, issues of racism among some transfeminists as well as transphobia among some Black feminists tended to arise, posing a challenge to working intersectionally (Kaas 2016, 149). However, Kaas notes that the project continued to be an important intersectional, coalitional work in progress.

These two intersectional feminist activist blogs in Brazil illustrate a gradual shift toward integrating intersectional politics into 2LGBTQ+ organizing in combined online and offline spaces that produce a multiplicity of complex, intersectional subjectivities. They also illustrate the internal social movement complexities of working generally, foregrounding one aspect of identity or oppression, such as 2LGBTQ+ rights, while also mobilizing around and accounting for intersectional axes of oppression and identity such as colonialism, racism, misogyny, and the like. Tensions and contradictions can arise from these complex entanglements, particularly when it comes to online and offline intersectional representations.

#Free_CeCe (USA)

Mia Fischer critically analyzes the use of social media and offline organizing in the case of the #Free_CeCe hashtag activism movement, in which CeCe McDonald, a transgender Black woman in Minneapolis, was charged with murder after defending herself from a transphobic racist attack. #Free_CeCe is an example of a movement in which the transmedia mobilization can be equated to the movement. Fischer (2016, 756) argues that "social media do not miraculously provide transformative civic and political engagement because intersecting oppressions, particularly the centrality of whiteness in organizing, continue to permeate online activism." The Support CeCe Committee used a range of media and organizing strategies, including a social media campaign consisting of the hashtag #Free_CeCe, a blog where CeCe herself shared observations and reflections, and a concerted effort to use the slow spread of social media to reach mainstream and large independent outlets such as *Democracy Now!* These social media and mainstream media initiatives were combined with on-the-ground organizing, including occupations, protests, court solidarity, and more.

Although Fischer acknowledges the crucial role social media played in the campaign, she also finds that it was not a panacea but tended to replicate the domination of whiteness in queer and trans organizing. For example, although the committee members were multiracial, they were rooted in the 2LGBTQ+ community and did little outreach to the communities of colour in which CeCe lived. At the same time, Fischer notes that CeCe's story did not go viral on social media right away, and instead developed its virality gradually as a slow burn. This, she argues, is "illustrative of the socioeconomic and cultural stratification processes not only impacting access to communication technologies in general, but who gets to participate in determining and shaping what is considered spreadable, valuable, and newsworthy" (Fischer 2016, 782).

She finds that online movements engaged in connective action (Bennett and Segerberg 2012) are not strictly as leaderless, horizontal, or decentralized as they may appear, with some individuals playing key roles that might be considered "soft leadership" and with mechanisms that enable some people to do the mobilizing while others are being mobilized. Further, contra Lance Bennett and Alexandra Segerberg (2012), Fischer (2016, 785) demonstrates that in social movement organizing "the formation of collective action and identity processes are still highly relevant." She suggests that the collective voice articulated by the #Free_CeCe movement was crucial to its success in reaching mainstream media, mobilizing international support, and achieving a greatly improved outcome. While originally facing forty years in prison, CeCe McDonald was convicted of second-degree manslaughter due to negligence, sentenced to a forty-one-month jail term, and released after serving eighteen months.

Although this case brought the violence experienced by trans people of colour in everyday life and the judicial-legal system to national and international visibility, trans rights and lives are still under threat in the streets and because of judicial prejudice in the courts, and not just in the United States, where former president Donald Trump banned trans people from joining the military, but in many other countries. The intersectional approach of the #Free_CeCe campaign was partially successful, as CeCe's trans identity was highlighted in the media more than her racialization, poverty, or incarceration, the key intersectional elements of her identity.

Body, Text, Technology

What Mangos with Chili, the Indignados movement, and the transfeminist approach to body as text have in common is that intersectional politics are translated into art and technologies of the self; bodies become subjects of creative militant action in performative, hacker, and other technopolitical approaches; and intersectional 2LGBTQ+ media and technologies converge on the body to create cyborgian intersectional, technopolitical outcomes.

Spanish trans activists Lucía Egaña and Miriam Solá (2016) mobilize the rhetoric of Gilles Deleuze and Felix Guattari's (1987) "war machine" as well as that of hackers and the free culture movement to engage in a collective process of critical analysis of several transfeminist art practices developed in Barcelona. They do so through a process of research-creation that is engaged in activism for social change, supplementing more traditional research and activist forms by conceiving of the materiality of the transfeminist body as a site of political contestation, creative action, militancy, research, and social transformation.

Their work began to take shape in 2009–10 with their participation in two conferences (the Granada Feminist Conference and the Transfeminist Conference that took place in a squatted social centre in Barcelona) and the publication of a manifesto (Manifesto for the Transfeminist Insurrection). In video interviews with fellow artists and activists, they "discern two articulated axes of analysis," which they characterize as "dissident bodies and representations of gender and sexuality," on the one hand, and "technologies, free software, transfeminist machines, and networks," on the other (Egaña and Solá 2016, 75–76).

The cultural work of dissident bodies, the first axis of analysis to emerge from their mutual co-interviews, is described as

> cultural, visual, and performative works that operate principally through the body as a locus for political work. This includes work that explicitly focuses on sex and sexuality (postporn); representations of bodies considered by the dominant culture to be abject and/or deviant (disabled, trans intersex, fat); and works that use the body as a basis for resistance to normalized hetero-binary strategies of gender, sex, and sexuality.
>
> (Egaña and Solá 2016, 76)

These dissident bodies in performance have resonances with the performance art of Mangos with Chili, using bodies as sites of representation and resistance that produce new subjugated and resistant knowledges on, in, and through bodies as media texts. Their transmachinic assemblages are "projects, spaces, and works of cultural production that address technology as a site for feminist and transfeminist activism. Such works emphasize autonomy, self-instruction, DIY, peer networking, and empowerment" (Egaña and Solá 2016, 76).

Taken together, these articulated approaches, Egaña and Solá (2016, 78) argue, emphasize how the "preoccupation with the body and the construction of sexuality results in a composite of artistic practices and machinic processes, grounded in new understandings of sovereignty as it pertains to the body and to machines . . . [in which] the technological is, together with the body, a space from which to transform reality." They further suggest that when concepts such as autonomy, DIY, and free- and open source hacking are translated into transfeminist artistic practices, they "provide a new framework for thinking, manipulating, and modifying bodies and desires outside the framework of compulsory heterosexuality" (Egaña and Solá 2016, 78).

These frameworks in turn provide opportunities to "enact new corporeal practices and knowledge production through creative expression. They make new uses of the body and technology, which are themselves arenas for political action." Indeed, they figure the transfeminist body as an autonomous technology of self, defined by a revolutionary "politico-aesthetic relation" (Egaña and Solá 2016, 78).

This approach allows people with non-normative, non-binary, or gender non-conforming expressions of genders, sexes, and sexualities to construct autonomous self-identities and empowered subjectivities within liberatory, autonomous socio-cultural spaces, including the squatted Can Vies Social Centre in Barcelona, where one of the originary transfeminist conferences took place. These kinds of spaces, like the queer world-making projects of Mangos with Chili, Gay Shame, and Queeruption, counter the oppression and silencing that takes place within mainstream cultural spaces and funding mechanisms and instead foster, nurture, and support the existence of alternative transgressive bodies and sexualities as communicative actions and technologies with intersectional resonances and entanglements. These projects call for deepening our understanding of the intertwined technologies of racially and gender non-normative bodies as performative texts, as technologies of the self.

2LGBTQ+ Intersectional Technopolitics

Following these debates, the key dimensions of 2LGBTQ+ intersectional technopolitics enacted in 2LGBTQ+ social movements and media projects are shown in Table 7.

First, in intersectional 2LGBTQ+ movements, activists are engaged in many issues, such as marriage equality, queer visibility, and anticapitalism. Within 2LGBTQ+ movements, they/we challenge heternormativity (sometimes critiquing marriage), homonormativity, and transnormativity. Movements contest gender and sexual norms in society, challenging trans pathologization and heteronormativity. They/we also challenge racism in QTPOC antiracist movements and colonialism in two-spirit Indigenous movements, as well as fight trans exclusion and transmisogyny in transfeminist affinities.

Second, in terms of distributed online-offline architectures and motility, 2LGBTQ+ movements feature online-offline movements of artistic expression exemplified by the *Gender Poo* art installation and the performance art group Mangos with Chili. Technologies of the self, self-identity, and self-expression online make blogs and vlogs important sites of resistance, protecting queer and trans youth by providing spaces of anonymity. At the

Table 7 Key dimensions of 2LGBTQ+ intersectional technopolitics

Dimension	*2LGBTQ+ Intersectional technopolitics*
Intersectional and anticapitalist	Marriage equality; queer visibility; non-binary and gender-ambiguous; against trans pathologization, heteronormativity, homonormativity, and transnormativity; anticapitalist, antiracist QTPOC, and anticolonial two-spirit movements
Distributed online-offline architectures and motility	Online-offline movements of artistic expression; distributive networks; technologies of the self; blogs and vlogs; critiques of EuroAmerican LGBTQ+ practices and conceptual frames
Multiplicities of technologies and spaces	Technologies of the trans body as mediatized gendered resistance; spaces and technologies analog to digital; technologies of politics of exclusion at the intersection of trans and feminist movements; multiplicity of expression in gender and sexuality galaxies
Translocal solidarity economies and technologies	Technologies of systemic violence and erasure; solidarities and affinities; economies of mutual aid; affective economies; translocal specificity of laws, cultural practices
Collective autonomy through direct action	Collective autonomy; autonomy of embodiment and embodiment of autonomy; direct action of toilet interventions; individuality within collective action

same time, engaged negotiations including critiques of EuroAmerican queer and trans practices and concepts have arisen in Asia and Latin America.

Third, there are multiplicities of technologies and spaces at play, extending technologies of trans, non-binary, and gender non-conforming bodies as mediatized gendered resistances. 2LGBTQ+ intersectional spaces and technologies range from analog creative expression to digital transmedia mobilizations. Technologies of the politics of exclusion at the intersection of trans and feminist movements are called into question. A multiplicity of expressions in gender, sex, and sexuality galaxies foster the unique expression of each person's gender, sex, and sexuality, as illustrated in the *Gender Poo* bathroom signs.

Fourth, translocal 2LGBTQ+ solidarity economies and technologies challenge systemic technologies of violence and erasure through the development of intersectional accomplices, solidarities, alliances, affinities, and mutual aid. 2LGBTQ+ movements can be limited in translocal mobilizations because of the national specificity of legal frameworks, as well as particularities of social, political, and cultural practices, such as the *khwaja sira* people in Pakistan and *travestis* in Brazil, who develop local modes of resistance in global contexts.

Fifth, 2LGBTQ+ groups organize in collectives to establish autonomy through direct action, for example, Mangos with Chili, expressing the autonomy of embodiment and the embodiment of autonomy through theatrical performances that insert QTPOC bodies into the public sphere. Trans and non-binary activists also engage in direct actions contesting the binarized technologies of toilets, with *Gender Poo*'s participatory art project providing space for expression of one's own body as text in a bathroom icon within a broader collective action calling binary gendered bathrooms into question.

Contradictions and Debates

In the foregoing analysis, I introduced global 2LGBTQ+ intersectional movements and technopolitical media practices. Below, I provide critical analysis of some of the contradictions under debate regarding these aspirationally transformative social movement and media practices.

Political Economy

Many 2LGBTQ+ projects and groups only have recourse to funding through the problematic structures and processes of the non-profit industrial complex (NPIC). This access has both advantages and disadvantages. Scholars have pointed out that the NPIC is not a sustainable method for supporting intersectional media and social movement work because of its inconsistency, tendency to privilege dominant groups for grants, provision of only short-term funding, and failure to acknowledge intersectional issues, instead insisting on maintaining funding silos (Costanza-Chock, Schweidler, and TMOP 2017; Jeppesen and Petrick 2018; Khoo 2014). Further, as Bev Lepischak (2004, 96) observes, "Unfortunately the conditions of funding from government programs and foundations means that monies can be used only in specific and prescribed ways," resulting in a paternalistic and dependent effect tantamount to a creeping social control. She suggests that, "demands related to acquiring this funding, such as writing funding applications, reporting to funders, organizing fundraising events, and managing a donor base, limit time available for program-related activities" (Lepischak 2004, 96). People with media activist skills are diverting their time to grant writing, forcing them to learn a new skill rather than using their expertise to produce media in what is an already constricted media ecology for intersectional activists and representations.

Costanza-Chock, Schwidler, and TMOP (2017) find a troubling contradiction in the misalignment of community projects and available funding sources. They studied 2LGBTQ+ organizations in the United States, from grassroots groups with little or no funding to well-established organizations with hundreds of thousands of dollars in funding for their media and communications strategies. Their findings indicate that many organizations engage in intersectional services and campaigns, including the following: violence against trans people of colour; push-out from high schools of non-binary, gender-variant, or queer students; disproportionate policing, incarceration, and suicide rates among the 2LGBTQ+ population; economic disenfranchisement, poverty, and homelessness of 2LGBTQ+ people; sex work; Indigeneity; immigration status; disability; and more. However, funding envelopes available in the NPIC for 2LGBTQ+ organizations are not intersectional but siloed, offering funding related to one single issue. Therefore, in completing funding applications, groups and organizations must downplay the intersectional dimensions of their work. Moreover, as noted by Khoo (2014, 16–17), the NPIC works as much to fund as it does to circumscribe and control grassroots social movements through negative funding decisions, exacerbating the deep social and political impacts of intersectional oppressions.

Mangos with Chili, the group researched by Khoo, encountered issues with grants and funding similar to those mentioned by Costanza-Chock,

Schweidler, and TMOP (2017), whereby they had limited grant access because of what they perceived, experienced, and named as intersectional capitalist oppression within funding structures: "We feel that our work does not neatly fit into the visions of funders who operate under the white supremacist hetero[-sexist] ableist patriarchy" (Khoo 2014, 17). This statement corroborates the findings of the Media Action Research Group (MARG) collective that intersectional grassroots media groups are less successful at attracting grants than white, heteronormative, middle-class, cis-male-dominated independent media makers, an experience they identified as systemic intersectional oppression (Jeppesen and Petrick 2018).

Moreover, Khoo (2014) points to the impossibility of sustainable funding under the NPIC model, which requires constant grant writing and is therefore inherently not stable. Some employees would find themselves in the position of writing a grant for funds that would pay for the continuation of that very employment (Jeppesen and Petrick 2018). This compulsion to write grants or otherwise procure funding relates back to the experiences of freelance journalists and other media labourers in the precarious gig economy discussed in the Introduction, where media activists must move beyond media production or journalism into entrepreneurial business management, multi-media self-promotion, and the like. Consequently, the political economy of intersectional 2LGBTQ+ media production is constrained through systemic barriers to funding.

Transnormativities

Stereotypical mainstream representations of trans and non-binary bodies and oppressive legal frameworks regarding trans and non-binary rights mean that what circulates in the public sphere about trans and non-binary people can be quite limiting. Referencing South Korean transgender singer Harisu, theorist and activist Ruin (2016) uses a transfeminist analysis to argue that several features of trans representations in Korea result in "trans-normativities," defined as the maintenance of hegemonic social norms and life narratives for trans people. Zhe (Ruin's preferred pronoun) posits four dimensions of transnormativities that must be challenged by global trans movements.

First, through the "erasure of lived temporalities," trans people become trapped in a narrative of an identity temporally fixed in the mainstream imaginary, through which "trans people become beings without a social context, trapped within the gender role set by society," thereby reinforcing transnormative expectations. Countering this, transfeminists need to "explore the local temporalities of lived transgender lives, and to trouble and disrupt normativizing and hegemonic temporalities" for 2LGBTQ+ counterpublics as well as mainstream publics (Ruin 2016, 203–4).

Second, identity narratives within trans communities are also shaped by transnormative life histories that position medical treatment or surgery as a necessary step, excluding those who choose not to have surgery or otherwise medicalize their bodies from this narrative. Ruin identifies a contradiction here: on one hand, it is important to question the transnormativizing pressure to move from one fixed gender to the so-called opposite fixed gender because this reifies the gender binary, while on the other, the gender binary is important for some trans people who "attempt to enact hegemonic gender norms in striving to survive" during and after transition. In this sense, the risk is that "transnormativity both naturalizes discordant lives within hegemonic gender norms and at the same time excludes lifestyles, gender practices, and voices of any trans person who does not adhere to the norms, thereby containing or eliminating ways of being and living that threaten the norms." This leaves trans communities stuck in a circular debate regarding gender binaries with no single position being adequate to account for all trans experiences and identities (Ruin 2016, 205).

To take the third dimension of transnormativity, within trans-exclusionary feminism, we find repeated reference to a stable female gender and sex being required to work against misogynist oppression. This brand of feminism accuses trans people of reinforcing the misogynist norms of hegemonic feminine gender through superficial constructions of femininity that, they claim, only serve masculine desire. In this critique, feminist ciswomen stake a claim in destabilizing gender binaries through devaluing the hetero-masculine desire that they assume trans women seek. Moreover, perhaps contradictorily, this position implies that ciswomen always-already successfully inhabit an untroubled, static, hegemonic feminine gender that trans women may aspire to but will never fully achieve (Ruin 2016, 207). These are aspects of transmisogyny, defined as a particular form of misogyny enacted against transgender and transsexual women. A decision by the Korean Supreme Court in 2006 to allow gender changes has led many cis-dominated Korean feminist groups to express support for new transgender rights organizations, reducing the original feminist transmisogynist backlash.

The final dimension of transnormativity articulated in the Korean context is the dominance of EuroAmerican perspectives in trans studies. Within Korea, Ruin (2016, 206–7) notes that "most nontrans/nonqueer Korean feminists treat queer and transgender topics as being merely private and

trivial personal interests, rather than being significant to the very formulation of gender." This both echoes an assimilationist perspective while highlighting a key difference between EuroAmerican and Korean feminism,
revealing the asymmetric power relations between what zhe refers to as
"US/European" and "non-US/European" scholars, where trans theories
emerging from non-US/European sites such as Korea are relegated to the
position of exotic case studies or field reports marked as "Other" (Ruin
2016, 208).

Imbricated in non-US/European theorizing is the importance of language
and the issue of translation. Ruin notes that zher article was originally written
in Korean and translated into English. In addition, the article had to present
detailed explanations of the Korean context, presuming a non-Korean reader
would need this information and would not take the time to do contextual
research themselves, whereas a Korean reader of a US/European paper must
provide the context and history through their own background research as
this context is presumed to be common knowledge among all readers. Ruin
notes that through and because of this process, "I feel myself becoming marginal within my own writing." Trans activists, theorists, and scholars from
US/European contexts are thus called upon to be attentive to "hierarchies of
language or knowledge that exist between nations . . . [and] the politics of
translation" in order not to make assumptions about the generalizability
of their research, or to invisibilize non-US/European scholars and activists in
the field (Ruin 2016, 209, 210).

An Affinity of Hammers

Sara Ahmed (2016) also addresses issues related to inclusions of trans issues
within 2LGBTQ+ and feminist movements. She encourages consideration
of the possibility of creating affinities and becoming accomplices across
meta-issue movements. In "An Affinity of Hammers," Ahmed critically analyzes the recent platforming of anti-trans sentiment within the feminist
movement in the United Kingdom through the lens of a radical rethinking
of affinity. She reveals how the language of "silencing" and "free speech" is
used to defend anti-trans positions in a problematic reversal of the mobilization of these discourses – typically used by marginalized groups to claim
the right to speak out against systemic oppression – now being used from a
dominant perspective to exclude and oppress trans people.

Trans people are now being called "bullies" when they use free speech to
insist on their right to exist and not be subjected to anti-trans discourse and
trans exclusion. "In such a schema," Ahmed (2016, 24–25) argues, "dominant

views become rearticulated as if they are minority views that we have to struggle to express" rather than the status quo that is digging in its heels to exclude trans people from feminism. "Racism," she continues, rather than being silenced, "is enacted by the claim that we are not free to be racist" (Ahmed 2016, 25). Put another way, "to point out harassment is to be viewed as the harasser; to point out oppression is to be viewed as oppressive" (Ahmed 2016, 28).

A second mechanism used by dominant groups is the tactic of labelling people who stand up for their rights as violent, ignoring the fact that they are standing up against long-term violence that has been directed at them. "So much violence directed against groups (that is, directed against those perceived as members of a group) works by locating that violence as coming from within those groups" (Ahmed 2016, 26). Because daily structural and inter-personal violence is not perceived among people who come from dominant groups or groups with privilege, they only see that the oppressed group is upset. The fact that oppressed people are standing up against structural violence (of racism, of trans exclusion) feels threatening to those with privilege, because it is their group being accused of this violence. Rather than owning the structural violence by taking responsibility, being accountable, and trying to change dominant structures, people with privilege refuse to see the basic originary violence – even though they themselves may be complicit in committing it. Thus, they turn the tables to claim that those standing up against violence are themselves violent. However, Ahmed (2016, 26) argues, "to give an account of trans people as causing violence (by virtue of being trans) is to cause violence against trans people."

Through these two mechanisms, the concept of free speech is turned into a "political technology" that is only available to those who already have power: "Whenever people keep being given a platform to say they have no platform, or whenever people speak endlessly about being silenced, you not only have a performative contradiction; you are witnessing a mechanism of power" (Ahmed 2016, 27). Ahmed uses a Foucauldian (1988) analysis of the incitement to discourse on trans and race issues to expose the ways in which TERFs use privilege and power to speak in order to establish that they have no privilege or power. It is the privilege they already have that allows them to engage in endless speaking and to enact the very power they claim not to have.

The third mechanism Ahmed points to is the uncritical reference by feminists to "Biology 101" to reaffirm the "scientific basis of female and male sex difference," to which she replies, "Biology 101? Patriarchy wrote that textbook!"

She thus identifies the troubling reversion to a patriarchal biological deter-minism, which feminists have been pushing back against for decades. Rather than belabouring this fact with evidence from early feminists such as Sim-one de Beauvoir and others, Ahmed points to an important aspect of the "Biology 101" mechanism. She suggests that there is a constant reinvention of old ideas disguised as new reasons to exclude trans and non-binary indi-viduals from feminism – ideas and arguments that she refers to as "moving targets," impossible to engage with because when one argument has been exposed there will be another inserted in its place. For example, "trans women will become not women because they were socialized as boys and men, or for some other reason that has yet to be invented" (Ahmed 2016, 30).

Building on these three mechanisms of trans exclusion, Ahmed draws a few tentative conclusions. The first is that the popular public call to trans people to just sit down and have a friendly dialogue with TERFs is impossi-ble, when their very existence has been called into question and they have been threatened with violence by TERFs. In this instance, "a refusal to have some dialogues and some debates is thus a key tactic for survival" (Ahmed 2016, 31).

The demand for such a debate can only really come from those who have not witnessed the everyday violence against trans people. Ahmed calls (2016, 31) this everyday violence a "hammering," a "system that is constantly chipping away at your being." Moreover, she argues unequivocally that "a feminism that participates in that chipping away is not worthy of the name" (Ahmed 2016, 31). Feminism needs to be an inclusive transfeminism to properly engage in sex, gender, and sexuality anti-oppression work, as women and trans people are subjected to misogynist violence and murder at alarmingly high rates (Zengin 2016).

The global justice, anti-austerity, ACAR, and 2LGBTQ+ movements examined thus far have all introduced intersectional approaches that account for gender. In the next chapter, global movements and media that foreground intersectional transfeminism will be considered.

6 Transfeminism

On January 21, 2017, the day after Donald Trump's inauguration as president of the United States, I participated in a protest in Ajijic, Mexico, that was a translocal mobilization of the Women's March on Washington. In Mexico, the northern border of which Trump planned to wall off, protesters denounced the wall, while resident Americans pledged to use their social position – their nation-of-origin privilege – to fight the wall from both sides. In Washington, DC, over one million participants protested Trump's election – more than had attended his inauguration by some counts. Many wore the iconic pink, knitted "pussyhats," a playful yet serious contestation of Trump's infamous statement that he likes to grab women "by the pussy" when he meets them. This statement was critiqued by activists for its misogynist sense of male entitlement to women's bodies as well as its transmisogynist assumption that all women have a "pussy." Hundreds of solidarity protests took place in North America, Africa, Asia, Europe, and Australia to contest the anti-immigrant racism, sexism, and transmisogyny evident in Trump's election campaign. The protests thus exemplify the translocal, intersectional, transfeminist movements this chapter explores.

We can understand the complexities of intersectional transfeminist movements through the lens of contestations of gender oppression (feminine, masculine, and non-binary) across intersectional identities and structures, including race, class, sexuality, disability, colonialism, and so on, as discussed in previous chapters. When I use the term "feminism" without adjectives, I am referring to transfeminism, in other words intersectional trans-inclusive feminism.

SlutWalk and #MeToo are two recent transfeminist movements that bear examination as contestations against sexual assault and rape culture with an explicit focus on intersectionality. Intersectionality has been popularized in public discourse by the #MeToo movement, including the #TimesUp protest at the 2018 Academy Awards, contesting systemic sexual harassment and abuse in the film industry, signalled by the arrest of Harvey Weinstein. During her 2018 Oscars speech, Ashley Judd explicitly mentioned intersectionality, drawing attention not only to sexist power abuses in Hollywood but also to the ways in which many Oscar contenders that year had explicitly addressed intersections of gender, 2LGBTQ+, race, disability, and other issues. Her speech featured a montage linking filmic representations to systemic power structures, making connections between #MeToo and the anti-racist #OscarsSoWhite hashtag.

This moment signalled a shift in feminist movements toward transfeminism, a global feminist movement that foregrounds race, trans and non-binary gender, queer sexualities, social class, and decolonization. It also points to the growing importance in transfeminist movements of hashtag activism – the circulation of social justice hashtags in social media by activists and non-activists alike. The hashtag activism of #MeToo is possible because "females aged between 18 and 29 are the 'power users of social networking'" (Munro 2013, 23). In Turkey, for example, "women make up 72 per cent of social media users" (Munro 2013, 23). Some of these female users, along with trans, non-binary, gender non-conforming, racialized, and/or queer individuals and groups, have used social media to become intersectional transfeminist digital media activists. In #MeToo, while the digital medium is the movement (to paraphrase McLuhan), transfeminist movements have a long history; they did not suddenly emerge in response to the misogyny of Trump or Weinstein, but have been contesting misogyny for years through grassroots groups, NGOs, student centres, community organizations, legal-support networks, and so on.

Transfeminism today is a controversial field, contested both externally and internally. Externally, there is a backlash from men's rights groups and anti-feminist men and women who characterize themselves as victims of oppression by transfeminist women, as well as a backlash from post-feminists, again both men and women, who believe feminism to be an obsolete movement that has achieved gender equality, which is simply not true. Internally within the feminist movement there is a backlash by trans exclusionary radical feminists (TERFs) who oppose trans inclusion in feminism, as discussed earlier – a position transfeminism rejects – as well as a push back from mainstream feminist organizations who do not always consider intersections of Black, Indigenous, and people of colour (BIPOC), 2LGBTQ+, social class, disability, and so on. These controversies form part of the context in which transfeminist movements and media activism take place.

Transfeminist Movements

Intersectional transfeminist movements are in action across the globe today. International Women's Day (IWD) is a great example to start with – a translocal protest that takes place on March 8th each year to promote women's rights and accomplishments. In Montreal, IWD has been organized by the group Women of Diverse Origins (WDO), making visible transfeminist contentions that foreground antiracism and additional global issues. As a member of the group Block the Empire/*Bloquez l'Empire* I have spoken at the IWD march organized by WDO in Montreal when I lived there.

IWD emphasizes global women's issues, whereas some transfeminist movements are specific to local contexts. The Gulabi Gang or Pink Saris movement in India, four-hundred-thousand–strong, fights gendered sexual violence by wielding bamboo sticks to attack rapists (Desai 2014). The Indigenous Kichwa ecofeminists in the Ecuador Amazon, whom I have worked with briefly, resist a masculinist-capitalist approach to oil exploitation. Mainstream feminists To Mov in Athens, whom the Media Action Research Group (MARG) interviewed, provide information for female refugees about specific rights for women. The queer transfeminist group in Italy called Smaschieramenti, mentioned in Chapter 1, whom MARG also interviewed, organizes workshops for self-reflection and theoretical development to challenge dominant forms of masculinity and gender binaries. Dotterbolaget in Sweden provides space for feminist comic artists to share creative work, often as paid labour; a member who is an Indigenous Chilean artist living in Sweden, whom MARG interviewed, has created comics as a method to start conversations with refugee women who are survivors of sexual assault and domestic abuse. These varied examples demonstrate how the collective identity of transfeminist movements has deepened and expanded to include specific local and global intersectional issues that connect with gender.

Collective identity is at stake in intersectional transfeminist movements. For Verta Taylor and Nancy Whittier (1998, 349), "Collective identity is the shared definition of a group that derives from members' common interests, experiences, and solidarity." Collective identity in social movement groups is defined by Francesca Polletta and James Jasper (2001, 285) as "an individual's cognitive, moral, and emotional connection with a broader community, category, practice, or institution," where the communities and institutions are social movement organizations (SMOs). Collective identity is created through social movement organizing and it is thus a key factor in understanding "the relationship between group consciousness and collective action" (Taylor and Whittier 1998, 349). The collective identities of intersectional transfeminist movements thus emerge from three sources: the specific experiences of intersectional oppressions; articulations of intersectional issues by SMOs; and specific modes of transfeminist organizing. Transfeminism is particularly generative of anticapitalist, BIPOC, and 2LGBTQ+ actions that shape specific transfeminist collective identities. These are based on shared interests, solidarities, and emotional connections developed through mobilizations and media practices, some of which have been discussed in previous chapters. Taking an intersectional transfeminist approach allows groups to build "solidarity through mutable alliances by acknowledging the disparate positions of power women occupy" in profoundly different experiences of gender oppression in the context of other intersecting oppressions and structures (Lotz 2003, 6).

Anticapitalist Transfeminism

Intersectional anticapitalist transfeminist movements focus on gender exploitation and empowerment in the context of anticapitalism. Within anticapitalist movements, transfeminist separatist or "caucus" strategies are sometimes used, where groups organize along lines of shared identity, as seen in the feminist caucus of *La Convergence des luttes anticapitalistes* (CLAC) in Montreal. At the same time, intersectional anticapitalist transfeminist movements can be inclusive of male-identified accomplices (Y.-Z. Chen 2014, 198; Shannon 2009), as seen in the anticapitalist queer transfeminist group Smaschieramenti which specifically engaged in consciousness-raising workshops with participants of all genders to unmask masculinities in anticapitalist movements.

Queer Transfeminism

Rejecting the gender binary and valuing the lived experience of non-binary genders, including trans gender, gender-queer, pan-gender, non-binary, intersex, and more, queer transfeminism centres all genders and sexualities taken together as mutually informing axes of identity, oppression, and liberation that do not need to be yoked together in gender normativity or heteronormativity. Two examples of this are the queer transfeminist theorizing of Burnt Bras in Athens, and the equality committees of the Indignados movement; we can also refer back to the intersectional anticapitalist BIPOC and 2LGBTQ+ groups covered in Chapters 4 and 5.

ACAR Transfeminism

Intersectional transfeminism foregrounds feminism while also accounting for the context of ACAR movements that address a range of gendered oppressions from the macro-structures of racist and colonial nation-states to the everyday experiences of micro-aggressions (Chanicka 2018). Activist media challenge the representational violence of silencing, symbolic annihilation, stereotypes, and misinformation regarding gendered BIPOC peoples in the public sphere. Black Lives Matter and Sisters in Spirit in support of missing and murdered Indigenous women, girls, and trans people are two examples of intersectional antiracist and anticolonial transfeminisms, respectively, discussed in Chapter 4, both of which foreground race and Indigenous identity in the context of gender oppression.

Below, I map out two global intersectional transfeminist movements, SlutWalk and #MeToo, paying particular attention to intersectional practices and critiques.

SlutWalk

On April 3, 2011, a police officer at a street-proofing workshop at York University's Osgoode Hall Law School told women the best way to avoid being raped was to "avoid dressing like sluts," and several thousand people took to the streets of Toronto to oppose "slut-shaming, sex-shaming and victim-blaming" in a movement they called SlutWalk (Carr 2013, 24).

Co-founded by Heather Jarvis and Sonya Barnett, SlutWalk has built on but deviated from earlier feminist night marches. Reclaim the Night was started in Brussels, Belgium, in 1976, where two thousand women from forty countries attending the International Tribunal on Crimes against Women marched to contest violence against women and advocate for the right of women to feel safe walking alone at night (Carr 2013, 29). It would go on to become a global movement, which I participated in as a university student. However, there is a much greater consciousness around rape culture today, including development of the term "rape culture" itself. Rape culture includes a myriad of problematic but normalized behaviours and attitudes: disrespectful talk about women in bars and men's locker rooms;

silencing, objectification, and symbolic annihilation of women in media, reducing women to bodies without personhood; violent sexual attacks, including acquaintance rape, date rape, marital rape, stranger rape, stalkers, domestic violence, and ex-partner violence; sex trafficking and sex slavery; underage marriage; female genital cutting; sexualization of very young girls evidenced through terms such as *kinderwhore* (where *kind* is German for "child") or *prostitot* (Egan and Hawkes 2008; Oppliger 2008), and more.

Opposing rape culture, SlutWalk promotes sex positivity for diverse genders from intersectional antiracist, anticapitalist, anticolonial, disability, and sex worker perspectives. Participants assert sex positivity and bodily autonomy, turning the lens from shaming victims to shaming (predominantly male) perpetrators who should be taught not to rape. As Majdoline Lyazadi (2013, n.p.), an organizer and participant in SlutWalk Morocco, articulated, "Shame has to switch sides!"

SlutWalk participants assert bodily autonomy by presenting bodies as texts, bodies that are no longer available as commodities for consumption in the gendered spectacle of consumer culture and, by doing so, contest capitalism. In Brazil, a sex worker described how she became empowered through the SlutWalk March and subsequently felt able to publicly challenge a federal deputy making anti-sex-worker comments at a political debate (de Castro Ferreira 2015, 213–14). SlutWalk was, for her, both intersectional and liberatory in its organizing modes and claims-making practices, opening a space for the articulation of the subject position of "slut" through sex positivity from an autonomous, sexual labour perspective. In mobilizing the body as text, intersectional SlutWalk protest participants reclaim the racialized-gendered body, rejecting capitalist commodification in the context of patriarchal, cis, racial, and colonial domination, while simultaneously regenerating bodies as sites of liberation, play, self-expression, political manifesto, and sensuality, generating a global, queer, antiracist, transfeminist, collective body politic responsive to and generative of the desires of a new generation.

Spreading globally from the first SlutWalk in Toronto, Canada, SlutWalks have taken place in over fifty cities globally, foregrounding local issues and events related to the overall contestation of rape culture, and, as such, exemplifying translocal mobilizations.

India

SlutWalks have taken place in India, where the word "slut" is used "against women who go out in the evening or take jobs at call centres" (Carr 2013,

26). This usage links women's empowerment through getting an education and achieving economic independence through work to a presumed negative sexuality, making her available as a potential victim for sexual assault. In India, "a group of young women were sexually attacked in a pub in Mangalore by men who called them sluts" (Carr 2013, 26). In New Delhi in 2012, twenty-three-year-old pharmacy student, Jyoti Singh, who had been out in the evening to see a movie with a friend, was brutally gang-raped and murdered on a bus, an incident reported extensively in global media. Intersectional systems such as patriarchal culture, class structures, and social norms, including the caste system, foster specific forms of violence against women in India that include "female infanticide, female feticide, dowry violence, and honor killings" (Carr 2013, 26). As Mary John (2020, 138) argues, women are "up against a state formation that is the most hostile to gender equality and social justice in the history of modern India." These issues were at stake in the SlutWalk in India, where organizers decided to drop the emphasis on adopting a "slut" identity in terms of the type of clothing embraced in the original Toronto SlutWalk: "Instead they would carry placards emphasizing the original message of the global SlutWalks, i.e. that all women have the right to safety, to not be harassed or sexually attacked regardless of how they are dressed" (Banerji 2011, n.p.). This connected the various India SlutWalks to the global movement contesting rape culture while expressing concerns in locally appropriate, autonomous ways, making it an example of a translocal mobilization.

Hong Kong

In Hong Kong in 2014, the Umbrella movement converged to embrace the strategy of SlutWalk. The practice of disorderly, aesthetic, feminist guerilla protests, like Bakhtin's carnivalesque that subverts the social order, does not always subvert the form of that which it calls into question. Instead, it aims to precipitate "unpremeditated social encounters or ideological debates" (Jacobs 2016, 823) generative of an "affective feedback loop" with the audience. This takes place both online and offline, in public spaces such as the squares occupied in the 2014 Umbrella movement and the SlutWalk movement in Hong Kong. The outpouring of images printed on cardboard placards worn by participants in the SlutWalk march reveals that this was a "multi-tiered movement in terms of a coalescence of different activist groups, age groups, ethnic and sexual minorities, media outlets, artist collectives and personalities who all at once were trying out various methods of activism" (Jacobs 2016, 825). Bodily guerilla images become "affective mediums that force viewers to interrogate their own subjectivity and emotions in relation to other subjects and other social formations" (Jacobs 2016, 823). The messages inscribed on the body are searching for an authentic, self-determined expression of sensuality and sexual pleasure while simultaneously documenting and denouncing sexual abuses that are often denied, silenced, or even perpetrated by functionaries of the state (Jacobs 2016, 824). The SlutWalk movement provided a script for non-binary bodies made available by and for participants – reclaiming bodily autonomy and refusing the logic of rape justification based on clothing choice.

United States

Transfeminists also engaged critically with SlutWalk. In the United States, the Black Women's Blueprint collective contested the very possibility of reclaiming the subject position of "slut" for racialized women. First, they argued that it is impossible for Black women to identify with the term "slut" because of the historical racialized-gendered experiences of Black women under slavery and its legacy: attitudes, behaviours, and representations through which "the trivialization of rape and the absence of justice . . . are tied to institutionalized ideology about our bodies as sexualized objects of property, as spectacles of sexuality and deviant sexual desire" (Black Women's Blueprint 2016, 10). Second, Black women's experiences and histories are often omitted from mainstream (white-dominated) feminist movements through "what has historically been the erasure of Black women and their particular needs, their struggles as well as their potential and contributions to feminist movements" (Black Women's Blueprint 2016, 11). Reclaiming the term "slut," moreover, rather than making Black women feel safer and shifting the attitudes and behaviours of men, retrenches hegemonic ideologies of women as sluts, which, they argue, is more dangerous for Black women than it is for other targets of gendered violence (e.g., white women), who do not experience the oppression of racism in the context of rape culture.

United Kingdom

In the United Kingdom, a negotiated antiracist intervention in SlutWalk drew attention to Islamophobia in the context of rape culture. Jason Lim and Alexandra Fanghanel (2013) conducted a participatory ethnography at the 2011 London SlutWalk, interviewing participants in a breakaway march called Hijabs, Hoodies and Hotpants (HHH), advocating the right to wear any type of clothing – slutty or modest, masculine or feminine – and be free from police brutality, street harassment, physical or sexual assault, and rape. HHH participants developed a negotiated decoding and re-encoding of SlutWalk to participate on their own terms, emphasizing racialized and religious intersectional transfeminist subject positions. They agreed with the organizers' anti-rape politics but, like organizers in India and the Black Women's Blueprint, they distanced themselves from the subject position and clothing choices linked to the term "slut." Three different clothing types indicated feminine Muslim (hijabs) and Western (hotpants) forms of dress, as well as masculine (hoodies) forms of dress that have played a role in police profiling of racialized-masculine bodies. This complexity is indicative of the broadening of transfeminist movements to account for the policing-through-objectification of racialized men's bodies and masculine gender issues more broadly.

Moreover, HHH pointed to the obvious myth, nonetheless often perpetuated, that rape is caused by clothing. As one participant, Aishah, said, rape "has absolutely nothing to do with what you wear, and loads of women that are covered head to toe get raped" (as cited in J. Lim and Fanghanel 2013, 211). Further, whether a woman is wearing a burqa or a miniskirt, as participant Saad notes, "she should not even get raped because it is her body, and she gets to choose what she wants to do with it" (as cited in J. Lim and Fanghanel 2013, 211). Another interviewee, Nadiyah, clarified that "being a slut is a state of sexuality, it is not a dress code at all. Even if a girl was to go out wearing a crop top and small shorts and heels . . . [it] doesn't make that woman a slut at all" (as cited in J. Lim and Fanghanel 2013, 213). In these arguments, the HHH participants are making an important distinction between sexuality and bodily presentation, including clothing, something they had felt was being conflated in the SlutWalk protest, which they challenged through their breakaway march.

Participants in HHH thus both embraced and rejected a "slut" subjectivity, contesting victim-blaming and clothing-profiling myths and foregrounding bodily autonomy. Their breakaway march also drew attention to the racialization of sexuality and gender, pointing to their double position within British society, contesting racialized-gendered violence in the context of Western Islamophobia. They suggested parallels by which "the feminine body is controlled and policed through rape discourses in both 'Western' and 'Islamic' contexts" (J. Lim and Fanghanel 2013, 212). This double position means that "if a certain distance is staked out from the hypocrisies of 'Western' liberal discourses, then it must be remembered that a certain distance is also being staked out from discourses of the 'good Muslim' and especially from the quiescence demanded by conventional constructions of the Muslim femininity" (J. Lim and Fanghanel 2013, 214). In other words, in joining SlutWalk in HHH, this group of youth proposed a rethinking of sites of pleasure and desire, "a deterritorialization that reminds us of the real and potential multiplicity of sexual expression" (J. Lim and Fanghanel 2013, 214). This negotiated subjectivity that accounts for genders, races, and religions embodies an intersectional transfeminist position.

The complex translocal discursive and embodied mobilizations of SlutWalk – including by groups who found it liberatory in Canada, Brazil, and Hong Kong; groups who mobilized oppositional antiracist critiques in the United States; and groups who negotiated their participation in Delhi and London – have raised important discussions about the intersections of gendered violence in the context of racism and religion. Moreover, they have raised questions regarding the continued dominance of whiteness in intersectional transfeminist movements. This dominance may inadvertently revert to ornamental intersectionality (Bilge 2016). The oppositional and negotiated engagements with SlutWalk work to centre antiracism and non-Western experiences and epistemologies in sexual assault and rape-culture contestation. The critiques brought by youth point to another axis of import: "Slut-Walks can also be situated within the recent wave of worldwide grassroots protest movements led by young people that appear to be organized through and fueled by social media" (Carr 2013, 29).

Transfeminist Technopolitics

Social media is fast becoming a dominant forum for feminist organizing, offering crucial affordances, including protest-media affordances mentioned in earlier chapters, as well as space for gendered self-expression and sociality and affective communication in community. Here, I consider the role of digital media and technologies in intersectional transfeminist movements. Feminist engagements with the body as a self-mediated text, and with social media, will be considered as part of an emergent feminist praxis of social reproduction and affective labour that recentres voices of intersectional BIPOC, 2LGBTQ+, and diversely gendered participants.

Recent waves of anticapitalist transfeminist contention have embraced networked technologies to support translocal feminist work within broader social movements, developing media practices that have played a significant role in shaping these broader waves of contention. Four entangled intersectional transfeminist media practices have emerged in conjunction with previously discussed modes of technopolitics: the gendered body as protest text, cyberfeminism in digital media, transfeminist technopolitics in 15M, and the intersectional hashtag activism of #MeToo.

The Gendered Body as Protest Text

"Bodies are powerful sites of resistance" (O'Keefe 2014, 3). While feminists have long advocated for bodily autonomy (Jeppesen and Nazar 2012), intersectional transfeminism challenges the policing of female and non-binary bodies through interventions imprinted on the body, quite literally embodying resistance. These imprinted messages are intersectional by design: "the body is very much a contextualized product of the relationship between capitalism, patriarchy, racism, colonialism and other systems of oppression" (O'Keefe 2014, 3). Already marked by intersectional identities, bodies intervene against intersectional oppressions, and in the process, "bodies in protest are important sources of knowledge for movement development" (O'Keefe 2014, 3). As such, they produce embodied, contestational epistemologies.

SlutWalk participants used their bodies to convey anti-rape-culture messages through clothing or other identifiers inscribed on the body. As noted in Chapter 3, Quebec Student Strike participants presented near-naked bodies-as-texts in the Naked March, drawing attention to student poverty in the context of gender. In Hong Kong, women have used full or partial nudity to contest misogyny in the pro-democracy Umbrella movement (Jacobs 2016). In the global justice movement, women arrested in Washington at the 2000 International Monetary Fund (IMF) protests, in which I was a participant, refused to enter the courtroom and, when forced to do so, stripped naked in protest. In Russia, Pussy Riot has created embodied spectacles to simultaneously draw attention to and close off readings of their bodies through balaclava masking and other performative tactics.

As these global examples illustrate, bodily contestation has a long feminist history. Examining "disorderly aesthetics," Katrien Jacobs (2016, 821), a cultural studies scholar at the Chinese University of Hong Kong, suggests that "actions are successful if they solicit reflection and dispute about the issues." In her study of feminist interventions against sexual abuse in China, she finds that "Chinese feminists have engaged in a type of 'fleeting' guerilla theatre or performance art in which they used their bodies, along with costumes and props, in order to intervene in public spaces" (Jacobs 2016, 821). Posting carefully curated photographs, they combine protest messages with new erotics to create "online nudity activism as a type of transient statement that stirs people to think about the body and its sexual pleasures or discontents" (Jacobs 2016, 822).

SlutWalk also engaged in a politics of gendered body as text: "To purposefully disrupt the normalising sexualising gaze upon the female body, the crowds at the SlutWalks dressed up in all manner of clothing," with body paint and artistic messages inscribed on bodies (Ringrose and Renold 2012, 334). Participants were creative and the bodies at play included "differently raced and classed, girls and women (and boys and men)" (Ringrose and Renold 2012, 335) and non-binary genders. This re-signified the word "slut" as a power position embraced by a multiply gendered collective subject, "refusing the destructive and projective force of 'slut shaming'" (Ringrose and Renold 2012, 335). Thus, the collective body-as-media-text asserts a collective identity that recodes and reconstitutes power relations: "The gendered body in protest can be used to manipulate, challenge and seize the power that seeks to confine and define it" (O'Keefe 2014, 4). At the same time, circulated images can risk reifying the heteronormative, cisnormative objectification of women in mass media, which can be intensified across race and other intersections. However, SlutWalk participants refigured themselves not as sexual objects for the commodification and consumption of others but as sexual subjects for their own autonomous pleasures and desires through body/self as text.

Mediatizing the reclaimed autonomous, transfeminist body (of all genders) opens a space for participants, liberated momentarily from rape culture, to become immersed in the play and pleasure of a multiplicity of embodied, sensual, self-expressed sexualities, sexes, and genders. Intersectional transfeminist movements using body-as-text are not just in the streets – they are also taking up digital spaces.

Cyberfeminism

Communications scholar Ellen Balka (1999, 1) recalls the work of "feminist information technology critics" of the 1970s who engaged in research and activism "aimed at assessing the impact on women of information technologies." In addition, they worked toward "mitigating the potentially adverse effects of new computer technologies on women" in the workplace and in the home. These skeptical critiques gave way in the 1990s to cyberfeminism.

The cyberfeminist movement emerged as a critique of anti-technology feminism. Donna Haraway (1991, 165) famously suggested that the cyborg is postgender, with the distinction between humans and machines blurring as we increasingly embed technologies in our bodies, collapsing the binary between not just body-text, as above, but also body-technology: "Communications technologies and biotechnologies are the crucial tools recrafting our bodies. These tools embody and enforce new social relations for women world-wide." She critiques the informatics of domination, a binary, Western, patriarchal, racist, imperialist, and technologically determinist technological system characterized by "a massive intensification of insecurity and cultural impoverishment, with common failure of subsistence networks for the most vulnerable" (1991, 172). To this informatics of domination, she opposes the transgressive intersectional politics of women in informatics and envisages "grounds for hope in the emerging bases for new kinds of unity across race, gender, and class" (1991, 173).

This intersectional vision of cyberfeminism goes beyond living a feminist life online. According to Carolina Branco de Castro Ferreira (2015, 201), cyberfeminism can "be defined as a set of aesthetic-political-communication strategies oriented towards electronic culture, and above all, the internet and digital technology." International development scholars Radhika Gajjala and Annapurna Mamidipudi (1999, 8) argued that "cyberfeminists share the belief that women should take control of and appropriate the use of Internet technologies in an attempt to empower themselves" beyond, as they humorously observe, "shopping via the Internet." Jessie Daniels (2009, 101) further suggests that, in cyberfeminism, "Internet technologies can be an effective medium for resisting repressive gender regimes and enacting equality."

These scholars, from a range of disciplines, generations, and global locations, collectively assert three key dimensions of cyberfeminism. First, cyberfeminism is a set of intersectional antiracist, anticolonial, queer, transfeminist strategies for communicative action. Second, these strategies are used by many different groups of feminists for collective empowerment through taking control of technologies, particularly the internet. This means that rather than seeing themselves as end-users of technology (e.g., online shoppers, social media users), cyberfeminists seize the means of production of technology, at the design and coding phases, mobilizing in the technopolitical movements of hacktivism, cyberactivism, and more. Third, these sociotechnical strategies are both aesthetic and political, culturally reinventing racialized-gendered digital image systems and challenging global power structures embedded in the racialized, colonialist binary sex-gender system.

Transfeminist Technopolitics in 15M

A specific example of cyberfeminism is the rise of intersectional transfeminist action in the 15M movement in Spain, discussed in Chapter 3, using the everyday body as text for protest messages, engaging a transfeminist technopolitics as a key component of the repertoire of communicative action: "The work of the feminist groups in the 15M was nourished by the activist legacy of the Spanish feminist movement during the first years of democracy, but also by an infrastructure that came into being in Spain in the 1990s, cyberfeminism" (Gámez Fuentes 2015, 362). This included online portals and spaces for feminists to engage in and contribute to the development of technopolitics. Transfeminist organizers thus had key impacts within the Indignados, including contributing pivotal organizational strategies and debate interventions (Gámez Fuentes 2015). But not at first.

At first, feminists in the 15M protest camps "encountered numerous difficulties in making themselves visible and heard" (Gámez Fuentes 2015, 360). They faced structural violence, both within the organizing of the protest camps in the squares and in discussions and decision making in the general assemblies (GAs). They identified six elements of structural gendered violence in the camps: (1) "lack of representation in committees and assemblies," (2) "patronising behavior," (3) "sexist stereotyping," (4) a rejection of women's demands as personal concerns rather than political issues, (5) "undermining of women's demands" once articulated, and (6) "sexual, sexist and homophobic aggression" (Gámez Fuentes 2015, 360). In Madrid, the Feminist Committee hung a banner that read "The revolution will be feminist or no revolution at all," and they read a statement at the GA that they would not spend any more nights in the camp because of their concerns and experiences (Gámez Fuentes 2015, 360). Other activists attempted to remove the banner and denounce the feminist concerns as not relevant to the 15M movement.

Promotion of transfeminist objectives, however, gained traction over time: "Feminist groups in the public protests and on the web have emerged as discordant voices, re-activating the Spanish feminist movement as political subjects and contributing to repositioning the very knowledge on social justice defended by the 15M" (Gámez Fuentes 2015, 361). Feminists within 15M engaged in a double militancy, promoting feminist concerns in shaping 15M's anticapitalist objectives, demands, and strategies while working in feminist movements to promote intersectional, anticapitalist, queer, and transfeminist issues, including antiracism, migrant and undocumented rights, and so on.

The double militancy of intersectional transfeminist activism was mobilized not just through protests and square occupations, which were organized on the ground using transfeminist strategies, according to activists whom MARG interviewed, but also through cyberfeminist engagements online as part of the free culture technopolitical approach of 15M. One of the key hacktivist groups in 15M was Xnet, a collective that supports internet freedoms, its members engaging in hacktivism, technopolitics, and guerrilla communications. Xnet integrated an intersectional transfeminist ethos into its transformative media practices, with several feminist women, men, and 2LGBTQ+ participants. It relied on three key practices: the 1–9–90 principle, the liberation of activists, and distributive organizing.

First, the 1–9–90 principle is the observation that 1 percent of internet users are producers who create content, including coding, digital design, text production, videos, podcasts, livestreaming, live tweeting, and so on; 9 percent are aggregators who comment, repost, retweet, aggregate content, and the like; and the majority, 90 percent, are passive lurkers who simply consume media. Xnet participated intentionally as the 1 percent, creating content at the deepest levels, including coding and shaping technologies through social organization.

Second, the liberation of activists is an explicitly anticapitalist practice in which individuals' subsistence is paid for a year, liberating them to participate freely in transformative media and movements as they see fit, without having to engage in exploitative wage labour in the capitalist economy.

Third, 15M was a distributed network, creating multi-nodal communicative patterns and opportunities from every node in the network to every other node. Monterde and colleagues (2015, 940) have found that "the 15M community creates an identity that cannot be confined to one or a few network subgraphs, for it emerges as a complex whole from a network of distributed interactions." There was no centralization or hierarchy, nor was there decentralization or coalescence of power into subgroups. Rather, in distributive networks, the objective is to distribute power equally among all nodes and all participants. Xnet producers attempted to move lurkers from the 90 percent into the 9 percent of aggregators by providing instructions for coordinated, engaged media practices to achieve trending topics, as described above in the anti-austerity chapter. Once in the 9 percent aggregator group, it would be easier for media activists to shift into the 1 percent by joining Xnet or other groups in which people played an active role in media content production, digital engagement, and movement mobilization.

Through this process, Xnet attempted to reshape the distribution of technopolitical practices toward the more fully expressed horizontality of distributed networks of media activists. A distributed network of translocal mobilizations also helped shape the #MeToo movement.

#MeToo

The global mobilizations of #MeToo have shaped and been shaped by the affordances of hashtag activism. Hashtag activism has grown from its previous conception as a form of armchair "slacktivism" by lurkers, or "clicktivists," who sign petitions with a click but do not engage in collective action. Hashtag activism now consists of much more intense and engaged forms of participation in which social transformation takes place through the process of digital participation itself. Communications scholars Kaitlynn Mendes, Jessica Ringrose, and Jessalynn Keller (2018, 237) find that "digital feminist activism is far more complex and nuanced than one might initially expect, and a variety of digital platforms are used in a multitude of ways, for many purposes."

As we have seen in the intersectional transfeminist mobilizations analyzed above, such as the cyberfeminists in 15M, digital media has become so integrated into social movement organizing that the 15M activists MARG interviewed all noted that the movement would not have been conceivable without its digital technologies and practices. This is the same with hashtag activism, particularly with the advent of #MeToo. The #MeToo movement is a hashtag – an ephemeral, virtual digital space, visible almost exclusively online. #MeToo has not organized protest marches; nor does it have chapters, camps, general assemblies, or other organizational structures; nor is it a hybrid movement with online-offline synergies or choreographies of contention as seen in 15M, the Arab Spring, Quebec Student Strike, or Black Lives Matter (BLM). In other words: the movement is the medium, and the medium is the movement.

If #MeToo is both a hashtag and a movement, we might ask: Where are the organizers, and who is mobilizing it? #MeToo is unique as a movement without organizers or an organization. But it does have two origin stories. The #MeToo hashtag was originally started in 2006 by Tarana Burke, a queer woman of colour from Brooklyn. According to Alison Gash and Ryan Harding (2018, 21), Burke envisaged creating empowerment through developing empathy with "a catchphrase to be used from survivor to survivor . . . [in] a movement for radical healing." Burke started #MeToo not because it would be an easy thing to say to someone disclosing sexual assault but because it often seems so difficult.

In Burke's conception of the hashtag, what we might call a "hashtag imaginary," she suggests that radical healing is challenging because it is hard to talk about sexual assault in the context of a general silencing. In this context, survivors (women, men, and non-binary) "are either forced to resolve, on their own, the cognitive dissonance of *appearing* unharmed while *feeling* brutalized, or risk being accused of lying or exaggerating when they seek assistance" (Gash and Harding 2018, 30). Burke's call for radical healing is also highlighted by the BLM movement, covered in Chapter 4, highlighting the intersectionality of both movements. For BLM and for Burke, radical healing can only take place when survivors speak out about their experiences, through instances of disclosure, collective speak-outs, storytelling, and narrativization in the context of movements for social justice. This narrativization is the modus operandi of the #MeToo movement. However, as Burke anticipated, it was difficult, as people did not see the point or the possibility of disclosing sexual assault online. The hashtag languished, gaining minimal tweets for more than a decade.

The second origin story was more of an explosion. On October 24, 2017, in the wake of Harvey Weinstein's arrest and revelations of the depth of sexual abuses in Hollywood, #MeToo was retweeted by celebrity Alyssa Milano, encouraging anyone who had experienced sexual assault to simply retweet it to show the depth of the issue. Her objective was to establish that Weinstein was not one bad apple but that sexual assault and abuse is a pervasive, systemic issue: "The hashtag was [then] used 12 million times in the first 24 hours alone" (Mendes, Ringrose, and Keller 2018, 236). Milano is often credited with starting the #MeToo movement. Both her social location as a white celebrity and her objective in tweeting #MeToo were different than Burke's. For Milano, "the purpose was to demonstrate the magnitude of the problem of sexual degradation" (Gash and Harding 2018, 23). Milano wanted to show that sexual abuse, harassment, assault, and rape were common, ongoing, systemic, global occurrences.

With these two origin stories, both Burke and Milano are often acknowledged as the two people who initiated the #MeToo movement. They appeared together on the *Today Show* in December 2017, when *Time* magazine announced "the silence breakers" as their person of the year. However, their two different approaches to #MeToo bear further attention.

Milano is involved in an offshoot of #MeToo, the Hollywood #TimesUp movement, which "seeks to fund legal action against perpetrators of sexual harassment, discrimination, and assault" (Rodino-Colocino 2018, 99), particularly men in positions of power whose workplace actions can limit or destroy career opportunities for those they target. Milano's "hashtag imaginary" in both #MeToo and #TimesUp focuses on recourse within the legal-justice system, funding cases to try to improve legal outcomes. Today, despite clear laws against sexual assault in many countries, very few survivors go forward with their cases, largely because of the ineffectual process of many legal systems, which often results in revictimization, victim blaming, disbelief, rejection of the facts, and low conviction rates. Additionally, if the perpetrator is known to the survivor, as in workplace or domestic cases, there may be a reluctance to prosecute because the survivor might lose their job or partner, both cases having economic repercussions. The focus in #TimesUp on bringing perpetrators to justice is therefore an uphill battle to change everyday practices in the legal-justice system to be in line with the letter and intent of laws achieved by second-wave feminists in the 1970s, or to change and improve sexual assault and harassment laws. This approach also faces hurdles in encouraging women experiencing workplace or domestic sexual abuse to risk coming forward when they have so much to lose.

Tarana Burke's approach focuses not on legal justice but on healing justice. She leads a project called Me Too (without the hashtag) that engages in face-to-face healing justice and sexual-assault support, focusing on survivors. Burke's community work "demands centering marginalized communities in public discourse to heal individuals and highlight systems of oppression that sexual violence serves" (Rodino-Colocino 2018, 98). Moreover, Burke aims to mobilize empathy that "incites one to action" (Rodino-Colocino 2018, 98). Her work focuses on consciousness raising and community activism in racialized communities that are even less likely than the general population to have success or trust in the legal system. Thus, Burke focuses on peer solidarity and support through community and interpersonal dialogues and workshops, mobilizing, as BLM does, a healing justice movement in which participants heal from sexual assault while also engaging in community organizing against rape culture.

Hashtag Imaginaries in #MeToo

To better understand the importance of these two distinct approaches to #MeToo, it is helpful to consider the concept of protest media imaginaries (Treré, Jeppesen, and Mattoni 2017). This concept brings together three distinct notions from three different fields: social movements, media practices, and the social imaginary. "Social imaginary" describes how a collectivity conceives of its social surroundings or "how shared meanings circulate among different groups" (Treré 2019, 106). If media practices are everyday interactions with media and technologies – and, for social movements, these take place in the context of communicative action – then considering movements, practices, and imaginaries together allows us to investigate how media activists imagine the media and technologies they are using, the myths created around them, and what they believe the specific technologies can achieve. Investigating hashtag imaginaries should, therefore, allow us to develop a deeper understanding of how hashtags are conceived, used, to what purposes, and why.

The two hashtag imaginaries of Burke and Milano, while coalesced around the same hashtag, can be seen to develop different myths, actions, motivations, and objectives. Tarana Burke's may be conceived of as a healing-justice hashtag imaginary, while Alyssa Milano's is a legal-justice hashtag imaginary. In practice, this double hashtag imaginary opens the door to a variety of media practices and movement objectives for participants, achieved through uses of the same hashtag, revealing the flexibility and malleability of hashtags, as we saw with the multi-valent objectives and outcomes of #SlutWalk and #BlackLivesMatter.

With the legal-justice and healing-justice hashtag imaginaries, the mechanisms invoked can at times be contradictory. On the one hand, putting legal discourse into circulation using terms such as "due process" reimagines the criminal aspects of sexual assault: "Those who use terms such as 'sexual assault' as a way of making sense of or naming their violence may be subjected to ongoing versions of law-bound, yet unregulated, interrogations" (Gash and Harding 2018, 25). In the legal-justice hashtag imaginary, survivors' experiences are narrativized; however, the narrative process is not autonomous and self-determined but shaped by an often-hostile prosecutor. The legal-justice hashtag imaginary thus imagines the possibility of shifting the legal process to be less hostile and more successful for survivors. On the other hand, the healing-justice hashtag imaginary includes consciousness raising through discussions and informal education about systemic oppression in rape culture and includes narrativizing one's experience in a compassionate environment, "establishing norms of support, empathy, and acceptance" (Gash and Harding 2018, 31). The healing-justice hashtag imaginary validates the narrator's experience, creating a space in which survivors can experience healing through both storytelling and witnessing.

These two narrative processes and the #MeToo hashtag imaginaries they constitute can be at odds with each other: "Paradoxically, in some circumstances, the force of law in the case of sexual violence is to undermine the goals and benefits of consciousness-raising" (Gash and Harding 2018, 23). In consciousness raising, the narrator is implicitly believed and supported, whereas in the courtroom the narrator must not be believed but rather subjected to an interrogation in which they must defend not just their narrative but also their sexual history, character, clothing choices, and so on. In both cases, the survivor is invited to put their experience into discourse and thus articulate a position of power – the power to speak out.

However, the hashtag imaginary positions the subject differently in relation to the narrative: "In the old consciousness-raising tactics, women formed political cohorts that debated and took far-ranging action for reproductive rights, equal pay, fair divorce, equal education, and other equity issues" (Larabee 2018, 8), thus extending the empowerment of discourse and healing into political, social, economic, and cultural action. The healing-justice hashtag imaginary thus envisions the subject's trajectory as moving through healing to political action, as we saw in BLM as well. However, in the legal-justice hashtag imaginary, the challenge is that within the social imaginary there is an expectation that women should be questioned on unrelated sexual behaviours, subjected to character assassination, victim blaming, slut shaming, and other rape myths. These ideas, long disproven by evidence-based research, are perpetuated in public legal discourse, including, importantly, "in the attitudes of legal officials" (Gash and Harding 2018, 29) such as judges, state attorneys, lawyers, and jury members. Therefore, the social imaginary of the legal-justice approach to #MeToo focuses on intersectional systemic oppressions that must be challenged by shifting not only this key institution that currently thwarts legal justice for survivors but conversely also the imbrication of legal discourse in the social imaginary.

Whereas the social imaginary of the healing-justice approach to #MeToo in some ways also acknowledges the systemic oppressions within the legal justice system, it instead focuses on challenging intersectional systemic oppressions through healing justice in the community, through participation in grassroots organizations and social movement spaces. Both #MeToo imaginaries converge in the shared objective of eliminating rape culture's pernicious intersectional effects on a systemic level, and thus both envision social justice outcomes. It can be argued, therefore, that both hashtag imaginaries are necessary to call for the complexities of intersectional systemic change required with respect to #MeToo, sexual assault, and the global workings of rape culture. Interesting, too, is the fact that these two hashtag imaginaries focus on dealing with sexual assault after the fact, whereas the impacts of #MeToo have far exceeded these two perspectives and, some may argue, include broad social, cultural, and political shifts in terms of consent, education, bystanders, and so on, critically analyzed below.

The legal-justice hashtag imaginary is increasingly necessary but also persistently resistant to change. The healing-justice hashtag imaginary has been crucial to #MeToo, but it, too, comes with contradictions. These two imaginaries, although at times oppositional, are not a binary pair but part of a larger constellation of hashtag imaginaries. As with all imaginaries, they are "inextricably related to practice" (Treré 2019, 107) and must be considered not in the abstract but rather in relation to the intersectional technopolitical practices they together construct, observable through the ways in which several challenges and contradictions have played out in #MeToo.

Challenges and Contradictions in #MeToo

While #MeToo has been broadly successful in generating a Twitter storm and shifting public discourse, tensions and contradictions within media activist practices have arisen with respect to political economy and intersectionality.

Political Economy

The hashtag #MeToo has arguably been an intensified site of affective labour. Media activist practices can be considered a form of media labour, as elaborated in Chapter 1. Part and parcel of media activist labour is the way in which it connects people to one another through sociality and relationship building. Affective labour is engagement in labour at the level of sociality, relationships, emotions, expressivity, and healing. Social movements have been characterized as a kind of affective labour, with transfeminist activists engaging in connective and communicative labour that has been largely invisibilized in movements such as Occupy (Boler and Phillips 2015). The invisibilized, intersectional, gendered, and racialized digital media labour commons can be understood as a form of cyberfeminism integrated into the technopolitical sphere. Whereas scholars have considered the political economy of platform structures (Dowling, Nunes, and Trott 2007; Fuchs 2013), few have examined the political economy of intersectional hashtag activism practices.

Here, I analyze three key dimensions of affective platform labour in #MeToo. The labour of online narrativizing of experiences of sexual assault is often paired with the labour of viewers witnessing these narratives. These mutually supportive dialogues may, in turn, be met by online threats creating disjunctive forms of affective labour. How might we understand these three dimensions of affective labour – narrativizing, witnessing, and costs – in the context of intersectional social media imaginaries and logics?

First, when narrativizing sexual assault in hashtag feminism, the healing-justice imaginary creates spaces for dialogues in which survivors may tell their stories, explaining emotional responses, which may include vulnerability, anger, betrayal, injustice, frustration, disempowerment, fear, nightmares, tears, sadness, anxiety, depression, and more. There may be a sense of finally being able to let go of something they had been holding inside and blaming themselves for. It can be cathartic, a relief, and a weight off their shoulders. This affective labour is not, however, all positive and may lead to negative experiences such as retraumatization if the narrative causes a reliving of the event. Mendes, Ringrose, and Keller (2018, 238) have found that "participating in a hashtag like #BeenRapedNeverReported is often both triggering and comforting to participants, a tension that was common among almost all our interviewees, and must be recognized as part of the complexity of doing digital feminist activism." The affective solidarity generated through the comfort of participating in #MeToo or other online movements and being believed and validated by other online participants, both known and unknown, is often paired with the negative affect of being overwhelmed at re-experiencing the event, which may provoke panic, anxiety, stress, depression, suicide ideation, and more. Therefore, the affective digital labour of narrativizing experiences must be understood as doubly valent.

Second, when witnessing other people's narrativizations online, many survivors report an "emotional 'tax' they experienced from listening to stories of abuse, harassment, misogyny and sexism" (Mendes, Ringrose, and Keller 2018, 238). As #MeToo digital activists provided support and solidarity for others through witnessing, they empathized with the distress of those reporting, meaning that the digital activism of witnessing could result in similar affective and mental health impacts to narrativizing. As I noticed in my own participation in #MeToo, the distinction between narrativizing and witnessing sometimes blurred as stories were exchanged, with participants both reporting their own experiences through narrativization and supporting the narrativizations of others through witnessing. In this sense, the #MeToo hashtag also includes an imaginary and a practice of reciprocity, which plays out in affective digital media labour.

Addressing the importance of reciprocity, Michelle Rodino-Colocino notes the importance of the non-passive empathy of shared participation, which she calls "transformative empathy," a key affective labour practice in transformative media activism. Transformative empathy "promotes listening rather than distancing or looking at speakers as 'others.' It requires self-reflexivity and potential transformation of one's own assumptions" (Rodino-Colocino 2018, 96). In this sense, it takes on some of the aspects of *Walking With Our Sisters*, mentioned in Chapter 4, in which participants must not simply watch from the sidelines but must step closer, put themselves in the shoes of others, empathize, be transformed, and in turn also witness the transformation of others. The risk is that when watching or witnessing is only passive, "in the Twittersphere, [it] may enable a 'consumption of the other,' similar to the process of 'eating the other' that bell hooks has theorized whereby marginalized people are viewed as exotic others to be consumed by gazing oppressors" (Rodino-Colocino 2018, 96).

Within narrativizing and witnessing, two key immaterial media practices of invisibilized, unpaid gendered-racialized digital labour of intersectional social movements, we find a third dimension we might think of as balancing the costs. As Mendes, Ringrose, and Keller (2018, 239) have found, "the labour involved in running these digital feminist campaigns is highly affective, precarious and exploitative – and as such, we raise questions about the sustainability of such unpaid labour in light of online abuse, burn-out and other issues around work-life balance in the digital age." While this goes beyond "work-life balance," a middle-class term implying access to full-time paid work, the concern regarding the emotional and material costs of precarity and exploitation is, nonetheless, valid. Burnout, for example, was a key challenge noted by research participants interviewed by MARG who often found themselves in precarious media labour situations attempting to address intersectional issues. Their digital emotional and immaterial labour, they observed, took place within structures of exploitation with greater negative impacts for women, BIPOC, and 2LGBTQ+ people. Many explained that they had made calculated trade-offs among spending time fully engaged in unpaid affective media labour; stepping back from media activism to focus on paid labour for their own economic well-being and that of their family (taking on more shifts or greater responsibility at non-media workplaces, for example); or stepping back from both work and social movements to improve their emotional well-being at the cost of their material conditions or economic situation. Often, activists explained, they did not have the capacity to take on more paid labour because they had to focus on healing, a particularly common discourse among racialized, gendered, Indigenous, and/or 2LGBTQ+ media activists. Balancing the material and affective costs of media labour, therefore, is a key factor in the imaginaries of media activists who increasingly conceive of their social media interactions as hypercapitalist labour exploited by social media platform corporations. Moreover, they noted that this exploitation was intersectional, and as such, they sought to foreground affective labour issues in their media practices, trying to find a balance between the legal-justice, healing-justice, and social justice opportunity structures of social media, while also contesting intersectional hypercapitalist exploitation.

The risk is that transfeminist hashtag activism movements, taking place on hypercapitalist platforms, run by corporations shown to be racist, misogynist, and heteronormative, are inadvertently undermining their own successes by contributing to the escalating profits of these corporations in the very moment that they achieve their greatest trending topics.

Non-consensual Affective Labour

The complexities of narrativizing, witnessing, and balancing the costs of affective digital media labour further connect to a fourth dimension of affective labour in hashtag activism – trolling. Many hashtag activists in #MeToo have experienced the "anxiety and fear of being attacked for their feminist views" (Mendes, Ringrose, and Keller 2018, 244) by trolls. Transfeminist hashtag activists, bloggers, journalists, academics, hacktivists, and others have been trolled in a myriad of ways: having their experiences denounced as lies; receiving violent rape and death threats; or having personal information doxed (released on the internet) with calls to do harm. This trolling tends to exacerbate already high levels of stress, anxiety, depression, and panic attacks or other health and mental health impacts from being triggered (Nagle 2013). While the affective labour of narrativizing and witnessing is engaged in voluntarily and with consent, the irony is that, in a movement calling for sexual consent, trolls are forcing those narrativizing and witnessing sexual assault to engage in unwanted affective labour without consent.

The backlash against #MeToo did not just take place on social media. Mainstream media often disputed research-based evidence brought forward by transfeminist scholars, journalists, and activists. For example, when then-President Barack Obama used the well-known and well-researched statistic that one in five women are sexually assaulted in their lifetimes, it was widely reported as the "so-called '1-in-5' statistic" in mainstream media, calling into question the validity of this statistic (Gash and Harding 2018, 39). Thus, mainstream reporting fuelled the flames of social media trolls.

However, despite transfeminist media activists using hashtag activism for positive change, there are also online impulses fuelling negative change. Basic social norms of civility and respect for human rights across difference often do not play out online, as "we increasingly see distinctly hierarchical gendered patterns in online behavior, often more rigidly policed along gender lines than those overtly hierarchical democratic institutions that are considered hopelessly stuffy and outdated by internet radicals" (Nagle 2013, 169). There is also an intensification of online sexual violence and targeted antifeminist hacking of the hacktivist group Anonymous through its 4chan/b/ site, permeated with oppressive gendered, racialized, and heteronormative visual and textual discourse (Coleman 2011; Friedman 2008; Nagle 2013). These targeted online attacks lead to non-consensual affective labour by transfeminist media activists forced by hackers in their own groups to confront misogynist trolling both online and off.

Activist practices have been developed to address this backlash. One set of examples encountered in our research took place in the 15M movement, including addressing antifeminist backlash through facilitated discussions in the squares; engaging in "calling-in" processes, encouraging antifeminists to consider how women's issues were important in anti-austerity politics; as well as foregrounding how the digital media and the activism of queer transfeminist activists had already played a key role in 15M. A second practice mentioned by a group MARG interviewed was for men to take on the role of confronting the misogynist trolls attacking female collective members by engaging in face-to-face conversations over coffee to explain how their racist and misogynist behaviour was negatively impacting people. This often resulted in verbal apologies, followed by the interlocutor stepping back from their role in the racist, misogynist online and offline groups. These offline practices – facilitated informal educational dialogues, calling in, publicly recognizing transfeminist activist work, and pro-feminist male solidarity – demonstrate how hashtag imaginaries can also encompass offline solidarity and relationship building actions in complex ways across difference both within and exterior to movements.

Another set of practices in response to antifeminist backlash includes bystander actions in mainstream and alternative journalism workplaces. This has been a huge issue, particularly when powerful people engage in sexual assault, harassment, or abuse in the workplace where those being targeted risk losing their jobs and having their careers destroyed if they speak up. In the case of activist projects, survivors risk losing access to the media collective. In both cases, in the past, bystanders often supported or hesitated to confront the powerful perpetrator. In contrast, in this media activist practice, bystanders or witnesses to sexual harassment, bullying, assault, and other gendered behaviours, particularly in meetings, are now stepping up to challenge them, slowly making change in media workplace culture.

A final media activist practice in response to trolling is what we might call "hacking back" or taking the fight back to the source in digital space. An example of this that predates #MeToo was the development of ggauto-blocker, a blocker bot designed by Randi Harper after the intense trolling she experienced during the Gamergate crisis (Harper 2014). When Harper called out the gaming industry for being male-dominated and misogynist, male gamers engaged in an intensified attack on her and her friends and accomplices through mass trolling, almost as if they were set-ting out to prove her right. Hacking back against the trolls, Harper designed a bot that would block people who followed a lot of misogynist sites linked with online trolling. Anyone could (and still can) download the ggautoblocker bot and install it on their Twitter feed (Burgess and Matamoros-Fernández 2016).

Subsequently, there was a backlash to Harper's hackback attack on the original backlash. Trolls blocked by ggautoblocker demanded they be unblocked, arguing that their right to free expression was being infringed upon. Harper's allies argued that ggautoblocker was the digital equivalent of walking out of a room; the trolls could express themselves freely but there is no law saying that anyone has to listen. In this technopolitical strategy, the technology created and freely shared – the blocker bot – was designed and coded with an embedded intersectional transfeminist liberatory politics.

Intersectionality in #MeToo

For Tarana Burke, Twitter seemed a natural space to mobilize on the issue of sexual assault using #MeToo. Twitter is a place for both disenfranchised cit-izens and celebrity culture, allowing Alyssa Milano's tweet to gain millions of retweets globally. This response raises a key issue, as a *Guardian* editorial notes, "who is heard, who is believed, who wins redress – are skewed by race and class as much as by gender" (*The Guardian* 2017). Women, girls, trans, and non-binary people who are racialized or in precarious or undocu-mented labour situations are more vulnerable to having their "economic, physical and emotional security" (*The Guardian* 2017) threatened through repeated sexual harassment, a fact corroborated by the EU Agency for Fun-damental Rights.

Similarly, Mendes, Ringrose, and Keller (2018, 237) have found that "although it may be technologically easy for many groups to engage in digital feminist activism, there remain emotional, mental or practical barriers which create different experiences, and legitimate some feminist voices, perspectives and experiences over others." Related to social class and the digital divide, which creates barriers to digital participation, lack of education can be a barrier to engaging in the feminist aspects of digital feminism. This is because "many women tend to encounter feminism at university. Women who do not go on to further education face a barrier when attempting to engage with those academic debates that drive feminism" (Munro 2013, 25).

Participation in hashtag activism nonetheless plays a key role for those who cannot protest in the streets or who do not want to confront misogyny face to face. Hashtag activism is available to people who might not be able to attend a protest or participate in feminist collective meetings because of health reasons, social capacities, reproductive and domestic labour obligations, rural or isolated social locations, cultural coercive control over the circulation of women and girls, fear of being publicly outed as trans or nonbinary, and so on. Age can also be a factor, whereby online activism has sometimes provided a safe space "for teenagers who found that practising feminism offline at school was extremely difficult to navigate" (Mendes, Ringrose and Keller 2018, 244). Online spaces such as Twitter are thus crucial for intersectional oppressed groups but may sometimes prove difficult to access for those very groups. Specifically, #MeToo has been critiqued for being a white-dominated group not accessible or meaningful to BIPOC activists and the concerns of their communities.

Even though #MeToo was started by Tarana Burke, many BIPOC people did not feel the hashtag was a place for them. Some found that once it became a celebrity space, it was not as hospitable to people of colour narrating their experiences of sexual assault and harassment in the context of racism. Muslim women, for example, had low participation rates in #MeToo because they felt they needed to defend their culture from Islamophobia while also critiquing rape culture within it, an issue articulated in the HHH breakaway march of London's SlutWalk.

In the #MeToo moment, critiques led to a breakaway hashtag #Mosque-MeToo. It was started by Mona Eltahawy to address Islamic feminism, challenging, on the one hand, misogyny and sexual assault in the context of Muslim communities and, on the other hand, experiences of Islamophobia within Western feminism (Eltahawy 2018). Eltahawy added the word

"Mosque" to the hashtag to foreground Muslim experiences of sexual assault in religious spaces by providing a space for Muslim women's voices to break the silence on their own terms. #MosqueMeToo problematizes "the ways that the contributions of women of colour can be sidelined, only to have the same ideas lauded when they are presented by women in higher-privileged communities" (Point 2019). There can be a tendency within inter-sectionality, Camille Point (2019) argues, to universalize individuals within specific groups, for example, assuming all Muslim women share experiences and political perspectives, leading to mainstream feminist groups tending to exclude the concerns of Muslim women, whom they perceive as non-feminist. At the same time, intersectionality can render Muslim women vul-nerable to accusations from within Muslim communities that, in joining forces with dominant white feminist concerns such as #MeToo, they are being whitewashed, foreclosing the possibility of contesting sexual assault from within the Muslim community. This backlash was experienced by Elt-ahawy when disclosing her experience through her hashtag.

This leaves Muslim feminists in a complex situation when narrativizing and witnessing sexual assault experiences in a Muslim antiracist, feminist, and religious space such as #MosqueMeToo, as they risk being condemned by both non-Muslim feminists and non-feminist Muslim community mem-bers alike. However, for Point, this is a fabricated binary against which the hashtag #MosqueMeToo articulates a space for the voices of Muslim women who denounce neither religion nor feminism but stake out a space for Islamic feminism, a space that can be integrated into the everyday lives of women who engage with hashtags in the private space of their phones. Through smartphones and #MosqueMeToo, hashtag activism is more acces-sible to Muslim women as "a woman can instantaneously communicate her experience" to a broader global community, with the "opportunity for par-ticipants to immediately position themselves within a larger visual body of work across the globe" (Point 2019). This establishes some of the complexi-ties of intersectional responses to sexual assault in the context of not just race and gender but religion as well.

Subsequent to the SlutWalk movement in India, #MeTooIndia also served as a negotiation of the premises of #MeToo. Women's development studies scholar in New Delhi, India, Mary E. John (2020, 137), identifies the complexities of feminism in "the contexts structuring and constraining young women students' aspirations, namely the peculiar twin developments of near parity in access to higher education coupled with one of the lowest female work participation rates in the world." Despite the rise of #MeToo in

India, John argues that the response has generally been to protect students from sexual assault by imposing earlier curfews and canceling social events, with reporting of sexual harassment or sexual assault to university authorities perceived by students as carrying the risk of expulsion rather than providing a path to justice. John and Narayanamoorthy Nanditha (2021) both also argue that intersectional identities play a role in education, employment, and sexual assault. Nanditha explores the hashtag #MeTooIndia, which, like #MosqueMeToo, takes a negotiated approach to EuroAmerica-dominated digital feminism. Particularly with respect to Dalit and lower-caste and -class women, trans women, 2LGBTQ+ communities, rural areas, and diversely gendered people, experiences of sexual abuse and involvement in #MeToo may be delimited by intersectional systems of oppression. In the "cyber-South," she argues, digital access is a site of colonial privilege, strictly regulated and controlled by men and capitalism, and breaking the silence comes at great cost.

Transfeminist Intersectional Technopolitics

Encapsulating this analysis, a tabulation of the five key dimensions of transfeminist intersectional technopolitics is provided in Table 8.

Table 8 Key dimensions of intersectional technopolitics in transfeminist movements

Dimension	Transfeminist intersectional technopolitics
Intersectional and anticapitalist	Contests global intersectional gender oppression; linked to power and capital; intersectional feminist movements; contests masculine-gendered digital dominance; participants of all genders
Distributed online-offline architectures and motility	Online-offline movements creating safer spaces; distributive leadership in multiple geo-social locations; offline spaces for consciousness raising and legal-support networks
Multiplicities of technologies and spaces	Multiple platforms and devices; body as gendered media text; digital hackback and digilante justice; the media is the movement; technopolitics of cyberfeminism
Translocal solidarity economies and technologies	Solidarities across borders and genders; digitally facilitated networks of transfeminist action; solidarity technologies of witnessing; feminist digital-communications labour commons
Collective autonomy through direct action	Collective autonomy in friend groups of disclosure and witnessing; asserting right to bodily autonomy; direct action of changing social norms (rather than making demands of the state)

First, movements are contesting global intersectional gender oppressions at the micro level of experience through SlutWalk marches and hashtags such as #MeToo, #MosqueMeToo, and #SayHerName, and at the macro level of structures of power that intersect with capitalism. Sexual abuses, particularly by rich and powerful men, are publicly contested, drawing attention to the ways in which systemic gender oppression is linked to power and capital. Gender and capital connect to other issues through meta-issue intersectional movements, bringing intersectional transfeminist concerns to the forefront in online and offline contestations.

Second, these online-offline movements create motility through safer spaces in debates and narrativization in the context of what historically was called consciousness raising both in person and through hashtags. Activists fight for the practice of believing people who are disclosing their experiences, providing healing justice, and offering distributive leadership affordances in multiple geo-social locations. This includes offline spaces for consciousness raising, legal-support networks, education of girls and women, and digital spaces on social media, blogs, and so on.

Third, digital feminist movements are run by participants who are tech-savvy and, as such, engage in multiple platforms and devices, not just creating social media content or hijacking algorithms to achieve trending topics but also engaging in hacktivism by coding technologies directly, using tactics such as digital hackbacks and digilante justice. They creatively reclaim the body as autonomous gendered media text through protest actions, interrupting the normative spectacle of capitalism that objectifies and commodifies women's bodies. In intersectional, technopolitical, transfeminist movements, media spaces are the movement itself in the new technopolitics of a remodelled cyberfeminism and hashtag activism.

Fourth, the online spaces of the movement generate translocal solidarities across borders and genders as people of all genders are interconnected through embodied actions. Digitally facilitated networks of transfeminist narrativization and protest actions map onto solidarity technologies of witnessing and technopolitical tactics in the transfeminist digital communications labour commons. Labour is a shared economic process of liberation rather than the extraction of surplus value from the racialized-gendered body.

Fifth, collective autonomy is developed in informal friend groups and online networks of narrativization and witnessing, as transfeminists of all genders assert the right to bodily autonomy. These assertions are a form of communicative direct action that changes social norms rather than making demands on states. In their media practices of technopolitics, queer and racialized transfeminists in 15M participated in groups such as the Feminist Committees in the squares and Xnet in the online sphere, adopting intersectional technopolitical practices that shifted both the feminist and the 15M movements through reciprocal influences.

SlutWalk, #MeToo, and #MosqueMeToo have taken up debates on rape culture and powerful men's sexual abuses of power, with legal, economic, and cultural implications in the global public sphere mapped out in, through, and within digital technologies.

Transfeminism Debates

Sexual assault, harassment, and violence have not come to a grinding halt since the #MeToo and SlutWalk and other cyberfeminist movements. The failure of many societies to adhere to legal frameworks persists based on "distrust of women complainants and commitment to male sexual access," along with the continuation of socialized "vestiges of gendered expectations and impositions regarding sexuality and sexual expression" (Gash and Harding 2018, 27). Nonetheless, there are debatably qualitative social transformations observable in the wake of contemporary transfeminist movements.

First, there has arguably been a shift in not just the volume but also the texture of public discourse on sexual assault: "The sheer volume of testimony that has emerged refutes the idea that the odd 'bad apple' needs to be removed but everything is otherwise fine. [#MeToo] has demonstrated that this is a widespread and structural issue" (*The Guardian* 2017). Media coverage now often uses a more nuanced discourse of systemic issues and calls for systemic change where the blame is much less often placed on the survivor.

A second qualitative metric is the transformation of social norms. Social norms both online and offline have transformed through the feminist 15M, SlutWalk, and #MeToo movements, in at least three specific ways. First, because of the space in the streets and in the digital sphere, survivors are coming forward to speak about their experiences, breaking the old social norm of silence and acceptance regarding sexual assault and harassment. Second, we now are more inclined toward supporting and believing people disclosing sexual assault and providing avenues for healing.

Third, the silence of bystander peers or colleagues is now understood to be directly supporting perpetrators, an understanding that has increasingly encouraged people to intervene when they witness sexual harassment or assault and to speak up against inappropriate behaviours that they have witnessed through hashtags such as #men4women. These normative transformations provide mechanisms for implicated individuals – survivors, receivers of reporting, and bystanders – to speak out and hold others accountable. They challenge the "societal forces and structures that legitimate and facilitate the use of sexual contact as a means of coercion and control" (Gash and Harding 2018, 31). Moreover, SlutWalk, #BeenRapedNeverReported, #TimesUp, and #MeToo have propelled shifts in discourses and social norms that "draw attention to structure – to the design of institutions and the content (and organizing principles) of culture" (Gash and Harding 2018, 32), systemic issues that have served to make sexual violence acceptable. These structures are therefore not only being called into question but also increasingly being understood as intersectional across race, colonialism, transmisogyny, misogynoir, class, disability, age, education, immigration, language, and so on, as "#MeToo and Times Up challenge the very systems of power that underlie harassment, discrimination, and assault" (Rodino-Colocino 2018, 96). This has profoundly transformed global collective social imaginaries (Gash and Harding 2018, 42).

A fourth qualitative metric, therefore, would be the accompaniment of the transformation of the social imaginary by systemic change. To this end, it is crucial that there is a "new international standard on violence and harassment in the world of work, currently under discussion by the UN's International Labour Organization" (*The Guardian* 2017). Examples provided by Rodino-Colocino illustrate how the ways in which power plays a role in workplace harassment can be challenged. In the restaurant industry, when tipping is not a social norm, as in some European countries, sexual harassment decreases. Sexual harassment also decreases in the workplace when BIPOC women are paid equally to white women and when all women are paid equally to men. When workplace power is equalized, the rate of sexual harassment in the workplace decreases (Rodino-Colocino 2018, 99). Structural workplace changes are qualitative outcomes of #MeToo that are still in progress.

These outcomes, particularly with respect to systemic changes, are preliminary, and many challenges remain. Online intersectional misogynist backlash continues to retrench the misogyny and entitlement of those in dominant groups (wealthy, white, heterosexual, cismen) to the bodies of those they see as inferior (poor, racialized, queer, trans, non-binary, women, etc.), with intersectional gradations and degradations. We see this in the growth of the misogynist hate group the Incels, or involuntary celibates; the escalation of misogynist and transmisogynist trolling on Twitter; the continued harassment of women in journalism, politics, gaming, high-tech industries; and so on.

What we can say with certainty is that intersectional transfeminist media practices engaging with digital media, social media, and online-offline hybrid media have been and must also continue to be generative of a transformative shift in media spaces and the public sphere.

7

Futures

A Greek media activist who was interviewed by the Protest Media Ecologies project mused that "Facebook is like a big mall." You can meet friends there and spend time there if you choose, but you are also constrained to behaving in certain ways. There are prescribed flows, expected actions, and always a capitalist imperative. To explore how an internal critique of technopolitics in the era of platform dominance might help activists develop more effective technopolitical strategies, this simile is worth considering.

Strategies such as hijacking the Facebook and Twitter trending algorithms to mobilize social movements by achieving virality may have some demonstrated efficacy, however, as we have seen, these algorithms are not technologically neutral and do not provide the same access, outcomes, and level of virality for all. In the #Free_CeCe movement, for example, nonbinary and trans activists of colour found that rather than an instantaneous virality, the virality they were eventually able to achieve took longer than other hashtags and was therefore characterized as a slow burn (Fischer 2016). In the #MeToo movement, African American Tarana Burke's tweet did not go viral until white celebrity Alyssa Milano retweeted it. Muslim women found that the #MeToo space did not adequately address their concerns in the context of race and religion, so a more specific hashtag, #MosqueMeToo, was started.

Moreover, TikTok's algorithm demotes posts by those not conforming to traditional beauty standards, such as being overweight, trans and non-binary, or Black, Indigenous, and people of colour (BIPOC) (Minarella 2021). Similarly, on the 2021 Missing and Murdered Indigenous Persons Awareness Day, also known as Red Dress Day, many activists found their posts deleted, part of a growing trend on Instagram called shadow banning, "where platforms restrict, limit, or hide content," such that the poster may be unaware of the ban, a process that Instagram denied in this instance, attributing it to a "global technical issue" (Monkman 2021). Racist-gendered algorithms create challenges for BIPOC transfeminists participating in social media activism.

At the same time, the SlutWalk movement resonated with people of many races, ages, and religions in many global locations; however, negotiation was required to make the movement their own. For example, in the Hijabs, Hoodies, and Hotpants breakaway march in London, organizers differentiated gendered and racialized clothing from sexualities in order to recentre Muslim identities and concerns, including racialized police profiling. In 15M, famous for its technopolitical strategies, transfeminists and 2LGBTQ+ participants intervened to foreground issues of gender, race, sex, and sexuality in the context of neoliberal capitalist austerity measures. Further, in Canada and the United States, Indigenous movements used digital media at times; however, they did so while recognizing the double digital danger of ex-partner stalking and police surveillance, in conjunction with the fact that some rural reserves might not have the infrastructure to provide adequate access to digital networks.

An additional intersectional issue of unequal digital access and outcomes from a political economy perspective was the finding that online activists experienced an emotional tax based in the material reality of unpaid digital affective labour. This labour was challenging materially and emotionally for activists and, moreover, was unequally distributed across race, class, gender, sex, sexuality, and Indigenous identities and structures. This tax, however, did not deter individuals and groups from digital participation; rather, it inspired them to be self-reflexive about their participation, developing community-oriented strategies of solidarity, mutual support, and healing justice. Indeed, digital affective labour became imbricated within the healing process in many cases, where, for example, expressions of multi-gendered transformative empathy in #MeToo, settler solidarity in #IdleNoMore, and non-Black solidarity in #BlackLivesMatter brought people closer together from across communities, transforming them through a connective healing process. Through the healing process, the very conception of community was transformed and extended, creating intersectional movements for healing justice.

In these movements, creative digital and analog media and arts-based practices were used to achieve objectives, pointing to the fact that the available technologies did not determine how the movements would be approached. These findings indicate that there is much greater agency involved in both the selected technologies and politics of technopolitics, located in a variety of intersectional subjectivities and their foregrounded collectively autonomous, self-determined political objectives. At the same time, digital technologies must not be ignored, as they have influenced the ways in which most groups have mobilized in transmedia and translocal mobilizations.

There are, however, many questions raised throughout these chapters regarding intersectional technopolitics. To return to the earlier question, what does it mean for the future of intersectional technopolitics to say that "Facebook is like a big mall"? Years ago, Douglas Kellner (2003, 183) suggested that "commercial interests are quickly converting [the internet] into a giant mall, thus commercializing the Internet and transforming it into a megaconsumer spectacle." If social media platforms are the new megaconsumer spectacles, with user data and labour non-consensually monetized and targeted advertising at every new click, have we recreated the society of the digital spectacle? And more importantly – who benefits from the digital spectacle? Although platform and activist objectives co-exist, we cannot assume that the spectacle, even when user-generated, is incidental or non-teleological within global capitalism. Is it possible for media activists to break through the noise of the spectacle so that participants are living up to the internet's potential to create stronger democracies through engaged civic participation (Curran, Fenton, and Freedman 2016)? But perhaps we need a different question based on the assumption of activist agency: How can social media be re-appropriated from capitalist economic and social control of the digital spectacle? Can we leave social media behind to create affordances for sociality, virality, reach, healing, and mobilization elsewhere in ways that foreground liberation, community, co-operation, solidarity, and equality? What do we make of the fact that alternative platforms such as Diaspora have had little uptake, and independent open editorial systems such as Indymedia, which opened this book and shifted so many media practices, are relegated to near invisibility except perhaps to the activists who produce them?

If we are stuck with social media "as-is," a broken and rejected object, do we have no choice online but to be interpellated as consumers rather than citizens? Can intersectional, technopolitical media practices interrupt the exploitative, anti-democratic monetization logics of hypercapitalist platform labour? What are the limits to social media as a space in which to issue challenges to the multiple exploitations and intersectional oppressive structures of communicative capitalism? Moreover, in 2021, how are political, cultural, economic, social, and communications fabrics and networks shifting globally in the pandemic era, the context in and through which social media circulate fake news, disinformation, and conspiracies so easily?

We can hang out in the Facebook mall as long as we follow social norms and don't interfere with its commercial imperative. We might, therefore, think of the media practice of hijacking the Facebook algorithm as akin to dumpster diving – eating the garbage of capitalism. Capitalism does discard some high-quality garbage, and many people have lived at least partially, and sometimes for many years, from dumpster diving, myself among them. However, living off capitalism's garbage, like hanging out in the Facebook mall, is not equally available or appealing to all people. Malls, like social media platforms, can have racist security guards or algorithms, misogynist and heteronormative objectification, transphobic and cisnormative bathrooms, and binary gendered clothing sections, all of which increasingly reproduce the systemic oppressions of intersectional capitalism.

Getting Mauled by Social Media

Are we getting mauled by Facebook, Instagram, TikTok, Twitter, and You-Tube when we participate in activist mobilizations, presuming we're engaged in transformative media practices? Technopolitical strategies depend on capitalist logics that are economically exploitative, but these logics, as we have seen, also deepen social, cultural, political, and economic inequalities on a structural level (van Dijck and Poell 2013). Many people can't get to the mall; others have chosen not to go there. There are many reasons people might not go to the social media mall: disconnectionist movements led by former platform developers; addiction and mental health issues from overuse of smartphones and social media; and a general wariness about the economics, surveillance, and social complications of online participation (Jurgenson 2013; Lanier 2018; Twenge 2017).

Moreover, platforms stop working in specific oppressive contexts for particular marginalized groups, for example, when transfeminists are verbally and physically attacked in the Facebook mall by violent transmisogynist trolls. This happened frequently for the people whom the Media Action Research Group (MARG) interviewed. Capitalist platforms might be effective spaces for mobilizing protests for some people, but they are not equally available and friendly to everyone. In many of the cases analyzed in this book, offline spaces were just as important as digital spaces. For example, Black Lives Matter has an online hashtag activism campaign, but BLM activists also run Freedom Schools for Black youth and engage in community organizing (Khan-Cullors and Bandele 2018). Burnt Bras in Athens, Greece, found its sporadic, in-person café meet-ups to be important spaces for building a sense of community and extending the longevity of the project. Offline caucus-type spaces were important for intersectionally marginalized groups who suffered from "space racism" or the tendency for dominant-race spaces to be better resourced than non-dominant-race spaces (Kendi 2019). There is a tendency for dominant spaces not to be amenable to transfeminist, antiracist, 2LGBTQ+, and/or anticolonial politics, despite claims to openness or horizontality (Costanza-Chock 2012; Wolfson 2013). Therefore, intersectionally marginalized groups have been resourceful in developing their own spaces, often outside the view or purview of dominant spaces, including dominant "alternative media" or contestation hashtag spaces. They work to create solidarity networks for capacity building and healing, by working on media activist projects that generate material and immaterial resources to both build organizational resilience and sustain individuals in their life trajectories (Alimahomed 2010; Jeppesen and Petrick 2018).

While platforms have been useful to technopolitical mobilizations, several problems with Web 3.0 architectures have been noted. Contacts and other data are not motile across platforms; for example, users cannot leave Facebook and take contact lists with them to spaces such as Diaspora (Toret and Calleja 2014, 19). When users do leave social media platforms, any photos, texts, videos, and other material will remain on the platform and cannot easily be ported to other platforms, downloaded to a personal device, or even deleted. Social media platform users are open to mass surveillance by police, trolls, exes, the alt-right, predators, the NSA, the CIA, the FBI, indeed, any group or individual who might not have the users' best interests at heart (Geist 2015; Grant et al. 2011; Hattery and Smith 2017; Kubitschko 2015; Milberry and Clement 2015). Profits derived by capitalist platforms through the participation of anticapitalist activists are fed back into capitalist ventures. These platforms are embedded in racialized, gendered, colonial, and heteronormative hierarchies, so that antiracist, feminist, anticolonial, and 2LGBTQ+ organizing and movements engaged on platforms, while contributing to the objectives of the movement, are also contributing to the objectives and material success of structures directly counter to their objectives. Intersectional technopolitics must, therefore, attempt to address the ways in which systemic inequalities play out in the Facebook mall, and scholars of such digital media uses must take seriously the intersectional complications of digital-platform labour in the production of activist user-generated content.

While some activists and scholars promote the capability of technopolitics activists to hijack the Facebook algorithm, many argue that it is still important for activists to develop autonomous, collectively self-owned, and self-determined spaces, collectives, and technologies. As Javier Toret (2012, n.p.) argues with respect to the deeply embedded technopolitics of 15M:

> It is also remarkable how the [protest] camping and DRY [Real Democracy Now website] used tools created based on free software. The one that served to organize, in addition to the blogs of tomalaplaza.net, has been N-1.cc, a free and self-managed social network, which went from having 3,000 users before 15M to more than 30,000 in just one month. At the same time, the movement set up an enormous amount of mailing lists, blogs and pages. Another really noteworthy point is how digital tools such as "propose," "stopdesahucios" and "oiga.me," were created in free software and planted both the autonomy of digital networks within the movement and the capacity to invent technopolitical devices which will facilitate the forms of decision, organization and collective action.

These free software technologies and practices need to be intersectional, or the risk is that open architectures, free open source software, and open horizontality structures will continue to be spaces of domination through openness, or openness for those who already experience intersectional privilege (Costanza-Chock 2012; Point 2019; Wolfson 2013), which I have written about elsewhere as "horizontality from above" (Aikawa, Jeppesen, and MARG 2020).

Toret (2012) argues that in addition to self-owned platforms, the affective engagement, knowledge production, and collective intelligence of 15M were part and parcel of its technopolitical practices. They were pivotal in "surprising and overcoming the control capabilities of the dominant powers. Collective intelligence concentrates attention and adds unique capabilities to a common power-environment" (Toret 2012, n.p.). Not just the global justice movement and 15M but also many ACAR, 2LGBTQ+, and transfeminist movements are engaged in an emergent intersectional technopolitics, where activists are attentive to complex cartographies of class, gender, race, sex, ethnicity, undocumented status, and so on in the generation of collective intelligence and common power in hybrid media ecologies (Treré 2019).

These multiplying cautions about the Facebook maul (sic) raise a series of contradictions that have led to at least six new interesting intersectional, technopolitical transformations in progress, the outcomes of which remain to be seen. Scholars and activists alike will want to be attentive to these contradictory processes, as they may play a pivotal role in the future of transformative media activism, particularly as we move through the COVID-19 pandemic and beyond to unknown futures.

From #OscarsSoWhite to *Hidden Figures?*

The first example comes from Hollywood film. At the 2018 Oscars, as noted above, Ashley Judd mentioned that intersectionality had been the promise of that year in filmmaking. Evidence was the slate of nominees, which included *Call Me by Your Name, Lady Bird,* and the ultimate winner, *The Shape of Water.* In 2017, *Moonlight* had won best picture, with *Hidden Figures* being nominated for three Oscars. These films address intersectional identities and oppression. *Lady Bird* features a working-class girl growing up in a complicated family situation. *The Shape of Water* features a mute woman working with a gay man to free another species from imprisonment and torture, taking intersectionality beyond the human world to challenge the violence of anthropocentrism. And *Hidden Figures* features three African American women protagonists, among them a professional mathematician whose work was pivotal in the NASA space race in the 1960s. This last film rewrites the history of NASA to reveal invisibilized or "hidden" intersectional accomplishments.

More recently, in 2019, we have examples of two films rewriting history in a different way – *BlacKKKlansman* and *Once upon a Time in Hollywood.* The latter, a Tarantino vehicle, rewrites the history of the Charles Manson cult killing of Sharon Tate so that the cultists are violently slaughtered (who is Tarantino, after all, without violence?). Critics are uncritical of that rewriting, understanding that the film is only heartbreaking because the audience already knows what really happened, with the rewriting providing momentary, fictional relief from the brutal reality of Tate's murder. The former, a Spike Lee Joint, rewrites the history of Ron Stallworth, an African American undercover police officer who spent years undercover in both Black Power and White Power groups. The truth was, as in Tarantino's film, quite different. Spike Lee, long understood to have been ostracized by Hollywood for his explicitly antiracist films, was called out by Black filmmaker Boots Riley for unrealistically deviating from the facts. However, if Spike Lee was refiguring Ron Stallworth as an antiracist hero who supported the Black Power movement and defeated the systemic racism of policing, was Lee not engaged in a similar project as Tarantino – re-imagining a better past? Is it allowable for a white director to do so but not a Black director? Must we always represent history exactly as it happened when we create fictional films and narratives, or is poetic license and poetic justice equally available to all directors? Do these Hollywood films risk audiences leaving the theatre with the takeaway message that racism and gender-based violence have been eradicated?

The question that these films, including the intersectional films of 2017, raise is one of great importance regarding the recording, rewriting, excavating, retelling, and reworking of intersectional histories. The question is not the seemingly obvious question regarding how people overcome intersectional oppressions in specific historical and contemporary contexts to excel in their chosen fields, albeit as the so-called hidden figures of history. Rather, the question is this: By which mechanisms do these figures *get hidden*, by whom, and in support of which power structures, so that their life histories are in need of excavating and retelling today because they have been made to become lost? Moreover, in this contemporary moment, it bears asking whether we are in the social process of both recovering hidden figures and simultaneously hiding troublesome figures. We do so as a society through mainstream media omissions that the projects covered in this book attempt to mitigate. We do so as researchers by not engaging in research at the level of granularity required to document and value the work of intersectionally oppressed marginalized groups, individuals, and networks, particularly those working hard to express transformative epistemologies and paradigms through social media and autonomous websites.

In the meantime, the hashtag #OscarsSoWhite and other similar antiracist hashtags continue to gain traction, demanding that the Oscars and Hollywood take on intersectionality at a deeper level, rather than simply moving on from their embarrassing Weinstein moment. But do they? In 2020, the only film nominated for best picture that went against the grain was also the winner, *Parasite*, a film about class divides in Korea. While a perhaps limited number of intersectional identities are appearing in mainstream film, this trend does not shift the capitalist intersectional structures of Hollywood. The intersectional controversies and accomplishments of recent best picture wins – *Green Book* in 2019 (critiqued for its white saviour trope), *Parasite* in 2020 (a first for a non-American film), and *Nomadland* in 2021 (with four Oscars including best director, a first for a woman of colour, Chloé Zhao) – signal that the unfinished project of intersectionality in Hollywood is a complicated and messy work-in-progress.

In communications scholarship, where these films might be critically analyzed, intersectional racialized hierarchies also exist, called into question by the hashtag #CommunicationSoWhite. Studies are increasingly revealing that intersectional hierarchies are still the prevailing norm in most universities (Henry, Dua, Kobayashi et al. 2017). Moreover, researchers who are not women, BIPOC, or 2LGBTQ+ often do not address intersectional issues. They may believe that doing so is a biased, subjective, or partial approach to research, a scenario in which (by corollary) objective, impartial research is more highly valued and presumed to be value-neutral, rather than supporting the status quo ideologically, while simultaneously doing the work to invisibilize, silence, and hide the figures and labour of intersectional movement and media activists. Are we thereby celebrating the "hidden figures" of history, excavating the historical contributions of BIPOC, women, and 2LGBTQ+ groups and individuals in mainstream Hollywood film, for example, while simultaneously erasing their contemporary contributions as we conduct research in the present moment by ignoring intersectionality in research?

To take one example, at a conference I recently attended, a researcher presented findings on the media activist work of the intersectional anticapitalist, antiracist, queer, transfeminist Brazilian group Mídia NINJA, which MARG has also interviewed. The presentation mentioned neither the meta-issues the group is active on nor the intersectional anticapitalist approach taken by Mídia NINJA in its organizing structure. When I asked about the group's intersectional politics, the political science scholar acknowledged that Mídia NINJA does such things but argued that the group's work was political only when it covered representations of elections and political parties. This scholar's research presentation thus did precisely the work of erasing the key intersectional meta-issue configurations foregrounded on the website and in the everyday organizing of Mídia NINJA, misrepresenting its members, for posterity, as hidden figures in their own project. This erasure is exceedingly common in research.

We can also see this mechanism in the literature on alternative media, which does not examine specifically who is contributing to the construction of media networks. While some scholars might aptly critique the elite soft-power structures silently encoded in horizontalism (Wolfson 2013), or the ways in which open access to meetings and digital technologies might privilege certain groups and individuals who already feel entitled to speak (Costanza-Chock 2012), at the same time, documentation of those with less privilege and access across intersectional lines is less frequent, with key exceptions (Breton et al. 2012b, 2012b; Costanza-Chock, Schweidler, and TMOP 2017; Jeppesen and MARG 2018; Jeppesen and Petrick 2018; Kidd, Barker-Plummer, and Rodriguez 2006).

Given the circulation of #CommunicationSoWhite, communication scholars need to continue accounting for the not-hidden but very present intersectional figures of contemporary media activism, or this unfinished process of documentation and theorization risks repeating a history of erasure and silencing of the very voices and movements we claim to be liberating and giving voice to. It raises the provocative question of whether Hollywood is doing a better job than communications scholarship at foregrounding racism, colonialism, gender, sex, disability, and more in the current intersectional moment. There is still a gulf between scholars engaged in intersectional antiracist, feminist, decolonizing, and/or 2LGBTQ+ research, particularly in media and communications, and those who are not. In this intersectional moment, it is crucial to incorporate intersectional concerns into research in order not to oversimplify, trivialize, silence, erase, or hide the figures engaged in political activism today.

It is not necessary to study #MeToo, #IdleNoMore, or #BlackLivesMatter in order to study gendered and racialized participation in media, technologies, and social movements. The Indignados, Occupy, the Arab Spring, the Quebec Student Strike – all of these movements included people engaged in antiracist, feminist, decolonizing, 2LGBTQ+, and disability organizing. For this reason, questions of collective identity in social movement and media scholarship must move beyond the universalized general subject (e.g., the Indignant ones, the 99%, the students) based on unwritten assumptions that everyone in a broad-based social movement of hundreds of thousands of people shares the same experiences and approaches to the movement (Crass 2013; Florini 2015; Jeppesen, Kruzynski, and Riot 2016; McDonald 2002; Polletta and Jasper 2001; Treré 2015).

From Embodied Technologies to Technologies of Embodiment

A second contradictory transformation taking place revolves around the concepts and practices circling bodies and technologies, originally broached by Donna Haraway's figure of the cyborg in "A Cyborg Manifesto" (Haraway 1994). Haraway figures cyborgs as "creatures simultaneously animal and machine" deriving from both social reality and science fiction, figures still available in both spheres today (Haraway 1994, 83). She does so in the interest of blurring boundaries and marking a time without gender within a time without time. In other words, a "postgender world" (Haraway 1994, 84) always-already exists in the liminal spaces between human and non-human animals, between organic and inorganic embodiments, and between material and virtual worlds. These are spaces in which embodied technologies are transgressed and where a virtual, inorganic, and beyond-human subjectivity may be achieved outside the gender binary. How do we move from this utopian, socialist-feminist, playfully ironic worldview that transgresses the boundaries of embodied technologies into the current technologies of affect and affective compulsion – in the sense of compulsive behaviour but also being compelled to produce affective expression? The embodied technologies of feminist cyborg utopian bodies as mediated texts have been translated through material processes into technologies of embodiment, recapturing the embodiments of liberatory practices through technopolitical, discursive, imagistic, experiential, and material modes of expression, expansion, and extension. These are what Foucault calls "technologies of the self" (Foucault 1988). Indeed, Foucault's objective was to "show people that they are much freer than they feel, that people accept as truth, as evidence, some themes which have been built up at a certain moment during history, and that this so-called evidence can be criticized and destroyed" (Foucault 1988, 10). Embodied technologies, the embodiments of the cyborg who transgresses so many boundaries, are a perfect example of this potential for the destruction of that which is no longer needed and that which is understood to be a regime of truth that does not hold.

Considering technologies of the self, the selfie stands as the quintessential example. The liberatory, embodied technologies of the cyborg utopian, non-binarized gender are under capture, surveillance, and erasure through the permanent selfie-fication of experience, the photo curation of virtual identities that even in the moment of taking the photo are not real. But in the moment of posting the not-real-identity photo, the platform translates it into the only-real-identity, capturing it through a technology of embodiment. The body (as mediatized text) moves from transgressive expressive to captured avatar, confined to the once limitless but now quite limited, bounded, and small frame of the Instagram post, the permanently disappearing Snapchat post, and the permanently captured Facebook post, which reappears as a technology of embodiment of memory years later. Technologies of self-control of behaviour are slipping away, replaced by technologies of control and erasure of the self, displaced on the timeline and news feed of the technologies of self, and ultimately becoming and not-becoming – at the same moment – technologies of the embodiment of control. The body itself is both left behind in the past and extended forward into the forever future but only in its captured technology of self-embodied control.

The question then becomes not just, "Can we use exploitative intersectional capitalist platforms to challenge intersectional exploitative capitalism by posting, curating, and recreating virtual selves that are controlled and seamlessly integrated into the current technologies of embodiment?" but also, "Can we use embodied technologies to escape the racialized, gendered, sexualized, colonialist technologies of capture of embodiment?" To use Foucault's (1978) language, "Can we transcend the regimes of truth about capitalism, gender, sexuality, race, and/or colonialism, if we stage and curate ourselves in platforms of dominance and capture?" And if so, "What does an intersectional technopolitics look like that does not get captured in the platformization of technologies of embodiment in everyday life?"

Because of these complex questions, the processes of intersectional hashtag activism – through antiracist anticolonial feminist 2LGBTQ+ liberations of embodiments – are a work-in-progress that may be becoming cyborg transgression and may also be, simultaneously, unbecoming virtual subsumption. Where this complicated give-and-take might one day emerge from the conflictual platformization, datafication, and virtualization of everything in the internet of things remains to be seen. It is this very struggle that is playing out on the ground in global intersectional technopolitics and transformative media movements.

From Technologies of Power to Empowering Technologies

Drawing attention to the technology-media-movements complex illustrates how scholars have moved toward developing more nuanced understandings of the ways in which technologies, media practices, and social movements are increasingly integrated (Fominaya and Gillan 2017). Discursive turns that capture this integration include the keywords addressed in this book, such as "protest media," "social media activism," "digital protest," "technopolitics," "hashtag activism," and more. "Hashtag activism" can be taken as the quintessential manifestation of this triangulation, as it is simultaneously all three – a digital technology, an everyday life media practice, and a social movement.

Technopolitics scholars consider the technologies used to mobilize an online-offline choreography of assembly in which specific media practices are embedded in the various structures and affordances of digital technologies available to activists. These practices have been determined to serve certain purposes for certain movements, engaging those online in specific ways and, to an extent, also shaping the digital actions of those in the streets. These technologies of choreography of assembly thus transmogrify into technologies of assembly but also assemblages, yoking together unlike items in Deleuze-and-Guattarian rhizomatic networks (Deleuze and Guattari 1987). These rhizomatic networks include nodes as materially distinct as the histories of protesters across generations and geographies; the politics of participants across intersectional identities; the technological practices across social media, print media, data activism, hacker spaces, and maker spaces; and the everyday lives of people across homelessness, unemployment, precarious labour, and more. Intergenerational, intersectoral, intersectional, interspersed assemblages are rhizomatically networked together from such dispersed discursive and material spaces and experiences and yet come together in discourse and action to develop social movement and media practices and strategies, doing real things in the world with the hope of contesting the embedded embodied technologies of capital, gender, race, sex, colonialism, and more.

Engaged in digital technologies, and exposed to surveillant sorting and dataveillance (Monahan 2009), these assemblages of protesters are afforded or denied specific benefits based on the invisibilized proprietary logics of social media; sublime algorithms; digital infrastructures; the motile architectures of technologies; and the mobile, unequal power relations or dynamic technologies of power. The question thus becomes not, "How do we empower our intersectional marginalized voices and bodies through digital technologies used by social movements to reclaim power?" but rather, "How can we empower communities through technologies when those technologies are also technologies of power?" What are the specific mechanisms and technologies for empowerment that now need to be developed to transcend, transgress, circumnavigate, and ultimately defeat the currently existing technologies of power? How do we continue to build toward empowering technologies when technologies are constructed through and as power and when, at the same time, access to technologies, always-already imbricated with power, continues to be figured and articulated by many states, corporations, researchers, and activists as the direct and only route to empowerment, even when scholars have revealed the depth of the contradictions within this assumption (Curran, Fenton, and Freedman 2016)?

From Technologies of Intersectionality to the Intersectionality of Technologies

If we consider that technological affordances are not equal across raced, classed, gendered, queered, trans-ed, and colonized identities, we must not only understand the technologies of power and oppression mentioned above, but we must also develop a different conception of what "technopolitics" actually means. This book has made some efforts to do so, but this has only resulted, it seems, in revealing more contradictions and tensions than it has resolved.

Technopolitics is not just the exceptional use tech-savvy groups such as Indymedia and 15M or translocal digital mobilizations such as #BlackLives-Matter, #Free_CeCe, and #IdleNoMore have made of digital media. Technopolitics includes the politics of both oppression and liberation enacted through digital and other art, media, and cultural forms across race, class, gender, sexuality, Indigeneity, and so on. What are the implications of these oppressive and liberatory enactments for our conception of technopolitics? This conception must consider the specificity not just of local technological capacities, such as whether people have access and training in digital technologies, but also such questions as, "What are activists capable of doing?" and moreover, "What are the potential unintended consequences of doing so using digital media?" Antiracists are stalked and trolled by racists, 2LGBTQ+ activists by homophobes, and Indigenous peoples by #upsettlers; racism and sexism are embedded in search engines; Instagram provides avenues for influencer status to self-objectifying young girls and women; meta-issue activists are considered domestic terrorists and put under state surveillance – all of which results in defining the limits of specific digital media affordances for intersectional movements. Instead of liberation, there is an intensification of the emotional tax, an intensification of experiences of affective, intersectional oppression in hybrid media action.

In other words, what are the new sociotechnical configurations of technologies with supplemental functionalities of the digital? Whereas a massive number of research studies focus on digital technologies, they tend to erase the importance of transmedia mobilizations that include residual, analog, print, radio, creative arts, performance, and other communicative actions that are particularly salient in hybrid intersectional movements today.

Technopolitics in popular and scholarly usage is often conceived of, even by those moving away from mediacentrism or technological determinism, as only engaging cutting-edge digital technologies, whereas my research shows that for the majority of meta-issue intersectional movement and media activists, a multiplicity of genres and forms are still relevant and must be accounted for in any theoretical framework of technopolitics.

We can return to our original definition of technopolitics as "a sophisticated form of communicative action that is a complex blend of technological knowledge and digital expertise used for radical political purposes with the technology itself seen as a site of contestation" (Treré, Jeppesen, and Mattoni 2017, 413). Elements of communicative action and technological knowledge are key dimensions of technopolitics in addition to digital expertise. It is also crucial to remember that the technologies themselves are sites of contestation; they are not neutral or uncontroversial but rather complex sites of resistance and co-optation that construct social meanings, and in which struggles over ownership, representation, surveillance, creeping, trolling, and more play out along racialized, gendered, colonial, and sexualized lines.

Technopolitical frameworks must therefore consider how technologies are appropriated, adapted, and adopted in ways that integrate intersectionality into sociotechnical assemblages that consist of a multiplicity of old and new technologies, media logics, and so on – the logic of connective action, social media logic, mainstream media logic, capitalist media logic, surveillant media logic, and so on. These logics may be more empowering for specific groups, individuals, and networks in a range of distinct social, cultural, political, economic, and geographical locations, comprising a complexity and depth that an oversimplified approach to a generalized free culture movement with a presumed universal subject may fail to account for. These failures lead to erasures of the key contributions of women, BIPOC, and 2LGBTQ+ individuals, groups, and networks, as academics write their histories without accounting for their specific collective identities, thus absenting them/us from the archives.

The questions once again shift away from delving into the cool and innovative ways in which some universal subjects have mobilized digital technologies in social movements to frames where we might need to shift our thinking, research, and activism about technologies of intersectional oppressions to develop intersectionally liberating technologies. Do we need to use oppressively structured and mobilized technologies, including their technologies of power and hierarchical structures, to do so? Is this a closed, oppressive loop or an open, liberatory assemblage with lines of flight out of oppression? Are there ways in which solidarity software and economies can reinscribe the intersections of technopolitics over and against the technologies of intersectional oppression in new formations that might expand creative expression, and open up the communicative labour commons in ways that can better instantiate social justice and sustain life?

From Technologies of Control to Control of Technologies

The first contradiction in this chapter focused on mainstream Hollywood film, a clear indication that the concerns, implications, and complications of intersectional technopolitics extend beyond grassroots social movements and media. This fifth contradiction zooms out to examine two high-level global technopolitical initiatives that seem to be attempting to mobilize technologies of control to exercise control over technologies.

The first initiative is Denmark's appointment, in 2017, of an ambassador to the tech industry (Brocklehurst 2019; Satariano 2019). Denmark has recognized that with half the world's population engaged on social media platforms, and with the communications industry dominated by the so-called FAANG corporations (Facebook, Apple, Amazon, Netflix, and Google), that "tech behemoths now have as much power as many governments – if not more" (Satariano 2019).

The first technology ambassador in the world emerged from the country that gave us the word *hygge*, meaning "a cozy hangout with friends or family in an atmosphere of warmth and conviviality" (Wiking 2017), and which is continuously named one of the happiest countries in the world, coming second after Finland in 2019 and 2020 (United Nations 2019, 2020). Much of this has to do with not just cultural practices but also political, economic, and social policy.

Enter the concept of the tech ambassador invented by Denmark as an attempt to acknowledge and address the domestic policy implications of foreign power blocks that are not countries but corporations. The world's first-ever tech ambassador, Casper Klynge, noted that technology platforms have a far greater influence on the everyday lives of citizens than the foreign policy of many countries. And yet, contradictorily, these platforms are not being developed by, for, or in consultation with, and remain largely unregulated within, the countries they are used in. Klynge is quoted in the *New York Times* as suggesting that "our values, our institutions, democracy, human rights, in my view, are being challenged right now because of the emergence of new technologies" (Satariano 2019). The implication is that the FAANGs are exercising what is seen by Klynge, and Denmark cannot be alone in recognizing this, as the equivalent power of a foreign policy maker. That's an extraordinary amount of power for technologies to control.

The government of Denmark aims to make inroads in developing nation-to-nation-like relationships with the tech industry to ensure, as Jeppe Kofod, Denmark's minister of foreign affairs, puts it, "that democratic governments set the boundaries for the tech industry and not the other way around" (Satariano 2019). Based on my research findings, and similar concerns coming out of both industry and academic research regarding the addictive qualities of social media and smartphones, including escalating mental health impacts, I had expected these health concerns might be addressed by such a tech ambassador. However, this is not the case. The list of issues to be addressed include cyber-security, data privacy, content moderation, misinformation, datafication, competition, and taxation (Brocklehurst 2019; Satariano 2019). These are clearly important issues in the wake of digital exposure events such as the Cambridge Analytica scandal, the Russian bot influence over the Trump election (Marineau 2020), massive data breaches (including the recent Life Labs hack of genetic data which is valuable on the Dark Web), and the virality of the New Zealand mosque shooter's first-person video. Indeed, if we look at any one of these issues in the light of the new logic of social media (Burnap and Williams 2016; Couldry and Campanella 2019; Milan 2017; van Dijck 2014; van Dijck and Poell 2013), there is cause for concern. Denmark is encouraging other countries to appoint tech ambassadors to increase their leverage and negotiating power at the table with big tech.

However, is this the right solution for increasing democracy and human rights in the context of technology? While Denmark is known for its democratic principles and values, what would happen if autocratic dictatorships stepped up and instituted tech ambassadors unilaterally, attempting to influence the FAANGs toward more dangerous and harmful ends, offering them tax incentives to develop technologies of social control, for example, or more invasive surveillance of citizens (though I am not sure what could be more invasive than smartphone and metadata tracking), or even to collect ethnic data for ethnic cleansing purposes, and the like? These are things that are already happening on social media, health tracking, and other types of digital datafication platforms. Although one tech ambassador from one democratic country seems innocuous, and perhaps even socially innovative, if we think this model through, it might have some loopholes that could be exploited in ways that would further intensify the attacks on democracy and human rights noted by Klynge himself.

Does the fact that technology power brokers are exercising monopolies of social control not call for a more concerted response? In the meantime, tech ambassadors are a fascinating idea, one that holds great promise if it plays out in the ways foreseen by and being pursued by Denmark. It can also be hoped that issues of mental health and social impacts in a variety of intersectional communities will make it onto the tech ambassador's agenda. The future of societies, after all, should not be socially engineered, outside of regulatory frameworks, by tech giants, including their programmers, coders, and systems designers who may be working in ways that shield them from understanding the unintended social impacts of the technologies they are developing. At the same time, this is starting to change as the mobilization of high-tech employee activists is on the rise. For example, a small group of Twitter employees put pressure on the company to ban Donald Trump after the Capitol riots on January 6, 2021. But this begs the question – where does the responsibility lie? One tech ambassador interested in shaping regulatory frameworks and technological developments for the common good of citizens is not nearly enough for the sheer volume of work that needs to be done to bring the FAANGs back in line with democratic and human-rights values. Where this so-called TechPlomacy initiative will lead is anyone's guess, as it is open to many contradictory directions, interpretations, and potential outcomes, many of which may have unforeseen consequences.

The second and somewhat related case of a high-level initiative to regulate and control social media and other digital platforms has arisen in response to the performance crime of the New Zealand mosque shooting (Besley and Peters 2020). A performance crime takes place when the performance, often video recorded and committed with specific audiences in mind, is part and parcel of the crime itself and even part of the motivation for committing that specific act: "New media performance [crime]s are usually created for small homogeneous audiences, but access is often unbounded due to their digital nature" (Surette 2015, 197). With emergent social media logics, performance crimes "are no longer rare events that are place and time bound to physical stages and scheduled broadcasts; they are now ephemeral renditions constantly created and repeatedly distributed in millions of social media interactions" (Surette 2015, 197).

The New Zealand mosque shooting in 2019 was one such example. An Islamophobic, white-supremacist, domestic terrorist shot and killed fifty people, injuring forty-eight others, in a carefully planned and orchestrated attack on two different mosques in Christchurch during Friday prayers (Besley and Peters 2020). The video that he made of the shooting was shared over two hundred thousand times on social media, in a "17-min live-stream video of the attack in a 1st-person shooter style similar to a video game for viewers to comment on in real time, a form of 'performance crime,' that was intended to inspire other alt-right followers as he posted on Facebook" (Besley and Peters 2020, 112). This shooter also belonged to an internet chat room, interestingly, the one that started the GamerGate harassment campaign against women in the gaming industry, mentioned earlier. As he livestreamed his attack, followers in this internet chat room "cheered along and encouraged him as innocent people died" (Duff 2019, n.p.), real people in real life, not a video game. Whereas "overtly racist and misogynist rhetoric and images would often be picked up and shut down on more mainstream channels like Discord, YouTube and Twitch, a live-streaming video platform where viewers could chat and comment on gameplay in real time" (Duff 2019, n.p.), the New Zealand mosque shooter's video was not detected before it was shared hundreds of thousands of times. The New Zealand government declared it illegal to share the video, deeming it "objectionable publication material" (Besley and Peters 2020, 112), but at the same time, clips of it were being shown on Australian TV, pointing to the difficulties in attempting to regulate violent terrorist content globally.

After this disturbing event and its even more disturbing mediatization, a debate raged about whether the tech giants whose platforms were being used to spread the video should be held accountable: "A Facebook vice president said fewer than 200 people saw the Christchurch massacre while it was being streamed live on the site. But the video was viewed about 4,000 times before Facebook removed it, he added. Countless more views occurred in the hours afterward, as copies of the video proliferated more quickly than online platforms like Facebook could remove them" (Schwartz 2019, n.p.). Sites such as 4chan and LiveLeak continued to host footage of the attacks, leading telecoms in New Zealand to decide to block those sites temporarily until the situation could be resolved (Schwartz 2019). In addition, "more than 1.2 million copies of the video were blocked at upload" by Facebook, and another 300,000 copies of the video were taken down in the twenty-four hours following the shooting. The upload or attempted upload rates seemed astronomical, with YouTube seeing "one upload every second," which one of their chief product officers called "unprecedented" (Schwartz 2019, n.p.). Either this was being done by pre-programmed hacker bots, a likely scenario given that this is how fake news and other misinformation typically spreads, or it is a sign of the intensification of racism and Islamophobia in global society. Either way, this is participatory culture gone wrong.

That it was tech companies that stepped in to block sites hosting the videos raises a whole host of regulatory questions. Who is responsible for making decisions about blocking content? What kind of content will they block, and how will they make those decisions in a way that is accountable and consistent with democratic governance? While this content clearly should not have been circulating, what happens when tech giants decide that people exercising the right to protest should be blocked, groups such as anarchists, socialists, anti-austerity protesters, Black Lives Matter, 2LGBTQ+ groups, feminists, or antiracist and Indigenous groups? Who decides and how can citizens contest being blocked? This is even more complicated with what is called "shadow banning," whereby a user can be blocked from a social media platform in such a way that they cannot tell.

Following calls for action subsequent to the mosque attack, Facebook, Microsoft, Twitter, and YouTube came together to form the Global Internet Forum to Counter Terrorism (GIFCT) to prevent the virality of livestreamed mass live-shootings by sharing hashes or unique digital fingerprints associated with the uploaded videos. According to its website, the objective is to "prevent terrorists and violent extremists from exploiting digital platforms." GIFCT is partnering with Tech Against Terrorism, a United Nations–led private-public partnership launched by the UN counterterrorism executive director in 2016. Specifically, as noted on the website, it is addressing the fact that "in some cases, terrorists have also developed their own technologies. Those of particular concern include social media, file-sharing, link-shortening, content storage, blockchain, video-sharing, content-pasting, archiving, blogging, fintech, e-commerce, encrypted messaging, VPNs, gaming, and email services." GIFCT is also establishing a high-level research network to investigate these issues.

The issue, however, is that GIFCT is its own supranational entity, making decisions under its own advisement, not accountable to any form of regulatory or democratic decision-making process or framework. Typically, counter-terrorism initiatives are undertaken domestically by those in policing or the military who have expertise in these areas, whereas Facebook, Microsoft, Twitter, and YouTube have neither the expertise nor the democratic frameworks. The consortium, moreover, contains a growing number of social media platforms such as Instagram, Reddit, and Twitter, and has logged over two hundred thousand hashes into its shared database. It has also developed its own "Content Incident Protocol" (see "Joint Tech Innovation" on its website). While GIFCT exercises massive corporate technological power, it has no power to compel all platforms to join its consortium or, for that matter, to compel anyone to abide by its Content Incident Protocol.

This initiative appears to be a positive, if complex, move by big tech to take responsibility for clamping down on the spread of violent terrorist images, videos, and discourses. At the same time, there is a deep contradiction embedded in the consortium. We have the high-tech, intersectional, capitalist organizations joining their considerable forces to lead us from technologies of control that they exercise over massive numbers of users into developing protocols for controlling these very technologies of control through top-down initiatives outside of democratic regulation that will be developed and implemented through more innovation in technologies of control. And all of this will be designed, developed, and coded by the same high-tech companies that have developed algorithms that are racist, sexist, homophobic, cisnormative, colonial, addictive, and in other ways socially insensitive, irresponsible, exploitative, and oppressive – as discussed throughout this book. Moreover, all of this will be done by a supra-national, supra-corporate consortium, outside any auspices of domestic policy and law, working toward accountability without any mechanism for democratic oversight and accountability and, moreover, also with inadequate education, training, and expertise in many of the issues and concerns expressed by media and movement activists engaged in intersectional technopolitics.

This high-tech consortium must therefore be understood as a consolidation of power at the highest level. But history and Hollywood have taught us nothing if not that a consolidation of power of this magnitude can be very dangerous for the democratic rights and freedoms of those who fall under its control. In this instance, the biggest red flag is the lack of any mechanism for democratic accountability. A call for technologies of control over these technologies of control is not a call for greater democratic control, in the same way that the global justice movement (GJM) was not a movement against globalization. Rather the GJM was a grassroots mobilization drawing attention to and calling into question the consolidation of power and undemocratic mechanisms of neoliberal capitalist globalization from above rather than democratic globalization for the common good of humanity. As with the movements and media projects analyzed in this book, despite contradictions and tensions, at root they are struggles for the betterment of society on a global scale. While GIFCT seems to have an eye on curtailing technologies of performance crime entailed by the livestreaming of mass shooting events, it may also be serving as a further entrenchment of EuroAmerican global intersectional capitalist hegemony and social control. Who has decided that this consortium should run things, on behalf of global citizens, in this particular way? Therein lies its deepest contradiction.

Where this consortium will lead is anybody's guess. But one thing we can be certain of is that there will be, as with all new technologies, some unintended consequences for technologies and democracies. Activists engaged in intersectional technopolitics will also, I suspect, want to confront these issues in what may be the next wave of political contention. Some are already doing so. And in doing so they will be forced to confront a quandary in terms of their repertoires of contention: How should they best take on platform power consolidation when they have come to rely heavily, if not exclusively, on social media platforms in their repertoires of contention? Which intersectional technopolitical practices will they need to develop to achieve the reach and audience afforded by the platforms they now depend on but under which they are also subsumed through technologies of control without control over these technologies?

The Technologies of Politics within Intersectional Technopolitics

Although this critical analysis of intersectional technopolitics aims to deepen our understanding of the more effective, complex, and nuanced uses of technologies and intersectional practices in meta-issue movements today, these movements are not without their complications and entanglements. Even within movements, technologies of politics can trouble the politics of technopolitics. Trolling and flaming can happen not just from outside movements, attacking a consolidated internal social movement front, but also from within groups, turning the anger at world politics and individual oppression inward on one another in a sometimes toxic call-out culture.

Admittedly, there is much to be angry about. As many feminist and anti-racist activists have argued, the anger that comes from experiences of oppression can be a resource if it is accessed in generative ways and focused on challenging the hegemonic structures of oppression.

At the same time, movements use strategies within and across global mobilizations, working toward and achieving deep transformations with very few resources, building movements that foster greater understanding across difference in configurations of affinity. Many activists work hard to understand perspectives outside their own experience, building, as we have seen, movements based on the shared risk and commitment taken on by accomplices rather than the tokenizing and potentially patronizing positioning of allies. In doing so, we must learn ways to stop turning our anger inward on ourselves in self-destructive technologies of self, and on our movements in destructive anti-oppression impulses. Internal attacks can be vicious and they can burn out movements when we should be creating relationships based on affinity, humility, respect, dignity, and the liberation of all. Despite best intentions, this does not always happen, and social media has exacerbated the problem. People in movements say they often feel like they are walking on eggshells, always worried that something they've said will turn up in a social media call-out. But where does affinity building come from, what does it offer, and how can we improve on it today, not to avoid internal conflict, but to handle it in such a way as to avoid burning out activists?

Anarchists and feminists have long organized through affinities, creating groups that construct political movements by building close personal relationships. The Spanish anarchists fighting in the revolution against Franco (some of whom, and/or their children and grandchildren, were later involved in Spain's 15M) organized using an affinity model in autonomous collectives, most often in workplaces. They collectivized not only boot makers, chocolate factories, and agrarian groups but also towns and infrastructure services, many of which joined a larger group called the Aragon Federation (Leval 2018). The Spanish collectives also included mass mobilizations of women, particularly a well-known group, Mujeres Libres, or Free Women of Spain (Ackelsberg 2005). Anarchists have continued building movements for gender, sex, and sexual liberation in the Spanish context and beyond (G. Brown 2007; Daring et al. 2012; Heckert and Cleminson 2011; Jeppesen 2010b, 2019; Jeppesen and Nazar 2013, 2018; Marsh 1978; Shannon 2009).

Anarchist collective movements are typically built on principles of affinity. Affinity groups organize for the most part using consensus models. As Dana Williams (2018, 120) suggests, "An affinity group may have a common purpose or goal (e.g., to publish a newspaper, support strike picket lines, or provide free food at protests), common background (having a similar political outlook or ideological sub-variant), or simply share a long-term association and friendship." Affinity groups are grassroots organizations based on organizing political activities together in small groups of from five to twenty people. As such, "the members are there to support each other and the group's objectives, to find effective ways of achieving success, and are a tangible way to participate in the broader anarchist movement" (D.M. Williams 2018, 120). Anarchist affinity groups also participate in broader meta-issue social movements.

While Williams emphasizes shared politics, feminist 2LGBTQ+ antiracist decolonial and/or anarchist affinity groups also share something more
in terms of community building and the creation of practices for egalitarian
participation. Martha Ackelsberg (2005, 204) has found that the affinity
groups of the Mujeres Libres structured themselves as "more or less egalitarian collectives, in which everyone could feel part of the community."
Community conscientization – defined as a process of coming to consciousness as empowered political subjects aware of the political means of oppression and creating collective means of contestation – is key in affinity groups.
This process acknowledges that affinity groups are important structures and
that "the interpersonal connections on which those structures were based
(and which they fostered) in turn sustained the group and its members"
(Ackelsberg 2005, 204). This is a support mechanism still discussed today
by media activists and social movement participants engaged in intersectional technopolitics. Activists examine and reflect on how they can sustain
their own lives through relationships of mutual support while also developing practices that foster sustainability and resilience for their collective projects and broader movements.

At the same time, as mentioned in Chapter 1, and illustrated throughout
this book, intersectional movements have been self-reflexive in considering
internal practices of power within organizing collectives, affinity groups, and
communities. However, "community" can be a fraught and amorphous term,
raising questions regarding who is included or excluded. As Martha Ackelsberg (2005, 204) notes, "The women of the Mujeres Libres were also aware of
the ambiguous nature of communities. Specifically, communities that ignore
or deny differences can perpetuate relations of hierarchy and domination
despite an ostensible commitment to equality." Ackelsberg argues that this
denial of difference and unwillingness to confront the tendency to develop
soft power or internal unspoken elites, as echoed by Todd Wolfson (2013) and
Sasha Costanza-Chock (2012a) in their studies of Indymedia and Occupy
media cultures, respectively, is a key struggle that already had its roots in the
Spanish anarchist feminist collectives. These collectives emphasized "relationships of mutuality and reciprocity, rather than of hierarchy and dominance" (Ackelsberg 2005, 204), relationships that are also valued in media
and movement projects today. Ackelsberg points to many levels of intersectionality in arguing that the exclusion of feminist concerns from mainstream
movements is related to the exclusion of the concerns of working-class women
and women of colour from feminist movements. The Mujeres Libres were
thus confronting the race to innocence through affinity group organizing.

Today, this anarchist feminist politics has been extended to address and counter the exclusion of trans and non-binary people from some feminist, anticolonial, queer, and antiracist movements. Despite fighting systemic oppression external to movements, the mechanisms of oppression in society at large continue to insert themselves within intersectional, anti-oppression, meta-issue social movements. This phenomenon seems to arise in new ways with every new wave of contention. It also plays out in different ways through variations in each wave's repertoires of communicative action. In contemporary digital movements, with the dominance of platform activism, mechanisms of identity policing, tone policing, call-out culture, flaming, and trolling, even within movements ostensibly built on shared affinities, have moved online, much to the detriment of close affinities and broader affinity building. As we have seen with the burnout and emotional tax associated with being trolled – for example, feminists being trolled by men's rights groups, or 2LGBTQ+ people being trolled by homophobic, cisnormative, and heteronormative attacks – burnout can also result from attacks within movements and even within affinity groups that can collapse as a result.

Ackelsberg (2005, 204) argues that the "Mujeres Libres understood empowerment as a communal process, [and] it also recognized that not all communities empower." Community building sometimes, therefore, needs to move outside of the structures of already existing communities. Ackelsberg (2005, 205) suggests that "societies structured hierarchically along lines of class, race, and gender, empower some while disempowering others," to which Spanish anarchist women responded with practices aimed, "through a focus on gender, to create a community that fully incorporates *all* its members." As such, they respected the ways in which women, men, 2LGBTQ+, and BIPOC people experienced and expressed similarities and differences, making space for all participants "to contribute their unique perspective to the movement and the new society" (Ackelsberg 2005, 205). The anarchist feminist affinity groups of the time focused on building bridges, networks, consciousnesses, and connections that could provide mechanisms and practices for empowerment and action for all members of society. This was done, as Ackelsberg (2005) notes, by creating affinities that did not insist everyone should be the same and share the same politics, as implied by Dana Williams (2018), but by respecting both differences and similarities to work together despite not entirely understanding one another's perspectives, with the shared objective of developing that understanding in the process.

This is not what is happening today through social media call-out culture and cancel culture. Call-out has taken root not just in mainstream society but also in social movement and media projects engaged in intersectional technopolitics, as articulated above in concerns regarding the race to innocence (Fellows and Razack 1998) and the Oppression Olympics (Dhamoon 2015). This was noted in MARG interviews by many participants who struggled to find mechanisms for building intersectional affinities across differences while also maintaining safe(r) spaces that could be inclusive of transfeminist, BIPOC, and 2LGBTQ+ participants and politics. This articulates a contradiction that movement and media activists are struggling with today – a commitment to building intersectional movements that bring people together to work across difference for widespread social transformation juxtaposed with practices such as policing the boundaries of participation, including some and excluding others, and turning anger internally toward those in affinity-based movements.

Movements also (despite statements, mandates, visions, and bases of unity to the contrary) often internalize oppressive structures, processes, and practices. And individuals, similarly, may also internalize oppressive belief systems. Thus, internal oppressions can be both structural and individualized. Not only do we turn our rage toward those we are struggling with, but we also turn it inward on ourselves. Thus, affinity building and movement building need to address intersectional oppressions on at least three levels – society, social movements, and individuals. This is where things get messy. We become entangled. We start hammering, as Sara Ahmed suggests, but maybe not always in the right direction.

In this context we can revisit Ahmed's argument, introduced in Chapter 5, that the constant, everyday hammering of many axes and structures of oppression that we experience may also be reversed, aimed outward, directed toward the systems of oppression themselves. We can thus take up hammering at the often-invisible walls of institutions, the technologies of power – the university system, gender binary systems, cis-centric systems, racialized and colonial systems, heteronormative systems, immigration systems, police violence systems, environmental destruction systems, state oppression systems, housing exclusion systems, and more – to render those walls visible to people with various axes of privilege who may have never come up against them. "Walls that are experienced as hard and tangible by some do not even exist for others," Ahmed (2016, 32) observes. However, some activists are in fact inadvertently engaged in (re)creating this type of wall. Specifically, Ahmed (2016, 33) is concerned with how some cis women, seeing trans and non-binary people chipping away at the walls that exclude them, should, instead of helping to maintain those walls, make an effort toward developing affinities by working together. She suggests we create an "affinity of hammers" to hammer down those walls. The removal of any wall of systemic oppression can be beneficial to all involved, regardless of whether we can see the wall or which side of the wall we may be on:

> We have to take a chance to combine our forces. There is nothing necessary about a combination. In chipping away, we come into contact with those who are stopped by what allowed us to pass through. We happen upon each other. We witness the work each other is doing, and we recognize each other through that work. And we take up arms when we combine our forces. We speak up; we rise up.
>
> (Ahmed 2016, 33)

Ahmed's affinity of hammers is thus a road map to being better accomplices and generating stronger 2LGBTQ+, antiracist, anticolonial, transfeminist, and anticapitalist intersectional coalitions and solidarities.

If the hammer is a metaphor for the technologies of politics of both oppression and resistance, it raises the question, What kinds of technologies and resistances are we building together? Can we find generative ways to stop hammering away at one another on social media, destructive processes that tear down relationships and affinities that are very fragile and take years to create and, instead, start hammering together to build an affinity of hammers that fosters respect for difference, healing justice, care and understanding, mutual learning, complex inter-connected globally-oriented epistemologies – in short, an intersectional technopolitics of resistance and liberation?

It seems clear that while the global justice and anti-austerity movements have focused on the politics of technologies in livestreaming protests, developing activist platforms, and hijacking social media activism, the new intersectional transfeminist, 2LGBTQ+, and BIPOC movements engage a broader consideration of the technologies of politics.

Building on anarchist feminists' and Ahmed's related affinity frameworks, I propose that it may be possible to build an affinity of hammers within and around intersectional technopolitics. Intersectionality opens up the complexities of relationships across difference, allowing us to see that there is much, in fact, that we cannot see, to know that there is much more that we cannot know, things that many others might see and know. This extension of our seeing and knowing can grow so much larger if we link it to that of others. Our knowledge and epistemologies can expand exponentially when linked with those of others.

An affinity framework also asks us to consider how and under which practices, structures, and technologies of power we might be responsible for causing harm, pain, exclusion, and other forms of oppression ourselves. Is there a way that people can assert their own empowerment without feeling the need to engage in the same old technologies of power over others that harm, exclude, and re-hierarchize? Can we move beyond a universal solidarity economy into an intersectional solidarity of technologies? Intersectionality, while sometimes resembling and (re)assembling a multiplicitous, internodal, rhizomatic assemblage or network connecting all categories and linking all differences through embedded similarities, also needs to be considered more simply in the everyday one-to-one relationships upon which all affinities, including an affinity of hammers, must be based.

As Foucault (1978) noted, power is exercised in mobile, unequal relationships in different spaces and times. But this exercise of power can also shift to create relationships of equality, not based on sameness, nor on affinities that include some and exclude others, but based on working with those whom we do not understand and with whom it might seem we have insurmountable differences. Can we shift from building movements of horizontalism from above, power elites from within, and horizontality from below, which establish fixed positions based on technologies of power, toward building movements that attempt to fundamentally challenge the continued existence of an above and a below? Can we shift from technologies of horizontal empowerment to horizontally empowering technologies of access, affordances, capacities, and structures? This is an invitation to dialogues that begin with an open mind, with the caution that, as discussed earlier, there must be a recognition that those with greater power and privilege must be willing to step back from their/our world view and listen. There must also be a recognition that these dialogues may have the potential to produce greater harm to those with less power and privilege, and must therefore be entered into in ways that create protective practices to foster their/our safe participation.

This book thus concludes by noting that terrains of transformation imbricated with the complexities of intersectional technopolitics play out in contradictory ways. In opening up these conversations, I acknowledge the book raises more questions than it resolves. Intersectional technopolitics is a mode of generative movement engagement that may foster an affinity of hammers, but it also comes with a set of contradictory, entangled promises and perils. Untangling these entanglements is the work of future movement and media activists and the scholars and researchers that work with them, with us, as accomplices.

Appendix

A partial and incomplete list of political groups and events participated in by the author that informed the empirical and theoretical frameworks of this book.

Protests and Mobilizations

1998 Toronto – Active Resistance
1998 Toronto – Hands Off Street Youth! protest
1998 Cologne – World Economic Forum protests
1998–2001 Toronto – Resist! collective
1998–2001 Toronto – Reclaim the Streets! protest
1999 Toronto – Resist! Jean Chrétien Welcoming Committee
2000 Toronto – Ontario Coalition Against Poverty (OCAP) anti-poverty protest
2000 Squamish – Elaho Valley Anarchist Horde (EVAH)
2001 Quebec City – anti-Free Trade Area of the Americas (FTAA) consultas and protests
2001 Toronto – direct-action training facilitator for anti-FTAA protests
2001 Windsor – Organization of American States (OAS) Shutdown Coalition
2001 Washington, DC – International Monetary Fund (IMF) protests
2001 Toronto – OCAP snake march
2011 Toronto – Occupy Toronto
2011 London – Occupy London

2012 Montreal – Quebec Student Strike

2016 Mexico – Women's March and Pussyhat protest

2017 Online and offline – #MeToo, #IdleNoMore, #BlackLivesMatter

Activist Media and Technology and Knowledge Production and Circulation

1995–2003 Zines – *Projectile, Wagenplatz, Skeleton Silk,* and *Scabies Guide to New York*

1996–2006 Canadian Union of Public Employees (CUPE) 3903 Toronto – Teaching Assistants, Research Assistants, and Sessional Instructors union

1996–97 Toronto – Who's Emma, anarchist punk record shop volunteer

1997–99 Mainz – Anti-neoliberalism Working Group

2000–01 Toronto – Random Anarchist Group

2001–02 Toronto – Toronto Anarchist Bookfair collective

2004–05 Toronto – Tao communications

2004–06 Toronto – Uprising Books

2004–06 Toronto – Guerrilla postering

2004–07 Toronto – Anarchist Free University

2008–09 Montreal – Montreal Anarchist Bookfair collective

Antiracism, Anticolonialism, Anti-poverty, Feminism

1997 Berlin – *Kein Mensch Ist Illegal* (No One Is Illegal)

1997–98 Mainz – Feminist working group

1998–2003 Toronto – OCAP

2000–03 Toronto – CUPE 3903 anti-poverty working group member

2004–06 Toronto – CUPE 3903 antiracism working group co-founder

2007–10 Montreal – Solidarity Across Borders

2007–08 Montreal – *Bloquez l'Empire*/Block the Empire

2016–18 Orillia – partnered with Orillia Native Women's Group (ONWG) to create a Storytelling Circle and Research Project

Politics of Everyday Life

1996–97 Toronto – Critical Mass bike ride

1997–98 Mainz – lived on a Wagenplatz squat

2007–08 Montreal – The People's Potato cook

2001–03 Toronto – Springhurst housing collective

2002–03 Toronto – DIY Care Collective

2013–15 Orillia – Community Gardens

Community-Engaged Research-Activism Projects That Inform This Book

2009–12 *Collectif de recherche sur l'autonomie collective* (CRAC; Research Group on Collective Autonomy). Initiated by Anna Kruzynski at Concordia University on anti-authoritarian social movements in Quebec and organized as an anti-authoritarian horizontal feminist research collective. Funded by a Social Sciences and Humanities Research Council of Canada (SSHRC) Standard Research Grant.

2014–16 **Protest Media Ecologies**. Organized with Alice Mattoni and Emiliano Treré at the Scuola Normale Superiore in Florence, Italy. The project studied protest media legacies during the anti-austerity protest movements that included 15M in Spain, the Aganaktismenoi in Greece, and the Anomalous Wave in Italy. Funded by a SSHRC Insight Development Grant.

2016–18 **Lakehead University Research Chair in Transformative Media and Social Movements**. Partnered with the Orillia Native Women's Group (ONWG) to develop a Storytelling Circle Research Project in conjunction with the ONWG Grandmothers Circle. Funded by Lakehead University.

2013–20 **Media Action Research Group** (MARG). A horizontal research collective at Lakehead University, Orillia, Canada. MARG conducted six focus groups across Canada, and ninety-six semi-structured interviews in eleven countries with media activist project participants who self-identified with our five pillars – intersectional anticapitalism, feminism, queer and trans liberation, antiracism, and anticolonialism. Funded by a SSHRC Insight Grant.

References

Ackelsberg, Martha A. 2005. *Free Women of Spain: Anarchism and the Struggle for the Emancipation of Women*. Oakland, CA: AK Press.

Ahmed, Sara. 2016. "An Affinity of Hammers." *TSQ: Transgender Studies Quarterly* 3 (1–2): 22–34. https://doi.org/10.1215/23289252-3334151.

Aikawa, Luiza, Sandra Jeppesen, and MARG. 2020. "Indymedia Legacies in Brazil and Spain: The Integration of Technopolitical and Intersectional Media Practices." *Media, Culture and Society* 42 (6): 1044–51. https://doi.org/10.1177/0163443720926055.

Alimahomed, Sabrina. 2010. "Thinking Outside the Rainbow: Women of Color Redefining Queer Politics and Identity." *Social Identities* 16 (2): 151–68. https://doi.org/10.1080/13504631003688849.

AMARC. 2007. *Community Radio Social Impact Assessment: Removing Barriers, Increasing Effectiveness*. Montreal: AMARC.

Amnesty International. 2004. *Stolen Sisters: A Human Rights Response to Discrimination and Violence against Indigenous Women in Canada*. London: Amnesty International.

Amnesty International. 2018. *#ToxicTwitter: Violence and Abuse against Women Online*. London: Amnesty International.

Andersson, Jonas. 2009. "For the Good of the Net: The Pirate Bay as a Strategic Sovereign." *Culture Machine* 10: 64–108.

Anzaldúa, Gloria. 1987. *Borderlands/La Frontera*. San Francisco: Aunt Lute Books.

Apoifis, Nicholas. 2017. *Anarchy in Athens: An Ethnography of Militancy, Emotions and Violence*. Manchester: Manchester University Press.

Appadurai, Arjun. 1990. "Disjuncture and Difference in the Global Cultural Economy." *Theory, Culture Society* 7 (2–3): 295–310. https://doi.org/10.1177/026327690007002017.

Araneta, Aitzole, and Sandra Fernández Garrido. 2016. "Transfeminist Genealogies in Spain." *TSQ: Transgender Studies Quarterly* 3 (1–2): 35–39. https://doi.org/10.1215/23289252-3334163.

Archibald, Linda, Vanessa Stevens, Jonathan Dewar, and Carrie Reid. 2012. *Dancing, Singing, Painting, and Speaking the Healing Story: Healing through Creative*

Arts – Scholars Portal Books. Ottawa: Aboriginal Healing Foundation. https:// books1.scholarsportal.info/viewdoc.html?id=532558.

Asara, Viviana. 2020. "Untangling the Radical Imaginaries of the Indignados' Movement: Commons, Autonomy and Ecologism." *Environmental Politics* (2020): 1–25. https://doi.org/10.1080/09644016.2020.1773176.

Atkinson, Joshua D. 2008. "Towards a Model of Interactivity in Alternative Media: A Multilevel Analysis of Audiences and Producers in a New Social Movement Network." *Mass Communication and Society* 11 (3): 227–47. https://doi. org/10.1080/15205430801919705.

Atton, Chris, and Emma Wickenden. 2006. "Sourcing Routines and Representation in Alternative Journalism: A Case Study Approach." *Journalism Studies* 6 (3): 347–59. https://doi.org/10.1080/14616700500132008.

Ayres, Jeffrey. 2004. "Framing Collective Action against Neoliberalism: The Case of the 'Anti-Globalization' Movement." *Journal of World-Systems Research* 10 (1): 11–34. https://doi.org/10.5195/jwsr.2004.311.

Azzellini, Dario. 2016. "Labour as a Commons: The Example of Worker-Recuperated Companies." *Critical Sociology* 44 (4–5): 763–76. https://doi.org/ 10.1177/0896920516661856.

Bailey, Jane, and Sara Shayan. 2016. "Missing and Murdered Indigenous Women Crisis: Technological Dimensions." *Canadian Journal of Women and the Law* 28 (2): 321–41. https://doi.org/10.3138/cjwl.28.2.321.

Bailey, Olga, Bart Cammaerts, and Nico Carpentier. 2008. *Understanding Alternative Media*. Bristol: Open University Press.

Balka, Ellen. 1999. "Where Have All the Feminist Technology Critics Gone?" Loka alert, November 11. http://www.loka.org/alerts/loka_alert_6.6.htm.

Banerji, Rita. 2011. "SlutWalk to Femicide: Making the Connection." *The WIP*, September 2. http://thewip.net/2011/09/02/slutwalk-to-femicide-making-the-connection/.

Bank Information Centre. n.d. "Samut Prakarn Wastewater Management Project." Bank Information Center. https://bankinformationcenter.org/en-us/project/samut -prakarn-wastewater-management-project/.

Baril, Alexandre. 2015. "Needing to Acquire a Physical Impairment/Disability: (Re)Thinking the Connections between Trans and Disability Studies through Transability." *Hypatia: A Journal of Feminist Philosophy* 30 (1): 30–48. https://doi. org/10.1111/hypa.12113.

Baú, Valentina. 2020. "Open Publishing, Decentralisation, and the Rise of New Media Platforms: Reflecting on the IMC Experience of Australia." *Media, Culture and Society* 42 (6): 1039–43. https://doi.org/10.1177/0163443720926045.

Bennett, W. Lance. 2004. "Social Movements beyond Borders: Understanding Two Eras of Transnational Activism." In *Transnational Protest and Global Activism*, edited by Donatella Della Porta and Sidney Tarrow, 203–26. New York: Rowman and Littlefield.

Bennett, W. Lance, and Alexandra Segerberg. 2012. "The Logic of Connective Action." *Information, Communication and Society* 15 (5): 739–68. https://doi.org/ 10.1080/1369118x.2012.670661.

–. 2013. *The Logic of Connective Action: Digital Media and the Personalization of Contentious Politics*. Cambridge: Cambridge University Press.

Berlant, Lauren, and Elizabeth Freeman. 1992. "Queer Nationality." *Boundary 2* 19 (1): 149–80. https://doi.org/10.2307/303454.

Berlant, Lauren, and Michael Warner. 1998. "Sex in Public." *Critical Inquiry* 24 (2): 547–66. https://doi.org/10.1086/448884.

Besley, Tina, and Michael A. Peters. 2020. "Terrorism, Trauma, Tolerance: Bearing Witness to White Supremacist Attack on Muslims in Christchurch, New Zealand." *Educational Philosophy and Theory* 52 (2): 109–19. https://doi.org/10.1080/00131857.2019.1602891.

Bilge, Sirma. 2016. "Intersectionality Undone: Saving Intersectionality from Feminist Intersectionality Studies." *Du Bois Review: Social Science Research on Race* 10 (2): 405–24. https://doi.org/10.1017/s1742058x13000283.

–. 2020. "The Fungibility of Intersectionality: An Afropessimist Reading." *Ethnic and Racial Studies* 43 (13): 2298–326. https://doi.org/10.1080/01419870.2020.1740289.

Black Women's Blueprint. 2016. "An Open Letter from Black Women to the SlutWalk." *Gender and Society* 30 (1): 9–13. https://doi.org/10.1177/0891243215611868.

Boellstorff, Tom, Mauro Cabral, Micha Cárdenas, Trystan Cotton, Eric A. Stanley, Kalaniopua Young, and Aren Z. Aizura. 2014. "Decolonizing Transgender: A Roundtable Discussion." *TSQ: Transgender Studies Quarterly* 1 (3): 419–39. https://doi.org/10.1215/23289252-685669.

Boler, Megan and Jennie Phillips. 2015. "Entanglements with Media and Technologies in the Occupy Movement." *Fibreculture Journal* 26: 236–67. https://doi.org/10.15307/fcj.26.197.2015.

Bonilla, Yarimar, and Jonathan Rosa. 2015. "#Ferguson: Digital Protest, Hashtag Ethnography, and the Racial Politics of Social Media in the United States: #Ferguson." *American Ethnologist* 42 (1): 4–17. https://doi.org/10.1111/amet.12112.

Bose, Pablo. 2004. "Critics and Experts, Activists and Academics: Intellectuals in the Fight for Social and Ecological Justice in the Narmada Valley, India." *International Review of Social History* 49 (12): 133–57. https://doi.org/10.1017/s0020859004001671.

Brah, Avtar, and Ann Phoenix. 2013. "Ain't I a Woman? Revisiting Intersectionality." *Journal of International Women's Studies* 5 (3): 75–86.

Brecher, Jeremy, Tim Costello, and Brendan Smith. 2000. *Globalization from Below: The Power of Solidarity*. Cambridge, MA: South End Press.

Breton, Émilie, Sandra Jeppesen, Anna Kruzynski, and Rachel Sarrasin. 2012a. "Feminisms at the Heart of Contemporary Anarchism in Quebec: Grassroots Practices of Intersectionality." *Canadian Woman Studies* 29 (3): 147–59.

–. 2012b. "Prefigurative Self-Governance and Self-Organization: The Influence of Antiauthoriatrian (Pro) Feminist Radical Queer, and Antiracist Networks in Quebec." In *Organize! Building from the Local for Global Justice*, edited by Aziz Choudry, Eric Shragge, and Jill Hanley, 156–72. Oakland, CA: PM Press.

Brocklehurst, Sean. 2019. "Hacking the Foreign-Policy Playbook: Tech-Diplomat Aims to Protect Democracy in Digital Age." CBC News, February 24. https://www.cbc.ca/news/technology/national-casper-klyge-tech-ambassador-1.4828015.

Brophy, Enda, and Greig de Peuter. 2007. "Immaterial Labor, Precarity, and Recomposition." In *Knowledge Workers in the Information Society*, edited by Catherine McKercher and Vincent Mosco, 177–92. Lanham, MD: Lexington Books.

Brown, Gavin. 2007. "Mutinous Eruptions: Autonomous Spaces of Radical Queer Activism." *Environment and Planning A: Economy and Space* 39 (11): 2685–98. https://doi.org/10.1068/a38385.

Brown, Gavin, Anna Feigenbaum, Patrick McCurdy, and Fabian Frenzel. 2017. *Protest Camps in International Context: Spaces, Infrastructures and Media of Resistance.* Bristol: Policy Press.

Brown, Melissa, Rashawn Ray, Ed Summers, and Neil Fraistat. 2017. "#SayHerName: A Case Study of Intersectional Social Media Activism." *Ethnic and Racial Studies* 40 (11): 1831–46. https://doi.org/10.1080/01419870.2017.1334934.

Browne, Rembert. 2016. "How Trump Made Hate Intersectional." *New York Magazine*, November 9. http://nymag.com/daily/intelligencer/2016/11/how-trump-made -hate-intersectional.html.

Burgess, Jean, and Joshua Green. 2013. *YouTube: Online Video and Participatory Culture.* Cambridge: Polity Press.

Burgess, Jean, and Ariadna Matamoros-Fernández. 2016. "Mapping Sociocultural Controversies across Digital Media Platforms: One Week of #gamergate on Twitter, YouTube, and Tumblr." *Communication Research and Practice* 2 (1): 79–96. https://doi.org/10.1080/22041451.2016.1155338.

Burke, Tarana. 2019. "'Our Pain Is Never Prioritized': #MeToo Founder Tarana Burke Says We Must Listen to 'Untold' Stories of Minority Women." *Time Magazine*, April 23. https://time.com/5574163/tarana-burke-metoo-time-100-summit/.

Burnap, Pete, and Matthew L. Williams. 2016. "Us and Them: Identifying Cyber Hate on Twitter across Multiple Protected Characteristics." *EPJ Data Science* 5 (11): 1–15. https://doi.org/10.1140/epjds/s13688-016-0072-6.

Byrd, Jodi A. 2011. *The Transit of Empire: Indigenous Critiques of Colonialism.* Minneapolis: University of Minnesota Press.

Caballero, Francisco Sierra, and Tommaso Gravante. 2017. *Networks, Movements and Technopolitics in Latin America: Critical Analysis and Current Challenges.* London: Palgrave Macmillan.

Caffentzis, George, and Silvia Federici. 2014. "Commons against and beyond Capitalism." *Community Development Journal* 49 (1): S92–S105. https://doi.org/10.1093/cdj/bsu006.

Cahill, Caitlin. 2007. "The Personal Is Political: Developing New Subjectivities through Participatory Action Research." *Gender, Place and Culture: A Journal of Feminist Geography* 14 (3): 267–92. https://doi.org/10.1080/09663690701324904.

Canella, Gino. 2017. "Social Movement Documentary Practices: Digital Storytelling, Social Media and Organizing." *Digital Creativity* 28 (1): 24–37. https://doi.org/10.1080/14626268.2017.1289227.

Carr, Joetta. 2013. "The SlutWalk Movement: A Study in Transnational Feminist Activism." *Journal of Feminist Scholarship* 4 (4): 24–38.

Carrier, Michael A. 2010. "The Pirate Bay, Grokster, and Google." *Journal of Intellectual Property Rights* 15: 7–18. https://doi.org/10.2139/ssrn.1481854.

Castells, Manuel. 2005a. "Toward a Sociology of the Network Society." *Contemporary Sociology* 29 (5): 693–99. https://doi.org/10.2307/2655234.

–. 2005b. "The Network Society: From Knowledge to Policy." In *The Network Society: From Knowledge to Policy*, edited by Manuel Castells and Gustavo Cardoso, 3–21. Washington, DC: Johns Hopkins Center for Transatlantic Relations.

–. 2010. *The Rise of the Network Society.* 2nd ed. Hoboken, NJ: Wiley-Blackwell.

Cavanagh, Sheila L. 2010. *Queering Bathrooms: Gender, Sexuality, and the Hygienic Imagination.* Toronto: University of Toronto Press.

CBC. 1967. "Trudeau: 'There's No Place for the State in the Bedrooms of the Nation.'" CBC Archives. http://www.cbc.ca/archives/entry/omnibus-bill-theres-no-place -for-the-state-in-the-bedrooms-of-the-nation.

Chander, Anupam. 2017. "The Racist Algorithm?" *Michigan Law Review* 115 (6): 1023–45.

Chanicka, Jeewan. 2018. "Racist Microaggressions Are Like Death by a Thousand Cuts." *Huffington Post,* March 19. http://www.huffingtonpost.ca/jeewan-chanicka/ microaggression-privilege-racism-discrimination_a_23387202/.

Chavez, Daniel Brittany. 2016. "Transmasculine Insurgency: Masculinity and Dissidence in Feminist Movements in Mexico." *TSQ: Transgender Studies Quarterly* 3 (1–2): 58–64. https://doi.org/10.1215/23289252-3334199.

Chen, Hsuan-Ting, Sun Ping, and Gan Chen. 2015. "Far from Reach but near at Hand: The Role of Social Media for Cross-National Mobilization." *Computers in Human Behavior* 53 (December): 443–51. https://doi.org/10.1016/j.chb.2015.05.052.

Chen, Yin-Zu. 2014. "How to Become a Feminist Activist after the Institutionalization of the Women's Movements: The Generational Development of Feminist Identity and Politics in Mexico City." *Frontiers: A Journal of Women Studies* 35 (3): 183–206. https://doi.org/10.5250/fronjwomestud.35.3.0183.

Christensen, C. 2009. "Political Documentary, Online Organization and Activist Synergies." *Studies in Documentary Film* 3 (2): 77–94.

Chun, Jennifer Jihye, George Lipsitz, and Young Shin. 2013. "Intersectionality as a Social Movement Strategy: Asian Immigrant Women Advocates." *Signs: Journal of Women in Culture and Society* 38 (4): 917–40. https://doi.org/10.1086/669575.

Clark, Natalie. 2016. "Red Intersectionality and Violence-Informed Witnessing Praxis with Indigenous Girls." *Girlhood Studies* 9 (2). https://doi.org/10.3167/ ghs.2016.090205.

Clayton, Thomas. 2004. "Competing Conceptions of Globalization Revisited: Relocating the Tension between World-Systems Analysis and Globalization Analysis." *Comparative Education Review* 48 (3): 274–94. https://doi.org/10.1086/421180.

Coates, Ken. 2015. *#IdleNoMore and the Remaking of Canada*. Regina: University of Regina Press.

Cohen, Jason. 2020. "#BlackLivesMatter Hashtag Averages 3.7 Million Tweets Per Day during Unrest." *PCMAG,* July 20. https://www.pcmag.com/news/ blacklivesmatter-hashtag-averages-37-million-tweets-per-day-during-unrest.

Cohen, Nicole S. 2013. "Commodifying Free Labour Online: Social Media, Audiences, and Advertising." In *The Routledge Companion to Advertising and Promotional Culture,* edited by Matthew P. McAllister and Emily West, 177–91. https:// doi.org/10.4324/9780203071434-25.

–. 2016. *Writers' Rights: Freelance Journalism in a Digital Age*. Montreal/Kingston: McGill-Queen's University Press.

Cole, Desmond. 2020. *The Skin We're In: A Year of Black Resistance and Power*. Toronto: Doubleday.

Coleman, Gabriella. 2011. "Anonymous: From the lulz to collective action." Mediacommons. Accessed May 21, 2017. http://mediacommons.futureofthebook.org/ tne/pieces/anonymous-lulz-collective-action.

–. 2014. *Hacker, Hoaxer, Whistleblower, Spy: The Many Faces of Anonymous*. London: Verso Books.

Collins, Patricia Hill. 1986. "Learning from the Outsider Within: The Sociological Significance of Black Feminist Thought." *Social Problems* 33 (6): S14–S32. https://doi.org/10.1525/sp.1986.33.6.03a00020.

–. 1998. "It's All in the Family: Intersections of Gender, Race, and Nation." *Hypatia* 13 (3): 62–82. https://doi.org/10.1111/j.1527-2001.1998.tb01370.x.

–. 2000. *Black Feminist Thought: Knowledge, Consciousness, and the Politics of Empowerment.* London: Psychology Press.

Collins, Patricia Hill, and Sirma Bilge. 2016. *Intersectionality.* Cambridge: Polity Press.

Combahee River Collective. 1977. *The Combahee River Collective Statement.* Accessed May 1, 2021. https://www.blackpast.org/african-american-history/combahee-river-collective-statement-1977/.

Correa Leite, Jose. 2003. "The Internationalisation of the World Social Forum and Its Future." *Convergence* 36 (3–4): 37–45.

Costanza-Chock, Sasha. 2012. "Mic Check! Media Cultures and the Occupy Movement." *Social Movement Studies* 11 (3–4): 375–85. https://doi.org/10.1080/14742837.2012.710746.

–. 2013. "Transmedia Mobilization in the Popular Association of the Oaxacan Peoples, Los Angeles." In *Mediation and Protest Movements*, edited by Bart Cammaerts, Alice Mattoni, and Patrick McCurdy, 96–114. Bristol: Intellect.

–. 2014. *Out of the Shadows, into the Streets! Transmedia Organizing and the Immigrant Rights Movement.* Cambridge, MA: MIT Press.

Costanza-Chock, Sasha, Chris Schweidler, and Transformative Media Organizing Project (TMOP). 2017. "Toward Transformative Media Organizing: LGBTQ and Two-Spirit Media Work in the United States." *Media, Culture and Society* 39 (2): 159–84. https://doi.org/10.1177/0163443716674360.

Couldry, Nick, and Bruno Campanella. 2019. "From the Mediated Centre to the Hollowing Out of the Social World: The Media and the Process of Datafication of Society." *MATRIZes* 13 (2): 77–87. https://doi.org/10.11606/issn.1982-8160.v13i2p77-87.

Cox, Jonathan. 2017. "The Source of a Movement: Making the Case for Social Media as an Informational Source Using Black Lives Matter." *Ethnic and Racial Studies* 40 (11): 1847–54.

Crass, Chris. 2013. *Towards Collective Liberation: Anti-racist Organizing, Feminist Praxis, and Movement Building Strategies.* Oakland, CA: PM Press.

Craven, Julia. 2016. "Black Lives Matter Toronto Stands by Pride Parade Shutdown." *Huffington Post*, July 6. Politics. https://www.huffingtonpost.com/entry/black-lives-matter-toronto-pride_us_577c15aee4b0a629c1ab0ab4.

Crenshaw, Kimberlé. 1989. "Demarginalizing the Intersection of Race and Sex: A Black Feminist Critique of Antidiscrimination Doctrine, Feminist Theory and Antiracist Politics." *University of Chicago Legal Forum* 1989 (1): 139–67. https://doi.org/10.4324/9780429500480-5.

–. 1991. "Mapping the Margins: Intersectionality, Identity Politics, and Violence against Women of Color." *Stanford Law Review* 43 (6): 1241–99. https://doi.org/10.2307/1229039.

–. 2011. "From Private Violence to Mass Incarceration: Thinking Intersectionally about Women, Race, and Social Control." *UCLA Law Review* 59: 1418–72.

Crenshaw, Kimberlé, Andrea Ritchie, Rachel Anspach, Rachel Gilmer, and Luke Harris. 2015. "Say Her Name: Resisting Police Brutality against Black Women." Centre for Victim Research. https://hdl.handle.net/20.500.11990/1926.

Cromwell, Jason. 2006. "Queering the Binaries: Transsituated Identities, Bodies, and Sexualities." In *The Transgender Studies Reader*, edited by Susan Stryker and Stephen Whittle, 509–20. New York: Routledge.

Cruells, Marta, and Sonia Ruiz García. 2014. "Political Intersectionality within the Spanish Indignados Social Movement." *Research in Social Movements, Conflicts and Change* 37: 3–25. https://doi.org/10.1108/s0163-786x20140000037001.

Cullors, Patrisse. 2016. "#BlackLivesMatter and Global Visions of Liberation." In *Policing the Planet: Why the Policing Crisis Led to Black Lives Matter*, edited by Jordan T. Camp and Christina Heatherton, 76–88. London: Verso.

Curran, James, Natalie Fenton, and Des Freedman. 2016. *Misunderstanding the Internet*. London: Routledge.

DaCosta, Jamaias. 2014. "#HASHTAG #REVOLUTION." *MUSKRAT Magazine*, March 14. http://muskratmagazine.com/hashtag-revolution/.

Dallabona-Fariniuk, Tharsila, and Rodrigo Firmino. 2018. "Smartphones, Smart Spaces? The Use of Locative Media in the Urban Space in Curitiba, Brazil." *EURE, Revista Latinoamericana de Estudios Urbano Regionales* 44 (133): 255–75. https://doi.org/10.4067/s0250-71612018000300255.

Daniels, Jessie. 2009. "Cyberfeminism(s): Race, Gender, and Embodiment." *Women's Studies Quarterly* 37 (1–2): 101–24. https://doi.org/10.1353/wsq.0.0158.

Daring, C.B., J. Rogue, Deric Shannon, and Abbey Volcano. 2012. *Queering Anarchism: Addressing and Undressing Power and Desire*. Oakland, CA: AK Press.

Davis, Angela Y. 2003. *Are Prisons Obsolete?* New York: Seven Stories.

Davis, Angela, and Gina Dent. 2001. "Prison as a Border: A Conversation on Gender, Globalization, and Punishment." *Signs* 26 (4): 1235–41. https://doi.org/10.1086/495654.

de Castro Ferreira, Carolina Branco. 2015. "Feminisms on the Web: Lines and Forms of Action in Contemporary Feminist Debate." *Cadernos Pagu* 44 (Jan–June): 199–228. https://doi.org/10.1590/1809-4449201500440199.

de Peuter, Greig, Nicole Cohen, and Enda Brophy. 2012. "Interns Unite! (You Have Nothing to Lose – Literally!)" *Briarpatch Magazine*, November 9. https://briarpatchmagazine.com/articles/view/interns-unite-you-have-nothing-to-lose-literally.

Dean, Jodi. 2005. "Communicative Capitalism: Circulation and the Foreclosure of Politics." *Cultural Politics* 1 (1): 51–74. https://doi.org/10.2752/174321905778054845.

–. 2009. *Democracy and Other Neoliberal Fantasies: Communicative Capitalism and Left Politics*. Durham, NC: Duke University Press.

–. 2014. "Communicative Capitalism and Class Struggle." *Spheres Journal for Digital Culture* 1: 1–14.

Deggans, Eric. 2011. "How the Rodney King Video Paved the Way for Today's Citizen Journalism." CNN, March 7. http://www.cnn.com/2011/OPINION/03/05/deggans.rodney.king.journalism/index.html.

Deleuze, Gilles, and Felix Guattari. 1987. *A Thousand Plateaus: Capitalism and Schizophrenia*. Minneapolis: University of Minnesota Press.

Delgado, Richard, and Jean Stefancic. 2017. *Critical Race Theory: An Introduction*. New York: NYU Press.

Dencik, Lina, Arne Hintz, and Jonathan Cable. 2016. "Towards Data Justice? The Ambiguity of Anti-surveillance Resistance in Political Activism." *Big Data and Society* 3 (2): 1–12. https://doi.org/10.1177/2053951716679678.

Denzin, Norman K., Yvonna S. Lincoln, and Linda Tuhiwai Smith, eds. 2008. *Handbook of Critical and Indigenous Methodologies*. New York: Sage.

Depelteau, Julie, and Dalie Giroux. 2015. "LGBTQ Issues as Indigenous Politics: Two-Spirit Mobilization in Canada." In *Queer Mobilizations: Social Movement Activism and Canadian Public Policy*, edited by Manon Tremblay, 64–81. Vancouver: UBC Press.

Dessewffy, Tibor, and Zsófia Nagy. 2016. "Born in Facebook: The Refugee Crisis and Grassroots Connective Action in Hungary." *International Journal of Communication* 10 (2016): 2872–94.

Deuze, Mark. 2012. *Media Life*. Cambridge: Polity.

Dhamoon, Rita Kaur. 2015. "A Feminist Approach to Decolonizing Anti-racism: Rethinking Transnationalism, Intersectionality, and Settler Colonialism." *Feral Feminisms* 1 (4): 20–36. https://feralfeminisms.com/rita-dhamoon/.

DiAngelo, Robin. 2018. *White Fragility: Why It's So Hard for White People to Talk about Racism*. Boston: Beacon Press.

Dowling, Emma, Rodrigo Nunes, and Ben Trott. 2007. "Immaterial and Affective Labour: Explored." *Ephemera: Theory and Politics in Organization* 7 (1): 1–7.

Downing, John. 1988. "The Alternative Public Realm: The Organization of the 1980s Anti-nuclear Press in West Germany and Britain." *Media, Culture and Society* 10 (2): 163–81. https://doi.org/10.1177/016344388010002003.

–. 2003. "Audiences and Readers of Alternative Media: The Absent Lure of the Virtually Unknown." *Media, Culture and Society* 25 (5): 625–45. https://doi.org/10.1177/01634437030255004.

Driskill, Qwo-Li. 2011. *Queer Indigenous Studies: Critical Interventions in Theory, Politics, and Literature*. Tucson: University of Arizona Press.

Duff, Michelle. 2019. "Gaming Culture and the Alt-Right: The Weaponisation of Hate." *Stuff*, March 24. https://www.stuff.co.nz/national/christchurch-shooting/111468129/gaming-culture-and-the-alt-right-the-weaponisation-of-hate.

Dupuis-Déri, Francis. 2019. *Les black blocs: La liberté et l'égalité se manifestent*. Montreal: Lux Éditeur.

Dwyer, Sonya Corbin, and Jennifer L. Buckle. 2009. "The Space Between: On Being an Insider-Outsider in Qualitative Research." *International Journal of Qualitative Methods* 8 (1): 54–63. https://doi.org/10.1177/160940690900800105.

Dyer-Witheford, Nick. 1999. *Cyber-Marx: Cycles and Circuits of Struggle in High-Technology Capitalism*. Champaign, IL: University of Illinois Press.

Edwards, Paul N., and Gabrielle Hecht. 2010. "History and the Technopolitics of Identity: The Case of Apartheid South Africa." *Journal of Southern African Studies* 36 (3): 619–39. https://doi.org/10.1080/03057070.2010.507568.

Egan, R. Danielle, and Gail L. Hawkes. 2008. "Endangered Girls and Incendiary Objects: Unpacking the Discourse on Sexualization." *Sexuality and Culture* 12 (4): 291–311. https://doi.org/10.1007/s12119-008-9036-8.

Egaña, Lucía, and Miriam Solá. 2016. "Hacking the Body: A Transfeminist War Machine." *TSQ: Transgender Studies Quarterly* 3 (1–2): 74–80. https://doi.org/10.1215/23289252-3334223.

Eldred, Jan, and Alan Tuckett. 2003. "Another World Is Possible." *Convergence* 36 (3–4): 99–110.

Ellison, Keith. 2016. Foreword to Sue Bradford Edwards and Duchess Harris, *Black Lives Matter*, 4–5. Minneapolis: Abdo Publishing.

Eltahawy, Mona. 2018. "#MosqueMeToo: What Happened When I Was Sexually Assaulted during the Hajj." *Washington Post*, February 15. https://www.washingtonpost.com/news/global-opinions/wp/2018/02/15/mosquemetoo-what-happened-when-i-was-sexually-assaulted-during-the-hajj/.

Erickson, Loree. 2007. "Revealing Femmegimp: A Sex-Positive Reflection on Sites of Shame as Sites of Resistance for People with Disabilities." *Atlantis: Critical Studies in Gender, Culture and Social Justice* 31 (2): 42–52.

–. 2015. "Unbreaking Our Hearts: Cultures of Un/desirability and the Transformative Potential of Queercrip Porn." PhD diss., York University. https://yorkspace.library.yorku.ca/xmlui/handle/10315/32089.

Espineira, Karine, and Marie-Hélène/Sam Bourcier. 2016. "Transfeminism: Something Else, Somewhere Else." *TSQ: Transgender Studies Quarterly* 3 (1–2): 84–94. https://doi.org/10.1215/23289252-3334247.

Evans, Sarah Beth, and Elyse Janish. 2015. "#INeedDiverseGames: How the Queer Backlash to GamerGate Enables Nonbinary Coalition." *QED: A Journal in GLBTQ Worldmaking* 2 (2): 125–50. https://doi.org/10.14321/qed.2.2.0125.

Ezquerra, Sandra. 2012. "Feminist Practice in the 15-M Movement: Progress and Outstanding Issues." *OpenDemocracy*, July 12. https://www.opendemocracy.net/en/feminist-practice-in-15-m/.

Farrow, Lynne, and Black Bear. 1977. "Feminism as Anarchism." *The Anarchist Library*. http://theanarchistlibrary.org/pdfs/letter/Lynne_Farrow__Feminism_As_Anarchism_letter.pdf.

Federici, Silvia. 2011. "Women, Land Struggles, and the Reconstruction of the Commons." *WorkingUSA* 14 (1): 41–56. https://doi.org/10.1111/j.1743-4580.2010.00319.x.

Feigenbaum, Anna. 2010. *Tactics and Technology: Cultural Resistance at the Greenham Common Women's Peace Camp*. Montreal/Kingston: McGill-Queen's University Press.

Feigenbaum, Anna, Fabian Frenzel, and Patrick McCurdy. 2013. *Protest Camps*. London: Zed Books.

Feinberg, Leslie. 2006. "Transgender Liberation: A Movement Whose Time Has Come." In *The Transgender Studies Reader*, edited by Susan Stryker and Stephen Whittle, 205–20. New York: Routledge.

Fellows, Mary, and Sherene Razack. 1998. "The Race to Innocence: Confronting Hierarchical Relations among Women." *Journal of Gender, Race and Justice* 1 (1998): 335–52.

Fenton, Natalie. 2020. "Indymedia and the Long Story of Rebellion against Neoliberal Capitalism." *Media, Culture and Society* 42 (6): 1052–58. https://doi.org/10.1177/0163443720926039.

Ferris, Melanie A. 2001. "Resisting Mainstream Media: Girls and the Act of Making Zines." *Canadian Woman Studies* 20–21 (Winter/Spring): 51–55.

Fischer, Mia. 2016. "#Free_CeCe: The Material Convergence of Social Media Activism." *Feminist Media Studies* 16 (5): 755–71. https://doi.org/10.1080/14680777.2016.1140668.

Florini, Sarah. 2015. "This Week in Blackness, the George Zimmerman Acquittal, and the Production of a Networked Collective Identity." *New Media and Society* 19 (3): 439–54. https://doi.org/10.1177/1461444815606779.

Fominaya, Cristina Flesher, and Kevin Gillan. 2017. "Navigating the Technology-Media-Movements Complex." *Social Movement Studies* 16 (4): 383–402. https://doi.org/10.1080/14742837.2017.1338943.

Foucault, Michel. 1978. *The History of Sexuality*. New York: Pantheon Books.

—. 1988. *Technologies of the Self: A Seminar with Michel Foucault*. Boston: University of Massachusetts Press.

France, David. 2012. "Pictures from a Battlefield." *New York Magazine*, March 23. http://nymag.com/news/features/act-up-2012-4/.

Freelon, Deen, Charlton D. McIlwain, and Meredith Clark. 2016. "Quantifying the Power and Consequences of Social Media Protest." *New Media & Society* 20 (3): 990–1011. https://doi.org/10.1177/1461444816676646.

Friedman, J. 2008. "Wack Attack: Giving the Digital Finger to Blog Bandits." *Bitchmedia*, March 3. https://www.bitchmedia.org/article/from-the-archive-wack-attack.

Fuchs, Christian. 2009. "Information and Communication Technologies and Society: A Contribution to the Critique of the Political Economy of the Internet." *European Journal of Communication* 24 (1): 69–87. https://doi.org/10.1177/0267323108098947.

—. 2010. "Social Software and Web 2.0: Their Sociological Foundations and Implications." In *Handbook of Research on Web 2.0, 3.0, and X.0: Technologies, Business, and Social Applications*, edited by San Murugesan, 764–89. Hershey, PA: Information Science Reference.

—. 2012. "The Political Economy of Privacy on Facebook." *Television and New Media* 13 (2): 139–59. https://doi.org/10.1177/1527476411415699.

—. 2013. "Theorising and Analysing Digital Labour: From Global Value Chains to Modes of Production." *Political Economy of Communication* 2: 3–27.

Fuster Morell, Mayo. 2012. "The Free Culture and 15M Movements in Spain: Composition, Social Networks and Synergies." *Social Movement Studies* 11 (3–4): 386–92. https://doi.org/10.1080/14742837.2012.710323.

Gajjala, Radhika, and Annapurna Mamidipudi. 1999. "Cyberfeminism, Technology, and International 'Development.'" *Gender and Development* 7 (2): 8–16.

Gámez Fuentes, María José. 2015. "Feminisms and the 15M Movement in Spain: Between Frames of Recognition and Contexts of Action." *Social Movement Studies* 14 (3): 359–65. https://doi.org/10.1080/14742837.2014.994492.

Garriga-López, Claudia Sofía. 2016. "Transfeminist Crossroads: Reimagining the Ecuadorian State." *TSQ: Transgender Studies Quarterly* 3 (1–2): 104–19. https://doi.org/10.1215/23289252-3334271.

Garza, Alicia. 2014. "A Herstory of the #BlackLivesMatter Movement." In *Are All the Women Still White? Rethinking Race, Expanding Feminisms*, edited by Janell Hobson, 23–28. Albany, NY: SUNY Press.

Gash, Alison, and Ryan Harding. 2018. "#MeToo? Legal Discourse and Everyday Responses to Sexual Violence." *Laws* 7 (2): 21–45. https://doi.org/10.3390/laws7020021.

Geist, Michael. 2015. *Law, Privacy and Surveillance in Canada in the Post-Snowden Era*. Ottawa: University of Ottawa Press.

Gentile, Haley, and Stacy Salerno. 2019. "Communicating Intersectionality through Creative Claims Making: The Queer Undocumented Immigrant Project." *Social Identities* 25 (2): 207–23. https://doi.org/10.1080/13504630.2017.1376279.

Gerbaudo, Paolo. 2012. *Tweets and the Streets: Social Media and Contemporary Activism.* London: Pluto.

Gilchrist, Kristen. 2010. "'Newsworthy' Victims? Exploring Differences in Canadian Local Press Coverage of Missing/Murdered Aboriginal and White Women." *Feminist Media Studies* 10 (4): 373–90. https://doi.org/10.1080/14680777.2010. 514110.

Gilio-Whitaker, Dina. 2018. "Settler Fragility: Why Settler Privilege Is So Hard to Talk About." *Beacon Broadside,* November 14. https://www.beaconbroadside.com/broadside/ 2018/11/settler-fragility-why-settler-privilege-is-so-hard-to-talk-about.html.

Giroux, Henry. 2002. "Neoliberalism, Corporate Culture, and the Promise of Higher Education: The University as a Democratic Public Sphere." *Harvard Educational Review* 72 (4): 425–64. https://doi.org/10.17763/haer.72.4.0515nr62324n71p1.

Goodman, Amy. 2004. "The Zapatista Uprising, 1994–2004: A Look at How an Indigenous Rebel Group from Chiapas Took on Mexico and Corporate Global-ization." *Democracy Now!* January 2. https://www.democracynow.org/2004/1/2/ the_zapatista_uprising_1994_2004_a.

Gordon, Uri. 2008. *Anarchy Alive! Anti-authoritarian Politics from Practice to Theory.* London: Pluto.

Government of Canada. 2020. "Indigenous People in Federal Custody Surpasses 30%." Office of the Correctional Investigator, April 16. https://www.oci-bec.gc.ca/ cnt/comm/press/press20200121-eng.aspx.

Grant, Jaime, Lisa Mottet, Justin Tanis, Jack Harrison, Jody L. Herman, and Mara Keisling. 2011. *Injustice at Every Turn: A Report of the National Transgender Discrimination Survey.* Washington: National Centre for Transgender Equality and National Gay and Lesbian Task Force. http://www.thetaskforce.org/injustice-every -turn-report-national-transgender-discrimination-survey/.

The Guardian. 2017. "The Guardian View on #MeToo: What Comes Next?" *The Guardian,* December 31. http://www.theguardian.com/commentisfree/2017/ dec/31/the-guardian-view-on-metoo-what-comes-next.

Gyenes, Natalie, Connie Moon Sehat, Sands Fish, Anushka Shah, Jonas Kaiser, Paola Villarreal, Simin Kargar, et al. 2017. "Fighting For, Not Fighting Against: Media Coverage and the Dakota Access Pipeline." *Global Voices,* March 1. https:// globalvoices.org/2017/03/01/fighting-for-not-fighting-against-media-coverage -and-the-dakota-access-pipeline/.

Halupka, Max. 2016. "The Rise of Information Activism: How to Bridge Dualisms and Reconceptualise Political Participation." *Information, Communication and Society* 19 (10): 1487–1503. https://doi.org/10.1080/1369118x.2015.1119872.

Haney-Lopez, Ian. 1994. "The Social Construction of Race: Some Observations on Illusion, Fabrication, and Choice." *Harvard Civil Rights–Civil Liberties Law Review* 29 (2): 1–62.

Hanke, Bob. 2005. "For a Political Economy of Indymedia Practice." *Canadian Journal of Communication* 30 (1): 41–64. https://doi.org/10.22230/cjc.2005v30n1a1479.

Haraway, Donna. 1991. *Simians, Cyborgs and Women: The Reinvention of Nature.* New York: Routledge.

–. 1994. "A Manifesto for Cyborgs: Science, Technology, and Socialist Feminism in the 1980s." In *The Postmodern Turn: New Perspectives on Social Theory,* edited by Steven Seidman, 82–116. Cambridge: Cambridge University Press.

Harding, Sandra. 1992. "Subjectivity, Experience and Knowledge: An Epistemology from/for Rainbow Coalition Politics." *Development and Change* 23 (3): 175–93. https://doi.org/10.1111/j.1467-7660.1992.tb00461.x.

–. 1998. "Multiculturalism, Postcolonialism, Feminism: Do They Require New Research Epistemologies?" *Australian Educational Researcher* 25 (1): 37–51. https://doi.org/10.1007/bf03219664.

Harding, Tom. 1998. "Viva Camcordistas! Video Activism and the Protest Movement." In *DiY Culture: Party and Protest in Nineties Britain,* edited by George McKay, 79–99. London: Verso.

Hargreaves, Allison. 2017. *Violence against Indigenous Women: Literature, Activism, Resistance.* Kitchener-Waterloo: Wilfrid Laurier University Press.

Harper, Randi. 2014. *ggautoblocker: Good Game Auto Blocker.* https://github.com/freebsdgirl/ggautoblocker.

Harris, Angela P. 2012. "Critical Race Theory." In *International Encyclopedia of the Social and Behavioral Sciences,* 2nd ed., edited by Neil Smelser, Paul Baltes, and James D. Wright, 2976–80. Amsterdam: Elsevier.

Harris, Douglas C., and Peter Millerd. 2010. "Food Fish, Commercial Fish, and Fish to Support a Moderate Livelihood: Characterizing Aboriginal and Treaty Rights to Canadian Fisheries." *Arctic Review on Law and Politics* 1 (1): 82–107.

Harris, Fredrick C. 2015. "The Next Civil Rights Movement?" *Dissent Magazine,* Summer. https://www.dissentmagazine.org/article/black-lives-matter-new-civil-rights-movement-fredrick-harris.

Harvey, David. 2011. "The Future of the Commons." *Radical History Review* 109: 101–7. https://doi.org/10.1215/01636545-2010-017.

Hattery, Angela J., and Earl Smith. 2017. *Policing Black Bodies: How Black Lives Are Surveilled and How to Work for Change.* Lanham, MD: Rowman and Littlefield.

Hebdige, Dick. 1979. *Subculture: The Meaning of Style.* London: Methuen.

Heckert, Jamie, and Richard Cleminson, eds. 2011. *Anarchism and Sexuality: Ethics, Relationships and Power.* London: Routledge.

Heckert, Jamie, Deric Michael Shannon, and Abbey Willis. 2012. "Loving-Teaching: Notes for Queering Anarchist Pedagogies." *Educational Studies* 48 (1): 12–29. https://doi.org/10.1080/00131946.2011.637258.

Henry, Frances, Enakshi Dua, Audrey Kobayashi, Carl James, Peter Li, Howard Ramos, and Malinda S. Smith. 2017. "Race, Racialization and Indigeneity in Canadian Universities." *Race Ethnicity and Education* 20 (3): 300–14. https://doi.org/10.1080/13613324.2016.1260226.

Herman, Edward S., and Noam Chomsky. 2010. *Manufacturing Consent: The Political Economy of the Mass Media.* New York: Random House.

Hermida, Alberto, and Víctor Hernández-Santaolalla. 2018. "Twitter and Video Activism as Tools for Counter-Surveillance: The Case of Social Protests in Spain." *Information, Communication and Society* 21 (3): 416–33. https://doi.org/10.1080/1369118x.2017.1284880.

Hintz, Arne. 2011. "From Media Niche to Policy Spotlight: Mapping Community-Media Policy Change in Latin America." *Canadian Journal of Communication* 36 (1): 147–59. https://doi.org/10.22230/cjc.2011v36n1a2458.

Hintz, Arne, Lina Dencik, and Karin Wahl-Jorgensen. 2018. *Digital Citizenship in a Datafied Society.* Cambridge: Polity.

hooks, bell. 1982. *Ain't I a Woman? Black Women and Feminism.* London: Pluto.

–. 1997. "Representing Whiteness in the Black Imagination." In *Displacing Whiteness: Essays in Social and Cultural Criticism,* edited by Ruth Frankenberg, 165–79. Durham, NC: Duke University Press. https://doi.org/10.1215/9780822382270-006.

Innes, Robert Alexander, and Kim Anderson. 2015. *Indigenous Men and Masculinities: Legacies, Identities, Regeneration.* Winnipeg: University of Manitoba Press.

Jacobs, Katrien. 2016. "Disorderly Conduct: Feminist Nudity in Chinese Protest Movements." *Sexualities* 19 (7): 819–35. https://doi.org/10.1177/1363460715624456.

Jarrett, Kylie. 2008. "Interactivity Is Evil! A Critical Investigation of Web 2.0." *First Monday* 13 (3): 34–41. https://doi.org/10.5210/fm.v13i3.2140.

Jenkins, Henry. 2006. *Convergence Culture: Where Old and New Media Collide.* New York: NYU Press.

Jeppesen, Sandra. 2010a. "Creating Guerrilla Texts in Rhizomatic Value-Practices on the Sliding Scale of Autonomy: Toward an Anti-authoritarian Cultural Logic." In *New Perspectives on Anarchism,* edited by Nathan J. Jun and Shane Wahl, 473–96. Lanham, MD: Rowman and Littlefield.

–. 2010b. "Queer Anarchist Autonomous Zones and Publics: Direct Action Vomiting against Homonormative Consumerism." *Sexualities* 13 (4): 463–78. https://doi.org/10.1177/1363460710370652.

–. 2016a. "Direct-Action Journalism: Resilience in Grassroots Autonomous Media." *Journal of Applied Media and Journalism Studies* 5 (3): 383–403. https://doi.org/10.1386/ajms.5.3.383_1.

–. 2016b. "Understanding Alternative Media Power: Mapping Content and Practice to Theory, Ideology, and Political Action." *Democratic Communiqué* 27 (1): 54–77. http://journals.fcla.edu/demcom/article/view/88322.

–. 2019. "Toward an Anarchist-Feminist Analytics of Power." In *Anarchist Imagination: Anarchism Encounters the Humanities and Social Sciences,* edited by Saul Newman and Carl Levy, 110–31. London: Routledge.

–. 2021. "Intersectional Technopolitics in Social Movement and Media Activism." *International Journal of Communication* 15 (2021): 1961–83. https://ijoc.org/index.php/ijoc/article/view/15766.

Jeppesen, Sandra, Toni Hounslow, Sharmeen Khan, and Kamilla Petrick. 2017. "Media Action Research Group: Toward an Antiauthoritarian Profeminist Media Research Methodology." *Feminist Media Studies* 17 (6): 1056–72. https://doi.org/10.1080/14680777.2017.1283346.

Jeppesen, Sandra, Jaina Kelly, and MARG. Forthcoming. "The Immaterial Commons: Sustaining Intersectional Horizontalism through Affective Digital Labour." In *Organizing Equality,* edited by Alison Hearn. Montreal/Kingston: McGill-Queen's University Press.

Jeppesen, Sandra, Anna Kruzynski, Aaron Lakoff, and Rachel Sarrasin. 2014. "Grassroots Autonomous Media Practices: A Diversity of Tactics." *Journal of Media Practice* 15 (1): 21–38. https://doi.org/10.1080/14682753.2014.892697.

Jeppesen, Sandra, Anna Kruzynski, and Coco Riot. 2016. "Queer and Trans People of Color Community Arts Collective." In *Artistic Citizenship: Artistry, Social Responsibility, and Ethical Praxis*, edited by David J. Elliott, Marissa Silverman, and Wayne D. Bowman, 213–32. Oxford: Oxford University Press.

Jeppesen, Sandra, Anna Kruzynski, Rachel Sarrasin, and Émilie Breton. 2013. "The Anarchist Commons." *Ephemera: Theory & Politics in Organization* 14 (4): 879–900. http://www.ephemerajournal.org/contribution/anarchist-commons.

Jeppesen, Sandra, and MARG. 2018. "Intersectionality in Autonomous Journalism Practices." *Journal of Alternative and Community Media* 3 (1): 1–16. https://doi.org/10.1386/joacm_00036_1.

Jeppesen, Sandra, and Holly Nazar. 2012. "Gender Sexualities in Anarchist Movements." In *The Continuum Companion to Anarchism*, edited by Ruth Kinna, 162–91. London: Bloomsbury.

–. 2018. "Anarchism and Sexuality." In *Brill's Companion to Anarchism and Philosophy*, edited by Nathan J. Jun, 216–52. Leiden, NL: Brill.

Jeppesen, Sandra, and Kamilla Petrick. 2018. "Toward an Intersectional Political Economy of Autonomous Media Resources." *Interface: A Journal for and about Social Movements* 10 (1–2): 8–37.

Jeppesen, Sandra, and Paola Sartoretto. 2020. "Mapping Questions of Power and Ethics in Media Activist Research Practices." In *Media Activist Research Ethics: Global Approaches to Negotiating Power in Social Justice Research*, edited by Sandra Jeppesen and Paola Sartoretto, 1–26. London: Palgrave Macmillan.

Jiwani, Yasmin. 2006. *Discourses of Denial: Mediations of Race, Gender, and Violence*. Vancouver: UBC Press.

Jiwani, Yasmin, and Mary Lynn Young. 2006. "Missing and Murdered Women: Reproducing Marginality in News Discourse." *Canadian Journal of Communication* 31 (4): 895–917. https://doi.org/10.22230/cjc.2006v31n4a1825.

John, Mary. 2020. "Feminism, Sexual Violence and the Times of #MeToo in India." *Asian Journal of Women's Studies* 26 (2): 137–58.

Johnson, E. Patrick, and Mae G. Henderson. 2005. *Black Queer Studies: A Critical Anthology*. Durham, NC: Duke University Press.

Jurgenson, Nathan. 2013. "The Disconnectionists." *New Inquiry*, November 13. https://thenewinquiry.com/the-disconnectionists/.

Kaas, Hailey. 2016. "Birth of Transfeminism in Brazil: Between Alliances and Backlashes." *TSQ: Transgender Studies Quarterly* 3 (1–2): 146–49. https://doi.org/10.1215/23289252-3334307.

Kadir, Nazima. 2016. *The Autonomous Life? Paradoxes of Hierarchy and Authority in the Squatters Movement in Amsterdam*. Manchester: Manchester University Press.

Kahn, Richard, and Douglas Kellner. 2007. "Globalization, Technopolitics, and Radical Democracy." In *Radical Democracy and the Internet: Interrogating Theory and Practice*, edited by Lincoln Dahlberg and Eugenia Siapera, 17–36. London: Palgrave Macmillan.

Kaijser, Anna, and Annica Kronsell. 2013. "Climate Change through the Lens of Intersectionality." *Environmental Politics* 23 (3): 417–33. https://doi.org/10.1080/09644016.2013.835203.

Keegan, Cael M. 2016. "On Being the Object of Compromise." *TSQ: Transgender Studies Quarterly* 3 (1–2): 150–57. https://doi.org/10.1215/23289252-3334319.

Kellner, Douglas. 2003. "Globalisation, Technopolitics and Revolution." In *The Future of Revolutions*, edited by John Foran, 180–94. London: Zed Books.

Kendi, Ibram X. 2019. *How to Be an Antiracist*. New York: Random House.

Kennedy, Brendan. 2020. "As Standoff at '1492 Land Back Lane' Heats up in Caledonia, Land Defenders Say, 'This Is a Moment for Our People to Say No.'" *Toronto Star*, October 23. https://www.thestar.com/news/gta/2020/10/23/as-standoff-at -1492-land-back-lane-heats-up-in-caledonia-land-defenders-say-this-is-a-moment -for-our-people-to-say-no.html.

Kerswell, Timothy. 2012. "Globalizing the Social Movements? Labour and the World Social Forum." *Theory in Action* 5 (3): 73–92. https://doi.org/10.3798/ tia.1937-0237.12023.

Khan, Faris A. 2016. "*Khwaja Sira* Activism: The Politics of Gender Ambiguity in Pakistan." *Transgender Studies Quarterly* 3 (1–2): 158–64. tsq/article-abstract/ 3/1-2/158/91715/Khwaja-Sira-ActivismThe-Politics-of-Gender.

Khan, Janaya. 2016. "Black Lives Matter Toronto Co-founder Responds to Pride Action Criticism." *NOW Magazine*, July 6. https://nowtoronto.com/exclusive -black-lives-matter-pride-action-criticism.

Khan-Cullors, Patrisse, and Asha Bandele. 2018. *When They Call You a Terrorist: A Black Lives Matter Memoir*. New York: St. Martin's Press.

Khoo, Anabel. 2014. "Mangos with Chili: Two-Spirit, Queer and Trans People of Colour Performance as Social Movement Building." Master's thesis, York University. http://yorkspace.library.yorku.ca/xmlui/handle/10315/29886.

Kidd, Dorothy. 2003. "Indymedia.org: A New Communications Commons." In *Cyber-Activism: Online Activism in Theory and Practice*, edited by Martha McCaughey and Michael D. Ayers, 47–70. New York: Routledge.

Kidd, Dorothy, Bernadette Barker-Plummer, and Clemencia Rodriguez. 2006. "Media Democracy from the Ground Up: Mapping Communication Practices in the Counter Public Sphere." *Necessary Knowledge for a Democratic Public Sphere Background Papers*.

Kornhaber, Spencer. 2018. "The Oscars' Gauzy Take on Intersectionality." *The Atlantic*, March 5. https://www.theatlantic.com/entertainment/archive/ 2018/03/academy-awards-shape-of-water-oscars-inclusion-intersectionality/ 554858/.

Kraus, Krystalline. 2010. "G8/G20 Communiqué: Tent City in Allan Gardens." *Rabble*, June 25. http://rabble.ca/blogs/bloggers/krystalline/2010/06/g8g20-communiqu %C3%A9-tent-city-allan-gardens.

Kubitschko, Sebastian. 2015. "The Role of Hackers in Countering Surveillance and Promoting Democracy." *Media and Communication* 3 (2): 77–87. https://doi. org/10.17645/mac.v3i2.281.

Kumanyika, Chenjerai. 2016a. "Learn How to Livestream at Social Justice Events." Workshop presented at Media Activism Research Conference, Orillia, May 13. https://www.youtube.com/watch?v=oxRr-aEmDvI.

—. 2016b. "Policing and the 'War on Black Bodies." *College Literature* 43 (1): 252–58. https://doi.org/10.1353/lit.2016.0015.

—. 2016c. "Livestreaming in the Black Lives Matter Network." In *DIY Utopia: Cultural Imagination and the Remaking of the Possible*, edited by Amber Day, 169–88. Lanham, MD: Lexington Books.

Kurban, Can, Ismael Peña-López, and Maria Haberer. 2017. "What Is Techno-politics? A Conceptual Scheme for Understanding Politics in the Digital Age." *Revista de Internet, Derecho y Politica* 24, February. https://raco.cat/index.php/IDP/article/view/n24-kurban-peña-haberer.

La Barbera, Maria Caterina. 2017. "Intersectionality and Its Journeys: From Counterhegemonic Feminist Theories to Law of European Multilevel Democracy." *Investigaciones Feministas* 8 (1): 131–49. https://doi.org/10.5209/infe.54858.

Lanier, Jaron. 2018. "How We Need to Remake the Internet." TED 2018, April. https://www.ted.com/talks/jaron_lanier_how_we_need_to_remake_the_internet.

Laperrière, Marie, and Eléonore Lépinard. 2016. "Intersectionality as a Tool for Social Movements: Strategies of Inclusion and Representation in the Québécois Women's Movement." *Politics* 36 (4): 374–82. https://doi.org/10.1177/0263395716649009.

Larabee, Ann. 2018. "Celebrity, Politics, and the 'Me, Too' Moment." *Journal of Popular Culture* 51 (1): 7–9. https://doi.org/10.1111/jpcu.12650.

Lebron, Christopher J. 2017. *The Making of Black Lives Matter: A Brief History of an Idea*. Oxford: Oxford University Press.

Leeuw, Sarah de. 2016. "Tender Grounds: Intimate Visceral Violence and British Columbia's Colonial Geographies." *Political Geography* 52 (May): 14–23. https://doi.org/10.1016/j.polgeo.2015.11.010.

Lepischak, Bev. 2004. "Building Community for Toronto's Lesbian, Gay, Bisexual, Transsexual and Transgender Youth." *Journal of Gay and Lesbian Social Services* 16 (3–4): 81–98. https://doi.org/10.1300/j041v16n03_06.

Leval, Gaston. 2018. *Collectives in the Spanish Revolution*. Oakland, CA: PM Press.

Levin, Sam, and Nicky Woolf. 2016. "A Million People 'Check In' at Standing Rock on Facebook to Support Dakota Pipeline Protesters." *The Guardian*, November 1. https://www.theguardian.com/us-news/2016/oct/31/north-dakota-access-pipeline-protest-mass-facebook-check-in.

Lim, Jason, and Alexandra Fanghanel. 2013. "'Hijabs, Hoodies and Hotpants'; Negotiating the 'Slut' in SlutWalk." *Geoforum* 48 (August): 207–15. https://doi.org/10.1016/j.geoforum.2013.04.027.

Lim, Merlyna. 2013. "Framing Bouazizi: 'White Lies,' Hybrid Network, and Collective/Connective Action in the 2010–11 Tunisian Uprising." *Journalism* 14 (7): 921–41. https://doi.org/10.1177/1464884913478359.

Lopez, Lori Kido. 2016. "A Media Campaign for Ourselves: Building Organizational Media Capacity through Participatory Action Research." *Journal of Media Practice* 16 (3): 228–44. https://doi.org/10.1080/14682753.2015.1116756.

Lotz, Amanda D. 2003. "Communicating Third-Wave Feminism and New Social Movements: Challenges for the Next Century of Feminist Endeavor." *Women and Language* 26 (1): 2–9.

Lyazadi, Majdoline. 2013. "SLUTWALK Morocco: The Interview." *According to Hind*, August 20. https://accordingtohind.wordpress.com/2011/08/20/slutwalk-morocco-the-interview/.

Mangum, George. 2015. "Live Streaming and Citizen Journalism." MIT Graduate Program in Comparative Media Studies, February 18. http://cmsw.mit.edu/live-streaming-and-citizen-journalism/.

Manuel, Kanahus Freedom, Skyler Williams, and Naomi Klein. 2020. "The Ransom Economy: What #ShutDownCanada Reveals about Indigenous Land Rights."

Yellowhead Institute, December 10. https://www.youtube.com/watch?v=UoS1UbY0Mrw.

Marchand, Laura. 2016. "World Social Forum Organizers Deem Controversial Event a Success." *Montreal Gazette*, August 15. http://montrealgazette.com/news/local-news/world-social-forum-organizers-deem-controversial-event-a-success.

Marineau, Sophie. 2020. "Fact Check US: What Is the Impact of Russian Interference in the US Presidential Election?" *The Conversation*, September 29. https://theconversation.com/fact-check-us-what-is-the-impact-of-russian-interference-in-the-us-presidential-election-146711.

Marsh, Margaret S. 1978. "The Anarchist-Feminist Response to the 'Woman Question' in Late Nineteenth-Century America." *American Quarterly* 30 (4): 533–47. https://doi.org/10.2307/2712299.

Martinez, Elizabeth Betita. 2000. "Where Was the Color in Seattle? Looking for Reasons Why the Great Battle Was So White." *Colorlines*, March 10. https://www.colorlines.com/articles/where-was-color-seattlelooking-reasons-why-great-battle-was-so-white.

Mattoni, Alice. 2013. "Repertoires of Communication in Social Movement Processes." In *Mediation and Protest Movements*, edited by Bart Cammaerts, Alice Mattoni, and Patrick McCurdy, 39–56. Bristol: Intellect.

Maynard, Robyn. 2017. *Policing Black Lives: State Violence in Canada from Slavery to the Present*. Winnipeg: Fernwood.

McDonald, Kevin. 2002. "From Solidarity to Fluidarity: Social Movements beyond 'Collective Identity': The Case of Globalization Conflicts." *Social Movement Studies* 1 (2): 109–28. https://doi.org/10.1080/1474283022000010637.

McNally, David. 2002. *Another World Is Possible: Globalization and Anti-Capitalism*. Winnipeg: Arbeiter Ring.

McRobbie, Angela. 2011. "Reflections on Feminism, Immaterial Labour and the Post-Fordist Regime." *New Formations* 70 (17): 60–76. https://doi.org/10.3898/newf.70.04.2010.

Mendes, Kaitlynn, Jessica Ringrose, and Jessalynn Keller. 2018. "#MeToo and the Promise and Pitfalls of Challenging Rape Culture through Digital Feminist Activism." *European Journal of Women's Studies* 25 (2): 236–46. https://doi.org/10.1177/1350506818765318.

Mertes, Tom, and Walden F. Bello. 2004. *A Movement of Movements: Is Another World Really Possible?* London: Verso.

Milan, Stefania. 2013. *Social Movements and Their Technologies: Wiring Social Change*. London: Palgrave Macmillan.

–. 2017. "Data Activism as the New Frontier of Media Activism." In *Media Activism in the Digital Age*, edited by Goubin Yang and Viktor Pickard, 151–63. New York: Routledge.

Milberry, Kate, and Steve Anderson. 2009. "Open Sourcing Our Way to an Online Commons: Contesting Corporate Impermeability in the New Media Ecology." *Journal of Communication Inquiry* 33 (4): 393–412. https://doi.org/10.1177/0196859909340349.

Milberry, Kate, and Andrew Clement. 2015. "Policing as Spectacle and the Politics of Surveillance at the Toronto G20." In *Putting the State on Trial: The Policing of Protest during the G20 Summit*, edited by Margaret E. Beare, Nathalie Des Rosiers, and Abigail C. Deshman, 243–45. Vancouver: UBC Press.

Milioni, Dimitra. 2009. "Probing the Online Counterpublic Sphere: The Case of Indymedia Athens." *Media Culture and Society* 31 (3): 409–31. https://doi.org/10.1177/0163443709102714.

Milkman, Ruth. 2017. "A New Political Generation: Millennials and the Post-2008 Wave of Protest." *American Sociological Review* 82 (1): 1–31. https://doi.org/10.1177/0003122416681031.

Min, Incheol. 2004. "Perceptions of the Audience by the Alternative Press Producers: A Case Study of the *Texas Observer*." *Media, Culture and Society* 26 (3): 450–58. https://doi.org/10.1177/0163443704042559.

Minarella. 2021. "TikTok's 'Beauty Algorithm' Makes It Impossibly Hard to Be a POC Creator: Society Deems 'White, Pretty, and Popular' as Viral-Worthy." *Better Marketing*. February 22. https://bettermarketing.pub/tiktoks-exposed-beauty-algorithm-makes-it-impossibly-hard-to-be-a-female-poc-creator-65316dd2438e.

Mirza, Heidi Safia. 2015. "Decolonizing Higher Education: Black Feminism and the Intersectionality of Race and Gender." *Journal of Feminist Scholarship* 7 (Fall): 1–12.

Monahan, Torin. 2009. "Dreams of Control at a Distance: Gender, Surveillance, and Social Control." *Cultural Studies ↔ Critical Methodologies* 9 (2): 286–305. https://doi.org/10.1177/1532708608321481.

Monkman, Lenard. 2021. "Indigenous Women's Instagram Stories on MMIWG Awareness Vanish on Red Dress Day." CBC News. May 6. https://www.cbc.ca/news/indigenous/instagram-stories-vanish-mmiwg-red-dress-day-1.6017113.

Monterde, Arnau, Antonio Calleja-Lopez, Miguel Aguilera, Xabier E. Barandiaran, and John Postill. 2015. "Multitudinous Identities: A Qualitative and Network Analysis of the 15M Collective Identity." *Information, Communication and Society* 18 (8): 930–50. https://doi.org/10.1080/1369118x.2015.1043315.

Monterde, Arnau, and John Postill. 2014. "Mobile Ensembles: The Uses of Mobile Phones for Social Protest by Spain's Indignados." In *The Routledge Companion to Mobile Media*, edited by Gerard Goggin and Larissa Hjorth, 429–38. London: Routledge.

Moore, Darnell L., and Patrisse Cullors. 2014. "5 Ways to Never Forget Ferguson – and Deliver Real Justice for Michael Brown." *The Guardian*, September 4. http://www.theguardian.com/commentisfree/2014/sep/04/never-forget-ferguson-justice-for-michael-brown.

Moore, Malcolm. 2008. "China Earthquake Brings Out Citizen Journalists." *The Telegraph*, May 12. https://www.telegraph.co.uk/news/worldnews/asia/china/1950212/China-earthquake-brings-out-citizen-journalists.html.

Mundt, Marcia, Karen Ross, and Charla M. Burnett. 2018. "Scaling Social Movements through Social Media: The Case of Black Lives Matter." *Social Media + Society* (Oct–Dec): 1–14. https://doi.org/10.1177/2056305118807911.

Munro, Ealasaid. 2013. "Feminism: A Fourth Wave?" *Political Insight* 4 (2): 22–25. https://doi.org/10.1111/2041-9066.12021.

Murillo, Mario. 2003. "Community Radio in Colombia: Civil Conflict, Popular Media and the Construction of a Public Sphere." *Journal of Radio Studies* 10 (1): 120–40. https://doi.org/10.1207/s15506843jrs1001_11.

Nagle, Angela. 2013. "Not Quite Kicking Off Everywhere: Feminist Notes on Digital Liberation." In *Internet Research, Theory and Practice: Perspectives from Ireland,* edited by Cathy Fowley, Claire English, and Sylvie Thouësny, 157–75. Dublin: Research-publishing.net.

Nanditha, Narayanamoorthy. 2021. "Exclusion in #MeToo India: Rethinking Inclusivity and Intersectionality in Indian Digital Feminist Movements." *Feminist Media Studies*. https://doi.org/10.1080/14680777.2021.1913432.

Nasser, Shanifa. 2017. "Canada's Largest School Board Votes to End Armed Police Presence in Schools." CBC News, November 22. http://www.cbc.ca/news/canada/toronto/school-resource-officers-toronto-board-police-1.4415064.

National Inquiry into Missing and Murdered Indigenous Women and Girls. 2019a. "Reclaiming Power and Place: The Final Report of the National Inquiry into Missing and Murdered Indigenous Women and Girls." https://www.mmiwg-ffada.ca/final-report/.

–. 2019b. "Timeline of Key Milestones: MMIWG." National Inquiry into Missing and Murdered Indigenous Women and Girls, February 10. https://www.mmiwg-ffada.ca/timeline/.

Neumayer, Christina, and David Struthers. 2018. "Social Media as Activist Archives." In *Social Media Materialities and Protest: Critical Reflections*, edited by Mette Mortensen, Christina Neumayer, and Thomas Poell, 86–98. London: Routledge.

Noble, Bobby. 2007. "Refusing to Make Sense." *Journal of Lesbian Studies* 11 (1–2): 167–75. https://doi.org/10.1300/j155v11n01_13.

Noble, Safiya Umoja. 2018. *Algorithms of Oppression: How Search Engines Reinforce Racism*. New York: NYU Press.

NOW. 2016. "Meet the Faces of Toronto's Black Lives Matter Tent City." *NOW*, April 4. https://nowtoronto.com/meet-the-faces-of-black-lives-matter-tent-city-toronto.

Obasogie, Osagie K., and Zachary Newman. 2016. "Black Lives Matter and Respectability Politics in Local News Accounts of Officer-Involved Civilian Deaths: An Early Empirical Assessment." *Wisconsin Law Review* 3: 541–75.

O'Donnell, Susan, Sonja Perley, Brian Walmark, Kevin Burton, Brian Beaton, and Andrew Sark. 2007. "Community-Based Broadband Organizations and Video Communications for Remote and Rural First Nations in Canada." In *Proceedings of the Community Informatics Research Network*, 1–11. Prato, Italy: CIRN.

O'Hara, Jason, dir. 2017. *State of Exception*. Documentary. Seven Generations Productions, Toronto.

O'Keefe, Theresa. 2014. "My Body Is My Manifesto! SlutWalk, FEMEN and Femmenist Protest." *Feminist Review* 107 (1): 1–19. https://doi.org/10.1057/fr.2014.4.

O'Neil, Cathy. 2016. *Weapons of Math Destruction: How Big Data Increases Inequality and Threatens Democracy*. New York: Crown.

Oppliger, Patrice A. 2008. *Girls Gone Skank: The Sexualization of Girls in American Culture*. Jefferson, NC: McFarland.

Ortner, Sherry B., and Harriet Whitehead. 1981. *Sexual Meanings: The Cultural Construction of Gender and Sexuality*. Cambridge: Cambridge University Press.

Perez, Caroline Criado. 2019. *Invisible Women: Exposing Data Bias in a World Designed for Men*. New York: Abrams Press.

Perry, Keisha-Khan Y. 2016. "Geographies of Power: Black Women Mobilizing Intersectionality in Brazil." *Meridians* 14 (1): 94. https://doi.org/10.2979/meridians.14.1.08.

Peterson-Withorn, Chase. 2019. "How Bernie Sanders, the Socialist Senator, Amassed a $2.5 Million Fortune." *Forbes,* April 12. https://www.forbes.com/sites/chasewithorn/2019/04/12/how-bernie-sanders-the-socialist-senator-amassed-a-25-million-fortune/?sh=3e64c42036bf.

Phillips, M. Ann. 1997. "Feminist Anti-racist Participatory Action Research: Research for Social Change around Women's Health in Brazil." *Canadian Woman Studies* 17 (2): 100–5.

Pickard, Victor W. 2006. "Assessing the Radical Democracy of Indymedia: Discursive, Technical, and Institutional Constructions." *Critical Studies in Media Communication* 23 (1): 19–38. https://doi.org/10.1080/07393180600570691.

Pickerill, Jenny. 2007. "'Autonomy Online': Indymedia and Practices of Alter-Globalisation." *Environment and Planning A: Economy and Space* 39 (11): 2668–84. https://doi.org/10.1068/a38227.

Pirbhai-Illich, Fatima, Shauneen Pete, and Fran Martin. 2017. *Culturally Responsive Pedagogy: Working towards Decolonization, Indigeneity and Interculturalism.* London: Palgrave Macmillan.

Pleyers, Geoffrey. 2020. "The Pandemic Is a Battlefield: Social Movements in the COVID-19 Lockdown." *Journal of Civil Society* 16 (4): 295–312. https://doi.org/10.1080/17448689.2020.1794398.

Poell, Thomas, and Erik Borra. 2012. "Twitter, YouTube, and Flickr as Platforms of Alternative Journalism: The Social Media Account of the 2010 Toronto G20 Protests." *Journalism* 13 (6): 695–713. https://doi.org/10.1177/1464884911431533.

Point, Camille. 2019. "#MosqueMeToo: Islamic Feminism in the Twitter Sphere." *Ada: A Journal of Gender, New Media, and Technology* 15 (3): n.p. https://doi.org/10.5399/uo/ada.2019.15.3.

Poitras, Laura, dir. 2014. *Citizenfour.* Praxis Films, Hong Kong.

Policy4Women. 2018. *Rising Incarceration Rates of Racialized Women.* Toronto: Centre for Feminist Research at York University.

Polletta, Francesca, and James M. Jasper. 2001. "Collective Identity and Social Movements." *Annual Review of Sociology* 27 (1): 283–305. https://doi.org/10.1146/annurev.soc.27.1.283.

Postill, John. 2014. "Spain's Indignados and the Mediated Aesthetics of Nonviolence." In *The Political Aesthetics of Global Protest: The Arab Spring and Beyond,* edited by Pnina Werbner, Martin Webb, and Kathryn Spellman-Poots, 341–67. Edinburgh: Edinburgh University Press.

Rauch, Jennifer. 2007. "Activists as Interpretive Communities: Rituals of Consumption and Interaction in an Alternative Media Audience." *Media, Culture and Society* 29 (6): 994–1013. https://doi.org/10.1177/0163443707084345.

Ravine, Jai Arun. 2014. "Toms and Zees: Locating FTM Identity in Thailand." *TSQ: Transgender Studies Quarterly* 1 (3): 387–401. https://doi.org/10.1215/23289252-685651.

Razack, Sherene. 2002. *Race, Space, and the Law.* Toronto: Between the Lines.

Razack, Sherene, Sunera Thobani, and Malinda Smith. 2010. *States of Race: Critical Race Feminism for the 21st Century.* Toronto: Between the Lines.

Reality Check. 2021. "Covid-19: Palestinians Lag Behind in Vaccine Efforts as Infections Rise." BBC News, March 22. https://www.bbc.com/news/55800921.

Rebick, Judy. 2011. "Defenders of the Land: Building a Powerful Grassroots Movement of Indigenous Peoples." Rabble.ca, June 15. http://rabble.ca/blogs/

bloggers/judes/2011/06/defenders-land-building-powerful-grassroots-network
-indigenous-peoples.

Rice, Carla, Karleen Pendleton Jiménez, Elisabeth Harrison, Margaret Robinson, Jen Rinaldi, Andrea LaMarre, and Jill Andrew. 2020. "Bodies at the Intersections: Refiguring Intersectionality through Queer Women's Complex Embodiments." *Signs: Journal of Women in Culture and Society* 46 (1): 177–200. https://doi.org/10.1086/709219.

Rigby, Joe. 2010. "Interview with No Borders in Calais." *Shift*, January 2: http://libcom.org/library/interview-no-borders-calais.

Ringrose, Jessica, and Emma Renold. 2012. "Slut-Shaming, Girl Power and 'Sexualisation': Thinking through the Politics of the International SlutWalks with Teen Girls." *Gender and Education* 24 (3): 333–43. https://doi.org/10.1080/09540253.2011.645023.

Riot, Coco. 2008. *Gender Poo.* https://www.cocoriot.com/cocoart#/ver-o-no-ver/.

Ritchie, Andrea J. 2017. *Invisible No More: Police Violence against Black Women and Women of Color.* Boston: Beacon Press.

Robé, Chris, and Todd Wolfson. 2020. "Reflections on the Inheritances of Indymedia in the Age of Surveillance and Social Media." *Media, Culture and Society* 42 (6): 1024–30. https://doi.org/10.1177/0163443720926056.

Robertson, Roland. 1995. "Glocalization: Time-Space and Homogeneity-Heterogeneity." In *Global Modernities,* edited by Mike Featherstone, Scott Lash, and Roland Robertson, 25–44. London: Sage.

Rodino-Colocino, Michelle. 2018. "Me Too, #MeToo: Countering Cruelty with Empathy." *Communication and Critical/Cultural Studies* 15 (1): 96–100. https://doi.org/10.1080/14791420.2018.1435083.

Rodriguez, Clemencia. 2001. *Fissures in the Mediascape: An International Study of Citizens' Media.* New York: Hampton Press.

Rodriguez, Clemencia, Benjamin Ferron, and Kristin Shamas. 2014. "Four Challenges in the Field of Alternative, Radical and Citizens' Media Research." *Media, Culture and Society* 36 (2): 150–66. https://doi.org/10.1177/0163443714523877.

Roediger, David R., and Kendrick C. Roediger. 1999. *The Wages of Whiteness: Race and the Making of the American Working Class.* London: Verso.

Roseneil, Sasha. 1995. *Disarming Patriarchy: Feminism and Political Action at Greenham.* Buckingham: Open University Press. http://eprints.bbk.ac.uk/10650/.

Rosner, Cecil. 2013. "Whistleblowers, Journalists and the Public's Right to Know." *JSource,* July 6. https://j-source.ca/article/whistleblowers-journalists-and-the-publics-right-to-know/.

Ross, Loretta. 2008. "Featured Activist: Loretta Ross." *The F-Word: A Feminist Handbook for the Revolution,* special "Outlaws" issue, edited by Melody Berger, 3: 4–9.

Ross, Marlon. 2005. "Beyond the Closet as Raceless Paradigm." In *Black Queer Studies,* edited by E. Patrick Johnson and Mae G. Henderson, 161–89. Durham, NC: Duke University Press.

Roy, Arundhati. 2004. *An Ordinary Person's Guide to Empire.* Boston: South End Press.

Ruin. 2016. "Discussing Transnormativities through Transfeminism: Fifth Note." *TSQ: Transgender Studies Quarterly* 3 (1–2): 202–11. https://doi.org/10.1215/23289252-3334391.

Salgado, Julio. n.d. "Julio Salgado: I Exist." Accessed January 18, 2018. https://www.juliosalgadoart.com/.

Sanchez Cedillo, Raul. 2012. "15M: Something Constituent This Way Comes." *South Atlantic Quarterly* 111 (3): 573–84. https://doi.org/10.1215/00382876-1596299.

Sandoval, Marisol. 2016. "Fighting Precarity with Co-operation? Worker Co-operatives in the Cultural Sector." *New Formations* 88 (Fall): 51–68. https://doi.org/10.3898/newf.88.04.2016.

Sandvig, Christian, Kevin Hamilton, Karrie Karahalios, and Cedric Langbort. 2016. "Automation, Algorithms, and Politics – When the Algorithm Itself Is a Racist: Diagnosing Ethical Harm in the Basic Components of Software." *International Journal of Communication* 10 (2016): 4972–90.

Santos, Boaventura de Sousa. 2015. *Epistemologies of the South: Justice against Epistemicide.* London: Routledge.

Saramo, Samira. 2016. "Unsettling Spaces: Grassroots Responses to Canada's Missing and Murdered Indigenous Women during the Harper Government Years." *Comparative American Studies: An International Journal* 14 (3–4): 204–20. https://doi.org/10.1080/14775700.2016.1267311.

Sartoretto, Paola. 2016. "Between Opportunities and Threats: An Analysis of Brazilian Landless Workers' Movement Experiences with New Media Technologies." *Observatorio* 10 (special): 35–53. https://doi.org/10.15847/obsobs0020161092.

Satariano, Adam. 2019. "The World's First Ambassador to the Tech Industry." *New York Times,* September 3. https://www.nytimes.com/2019/09/03/technology/denmark-tech-ambassador.html.

Schudson, Michael, and Chris Anderson. 2009. "Objectivity, Professionalism, and Truth Seeking in Journalism." In *The Handbook of Journalism Studies,* edited by Karin Wahl-Jorgensen and Thomas Hanitzsch, 88–101. London: Routledge.

Schwartz, Matthew. 2019. "Facebook Admits Mosque Shooting Video Was Viewed at Least 4,000 Times." NPR.org, March 19. https://www.npr.org/2019/03/19/704690054/facebook-admits-mosque-shooting-video-was-viewed-at-least-4-000-times.

Sedgwick, Eve Kosofsky. 1990. *Epistemology of the Closet.* Oakland: University of California Press.

Sefa Dei, George J. 2017. *Reframing Blackness and Black Solidarities through Anti-colonial and Decolonial Prisms.* Toronto: Springer.

Semali, Ladislaus M., and Joe L. Kincheloe. 2002. *What Is Indigenous Knowledge? Voices from the Academy.* London: Routledge.

Shannon, Deric. 2009. "Articulating a Contemporary Anarcha-Feminism." *Theory in Action* 2 (3): 58–74. https://doi.org/10.3798/tia.1937-0237.09013.

Shannon, Deric, J. Rogue, C.B. Daring, and Abbey Volcano. 2013. *Queering Anarchism: Addressing and Undressing Power and Desire.* Oakland, CA: AK Press.

Shirky, Clay. 2008. *Here Comes Everybody.* New York: Penguin.

Siapera, Eugenia. 2016. "Digital Citizen X: XNet and the Radicalisation of Citizenship." In *Negotiating Digital Citizenship: Control, Contest and Culture,* edited by Anthony McCosker, Sonja Vivienne, and Amelia Johns, 72–83. London: Rowman and Littlefield.

Sideris, Sotiris. 2018. "Mapping the Dominance of Airbnb on Athens." *Athens Live,* August 23. https://medium.com/athenslivegr/mapping-the-dominance-of-airbnb-in-athens-4cb9e0657e80.

Silva, Joseli Maria, and Marcio Jose Ornat. 2016. "Transfeminism and Decolonial Thought: The Contribution of Brazilian *Travestis*." *TSQ: Transgender Studies Quarterly* 3 (1–2): 220–27. https://doi.org/10.1215/23289252-3334415.

Silver, Marc. 2015. "If You Shouldn't Call It the Third World, What Should You Call It?" *Goats and Soda*, NPR. January 4. https://www.npr.org/sections/goatsandsoda/2015/01/04/372684438/if-you-shouldnt-call-it-the-third-world-what-should-you-call-it?t=1620065580177.

Slagle, R. Anthony. 1995. "In Defense of Queer Nation: From Identity Politics to a Politics of Difference." *Western Journal of Communication* 59 (2): 85–102. https://doi.org/10.1080/10570319509374510.

Smith, Gaye. 2013. "Blockades Are Illegal and Hold Our Economy for Ransom." *Simcoe*, January 16. https://www.simcoe.com/opinion-story/8406849-blockades-are-illegal-and-hold-our-economy-for-ransom/.

Smith, Linda Tuhiwai. 1999. *Decolonizing Methodologies: Research and Indigenous Peoples*. London: Zed Books.

Solomon, Akiba. 2014. "Get on the Bus: Inside the Black Life Matters 'Freedom Ride' to Ferguson." *Colorlines*, September 5. https://www.colorlines.com/articles/get-bus-inside-black-life-matters-freedom-ride-ferguson.

Spade, Dean. 2006. "Mutilating Gender." In *The Transgender Studies Reader*, edited by Susan Stryker and Stephen Whittle, 315–32. New York: Routledge.

Spiegel, Jennifer. 2015. "Of Spectacle and Collective Resistance: Rethinking the Relationship between 'Symbolic' and 'Direct' Action in Radicalism." *Action radicale, sujet radical: Racines, représentations, symboles et créations/Radical action, radical subject: Roots, representations, symbols and creations*. Conference proceedings, edited by Nicholas Giguère and Dominque Hétu, 51–59. Sherbrooke: Éditions de l'Université de Sherbrooke (ÉDUS). https://doi.org/10.17118/11143/8370.

Starks, Sandra, Halaevalu F. Ofahengaue Vakalahi, M. Jenise Comer, and Carmen Ortiz-Hendricks. 2010. "Gathering, Telling, Preparing the Stories: A Vehicle for Healing," *Journal of Indigenous Voices in Social Work* 1 (1): 1–18. http://hdl.handle.net/10125/15118.

Starr, Amory, Luis A. Fernandez, and Christian Scholl. 2011. *Shutting Down the Streets: Political Violence and Social Control in the Global Era*. New York: NYU Press.

Stote, Karen. 2017. "Decolonizing Feminism: From Reproductive Abuse to Reproductive Justice." *Atlantis: Critical Studies in Gender, Culture and Social Justice* 38 (1): 110–24.

Sullivan, Nikki. 2003. *A Critical Introduction to Queer Theory*. New York: NYU Press.

Sunkel, Osvaldo, and Cherita Girvan. 1973. "Transnational Capitalism and National Disintegration in Latin America." *Social and Economic Studies* 22 (1): 132–76.

Surette, Raymond. 2015. "Performance Crime and Justice." *Current Issues in Criminal Justice* 27 (2): 195–216. https://doi.org/10.1080/10345329.2015.12036041.

Sycamore, Mattilda Bernstein. 2008. *That's Revolting! Queer Strategies for Resisting Assimilation*. New York: Soft Skull Press.

Tabobondung, Rebeka. 2014. "Interview with Métis Artist Christi Belcourt on Walking With Our Sisters." *Muskrat Magazine*, March 14. http://muskratmagazine.com/interview-with-metis-artist-christi-belcourt-on-walking-with-our-sisters/.

Tadem, Theresa S. Encarnacion. 2012. "Creating Spaces for Asian Interaction through the Anti-globalization Campaigns in the Region." *Modern Asian Studies* 46 (2): 453–81. https://doi.org/10.1017/s0026749x11000928.

Talaga, Tanya. 2020. "Caledonia's 1492 Land Back Lane Camp Is a Monument to the Justice Canada Has Denied." *Globe and Mail*, November 19. https://www.theglobeandmail.com/opinion/article-caledonias-1492-land-back-lane-camp-is-a-monument-to-the-justice/.

Talcott, Molly, and Dana Collins. 2012. "Building a Complex and Emancipatory Unity: Documenting Decolonial Feminist Interventions within the Occupy Movement." *Feminist Studies* 38 (2): 485–506.

TallBear, Kim. 2019. "Feminist, Queer, and Indigenous Thinking as an Antidote to Masculinist Objectivity and Binary Thinking in Biological Anthropology." *American Anthropologist* 121 (2): 494–96. https://doi.org/10.1111/aman.13229.

TallBear, Kim, and Angela Willey. 2019. "Critical Relationality: Queer, Indigenous, and Multispecies Belonging beyond Settler Sex and Nature." *Imaginations: Journal of Cross-Cultural Image Studies* 10 (1): 5–15. https://doi.org/10.17742/image.cr.10.1.1.

Tallie, T.J. 2014. "Two-Spirit Literature: Decolonizing Race and Gender Binaries." *TSQ: Transgender Studies Quarterly* 1 (3): 455–60. https://doi.org/10.1215/23289252-685705.

Tankovska, H. 2021a. "Facebook's Revenue and Net Income from 2007 to 2020." *Statista*, February 5. https://www.statista.com/statistics/277229/facebooks-annual-revenue-and-net-income/.

–. 2021b. "Worldwide Revenue of Twitter from 2010 to 2020." *Statista*, March 26. https://www.statista.com/statistics/274568/quarterly-revenue-of-twitter/.

–. 2021c. "Worldwide Advertising Revenues of YouTube from 2017 to 2020." *Statista*, February 11. https://www.statista.com/statistics/289658/youtube-global-net-advertising-revenues/.

Taylor, Verta, and Nancy E. Whittier. 1998. "Collective Identity in Social Movement Communities: Lesbian Feminist Mobilization." In *Social Perspectives in Lesbian and Gay Studies*, edited by Peter M. Nardi and Beth E. Scheider, 349–65. New York: Routledge.

Thomas, Victoria E. 2019. "Gazing at 'It': An Intersectional Analysis of Transnormativity and Black Womanhood in *Orange Is the New Black*." *Communication, Culture and Critique* 13 (4): 519–35.

Thorburn, Elise Danielle. 2014. "Social Media, Subjectivity, and Surveillance: Moving on from Occupy, the Rise of Live Streaming Video." *Communication and Critical/Cultural Studies* 11 (1): 52–63. https://doi.org/10.1080/14791420.2013.827356.

Tiny House Warriors. 2019. "Tiny House Warriors." http://www.tinyhousewarriors.com/.

Tolley, Bridget, Sue Martin, and Kristen Gilchrist. 2012. "Families of Sisters in Spirit: Solidarity and Relationship Building in the Family-Led Movement on Behalf of Missing and Murdered Indigenous Women." *Our Schools/Our Selves* 21 (3): 133–40.

Tompkins, Avery Brooks. 2014. "'There's No Chasing Involved': Cis/Trans Relationships, 'Tranny Chasers,' and the Future of a Sex-Positive Trans Politics." *Journal of Homosexuality* 61 (5): 766–80.

Toret, Javier. 2012. "A Technopolitical Look at the Early Days of #15M." *Technopolítica*, March 12. http://tecnopolitica.net/node/14.

Toret, Javier, and Antonio Calleja. 2014. "Collective Intelligence Framework." *Decentralized Citizens Engagement Technologies (D-CENT)*, 1–89. https://dcentproject.eu/articles/.

Toret, Javier, Antonio Calleja, Oscar Marin Miro, Pablo Aragon, Miguel Aguilera, and Alberto Lumbreras. 2013. *Tecnopolitica: La potencia de las multitudes conectadas.* [Technopolitics: The power of the connected multitudes.] Internet Interdisciplinary Institute Working Paper Series, Universitat Oberta de Catalunya. Barcelona, Spain. doi:10.7238/in3wps.v0i0.1878.

Treré, Emiliano. 2015. "Reclaiming, Proclaiming, and Maintaining Collective Identity in the #YoSoy132 Movement in Mexico: An Examination of Digital Frontstage and Backstage Activism through Social Media and Instant Messaging Platforms." *Information, Communication and Society* 18 (8): 901–15. https://doi.org/10.1080/1369118x.2015.1043744.

–. 2019. *Hybrid Media Activism: Ecologies, Imaginaries, Algorithms.* London: Routledge.

Treré, Emiliano, and Alejandro Barranquero. 2018. "Tracing the Roots of Technopolitics: Towards a North-South Dialogue." In *Networks, Movements and Technopolitics in Latin America,* edited by Francisco Sierra Caballero and Tommaso Gravante, 43–63. London: Palgrave Macmillan. https://doi.org/10.1007/978-3-319-65560-4_3.

Treré, Emiliano, Sandra Jeppesen, and Alice Mattoni. 2017. "Comparing Digital Protest Media Imaginaries: Anti-austerity Movements in Greece, Italy and Spain." *TripleC: Communication, Capitalism and Critique* 15 (2): 404–22. https://doi.org/10.31269/triplec.v15i2.772.

Truth and Reconciliation Commission of Canada. 2015. *Truth and Reconciliation Commission of Canada: Calls to Action.* Winnipeg: Truth and Reconciliation Commission of Canada.

Tuck, Eve, and K. Wayne Yang. 2012. "Decolonization Is Not a Metaphor." *Decolonization: Indigeneity, Education and Society* 1 (1): 1–40.

Tufekci, Zeynep. 2017. "We're Building a Dystopia Just to Make People Click on Ads." Filmed September 2017 in New York, NY: TEDGlobal video, 22:46, https://www.ted.com/talks/zeynep_tufekci_we_re_building_a_dystopia_just_to_make_people_click_on_ads.

Twenge, Jean M. 2017. "Have Smartphones Destroyed a Generation?" *The Atlantic,* September. https://www.theatlantic.com/magazine/archive/2017/09/has-the-smartphone-destroyed-a-generation/534198/.

Uberti, David. 2016. "Philando Castile, Facebook Live, and a New Chapter for Citizen Journalism." *Columbia Journalism Review,* July 7. https://www.cjr.org/analysis/philando_castile_minnesota_facebook_live.php.

UNDRIP. 2007. "United Nations Declaration on the Rights of Indigenous Peoples / United Nations for Indigenous Peoples." Accessed March 21, 2018. https://www.un.org/development/desa/indigenouspeoples/declaration-on-the-rights-of-indigenous-peoples.html.

United Nations. 2019. *World Happiness Report, 2019.* New York: United Nations. http://worldhappiness.report/ed/2019.

–. 2020. *World Happiness Report, 2020.* New York: United Nations. http://worldhappiness.report/ed/2020.

Vade, Dylan. 2005. "Expanding Gender and Expanding the Law: Toward a Social and Legal Conceptualization of Gender That Is More Inclusive of Transgender People." *Michigan Journal of Gender and Law* 11 (2): 253–316.

van der Haak, Bregtje, Michael Parks, and Manuel Castells. 2012. "The Future of Journalism: Networked Journalism." *International Journal of Communication* 6: 2923–38.

van Dijck, José. 2014. "Datafication, Dataism and Dataveillance: Big Data between Scientific Paradigm and Ideology." *Surveillance and Society* 12 (2): 197–208. https://doi.org/10.24908/ss.v12i2.4776.

van Dijck, José, and Thomas Poell. 2013. "Understanding Social Media Logic." *Media and Communication* 1 (1): 2–14. https://doi.org/10.17645/mac.v1i1.70.

van Leeckwyck, Robin, Pieter Maeseele, Maud Peeters, and David Domingo. 2020. "Indymedia in Belgium: The Delicate Balance between Media Activism and Political Activism." *Media, Culture and Society* 42 (6): 1031–38. https://doi.org/10.1177/0163443720926047.

Vlachokyriakos, Vasilis, Clara Crivellaro, Christopher A. Le Dantec, Eric Gordon, Pete Wright, and Patrick Olivier. 2016. "Digital Civics: Citizen Empowerment with and through Technology." *Proceedings of the 2016 CHI Conference Extended Abstracts on Human Factors in Computing Systems 16*, 1096–99. New York: Association for Computing Machinery. https://doi.org/10.1145/2851581.2886436.

Vlachokyriakos, Vasilis, Clara Crivellaro, Pete Wright, Antonio Krüger, Johannes Schöning, Matt Jones, Shaun Lawson, Evika Karamagioli, Eleni Staiou, Dimitris Gouscos, Rowan Thorpe, and Patrick Olivier. 2017. "HCI, Solidarity Movements and the Solidarity Economy." In *Proceedings of the 2017 CHI Conference Extended Abstracts on Human Factors in Computing Systems 17*, 3126–37. New York: Association for Computing Machinery. doi:10.1145/3025453.3025490.

Wachter-Boettcher, Sara. 2017. *Technically Wrong: Sexist Apps, Biased Algorithms, and Other Threats of Toxic Tech*. New York: Norton.

Walking With Our Sisters. n.d. "Walking With Our Sisters." http://walkingwithoursisters.ca/.

Wallace, Tim, and Alicia Parlapiano. 2017. "Crowd Scientists Say Women's March in Washington Had 3 Times as Many People as Trump's Inauguration." *New York Times,* January 22. https://www.nytimes.com/interactive/2017/01/22/us/politics/womens-march-trump-crowd-estimates.html.

Ward, Tara. 2011. "The Right to Free, Prior, and Informed Consent: Indigenous Peoples' Participation Rights within International Law." *Northwestern University Journal of International Human Rights* 10: 54. http://heinonline.org/HOL/Page?handle=hein.journals/jihr10&id=54&div=&collection=.

Warner, Michael. 1993. *Fear of a Queer Planet: Queer Politics and Social Theory*. Minneapolis: University of Minnesota Press.

Watson, Kaitlyn, and Sandra Jeppesen. 2020. "Settler Fragility: Four Paradoxes of Decolonizing Research." *Revista de Comunicação Dialógica* 1(4): 78–109. https://doi.org/10.12957/rcd.2020.55392.

Weissinger, Sandra E., Dwayne A. Mack, and Elwood Watson. 2017. *Violence against Black Bodies: An Intersectional Analysis of How Black Lives Continue to Matter*. New York: Routledge.

Wesley-Esquimaux, Cynthia. 2009. "Trauma to Resilience: Notes on Decolonization." In *Restoring the Balance: First Nations Women, Community, and Culture*, edited by Gail Guthrie Valaskakis, Madeleine Dion Stout, and Eric Guimond, 13–34. Winnipeg: University of Manitoba Press.

West, Isaac. 2013. *Transforming Citizenships: Transgender Articulations of the Law*. New York: NYU Press.

White, Melissa Autumn. 2013. "Ambivalent Homonationalisms: Transnational Queer Intimacies and Territorialized Belongings." *Interventions* 15 (1): 37–54. https://doi.org/10.1080/1369801x.2013.770999.

Whitehead, Harriet. 1981. "The Bow and the Burden Strap: A New Look at Institutionalized Homosexuality in Native North America." In *Sexual Meanings: The Cultural Construction of Gender and Sexuality,* edited by Sherry B. Ortner and Harriet Whitehead, 80–115. Cambridge: Cambridge University Press.

Wiking, Meik. 2017. *The Little Book of Hygge: Danish Secrets to Happy Living.* New York: William Morrow.

Wilkins, Denise J., Andrew G. Livingstone, and Mark Levine. 2019. "Whose Tweets? The Rhetorical Functions of Social Media Use in Developing the Black Lives Matter Movement." *British Journal of Social Psychology* 58 (4): 786–805.

Williams, Dana M. 2018. "Tactics: Conceptions of Social Change, Revolution, and Anarchist Organisation." In *The Palgrave Handbook of Anarchism,* edited by Carl Levy and Matthew S. Adams, 107–24. London: Palgrave Macmillan.

Williams, Sherri. 2016. "#SayHerName: Using Digital Activism to Document Violence against Black Women." *Feminist Media Studies* 16 (5): 922–25. https://doi.org/10.1080/14680777.2016.1213574.

Williamson, Kenneth. 2015. "Some Things Cannot Be Separated: Intersectionality in the Lives of Black Women Activists in Salvador, Brazil." *African and Black Diaspora: An International Journal* 8 (1): 86–101. https://doi.org/10.1080/17528631.2014.972702.

Wilson, Dean Jonathon, and Tanya Serisier. 2010. "Video Activism and the Ambiguities of Counter-Surveillance." *Surveillance and Society* 8 (2): 166–80. https://doi.org/10.24908/ss.v8i2.3484.

Windpassinger, Gwendolyn. 2010. "Queering Anarchism in Post-2001 Buenos Aires." *Sexualities* 13 (4): 495–509. https://doi.org/10.1177/1363460710370657.

Wolfsfeld, Gadi, Elad Segev, and Tamir Sheafer. 2013. "Social Media and the Arab Spring: Politics Comes First." *International Journal of Press/Politics* 18 (2): 115–37. https://doi.org/10.1177/1940161212471716.

Wolfson, Todd. 2013. "Democracy or Autonomy? Indymedia and the Contradictions of Global Social Movement Networks." *Global Networks* 13 (3): 410–24. https://doi.org/10.1111/glob.12030.

Yang, Guobin. 2016. "Narrative Agency in Hashtag Activism: The Case of #BlackLivesMatter." *Media and Communication* 4 (4): 13–17. https://doi.org/10.17645/mac.v4i4.692.

Ye, Shana. 2016. "Reconstructing the Transgendered Self as a Feminist Subject: Trans/Feminist Praxis in Urban China." *TSQ: Transgender Studies Quarterly* 3 (1–2): 259–65. https://doi.org/10.1215/23289252-3334475.

Zengin, Aslı. 2016. "Mortal Life of Trans/feminism: Notes on 'Gender Killings' in Turkey." *TSQ: Transgender Studies Quarterly* 3 (1–2): 266–71. https://doi.org/10.1215/23289252-3334487.

Zimonjic, Peter. 2020. "NDP Leader Jagmeet Singh Booted from Commons for Calling Bloc MP a Racist." *CBC,* June 17. https://www.cbc.ca/news/politics/ndp-jagmeet-singh-rota-racist-therrien-1.5616661.

Zuboff, Shoshana. 2019. *The Age of Surveillance Capitalism: The Fight for a Human Future at the New Frontier of Power.* New York: Public Affairs.

Index

(t) after a page number indicates a table.